MATHEMATICAL

SOFTWARE

TOOLS IN C++

MATHEMATICAL

SOFTWARE

TOOLS IN C++

Alain Reverchon and **Marc Ducamp**

Translators
Veronique Fally and **Sara Schaer**

JOHN WILEY & SONS
Chichester · New York · Brisbane · Toronto · Singapore

Mathematical Software Tools in C++ by Alain Reverchon and Marc Ducamp is a translation of the French book *Outils mathématiques en C++* © Armand Colin Éditeur, 1993

Other Wiley Editorial Offices

John Wiley & Sons, Inc., 605 Third Avenue,
New York, NY 10158-0012, USA

Jacaranda Wiley Ltd, G.P.O. Box 859, Brisbane,
Queensland 4001, Australia

John Wiley & Sons (Canada) Ltd, 22 Worcester Road,
Rexdale, Ontario M9W 1L1, Canada

John Wiley & Sons (SEA) Pte Ltd, 37 Jalan Pemimpin #05-04,
Block B, Union Industrial Building, Singapore 2057

Library of Congress Cataloging-in-Publication Data

Reverchon, Alain.
    [Outils mathématiques en C++. English]
    Mathematical software tools in C++ / Alain Reverchon and Marc
Ducamp.
        p.   cm.
    Includes bibliographical references (p.   ) and index.
    ISBN 0 471 93792 4
    1. C++ (Computer program language)   2. Computer software.
I. Ducamp. Marc.   II. Title.
QA76.73.C153R48   1993
519.4'0285'5133—dc20   93-13741
                                                                CIP

British Library Cataloguing in Publication Data

A catalogue record for this book is available
from the British Library

ISBN 0 471 93792 4

Produced from camera-ready copy supplied by the author.
Printed and bound in Great Britain by Redwood Books Ltd, Trowbridge, Wiltshire

Contents

Preface

The development of computer science, as well as the recent arrival of workstations and microcomputers, has made numerical analysis essential to most scientists, researchers, engineers and students.

Though many texts discussing the theoretical and algorithmic aspects of numerical analysis have been published, very few books on the operational programming of numerical methods are available today.

On the other hand, we have made progress in the domain of development languages. Fortran, long considered the language of reference for scientific programming, is now giving way to highly structured languages such as Pascal and C, as well as to their object-oriented extensions, C++ in particular.

Structured programming allows one to write programs in a much more rational manner than Fortran. This is largely due to software tools, which are at the core of modern programming methods. Software tools significantly reduce development time, and increase the reliability of programs as well.

Our book has two goals: first, to allow computer science students to learn and to master the development of mathematical software in C++; second, to build a library of mathematical tools accessible to engineers and researchers who are not computer science specialists, but who need to solve problems using a computer.

This is why we have adopted a very operational approach. Each chapter is independent, and may be consulted as needed without knowledge of the entire book. The first four chapters, however, must be assimilated first. They review the object of numerical analysis, discuss calculation errors, and describe the general architecture of the programs in the book.

Then, a number of methods are described for each topic. We review the algorithm, describe the calculation tool, and provide examples which illustrate the application and the precision of the calculations.

The different tools described in this book may be used independently, as in a mechanical or thermic simulation program, or may be combined within one mathematical software program. This allows one to process most common calculation needs.

Some topics deserve special attention. The function interpreter, for example, transforms mathematical expressions entered by the program user into objects which the computer can use. The formal derivation program for a numerical function is important, as well as the formal calculations using polynomials and rational fractions. In addition, any result obtained in the form of a series of values may be represented graphically; for example, the solution of a differential equation.

Finally, we note that the programs were written on a microcomputer in Borland C++, but with a constant regard for portability. They can very easily be adapted to the Microsoft C++ compiler, or to a compiler on VAX or HP.

1

Numerical Analysis and Software Tools

The field of numerical analysis has expanded rapidly with the appearance of electronic calculators and greater familiarisation with computers. Today, the vast majority of engineers, scientists, researchers and students have access to central computers, minicomputers, workstations or microcomputers. As a result, numerical analysis has become both accessible and indispensable for this group of users.

Though methods of numerical analysis have been studied from theoretical and algorithmic points of view, few publications actually go on to examine how to write the program itself.

In addition, the recent progress in the area of computer languages has revolutionized numerical analysis programs, opening up possibilities other than Fortran. Structured languages such as Pascal and C++, increasingly popular within the scientific and technical communities, allow the user to write calculation programs in a far more rational manner.

Software tools are particularly important for structured programming. The availability of software tools libraries in many fields, especially graphic interfaces, has significantly reduced development time by offering the programmer functions which are already perfected and ready to use.

The aim of this book is to show how to build a library of numerical tools, in order to permit the user to solve numerous scientific problems without having to do all the programming associated with the project. The book can serve as an introduction to the programming of numerical tools, but also as a complete library of tools at the disposition of the programmer during a project.

Before beginning our study of numerical tools, we will describe the objectives of numerical analysis and its role in the resolution of modern problems. Then we will identify and evaluate the various sources of error which can distort the results of numerical calculations. Finally, we will define software tools, attempting to show why this concept is essential for all software development, and in particular for scientific and technical programs.

1   Objectives of Numerical Analysis

1.1 Why Numerical Analysis?

Let us start with a brief historical review. We have long known that the resolution of scientific problems involves the mathematical representation of the relevant phenomena. However, they are generally so complicated that in so doing, we are led to neglect some less important events and to simplify others. Despite these simplifications, the resulting equations are often impossible to solve using known algebraic methods.

In order to bypass the obstacle caused by the exact mathematical resolution of these problems, we must resort to numerical methods. The latter have appeared as a result of three simultaneous phenomena:
- first, most simple problems have been solved, and we are now confronted by increasingly complicated problems which cannot be solved using traditional mathematics;
- since 1945, computers have developed rapidly, and are now available to a large, growing number of users. This is particularly true since the introduction of microcomputers;
- finally, mathematicians have developed increasingly efficient techniques of numerical resolution which can be applied to a growing variety of mathematical problems.

However, there are two restrictions to the utilisation of numerical analysis, even though the latter does increase the field of solvable problems.

Some programs are so complex and demand so much calculation power, that they exceed the capacity of the standard computer; either the data exceeds memory limits, or the resolution takes too much time. This changes the mathematical problem into an economic question: how much are we prepared to pay to solve the problem?

This issue is common in high technology. In aeronautics, for example, the cost of supercomputers remains financially attractive because the numerical simulation of the phenomena is less expensive than the construction of models and their study in a wind tunnel. In another example, the information which one obtains using meteorological calculations is of such great importance that the use of sophisticated numerical techniques is justified.

The second main limitation of numerical analysis stems from the fact that certain problems do not yet have a complete and precise mathematical model which would permit their resolution with a computer.

1.2 Algorithmic Process

The first step in resolving a numerical analysis problem is to determine the algorithm. The algorithm is the method that will be used to obtain the result. It is built, using the raw data, through a series of more or less complex stages.

When developing an algorithm, one usually has to reduce or simplify the original problem because it is too difficult to find an exact solution. The desired result is then an approximated value of the theoretical, exact result. The difference between these two results must be less than a predetermined value called the tolerated error. This tolerated error is associated with two aspects of the resolution:

– when solving a problem P, one can solve another problem P', different from P, whose solution is sufficiently close to the solution of P;

– the choice of method depends on the precision of which the computer is capable: it would be useless to use a sophisticated method if the added precision it brought were destroyed by numerical errors.

In fact, a great number of problems can be solved by solving similar but simpler problems in which the complex functions of the first problems are replaced with easier–to–calculate functions (a polynomial or a rational fraction). For example, in order to interpolate a function or calculate its integral, one usually replaces the function with a polynomial. The calculation is then based on the polynomial (or its integral).

The two following methods are generally used to solve the simplified problem:

The *direct method*, which allows users to find the exact solution to the problem (not considering errors due to the rounding–off of numbers). It uses a finite number of elementary calculations. The Gauss–Jordan method of matrix inversion is an example of a direct method.

The *iterative method*, which proceeds by applying the same calculation sequence a number of times. This sequence uses an approximate value of the solution to find another – but more accurate – approximate value. In order to use such a method, it is first necessary to examine the convergence of the process and the speed of this convergence. One should avoid using a slow iterative method as it might result in large errors due to the rounding–off of numbers.

For example, let us examine the calculation of the exponential based on the truncated series. The degree n will be such that:

$$| \frac{\text{Est}_n(e^x) - e^x}{e^x} | < \varepsilon$$

The calculation of e^x has been replaced by the calculation of a polynomial.

1.3 Capacities and Limitations of Computers

The contribution of computers to the development of numerical analysis has been essential. Indeed, the use of calculators has allowed users to solve problems that were inaccessible when calculations were done only by hand. The three main improvements brought by computers are:

– the capacity to calculate at great speed;
– the capacity to store information;
– the capacity to save calculation programs.

These new possibilities have completely modified the resolution of problems and the numerical methods which are used. Therefore, numerical analysis has evolved, and today is a part of computer science as well as mathematics.

This evolution has tended to give the advantage of the actual resolution of problems over pure theoretical reasoning. For example, in numerical analysis, an elegant but impractical method will not do. The goal is to search not for the theoretical solution to a problem, but for an approximate solution.

However, computers do have handicaps. The following are their main limitations.

For each result, there is a problem of precision. Due to the structure of computers and to the way they work with numbers, a certain number of errors can occur and modify the result. These errors are the subject of section 2.

The other major limitation of computers is their calculation speed. Though computers today calculate very rapidly, they do not allow the use of certain methods that require a great number of calculations because the result cannot be obtained quickly enough.

1.4 Algorithm Evaluation

It is often possible to find the solution to a given problem using several different numerical methods. Thus, the difficulty lies in the choice of the algorithm.

Generally, one can evaluate the qualities of an algorithm on the basis of the following characteristics:

precise it is not sensitive to approximation or truncation errors;
general it works with a wide range of problems;
reliable there is no discontinuity on the limits of its application field;
adapted it is possible to evaluate its applicability to the given problem;
fast it requires few calculation resources.

In section 2 we will examine the different factors that decrease the precision of a given calculation method. In particular, we will distinguish between the two main sources of imprecision.

The first, calculation error, is due to the computer. The second, method or truncatory error, can be blamed on the algorithm.

According to the type of problem one wishes to solve and the constraints that one must take into account, the importance of the different criteria in the choice of the algorithm may vary. In some cases, precision will be given priority. However, when the calculation's speed is critical, one will tend to choose a rapidly convergent algorithm, even if it leads to a result that is less precise.

For iterative methods, convergence speed is often essential. The calculation of e^x, for example, is never done by using the sum of the truncated series because the number of terms to take into account is too great to obtain a result with acceptable precision. Furthermore, two contradictory factors appear in such methods: the complexity of each iteration and the number of iterations. One can often use either a simple but slowly convergent iterative method or a more complex but more rapidly convergent iterative method. It is generally better to choose the former as long as the number of iterations remains acceptable.

In order to reduce the number of iterations and thus the calculation time, one may rely on accelerated convergence formulas. These formulas use a series of calculated values x_1, x_2, ... x_n to generate another series y_1, y_2 ... y_n which converges toward the desired solution more quickly. The Romberg method, which is used for calculating integrals and is described in chapter 14, uses this process.

Finally, we must point out that in some cases, the algorithm that is used depends heavily on the available computer system. If for example the computer's central memory (RAM) is too restricted to contain all of the data, it becomes necessary to store this data on a peripheral, usually a magnetic disk. Due to the relatively large amount of time needed to access such a peripheral, compared to the central memory, it is important to limit the number of accesses to the magnetic disk during problem resolution.

2   Precision in Numerical Calculations

The above considerations have introduced the notion of error. This notion is omnipresent in numerical analysis, as it is based on the calculation of approximated values.

Through the use of the computer, one of the main causes of error in numerical analysis, the copying of intermediate results by hand, has disappeared. However, two new causes of error have appeared: the truncation error, also known as the method error, and the round sum error, also known as the numerical error.

The method error stems from the algorithm's precision. It is generally linked to the study of the algorithm itself. Most often, the programmer has pertinent information in this area when he chooses an algorithm.

However, errors involving the computer are seldom mentioned. We shall therefore discuss that aspect now.

We will first explain the way numbers are coded in the computer's memory. Then, we will examine how this affects the calculated results in terms of overflow errors, round number errors and cumulated errors.

Subsequently, we will provide a brief review of truncation errors. This will enable us to compare the influence of numerical errors with the influence of method errors. Such a comparison is necessary in order to dissociate the two types of errors when analysing a result given by the computer.

2.1 Number Representation

In order to fully understand where the lack of precision in numerical calculations comes from, we must examine how numbers – whole and real numbers as far as we are concerned – are coded in the computer's memory.

2.1.1 Binary Representation

The technology used in the construction of computers today allows users to store information only in the form of a succession of binary states. The computer can handle only the two logical states 0 and 1, which correspond to the presence or the absence of electrical current.

The representation of more complex information is done through the assemblage of several binary digits called bits. A series of eight bits is called a byte (symbolised by the letter B). This unit is often mentioned in relation to the storage capacity of computers: for example, a 640 KB central memory (or RAM: Random Access Memory), a 720 KB diskette or a 80 MB hard disk drive. The K stands for "Kilo" and represents a value of $1\,024 = 2^{10}$; the M stands for "Mega" and represents a value of $1\,048\,576 = 2^{20}$.

Because of the architecture of computers, the base unit used for the storage of high level information is the byte. The storage of an ASCII character usually uses one byte, while the storage of a whole number uses up to four bytes and the storage of a real number uses four, eight or sixteen bytes.

2.1.2 Integer Representation

In Borland C++, there are two modes of integer representation: the `short int` mode and the `long int` mode. In `short int` mode, whole numbers are coded on two bytes, or sixteen bits, representing 2^{16} or 65 536 possible values. It is therefore easy to code whole numbers between –32 768 and 32 767. There is a third mode, called `unsigned int`, which only codes positive whole numbers between 0 and 65 535.

The second mode, `long int`, is coded on four bytes, which allows one to enlarge the representation interval. It is thus possible to code whole numbers between –2 147 483 648 and 2 147 483 647.

The number of bytes used for coding numbers is set only once by the types of variables available. This limits the size of the numbers that can be coded, setting the stage for overflow error. Overflow error happens, during a calculation, for example, when there is a number located beyond one of the two limits. We will analyse this error and its consequences more precisely in the next section.

2.1.3 Real Number Representation

Before presenting the types of real numbers available in C++, we will first describe the representation of floating point real numbers.

Any real number has only one approximation of the following form (the first digit after the point being different from 0):

$$0.DDDDDDDDDD . 10^N$$

The series of decimal figures DDDDDDDDDD is called a mantissa and contains the significant figures of the number. N is the exponent and represents the number's degree. For example:

2.8	is	$0.28 . 10^1$
256	is	$0.256 . 10^3$
0.0048	is	$0.48 . 10^{-2}$

Let us note that in this representation, the mantissa is always greater than $\frac{1}{10}$ and smaller than 1 (it is always possible to bring it back into this interval by changing the exponent).

We have said that the computer uses binary, not decimal, representation. Therefore, real numbers are not coded in memory according to their base 10 representation, but are converted to base 2. Thus, any real number can be represented under the following form (the first digit after the decimal point being different from 0):

$$0.BBBBBBBBBB . 2^N$$

In this case, the mantissa and the exponent are made up of binary digits. The mantissa is greater than $\frac{1}{2}$ and smaller than 1. Each one of its digits is associated with a power of $\frac{1}{2}$:

0,	B	B	B	B	B	B	B	B	B	B	...
	$\frac{1}{2^1}$	$\frac{1}{2^2}$	$\frac{1}{2^3}$	$\frac{1}{2^4}$	$\frac{1}{2^5}$	$\frac{1}{2^6}$	$\frac{1}{2^7}$	$\frac{1}{2^8}$	$\frac{1}{2^9}$	$\frac{1}{2^{10}}$	

Here are a few examples of real numbers coded in binary floating point:

1	is	$0.5 . 2^1$	mantissa:	0.1	exponent:	1
4	is	$0.5 . 2^3$	mantissa:	0.1	exponent:	11
12.5	is	$0.78125 . 2^4$	mantissa:	0.11001	exponent:	100

This form of representation has one fault: it does not allow exact storage of all rational numbers.

Let us visualise this effect by representing the number $\frac{1}{5} = 0.2$ in binary floating point. First, we wish to determine the value of the exponent:

$$0.2 = 0.8 . 2^{-2}$$

We then decompose the mantissa 0.8 into powers of 1/2; the binary result is the following:

0.1100 1100 1100 1100 ...

The series of powers of $\frac{1}{2}$ necessary to form the number 0.8 is infinite.

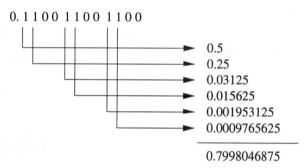

0. 1 1 0 0 1 1 0 0 1 1 0 0

| | 0.5
| | 0.25
| | 0.03125
| | 0.015625
| | 0.001953125
| | 0.0009765625

0.7998046875

As the storage capacity of a computer is necessarily limited, the series has to be truncated. This operation induces an error. Above, we have represented the mantissa with twelve bits. We obtain a medium precision, with only three significant figures.

In order to obtain a more acceptable precision, it is necessary to increase the number of bits used for coding the mantissa. In Borland C++, the `double` type coded on 64 bits, of which 53 are used by the mantissa, allows a 16 significant digit precision.

The exponent is coded on 11 bits, which allows an interval of variation limited by:

$$2^{-1022} \quad \text{and} \quad 2^{+1024}$$

which correspond to the following numbers, using decimal notation:

$$2.23 . 10^{-308} \quad \text{and} \quad 1.79 . 10^{+308}$$

Normally, the limits are rounded off at the values 10^{-308} and 10^{+308}, to facilitate the storage. We have defined the `ar_double` type which allows to use `long double` (16 bytes) instead of `double` (8 bytes) just by replacing the line:

```
#define ar_double double
```
by
```
#define ar_double long double
```

2.2 Numerical Errors

2.2.1 Overflow Errors

Be it for whole numbers or real numbers, we have seen that their representation, on a set number of bits, creates a limited interval of use.

An overflow error occurs when, in the middle of a calculation, the result goes beyond the imposed interval.

For real numbers, exceeding the upper limit (10^{+308}) forces the program to stop and an error message appears. On the other hand, when exceeding the lower limit (10^{-308}), the program continues; however, the result is rounded off to 0, which can be a problem in certain calculations.

For whole numbers, the situation is much worse: no error is detected by the computer. The result of the calculation is truncated before being stored in the variable, and the stored value is completely false. This can greatly damage the program's execution.

The following program illustrates the computer's behaviour when faced with an overflow. Notice that in our example, the final result is between the limits imposed by the integer type. However, the overflow results from an intermediate calculation.

This rather frequent case can be easily avoided by inverting the order of the calculations or by placing parentheses at the proper locations.

```
#include <stdio.h>

main ()
{
   int a = 500, b = 400, c = 200, d;

   d = a * b / c;    cout << "d = " << d << "\n";
   d = b / c * a;    cout << "d = " << d << "\n";
   d = a * (b / c);  cout << "d = " << d << "\n";
}
```

The first result given by the program is completely false (16), whereas the two last results are correct (1000 and 1000).

Therefore, when writing a program, one must take into consideration the limit cases in order to detect the overflows which can take place and make the necessary corrections.

2.2.2 Approximation Errors

This type of error involves only real numbers. We have seen that floating point representation induces a systematic truncation error for some real numbers: only the first significant digits are preserved. For example, for the real number $\frac{1}{3}$, the computer writes the value 0.3333333333333334. The last digit is incorrect. Generally, we can never consider that the last digit is correct, because of the approximation error.

This phenomenon occurs most frequently when the calculations use numbers with very different degrees. A small result, obtained through the difference between two large values, is often subject to an important approximation error. Here is a simple example of this phenomenon.

Let $x = 10^{25}$, $y = 50$, $z = -10^{25}$. The sum $w = x + y + z$ theoretically amounts to 50. However, the result given by the computer is 0. The relative error is small but can be catastrophic when located inside an iterative process. If the computer had calculated $w = x + z + y$, it would have found the correct result. From a numerical point of view, the sum of real numbers is not associative!

In order to eliminate the influence of approximation errors, some scientific programs transform the data so that the different degrees it contains become closer. The opposite transformation is performed on the results. It is sometimes necessary to use 12 significant digits in a calculation in order to obtain 5 or 6 correct digits in the result.

Let us consider the approximation of the value of a derivative at a given point. The well–known theoretical formula is the following:

$$f(x_0) = \lim \frac{f(x) - f(x_0)}{x - x_0} \qquad \text{when } x \text{ approaches } x_0.$$

We can use the following 2nd degree approximation formula:

$$f(x_0) = \frac{f(x_0+h) - f(x_0-h)}{2h}$$

The precision of the result should be better if the value of h is small. However, if h is very small, the values $f(x_0+h)$ and $f(x_0-h)$ are extremely close. Consequently, the last decimals of the difference between these two values are very significant. There may be few significant digits in the result of the calculation, and perhaps none if the representations of the numbers $f(x_0+h)$ and $f(x_0-h)$ are identical.

This phenomenon is also known as the evanescent differences phenomenon. It is necessary to find an optimal value for h which is satisfactory for the theoretical formula and at the same time permits one to achieve suitable calculation precision.

We will examine this example in greater detail in section 2.4.

2.2.3 Cumulative Errors

Cumulated errors are directly linked to approximation errors. They appear when the result is obtained through a large number of calculations.

After each calculation, the computer makes an approximation error. Because the result is generally obtained using the intermediate results, errors accumulate and can impair the precision.

This phenomenon becomes more serious when the magnitude of the problem increases. The cumulation of approximation errors when calculations are very numerous can completely transform the result. Some resolution methods that prove satisfactory for small problems are not suitable for large problems.

Let us consider the calculation of the sum of a series. If the series converges rapidly, the sum of about a hundred terms yields the greatest precision that a computer can achieve.

On the other hand, if the series converges slowly, one must use a greater number of terms (100 000, for example). Since each term is only an approximation, uncertainties accumulate after each sum and may impair the final result's precision.

One must, then, use a large enough number of terms without allowing numerical errors to become predominant. This compromise between numerical errors and method errors will be described in greater detail in the next section.

2.2.4 The Notion of Numerical Zero

Let us consider two numerical values A and B obtained after a number of arithmetic calculations. Even if these two values are theoretically identical, they are generally different. Naturally, this difference is due to approximation errors.

To determine whether these two values are equal, one cannot just compare the difference $A-B$ to zero. One could compare $|A-B|$ with a value ε, negligible relative to A and B, and chosen according to the proportion of approximation errors. This value ε is called "numerical zero". If the difference $|A-B|$ is less than ε, then it is considered equal to zero and A and B are considered equal.

The main interest of the numerical zero is that it can, in some cases, reduce the propagation of approximation errors. If each intermediate result less than ε is forced to zero, approximation errors that appear during the calculation of this intermediate value are eliminated. Unfortunately, the notion of numerical zero is difficult to handle because ε must be chosen according to the calculation plan as well as to the problem's data.

2.3 Method Errors

We have just reviewed the main causes of numerical errors, whch are all errors made by the computer. There is another type of error which is associated with the calculation method that is used.

To limit the calculation time and the memory space needed to run a numerical calculation algorithm, the programmer must make simplifications and approximations. These voluntary, known simplifications and approximations impair the result's precision.

These errors are called method errors. They are a result only of the chosen resolution method, and not of the hardware that is used.

The most frequent method error is the truncatory error. We have seen that the resolution of most problems is done by replacing the initial problem by a similar one that is easier to solve. Sometimes, the resolution of the second problem neglects or simplifies part of the first problem. This error is called truncation error.

For example, let us examine the calculation of the sum of a series: one merely adds up a finite number of terms. When calculating an integral, one replaces the function with a polynomial. When solving a differential equation with initial conditions, one obtains the point y_{n+1} using the point y_n and an approximative formula.

In general, it is possible to calculate theoretically the upper limit of the error induced by this substitution. However, the exact calculation of this limit is not always easy.

2.4 Numerical Errors and Method Errors

When perfecting an algorithm, one must study the error induced by the method and compare it with the numerical errors made by the computer.

In the previous example of the calculation of a derivative, we saw that one must find a compromise between the value of h necessary to obtain a precise theoretical formula, and the number of significant digits needed to obtain a suitable numerical value. In this example, the numerical error superseded the method error when the value of h was reduced.

This effect is visible in the following figure:

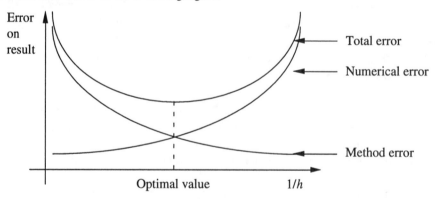

This is also true for the sum of a series: if we increase the number of terms added, the method error decreases, but the numerical error increases. The precision of the final result is subject to these two sources of error.

In conclusion, it is useless to develop a very precise algorithm if its precision is destroyed by numerical errors. It is indispensable to know how to distinguish between the types of errors, in order to decide which parameters must be modified to increase precision.

Example: calculation of a derivative

We will calculate the approximate value of the derivative of a numerical function at one point by using the following approximation:

$$f'(x_0) = \frac{f(x_0+h) - f(x_0-h)}{2h}$$

Of course, the smaller h is, the better our approximation. However, when h is very small, the values $f(x_0+h)$ and $f(x_0-h)$ are very close and, due to the approximation error, there are only a few significant digits in their difference.

Let us visualise this phenomenon by using the following program:

```
#include <stdio.h>
#include <math.h>
#include <iomanip.h>

/*--------------------- Definition of the function */
double f (double x)
{
  return (exp (x));
}

main ()
{
  double h, x = 0;
  do  {
    cout << "h = "; cin >> h;
    if (h != 0)
      cout << "f'(0) = " << setw (18) << setprecision (15)
           << (f (x + h) - f (x - h)) / 2 / h << "\n";
  }  while (h != 0);
}
```

Let us run the program using different values for h; we obtain the following results:

```
h = 1          f'(0) = 1.175201193643801
h = 0.1        f'(0) = 1.00166750019844
h = 0.01       f'(0) = 1.00001666675
h = 0.001      f'(0) = 1.000000166666675
h = 1e-4       f'(0) = 1.000000001666666
h = 1e-5       f'(0) = 1.000000000016664
h = 1e-6       f'(0) = 1.000000000000106
h = 1e-7       f'(0) = 0.999999999999482
h = 1e-8       f'(0) = 0.999999999999482
h = 1e-9       f'(0) = 0.99999999993443
h = 1e-10      f'(0) = 1.000000000069955
h = 1e-11      f'(0) = 0.999999996004197
h = 1e-12      f'(0) = 0.999999968899143
h = 1e-13      f'(0) = 0.99999950811322
h = 1e-14      f'(0) = 0.999997610759418
h = 1e-15      f'(0) = 0.999932558629068
h = 1e-16      f'(0) = 0.999634403031635
```

It is clear that the optimal value for h is around 10^{-6}. For this value, the method error and the numerical error are of the same degree, and the global precision is almost equal to the maximum possible precision.

2.5 Program Validation

It is relatively easy to evaluate method errors theoretically, but numerical errors are harder to evaluate. Furthermore, an errorless program is very rare.

This is why one must verify the results obtained by running the program with various sets of data for which theoretical results are known. The values calculated by the program must then be analysed. If there is disagreement, it can be due to one or several of the following errors:

– numerical error by the computer;

– method error (this error does not apply in our example);

– data error

– undetected programming error.

In this book, each algorithm comes with annotated examples. When disparities between theoretical and calculated values appear, their causes are analysed.

Programs presented in this book have been validated for use in the cases discussed in the text. This does not mean that programs are valid for other uses.

Using an algorithm in situations that were not initially planned may lead to abnormal results.

3   Numerical Tools

When teaching numerical analysis, most people focus on the algorithmic and mathematical aspects and neglect the programming side. Many programmers who use numerical calculation methods are better at calculating the errors than at programming.

For this reason, we have decided to focus on the aspects of programming by using the very powerful concept of software tool.

3.1 Software Tool and Toolbox

A software tool is a small program which is very good at performing a limited number of tasks. Its small size facilitates testing, error detection and performance optimisation.

The interfaces between software tools and users are perfectly defined. Knowledge of these interfaces makes the tools simple to use, on their own or as a whole; as a result, programmers do not hesitate to rely on them.

Thus, programs developed using these tools are written and perfected more rapidly. Using a toolbox, one can write a short, legible, simply maintained program, instead of writing a long, inflexible, complex program.

This is why toolboxes, which are very common due to structured languages such as Pascal and C, are more useful in the development of graphic tools or interfaces, for example, than in numerical analysis. When an engineer must solve a differential equation during the simulation of a physical phenomenon, he usually develops his own program. Most often, he does not systematically seek to optimise it, nor to use tools which are already functional.

Thus, numerical analysis programs have the reputation of being used only once. Since they are not particularly well written, they are not sufficiently clear or modular to be easily adaptable to new problems. Experienced programmers know that 1000–line functions containing many overlapping GOTO commands are not the best way to write a flexible program.

There are numerical toolboxes which implement the main methods of analysis, but the latter usually run on mainframe or mini–computers. Because increasing numbers of engineers and scientists use workstations or microcomputers, access to these toolboxes managed by computer services is disappearing. In addition, the intermediate code, necessary for the input and the output of data or for modifying the format of the data between two tools, must be constantly rewritten.

3.2 The Approach of This Book

The aim of this book is to show how to apply software tools to programming in numerical analysis, and to provide the engineer or the student with a complete, coherent set of tools. All the tools in this book were made to work together, in order to form a toolbox of C++ functions which complete existing libraries. We also show how to use exploitation tools to build a program. Thus, even the adaptation to the specific program is facilitated.

The interface between the tools and the user has voluntarily been greatly simplified, so as to limit the parameters to be learned for each tool. The same applies to the representation of numbers and mathematical expressions: very powerful tools have been developed to facilitate the writing of a program by the user.

Thus, an application program contains a limited number of calls to certain tools. This replaces many lines of programming.

3.3 Utilisation of C++

Though FORTRAN has long been the inevitable language of numerical analysis, it has not had the same success on microcomputers or on workstations used for scientific purposes. However, the growing development of systems using UNIX in scientific and technical environments has made C and its extension C++ into a universal language for high level programming. Further, C is not restricted to the programming of system software.

Today, a version of a C++ compiler exists on almost all workstations and microcomputers, and the conversion of programs from one version to another involves only slight modifications. In addition, several engineering schools and universities have chosen to teach C.

Thus, C is now a reference language in the scientific and technical worlds. Among its qualities, other than its ease of structure and portability, is the speed of the programs which it generates. C possesses instructions "close to the machine" which may be translated by as little as one line of assembler. This speed is essential for scientific programs which often demand instant results (real time), or long and complex resolutions of differential systems.

One of the reasons C can generate such efficient code is that it makes no implicit verifications. In other words, it considers only the tests which are explicitly written into the programs. Thus, unlike Pascal, C does no variable comparisons with given intervals, and no coherence verifications.

The major drawback of C is summarised in the following remark: though it is possible to create very effective programs, using all the resources of the material, and of the processor in particular, it is also very easy to commit programming errors which are extremely difficult to detect. Specifically, insufficient mastery of the mechanism of dynamic memory allocation can lead to problems which cause difficulties at any moment, except during the execution of the command by the processor.

This explains why with C, unlike Pascal, one needs to have considerable programming experience in order to assimilate all the nuances and subtlety, especially in the case of scientific real–time programs.

4   The Advantages of C++ Over C

4.1 The Advantage of Object Programming

The major advantage of C++ compared to C lies of course in its manipulation of the object–oriented mechanisms. This allows one to implement the encapsulation and abstraction of the data.

For example, whether a matrix is represented by a table or by a string will be perceived only when the class `matrix` is declared.

During subsequent use of this new object, this choice of representation will be ignored. In particular, one is thus enabled to modify it later without affecting all programs using matrices.

4.2 Passing Parameters by Reference

Among other reasons, C is awkward because it is impossible to pass variables by "address" or by "variable" like one can in Pascal. Each C parameter must be passed by value. This necessitates the intensive use of pointers, even when the pointers are not useful functionally or algorithmically.

C++ eliminates this serious limitation by offering the possibility of passing a parameter "by reference". This automatically transmits the *address* of this parameter to the called procedure, instead of transmitting its *value*.

The following example illustrates the difference using a concrete case. This small program calculates the square of *i* and assigns it to *n*.

In C :

```
main ()
{
   int i = 2, n;
   square (i, &n);
}

square (int i, int *n)
{
   *n = i * i;
}
```

In C++ :

```
main ()
{
   int i = 2, n;
   square (i, n)
}

square (int i, int &n)
{
   n = i * i;
}
```

In C++, the fact that the function `square` modifies the parameter n only comes into play once, during the definition of the header of `square`.

In C, however, one must specify this particularity again each time n is used, be it in `main ()` or in `square ()`.

If one forgets just once, an integer is assigned to a pointer instead of the pointed variable, and pandemonium ensues...

4.3 Mandatory Prototyping

The function prototyping mechanism allows one to ask the compiler to verify that the types of variable passed as parameters are correct.

This mechanism already exists in C, but it is optional. In C++, prototyping becomes mandatory, which avoids errors that are extremely difficult to detect.

4.4 Operator Overload

C++ enables one to rewrite the basic functions, such as multiplication, for the new objects in use. In chapter 9, for example, we have overloaded the multiplication of matrices. This allows one to write very simply:

```
m3 = m1 * m2;
```

This instruction, in which `m1`, `m2` and `m3` are three variables of the class `matrix`, executes the multiple operations which are necessary in a transparent manner.

2

Using the Tools in This Book

In chapter 1, we examined the concept of tools and their importance in object oriented programming. Now we will study the utilisation of the tools which are presented in this book.

Though you are most probably eager to integrate certain tools into your own programs, we strongly recommend that you do more than skim this general chapter. If you do, you will get more out of the specific tools which interest you.

We will begin by reviewing the philosophy behind the development of applications in C++. Then, we will introduce the general software architecture, namely the tool typology and the distribution of the source modules throughout the different files and directories.

Portability and Borland C++ compilers will be examined in more detail.

Subsequently, we will discuss different approaches to the utilisation of these tools, from the integration of one sole tool into a program, to the creation of a complete mathematical software program. We pay particular attention to the practical application of these methods.

Lastly, we will provide printouts of the general modules.

1   Software Architecture

1.1 Development Principles for an Application in C++

The following diagram symbolizes the program construction process. This diagram is more complicated for the creation of a Windows program. In the latter case, the executable program itself is mixed with one or more Windows resource files.

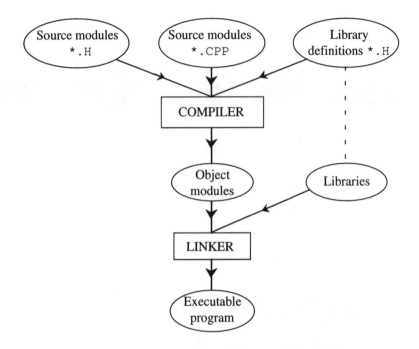

Now we will explain the different concepts used by this representation.

A software program written in C++ is composed of several source modules which fall into two categories:

- the modules whose names end in .CPP, and which contain functions written in C++,
- the modules whose names end in .H, and which contain constants, structure types, predefinitions, and particular objects.

The source modules take on concrete form, after compilation, as executable binary instructions. On the other hand, the data contained in the *.H modules is used only during compilation, to determine the nature or the value of certain objects.

The example below illustrates this composition. The program calculates the circumference of a circle with a given radius. It is made up of two modules, CIRCLE.CPP and TRIGO.H.

Contents of the module CIRCLE.CPP:

```
#include <stdio.h>
#include <iomanip.h>
#include "trigo.h"

main ()
{
    int  r, circ;
```

```
cout << "Enter the radius of the circle : "; cin >>r;
circ = 2 * PI * r;
cout << "\nThe circumference is : " << circ << "\n";
}
```

Contents of the module `TRIGO.H`:

```
#define  PI  3.1415926535
```

The separation of the constants and predefinitions from the functions allows one to form `*.H` modules which are common to several programs. Thus, in the previous example, the exact value of `PI` is only defined once in the module `TRIGO.H`. Other programs can use this value without redefining it, but using the module `TRIGO.H`.

Writing an inclusion command `#include` on a line is just like replacing the line with the entire file to which it refers.

Using these source modules `*.CPP` and `*.H`, the compiler produces *object* modules. An object is produced for each source module. For example, the name of the object module associated with the source module `CIRCLE.CPP` is `CIRCLE.OBJ`. These object modules contain the machine language code which is generated from the source module. They also contain relocation information, which allows unknown objects to be referenced. Since a program written in C++ is composed of several source modules, the location in memory of the functions called on by a given module is unknown during the compilation of this module.

At the last stage of final program construction, the linker places all the object modules end to end, and solves the set of memory references.

Using libraries during the linking phase enables one to call on often-used functions within the source modules which are already written and perfected. The linker will take responsibility for extracting the referenced modules from the libraries, and for including them in the final program.

The nucleus of C++ is intentionally poor in available functions. On the contrary, the style of the language is to build libraries using a nucleus of basic instructions which are elementary but powerful.

The linker provides the program executable by the computer in the form of a module ending in `EXE`. In the previous example, the program will be `CIRCLE.EXE`.

1.2 The Four Tool Levels

The tools presented in this book may be grouped into four levels:
  – basic general tools, like the function `ar_calc_rational` which allows one to compute the rational approximation of a real number, or the function `ar_gcf`, which calculates the GCF of two numbers. These tools are collected in the module `ARMATH.CPP`, described in chapter 3;

- more elaborate general tools, each needing a complete source module. For example, the data entry module, which allows one to enter a set of variables which may be integers, real numbers, or alphanumeric characters, with error correction. These tools are presented in chapters 3 and 4;
- mathematical calculation tools, adapted to the resolution of a particular numerical problem. For example, the module for numerical calculation of integrals using the Romberg method, or the module for formal derivation of a function. These tools form the heart of the text and are introduced throughout the specific chapters;
- mathematical "exploïtation tools" which allow one to solve a problem completely, from the entry of the basic data needed for the calculation, to the display of the results, calling on the pure calculation tool along the way. We have written an exploitation tool for every calculation tool. These tools are collected at the end of each specific chapter.

1.3 Files and Directories Used

We have filed the roughly 200 tools presented in this book in a hierarchical structure with two directory levels.

The main directory contains the general tools.

Then, a subdirectory for each specific chapter of the book contains all the calculation and exploitation tools relevant to the chapter.

The name of the file which contains the exploitation tool is formed by placing the letter U in front of the name of the file containing the mathematical tool. For example, the calculation tool for arcs is in the file ARC.CPP and the corresponding exploitation tool is in the file UARC.CPP.

We suggest that you create a directory on your hard disk which is reserved for the tools in this book. You may call this directory \MATHCPP.

This directory \MATHCPP contains the following subdirectories:

```
COMPLEX     <DIR>
CURVES      <DIR>
DERIV       <DIR>
PSE         <DIR>
EQUADIFF    <DIR>
EQUATION    <DIR>
FOURIER     <DIR>
FRAC        <DIR>
GEO         <DIR>
INTEGRAL    <DIR>
MAT         <DIR>
OUTPUT      <DIR>
POL         <DIR>
SURFACES    <DIR>
```

as well as the following files, whose contents will be introduced in detail throughout the book.

`ARMATH.CPP`	Basic general tools
`ARMATH.H`	Constants and predefinitions for the entire book
`ARPORT.CPP`	Portability functions
`ARPORT.H`	Portability constants and predefinitions
`GRAFPORT.CPP`	Portability functions for graphics
`ENTRY.CPP`	Specific data entry tools for variables
`BUFFER.CPP`	Specific tools permitting data communication
`FUNCTION.CPP`	Specific tools for function analysis and manipulation
`GRAPHICS.CPP`	Specific tools for graphics utilisation
`NUMBER.CPP`	Management of the `ar_number` class which permits formal calculations using rational numbers
`ANALYSI.CPP`	Module providing access to all analysis tools
`ALGEBRA.CPP`	Module providing access to all algebra tools

1.4 Different User Approaches

Now we will examine different approaches to using the tools in this book.

The architecture presented here meets the user's need for a "toolbox", from the integration of one tool into a software program, to the creation of a complete mathematical software program by using several tools from a library.

2 Portability

No language is 100% portable. Even though C++ is well known for its high degree of portability, there is a slight adaptation to make when one transfers the program from one machine to another, or even when one changes compilers (for example, using Microsoft C++ instead of Borland C++).

In this book, we have collected all the functions and constants specific to the machine or compiler in use, into the three files `ARPORT.CPP`, `ARPORT.H` and `GRAFPORT.CPP` (the letters `PORT` stand for portability).

The portability files presented at the end of the chapter are those which permit the use of Borland C++ on a PC compatible computer. If you are using other equipment, or another compiler, you must complete these two files in order to be able to implement (or to modify the implementation of) functions which differ from one system to another. For example, if you are using the Microsoft C++ compiler, you need only replace the two portability files by the following:

File ARPORT.CPP:

```
/*===========================================================
                       ARPORT.CPP :
                   MICROSOFT C++ SPECIFIC
===========================================================*/

#include <armath.h>

void ar_beep (int frequency, int duration)
{
  cout << "\007";
}

void clrscr ()
{
  int i;

  for (i = 1; i <= 25; i++)
    cout << "\n";
}

double pow10 (double r)
{
  return pow (10, r);
}

complex operator / (complex &z1, complex &z2)
{
  double r = norm (z2);
  if (r == 0) {errno = 1; return 0;}

  return complex ((z1.x * z2.x + z1.y * z2.y) / r,
            (- z1.x * z2.y + z1.y * z2.x) / r);
}

complex  exp (complex &z)
{
  double  x = real (z), y = imag (z);
  return complex (exp (x) * cos (y), exp (x) * sin (y));
}

complex  log (complex &z)
{
  double  x = real (z), y = imag (z);
  if (x == 0) {errno = 1; return 0;}
  return complex (log (x * x + y * y) / 2, atan (y / x));
}
```

```
complex  pow (complex &z1, complex &z2)
{
  return  exp (z2 * log (z1));
}

complex  sqrt (complex &z)
{
  double  x = real (z), y = imag (z);
  double  r = sqrt (x * x + y * y);
  double s = sqrt ((r - x) / 2);
  return complex (sqrt ((r + x) / 2), ((y > 0) ? s : - s));
}

complex  sin (complex &z)
{
  double  x = real (z), y = imag (z);
  return complex (sin (x) * cosh (y), cos (x) * sinh (y));
}

complex  cos (complex &z)
{
  double  x = real (z), y = imag (z);
  return complex (cos (x) * cosh (y), - sin (x) * sinh (y));
}

complex  tan (complex &z)
{
  return  (sin (z) / cos (z));
}

complex  sinh (complex &z)
{
  double  x = real (z), y = imag (z);
  return complex (sinh (x) * cos (y), cosh (x) * sin (y));
}

complex  cosh (complex &z)
{
  double  x = real (z), y = imag (z);
  return complex (cosh (x) * cos (y), sinh (x) * sin (y));
}

complex  tanh (complex &z)
{
  return  (sinh (z) / cosh (z));
}
```

```
complex  asin (complex &z)
{
  return  (complex (0, -1) * log (
    complex (0, 1) * z + sqrt (complex (1, 0) - z * z)));
}

complex  acos (complex &z)
{
  return  (complex (0, -1) * log (
          z + sqrt (z * z - complex (1, 0))));
}

complex  atan (complex &z)
{
  return  (complex (0, 0.5) * log (
    (complex (1, 0) + complex (0, 1) * z) /
    (complex (1, 0) - complex (0, 1) * z)));
}
```

File ARPORT.H:

```
/*===========================================================
                         ARPORT.H:
               PORTABILITY: CONSTANTS MODULE
                       MICROSOFT  C++
   =========================================================*/

#include <stdlib.h>
#include <string.h>
#include <math.h>
#include <iostream.h>
#include <iomanip.h>

#define AR_PI          3.14159265358979323846
#define AR_PI2         1.57079632679489661923

void  clrscr       (void);
double      pow10 (double);

class complex {

  double  x, y;

public:
  complex (double _x, double _y = 0) {x = _x; y = _y;};
  complex () {x = 0; y = 0;};
```

```
    friend double    real  (complex &);
    friend double    imag  (complex &);
    friend double    norm  (complex &);
    friend double    arg   (complex &);
    friend complex   polar (double, double);

    friend complex   operator + (complex  &, complex  &);
    friend complex   operator - (complex  &, complex  &);
    friend complex   operator * (complex  &, complex  &);
    friend complex   operator / (complex  &, complex  &);

    complex  & operator += (complex  &);
    complex  & operator -= (complex  &);
    complex  & operator *= (complex  &);
    complex  & operator /= (complex  &);
};

    complex  sqrt (complex &);
    complex  exp   (complex &);
    complex  log   (complex &);
    complex  pow   (complex &, complex &);
    complex  sin   (complex &);
    complex  cos   (complex &);
    complex  tan   (complex &);
    complex  asin (complex &);
    complex  acos (complex &);
    complex  atan (complex &);
    complex  sinh (complex &);
    complex  cosh (complex &);
    complex  tanh (complex &);

inline complex& complex::operator += (complex &z)
{
    *this = *this + z;
    return *this;
}

inline complex& complex::operator -= (complex &z)
{
    *this = *this - z;
    return *this;
}

inline complex& complex::operator *= (complex &z)
{
    *this = *this * z;
    return *this;
}
```

```
inline complex& complex::operator /= (complex &z)
{
  *this = *this / z;
  return *this;
}

inline double real (complex &z)
{
  return  z.x;
}

inline double imag (complex &z)
{
  return  z.y;
}

inline double norm (complex &z)
{
  return  z.x * z.x + z.y * z.y;
}

inline double arg (complex &z)
{
  if (z.y == 0)  return  0;
  if (z.x == 0)  return  AR_PI2;
  return  atan (z.y / z.x);
}

inline complex polar (double mod, double ang)
{
  return complex (mod * cos (ang), mod * sin (ang));
}

inline complex operator + (complex &z1, complex &z2)
{
  return complex (z1.x + z2.x, z1.y + z2.y);
}

inline complex operator - (complex &z1, complex &z2)
{
  return complex (z1.x - z2.x, z1.y - z2.y);
}

inline complex operator * (complex &z1, complex &z2)
{
  return complex (z1.x * z2.x - z1.y * z2.y,
            z1.x * z2.y + z1.y * z2.x);
}
```

This technique involves isolating all the concepts which are not directly portable in a small number of modules. It allows one to rapidly adapt the tool library presented in this book to a wide range of compilers and computers, from an IBM-PC to a DEC minicomputer or IBM mainframe.

For the users of Borland C++, we note that in addition, the graphic interface file which corresponds to the graphics card in use (`xxxxx.BGI`) must be present in the current directory during the execution of the program, if one wishes to use the graphic functions.

---

3   Integrating a Tool Into a Program

Let us suppose that inside the module of an existing software program, we wish to call on the equation–solving tool `ar_dichotomies`. We will now provide in detail the different operations which must be done in order to integrate this tool into the existing software program.

The existing software program is made up of several source modules `*.CPP` and `*.H`. Most often, it also contains a project management file or a linking file, which gives an exhaustive list of the object modules that will compose the executable program, as well as the list of libraries to use during linking.

The integration of a software tool happens in four steps:
- a call to the tool, with the adapted parameters,
- insertion of `ar_init_math ()` instruction,
- inclusion of the file of mathematical constants,
- addition of all the object modules needed to the project file.

The tool call line resembles all function calls in C++.

The fact that C is so permissive when the type of parameters passed to a function was incorrect led to many errors which were difficult to detect. C++, however, demands that all functions be predefined and refuses to compile a program if there is a lack of coherence.

The predefinition lines for all the tools in the book are grouped in the file `ARMATH.H`.

One must add a line providing for the inclusion of the constants and predefinition file to the beginning of the module which uses the tool:

```
#include <armath.h>
```

This file is long (it has several hundred lines).

We could have distributed the predefinitions among several files of constants. However, we found it preferable to create only one file for the entire group of mathematical tools. This approach makes the inclusion line systematic and unique, thereby simplifying the utilisation of the tool.

After modifying the source module in question, by adding the tool call line and the inclusion line for the constants file, one must complete the project file.

One must systematically add three modules to this list: ARPORT, ARMATH, and the module containing the tool in use. One must often attach other modules to this list: those which contain the sub-tools of the tool which is called, or the modules containing the general tools (entry of variables ENTRY, manipulation of user functions FUNCTION).

We will see that using a library frees one from the constraint of having to search for the useful modules.

Cancelling Double Definition Errors

In our book, all constants and all tools start with the three characters ar_ (analysis routines). For example, the tool for integration using the Romberg method is called ar_integral_romberg.

This specificity allows one not only to easily identify the tools of the mathematical library, but also to eliminate double definition errors.

Let us suppose that you would like to add the tool for integration using the Romberg method to a program for solving a complex physical phenomenon, which you own. Though this tool does not use the constant PI directly, the latter is in the constants file. If PI is also defined in your program, a conflict due to double definition will arise during compilation. This also happens with the tools. If the tool ar_gcf () which is in the general basic tools file (ARMATH.CPP) were called (), and if your program had a similar function with the same name, there would be an error during compilation.

4   Constitution and Use of a Library

4.1 Advantages of Using a Library

One module is rarely sufficient in order to use a given tool. For example, the multiplication of two rational fractions demands the specific module for the multiplication of two fractions, as well as the following modules:

– multiplication of two polynomials,
– division of two polynomials,
– calculation of the GCF of two polynomials,
– simplification of a rational fraction,
– general mathematical module (ARMATH),
– portability module (ARPORT).

Suppose we would like to use the fraction multiplication tool in a software application. According to the approach described above, seven files must be specified in the project management file. If, later on in the development process, one decides to use a different method, the seven files must be eliminated from the project management module.

Using a library eliminates concerns about files not directly related to the tool one wishes to use. The linker takes responsibility for this task. During the creation of the executable program, the linker will look up the necessary modules in the library.

In addition to the modularity which it engenders, using a library frees the user from the management of all source modules and compiled modules, and allows these modules to be erased from the disk. Only the library file and the constants file must be kept.

We will describe how to build and use a library, using a set of object modules which have already been perfected.

4.2 How to Build a Library

The library can be built only when all of the modules have been correctly compiled. We suggest that you call the tool library ARMATH.LIB.

Each compiler has its own library management program. Though these programs have different syntaxes, they all use the same principle: the object modules can be added or withdrawn from a library, or replaced. The initial construction of a library is done by adding the compiled modules one by one.

For example, the management utility for libraries in Borland C++ is called TLIB. Adding an object module is done like this:

```
TLIB ARMATH.LIB +NAME.OBJ
```

or more simply (the extensions are known by default):

```
TLIB ARMATH +NAME
```

A long list of modules can simultaneously be placed in the library by using an intermediate file ARMATH.RSP, which contains the names of all of the modules. The instruction, issued from the OUTPUT directory:

```
TLIB ARMATH.LIB ..\@ARMATH.RSP
```

then creates the complete library. A file containing the names of all the compiled modules in this book comes with the diskette, so that partial or enriched libraries can be modified and generated.

When the library ARMATH.LIB has been created, it must be placed in the directory of the compiler which contains the libraries. With Borland C++, this directory is by default \BORLANDC\LIB.

The file of constants and predeclarations ARMATH.H must also be kept, and placed in the directory of the compiler which contains the files of constants. With Borland C++, this directory is \BORLANDC\INCLUDE by default.

4.3 How to Use a Library

Using a mathematical tool with a library is almost as simple as using a standard library function in C++.

When one uses the sine calculation function `sin` in a program in C++, it suffices to include the file of constants `math.h` at the beginning of this program, through the instruction `#include <math.h>`.

The brackets around the file name mean that the compiler must seek this file in the directory which contains the files of constants, not in the current directory.

Similarly, using a mathematical tool in any program will only necessitate one extra instruction: the line `#include <armath.h>` at the beginning of this program.

However, because the linker only knows standard libraries, the name of the mathematical library must be specified for it. With Borland C++, this is done by adding a line `armath.lib` to the project file. The presence of the extension `.lib` is sufficient for Borland C++ to know that it is not dealing with a module to be compiled, but with a library which must be taken into account during linking.

In the following example, we show how using a library makes things simpler: consider a program for the calculation of mechanical structures, which must calculate an integral using the Simpson method. This calculation calls for only two additional lines:

One in the program:

```
// ------------ Structures calculation program

 . . . .


// ------------ Inclusion of the constants file
#include <armath.h>


 . . . .

main ()
{
  . . . .

// ------------- Use of a tool
  resul = ar_integral_simpson (f, 20, 30, 100);


  . . . .
}
```

In the project description file:

```
// ------------- Inclusion of the mathematical library
armath.lib
```

4.4 Necessary Precautions

A library contains modules which were compiled under a certain compiler configuration; for example, a particular type of addressing, target processor, and emulation of a mathematical coprocessor.

The configuration used during the compilation of the modules which form the software program being developed must be identical to the configuration used during the creation of the library.

This explains the presence of several standard libraries in the environment of a C compiler. There is one library for each type of addressing which is used (one LARGE library, one SMALL library). In Borland C++, there are 6 of these standard libraries.

This obligation demands great caution while using libraries, in order to avoid inexplicable errors during linking. Suppose that a software developer in a Borland C++ environment on a microcomputer 386 creates a library using instructions specific to 80386 processors (by modifying the corresponding compiler option). If another developer has access only to a 286 microcomputer he will be unable to use this library.

The Borland C++ library provided on the disk is made up of modules compiled with the LARGE addressing type option, and instructions 80386.

5 Creation of a Complete Mathematical Software Program

It is possible to construct an entire program giving access to all of the tools described in this book.

To facilitate utilisation, especially where the general menu and the size of executable programs are concerned, we have decomposed this program into two modules: one associated with analysis and the other with algebra.

Through a menu, the module ANALYS.CPP gives access to all of the tools associated with analysis (graphing, equations, derivatives, integrals, surfaces, Fourier series, differential equations).

Like the others, this module must be compiled and placed in the list of modules to be taken into account during linking.

Similarly, the module ALGEBRA.CPP gives access to all the tools associated with geometry and algebra (complex numbers, polynomials, rational fractions, expansion series, matrices, vectors).

6   Printout of General Modules

The following module contains the constants and predefinitions for the entire book. It must be stored in the file ARMATH.H.

```
/*=======================================================
                         ARMATH.H:
              CONSTANTS AND BASIC PREDEFINITIONS
=======================================================*/

#include <stdio.h>
#include "arport.h"

#define   AR_MAXFIELD     200
#define   AR_MAXLONG      2147483646L

#define   AR_SMALL 1E-8
#define   AR_LARGE 1E9

#define   AR_MAXBAIRSTOW 40
#define   AR_MAXFACT      10

#define   AR_MAXBUFFER    10

#ifndef   TRUE
#define   TRUE            1
#endif

#ifndef   FALSE
#define   FALSE           0
#endif

#ifndef max
#define max(a,b)     (((a) > (b)) ? (a) : (b))
#endif

#ifndef min
#define min(a,b)     (((a) < (b)) ? (a) : (b))
#endif

#define ar_nl        cout << "\n";

#define ar_double    double

/* ---------------------------- ARPORT.CPP tools */
extern  void  ar_beep   (int, int);
```

```
/* --------------------------- ARMATH.CPP tools */
extern  char   ar_temp [];

extern  int    ar_init_math (void);
extern  void   ar_pause (void);
extern  int    ar_stop_asked (void);
extern  void   ar_calc_rational (ar_double, long*, long*);
extern  char*  ar_rational (ar_double);
extern  int    ar_strfind  (char *, char);
extern  long   ar_gcf      (long, long);

/* -----------------------------------------------------
                    ENTRY TOOLS
   ------------------------------------------------- */

enum {AR_TSTR, AR_TINT, AR_TLON, AR_TBOO, AR_TDOU, AR_TNUM,
      AR_TFUN, AR_TFYI};

typedef struct  {
  int ftype;
  void        *val;
  char        txt [30];
} AR_FIELD;
extern  AR_FIELD *ar_ch;
extern  int       ar_read        (char*, void*, int);
extern  void      ar_init_entry  (char*);
extern  int       ar_fill_entry  (char*, void*, int);
extern  int       ar_do_entry    (void);

/* -----------------------------------------------------
                 BUFFERS MANAGEMENT
   ------------------------------------------------- */

class ar_buffer {

  ar_double *x, *y;
  int          empty;

public:
  int        start, end, cur;
  char             title [80];

  inline ar_buffer (void)   {empty = TRUE;}
  inline ~ar_buffer (void)  {close ();}

  int        nbelts   (void);
  int        open     (char *, int, int);
  void       close    (void);
```

```
  ar_double     readx       (int);
  ar_double     ready       (int);
  void          writex      (int, ar_double);
  void          writey      (int, ar_double);
  void          writecouple (int, ar_double, ar_double);
  void          addcouple   (ar_double, ar_double);
  void          load        (void);
  void          save        (void);
};

ostream& operator << (ostream&, ar_buffer&);
istream& operator >> (istream&, ar_buffer&);

extern  ar_buffer  ar_buff [];

void  ar_erase_buffer  (void);
void  ar_list_buffer   (void);

int   ar_digitize_function (
             ar_double (*) (ar_double), ar_buffer &,
             ar_double, ar_double, int, int);

/* ------------------------------------------------------------
             FUNCTIONS ANALYSIS AND EVALUATION
   ------------------------------------------------------ */

enum ar_unary_op {FMINUS, FPLUS, FSIN, FCOS, FTAN, FARCSIN,
   FARCCOS, FARCTAN, FSH,  FCH, FTH, FARGSH, FARGCH, FARGTH,
   FABS, FINT, FFRAC, FFACT, FEXP, FLOG, FSQRT};

class ar_function {

  char  *start;
  int   maxlen;

public:

  inline ar_function (int n = 100) {open (n);}
  inline ~ar_function ()    {if (start) delete[]start;}

  void        open        (int);
  void        operator =   (ar_function &);
  ar_double   operator ()  (ar_double (*) (int));
  int         operator []  (ar_function &);
  int         analyse      (char *, int (*) (char *, int));
  void        anal_std_x   (char *);
  void        anal_std_xyi (char *);
  void        decompile    (char *);
```

```
  friend   int   fastanal          (char [], ar_function *);
  friend   int   ar_derive_char (char *,   ar_function *);
};

extern   unsigned int   ar_funclen (char *);

extern   ar_double       ar_val_var (int);
extern   ar_double       ar_val_arr (int);

extern   ar_function     ar_glob_f, ar_glob_g;
extern   ar_double       ar_glob_x, ar_glob_y, ar_glob_arr_y [];
extern   int             ar_glob_dim;

extern   ar_double       ar_eval_f    (ar_double);
extern   ar_double       ar_eval_g    (ar_double);
extern   ar_double       ar_eval_fxy  (ar_double, ar_double);
extern   ar_double       ar_eval_gxy  (ar_double, ar_double);
extern   ar_double       ar_eval_fyi  (ar_double, ar_double []);

/* -------------------------------------------------------
                        GRAPHICS
   ------------------------------------------------------- */

extern int        ar_maxlig;
extern int        ar_maxcol;
extern ar_double  ar_round;

extern   void   ar_init_graph     (void);
extern   void   ar_close_graph    (void);

extern   void   ar_line           (int, int, int, int);
extern   int    ar_getpixel       (int, int);
extern   void   ar_putpixel       (int, int, int);

extern   void   ar_outtext        (char *);
extern   void   ar_setcolor       (int);
extern   int    ar_getmaxcolor    (void);
extern   void   ar_closegraph     (void);

extern   unsigned ar_imagesize   (int, int, int, int);
extern   void     ar_getimage    (int, int, int, int, char *);
extern   void     ar_putimage    (int, int, char *, int);

extern   void   ar_grgotoxy       (int, int);
extern   void   ar_grread         (char*);
extern   void   ar_load_graph     (char*);
extern   void   ar_save_graph     (char*);
extern   void   ar_erase_char     (void);
```

```
extern  void    ar_erase_line     (int);
extern  void    ar_disp_graph     (void);
extern  void    ar_hardcopy       (int);
extern  void    ar_hardcopy_laser (char *, int, int, int);

/* --------------------------------------------------------
                        EQUATIONS
   ------------------------------------------------------ */

extern  void    ar_dichotomies (
                ar_double(*)(ar_double),
                ar_double, ar_double, int,
                ar_double, ar_buffer &);

extern  ar_double ar_newton (ar_double(*)(ar_double),
                            ar_double, ar_double);

extern  void    ar_non_linear_system (
        ar_double(*) (ar_double, ar_double),
        ar_double(*) (ar_double, ar_double),
        ar_double, ar_double, ar_double,
        ar_double&, ar_double&);

extern void  ar_use_dichotomies      (void);
extern void  ar_use_newton           (void);
extern void  ar_use_non_linear_syst  (void);

/* --------------------------------------------------------
                       DERIVATIVES
   ------------------------------------------------------ */

extern  ar_double ar_derivative (ar_double(*)(ar_double),
                ar_double, int, ar_double);

extern  void      ar_discrete_derivative (ar_function &,
                  ar_buffer &, ar_double, ar_double,
                  int, int, int);

extern  int       ar_derive_function (char *, ar_function *);

extern  void      ar_simplify_function (char *);

extern void  ar_use_derivative          (void);
extern void  ar_use_discrete_derivative (void);
extern void  ar_use_formal_derivative   (void);

extern void  ar_use_pse_xo              (void);
```

```
/* --------------------------------------------------------
                        INTEGRALS
   ---------------------------------------------------- */

extern ar_double  ar_integral_simpson (
       ar_double(*)(ar_double), ar_double, ar_double, long);

extern ar_double  ar_integral_villarceau
       (ar_double(*)(ar_double), ar_double, ar_double, long);

extern ar_double  ar_integral_romberg
       (ar_double(*)(ar_double), ar_double, ar_double,
       ar_double, ar_double&, int, int, int);

extern void    ar_primitive (ar_double(*) (ar_double),
       ar_buffer&, ar_double, ar_double, ar_double, int, int,
       int);

extern ar_double  ar_integral_discrete (ar_buffer &);

extern  void    ar_use_simpson           (void);
extern  void    ar_use_villarceau        (void);
extern  void    ar_use_romberg           (void);
extern  void    ar_use_integral_discrete (void);
extern  void    ar_use_primitive         (void);

/* --------------------------------------------------------
                   CURVES AND SURFACES
   ---------------------------------------------------- */

extern  void   ar_draw_axes (ar_double &, ar_double &,
               ar_double &, ar_double &, ar_double &,
               ar_double &, int &, int &, int, int, int);

extern  void   ar_curve_discrete (ar_buffer&, ar_double,
               ar_double, ar_double, ar_double, int, int,
               int);

extern  void   ar_curve_yfx (ar_double (*)(ar_double),
               ar_double, ar_double, ar_double, ar_double,
               int, int, int);

extern  void   ar_curve_parametric (ar_double (*)(ar_double),
               ar_double (*)(ar_double), ar_double,
               ar_double, ar_double, ar_double, ar_double,
               ar_double, int, int, int);

extern  void   ar_curve_cycloid (int, int, int);
```

```
extern  void  ar_perspective (ar_double(*)(ar_double,
              ar_double), int, int, ar_double, ar_double,
              ar_double, ar_double, ar_double, ar_double,
              ar_double, ar_double, int);

extern void   ar_use_curve_yfx        (void);
extern void   ar_use_curve_discrete   (void);
extern void   ar_draw_buffer          (ar_buffer &);
extern void   ar_use_curve_parametric (void);
extern void   ar_use_curve_polar      (void);
extern void   ar_use_curve_cycloid    (void);

extern void   ar_use_perspective      (void);

/* -----------------------------------------------------------
                   FOURIER SERIES
   -------------------------------------------------------- */

extern void  ar_fourier_discrete (ar_buffer &, int,
             ar_double &, ar_double &);

extern void  ar_fourier_analytic (ar_function *, ar_double *,
             int, int, int, ar_double &, ar_double &,
             ar_double &, int);

extern void  ar_fourier_spectrum (ar_buffer &, int);

extern void  ar_fourier_synthesis (ar_buffer &, int,
             ar_double, ar_double, ar_double, ar_double,
             ar_double, int, int, int);

extern void  ar_use_fourier_discrete  (void);
extern void  ar_use_fourier_analytic  (void);
extern void  ar_use_fourier_spectrum  (void);
extern void  ar_use_fourier_synthesis (void);

/* -----------------------------------------------------------
                 DIFFERENTIAL EQUATIONS
   -------------------------------------------------------- */

extern void ar_equadiff_11 (
       ar_double(*)(ar_double, ar_double),
       ar_buffer &,
       ar_double, ar_double, ar_double,
       int, int, int);

extern void ar_equadiff_pc (
       ar_double(*)(ar_double, ar_double),
```

```
        ar_buffer &,
        ar_double, ar_double, ar_double,
        int, int, int);

extern void ar_equadiff_1n (
        ar_double(*)(ar_double, ar_double []),
        ar_buffer &,
        ar_double, ar_double, ar_double [],
        int, int, int, int);

extern void ar_equadiff_p1 (
        ar_double(*[])(ar_double, ar_double []),
        ar_buffer &, ar_buffer &,
        ar_double, ar_double, ar_double [],
        int, int, int, int);

extern void  ar_use_equadiff_11        (void);
extern void  ar_use_equadiff_pc        (void);
extern void  ar_use_equadiff_1n        (void);
extern void  ar_use_equadiff_p1        (void);

/* ---------------------------------------------------------
                     RATIONAL NUMBERS
   --------------------------------------------------- */

class ar_number {

public:
  int            real;
  ar_double      value;
  long           p, q;
  ar_number      (long = 0, long = 1);
  ar_number      (char *ch);
  int   zero     (void);
  int   positive (void);
  int   small    (void);

  ar_number  operator - ();

  friend int        operator == (ar_number &, ar_number &);
  friend int        operator != (ar_number &, ar_number &);

  friend ar_number operator +  (ar_number, ar_number);
  friend ar_number operator -  (ar_number, ar_number);
  friend ar_number operator *  (ar_number, ar_number);
  friend ar_number operator /  (ar_number, ar_number);
  ar_number & operator += (ar_number);
  ar_number & operator -= (ar_number);
```

```
   ar_number & operator *= (ar_number);
   ar_number & operator /= (ar_number);
};

ostream&    operator << (ostream&, ar_number&);

extern ar_number N0, N1;

/* ----------------------------------------------------------
                        GEOMETRY
   -------------------------------------------------------- */
ar_number ar_calc_surf (ar_number [], ar_number [], int);

void       ar_circle (
           ar_double&, ar_double&, ar_double&,
           ar_double&, ar_double&, ar_double&);

void       ar_triangle   (
           ar_double&, ar_double&, ar_double&, ar_double&,
           ar_double&, ar_double&, ar_double&, int&);

void       ar_conic_reduction (
           ar_double, ar_double, ar_double, ar_double,
           ar_double, ar_double, int&, ar_double&, ar_double&,
           ar_double&, ar_double&, ar_double&, ar_double&,
           ar_double&, ar_double&, ar_double&, ar_double&,
           ar_double&, ar_double&, ar_double&, ar_double&,
           ar_double&, ar_double&, ar_double&);

extern  int ar_conic_find (ar_number  *, ar_number *,
           ar_number *);

extern  void  ar_use_geo_surface       (void);
extern  void  ar_use_geo_circle        (void);
extern  void  ar_use_geo_reduc_conic   (void);
extern  void  ar_use_geo_find_conic    (void);
extern  void  ar_use_geo_triangle      (void);

/* ----------------------------------------------------------
                        POLYNOMIALS
   -------------------------------------------------------- */

class ar_polynomial {

   int        empty;
   int        maxdegree;
   ar_number  *ptcoeff;
```

```
public:
  int           degree;

  inline ar_polynomial::ar_polynomial ()   {empty = TRUE;};
  inline ar_polynomial::~ar_polynomial () {close ();};

  int           open        (int);
  void          close       (void);
  void          operator =  (ar_polynomial &);
  ar_number &   readcoeff   (int);
  void          writecoeff  (int, ar_number &);

  int           zero        (void);
  void          clear       (void);
  void          reduce      (void);

  ar_number     operator () (ar_number &);

  ar_polynomial & operator += (ar_polynomial &);
  ar_polynomial & operator -= (ar_polynomial &);
  ar_polynomial & operator *= (ar_polynomial &);
  ar_polynomial & operator *= (ar_number  &);
  ar_polynomial & operator /= (ar_polynomial &);
};

ostream& operator << (ostream&, ar_polynomial&);
istream& operator >> (istream&, ar_polynomial&);

int   operator == (ar_polynomial&, ar_polynomial&);
int   operator != (ar_polynomial&, ar_polynomial&);

ar_polynomial& operator +   (ar_polynomial&, ar_polynomial&);
ar_polynomial& operator -   (ar_polynomial&, ar_polynomial&);
ar_polynomial& operator *   (ar_polynomial&, ar_polynomial&);
ar_polynomial& operator *   (ar_number &,    ar_polynomial&);
ar_polynomial& operator /   (ar_polynomial&, ar_polynomial&);
ar_polynomial& ar_subst_pol (ar_polynomial&, ar_polynomial&);
ar_polynomial& ar_div_pol   (ar_polynomial&, ar_polynomial&,
ar_polynomial&);
ar_polynomial& ar_dcr_pol   (ar_polynomial&, ar_polynomial&,
int, ar_polynomial&);
ar_polynomial& ar_der_pol   (ar_polynomial&, int);
ar_polynomial& ar_gcf_pol   (ar_polynomial&, ar_polynomial&);
ar_polynomial& ar_lcm_pol   (ar_polynomial&, ar_polynomial&);

int   ar_bairstow (ar_polynomial&, complex[], ar_double,
                   ar_double, ar_double);
```

```
extern   void   ar_use_pol_evaluation            (void);
extern   void   ar_use_pol_multiplication        (void);
extern   void   ar_use_pol_lincomb               (void);
extern   void   ar_use_pol_substitution          (void);
extern   void   ar_use_pol_division              (void);
extern   void   ar_use_pol_division_increasing   (void);
extern   void   ar_use_pol_gcf                    (void);
extern   void   ar_use_pol_derivation            (void);
extern   void   ar_use_bairstow                   (void);

/* ----------------------------------------------------------
                   POWER SERIES EXPANSIONS
   --------------------------------------------------------- */

extern void   ar_pse_mul   (ar_polynomial &, ar_polynomial &,
              ar_polynomial &);
extern void   ar_pse_div   (ar_polynomial &, ar_polynomial &,
              ar_polynomial &);
extern void   ar_pse_comp  (ar_polynomial &, ar_polynomial &,
              ar_polynomial &);

extern int    ar_entry_pse (ar_polynomial &, int, char, char);

extern void   ar_use_pse_mul    (void);
extern void   ar_use_pse_div    (void);
extern void   ar_use_pse_comp   (void);

/* ----------------------------------------------------------
                     RATIONAL FRACTIONS
   --------------------------------------------------------- */

//------------------- ar_fraction class definition

class ar_fraction  {

public:
  ar_polynomial   numer, denom;

  void            operator =  (ar_fraction &);

  int             zero  (void);
  void            clear (void);

  ar_number       operator () (ar_number &);
  void            simp        (int);

  ar_fraction & operator += (ar_fraction &);
  ar_fraction & operator -= (ar_fraction &);
```

```
   ar_fraction & operator *= (ar_fraction &);
   ar_fraction & operator *= (ar_number  &);
   ar_fraction & operator /= (ar_fraction &);
};

//------------------- Operators on class ar_fraction

ostream&       operator <<    (ostream&, ar_fraction&);
istream&       operator >>    (istream&, ar_fraction&);

int            operator ==    (ar_fraction&, ar_fraction&);
int            operator !=    (ar_fraction&, ar_fraction&);

ar_fraction&   operator +     (ar_fraction&, ar_fraction&);
ar_fraction&   operator -     (ar_fraction&, ar_fraction&);
ar_fraction&   operator *     (ar_fraction&, ar_fraction&);
ar_fraction&   operator *     (ar_number &,  ar_fraction&);
ar_fraction&   operator /     (ar_fraction&, ar_fraction&);
ar_fraction&   operator ~     (ar_fraction&);
ar_fraction&   ar_subst_frac  (ar_fraction&, ar_fraction&);
ar_fraction&   ar_der_frac    (ar_fraction&, int);

//--------------- Interface tools of rational fractions

extern  void   ar_use_frac_evaluation         (void);
extern  void   ar_use_frac_multiplication      (void);
extern  void   ar_use_frac_lincomb             (void);
extern  void   ar_use_frac_inversion           (void);
extern  void   ar_use_frac_substitution        (void);
extern  void   ar_use_frac_simplification      (void);
extern  void   ar_use_frac_derivation          (void);
extern  void   ar_use_frac_partial             (void);

/* ---------------------------------------------------------
                         VECTORS
   --------------------------------------------------- */

class ar_vector {

   int        empty;
   ar_number  * ptcoeff;

public:
   int        lig;
   char       title [3];

   inline ar_vector::ar_vector ()
                          {empty = TRUE; title[0] = 0;};
```

```
    inline ar_vector::ar_vector (char *ch)
                        {empty = TRUE; memcpy (title, ch, 3);};
    inline ar_vector::~ar_vector () {close ();};

    int         open        (int);
    void        close       (void);
    void        operator =  (ar_vector &);

    ar_number & readcoeff   (int);
    void        writecoeff  (int, ar_number &);

    void        clear       (void);

    friend int  operator == (ar_vector&, ar_vector&);

    ar_vector & operator += (ar_vector &);
    ar_vector & operator -= (ar_vector &);
    ar_vector & operator *= (ar_vector &);
    ar_vector & operator *= (ar_number  &);
};

ostream& operator << (ostream&, ar_vector&);
istream& operator >> (istream&, ar_vector&);

int   operator != (ar_vector&, ar_vector&);

ar_vector&  operator + (ar_vector&, ar_vector&);
ar_vector&  operator - (ar_vector&, ar_vector&);
ar_vector&  operator * (ar_number&, ar_vector&);
ar_number   operator * (ar_vector&, ar_vector&);
ar_vector&  operator ^ (ar_vector&, ar_vector&);
ar_number   ar_mix_vec (ar_vector&, ar_vector&, ar_vector&);

/* -----------------------------------------------------------
                    MATRICES
   ----------------------------------------------------- */

//--------------------- class ar_matrix definition

class ar_matrix {

    int         empty;
    ar_number   * ptcoeff;

public:
    int         lig, col;
    char        title [3];
```

```
inline ar_matrix::ar_matrix ()
                            {empty = TRUE; title[0] = 0;};
inline ar_matrix::ar_matrix (char *ch)
                    {empty = TRUE; memcpy (title, ch, 3);};
inline ar_matrix::~ar_matrix () {close ();};

int         open        (int, int);
void        close       (void);
void        operator =  (ar_matrix &);

ar_number & readcoeff   (int, int);
void        writecoeff  (int, int, ar_number &);

void        clear       (void);

friend int          operator == (ar_matrix&, ar_matrix&);
friend ar_matrix&   operator ^  (ar_matrix&, long);

ar_matrix & operator += (ar_matrix &);
ar_matrix & operator -= (ar_matrix &);
ar_matrix & operator *= (ar_matrix &);
ar_matrix & operator *= (ar_number &);

ar_vector & operator [] (ar_vector &);

ar_number trace (void);
};

//-------------------- Operators on class ar_matrix

ostream&    operator << (ostream&,    ar_matrix&);
istream&    operator >> (istream&,    ar_matrix&);

int         operator != (ar_matrix&, ar_matrix&);

ar_matrix&  operator +  (ar_matrix&, ar_matrix&);
ar_matrix&  operator -  (ar_matrix&, ar_matrix&);
ar_matrix&  operator *  (ar_matrix&, ar_matrix&);
ar_matrix&  operator *  (ar_number&, ar_matrix&);

ar_matrix&  ar_inv_mat  (ar_matrix&, int&,
ar_number&);
ar_vector&  ar_lin_sys  (ar_matrix&, ar_vector&,
ar_number&);

int     ar_eigen_values (ar_matrix&, complex [],
                ar_double, ar_double, ar_double);
```

```
//--------------- Interface tools for vectors and matrices

void  ar_use_combination_vector      (void);
void  ar_use_scalar_product          (void);
void  ar_use_vectorial_product       (void);
void  ar_use_mixed_product           (void);
void  ar_use_combination_matrix      (void);
void  ar_use_multiplication_matrix   (void);
void  ar_use_raising_matrix          (void);
void  ar_use_determinant_matrix      (void);
void  ar_use_inversion_matrix        (void);
void  ar_use_trace_matrix            (void);
void  ar_use_eigen_values            (void);
void  ar_use_image_vector            (void);
void  ar_use_linear_system           (void);

//------- Partial fraction decomposition

class ar_factor  {

public:
  ar_number  a, b, c;
  int        power;
};

int  ar_partial_fraction (ar_polynomial&, int, ar_factor [],
                          ar_polynomial&, ar_vector&);

/* ------------------------------------------------------
                    COMPLEX NUMBERS
   ---------------------------------------------------- */

extern  int   ar_system_complex (
              ar_matrix &, ar_matrix &,
              ar_vector &, ar_vector &,
              ar_vector &, ar_vector &);

extern  void  ar_equation_complex (
              complex&, complex&, complex&,
              complex&, complex&);

extern  void  ar_use_complex_calculator   (void);
extern  void  ar_use_complex_equation      (void);
extern  void  ar_use_complex_system        (void);
```

The two following modules give all of the functions and constants specific to the use of the Borland C++ compiler.

File ARPORT.CPP:

```
/*=============================================================
                        ARPORT.CPP:
                    BORLAND C++ SPECIFIC
=============================================================*/

#include <dos.h>
#include <iostream.h>

void ar_beep (int frequency, int duration)
{
#ifdef _Windows
  cout << "\007";
#else
  sound (frequency);
  delay (duration);
  nosound ();
#endif
}
```

File ARPORT.H:

```
/*=============================================================
                        ARPORT.H:
              PORTABILITY: CONSTANTS MODULE
                    BORLAND C++ SPECIFIC
 =============================================================*/

#include <stdlib.h>
#include <string.h>
#include <complex.h>
#include <iomanip.h>
#define   AR_PI      M_PI
#define   AR_PI2     M_PI_2
```

The following module gives access to all the analysis tools. It must be stored in the file ANALYSI.CPP.

```
/*=============================================================
                        ANALYSI.CPP:
            MATHEMATICAL SOFTWARE TOOLS IN C++
                      ANALYSIS TOOLS
=============================================================*/

#include <conio.h>
#include "armath.h"

#define   LINE   cout << setfill ('-') <<  setw (79) \
                   << " " << "\n" << setfill (' ');
```

```
extern unsigned _stklen = 32000U;

void main ()
{
  int       i, choice;
  ar_double  r;

  if (ar_init_math   ()) exit (1);

  do {
    clrscr ();

    LINE
    cout << "  MATHEMATICAL SOFTWARE TOOLS IN C++ 1/2 ";
    cout << " - A.Reverchon and M.Ducamp, 1993" << "\n";
    LINE

    cout << "|  1: Analytical curves (y = f (x))      |";
    cout << " 20: Fourier Analysis (discrete case) |\n";
    cout << "|  2: Discrete curves                    |";
    cout << " 21: Fourier Analysis (analytic case) |\n";
    cout << "|  3: Parametric curves                  |";
    cout << " 22: Fourier : Spectrum               |\n";
    cout << "|  4: Polar curves                       |";
    cout << " 23: Fourier : Signal synthesis       |\n";
    cout << "|  5: Cycloid curves                     |";
    cout << " 24: Diff. equations (Runge-Kutta)    |\n";
    cout << "|  6: Surfaces drawing                   |";
    cout << " 25: Diff. equations (predict/correct)|\n";
    cout << "|  7: Dichotomies (functions roots)      |";
    cout << " 26: Diff. equations - order n         |\n";
    cout << "|  8: Newton (functions roots)           |";
    cout << " 27: Differential systems              |\n";
    cout << "|  9: Non linear systems                 |";
    cout << " 28:                                   |\n";
    cout << "| 10: Derivatives at a point             |";
    cout << " 29: List of present buffers           |\n";
    cout << "| 11: Discrete derivatives               |";
    cout << " 30: Draw a buffer                     |\n";
    cout << "| 12: Formal derivatives                 |";
    cout << " 31: Input buffer                      |\n";
    cout << "| 13: Power series expansions            |";
    cout << " 32: Load buffer                       |\n";
    cout << "| 14: Integrals : Simpson's method       |";
    cout << " 33: Display buffer                    |\n";
    cout << "| 15: Integrals : Villarceau's method    |";
    cout << " 34: Load graph                        |\n";
    cout << "| 16: Integrals : Romberg's method       |";
```

```
cout << " 35: Save buffer                     |\n";
cout << "| 17: Discrete integration           |";
cout << " 36: Evaluate a number               |\n";
cout << "| 18: Primitives                     |";
cout << " 37: Erase a buffer                  |\n";
cout << "| 19:                                |";
cout << " 0 : EXIT                            |\n";

LINE

if (ar_read ("Your choice : ", &choice, AR_TINT)) return;

clrscr ();
switch (choice)  {
  case  1 : ar_use_curve_yfx              (); break;
  case  2 : ar_use_curve_discrete         (); break;
  case  3 : ar_use_curve_parametric       (); break;
  case  4 : ar_use_curve_polar            (); break;
  case  5 : ar_use_curve_cycloid          (); break;
  case  6 : ar_use_perspective            (); break;
  case  7 : ar_use_dichotomies            (); break;
  case  8 : ar_use_newton                 (); break;
  case  9 : ar_use_non_linear_syst        (); break;
  case 10 : ar_use_derivative             (); break;
  case 11 : ar_use_discrete_derivative    (); break;
  case 12 : ar_use_formal_derivative      (); break;
  case 13 : ar_use_pse_xo                 (); break;
  case 14 : ar_use_simpson                (); break;
  case 15 : ar_use_villarceau             (); break;
  case 16 : ar_use_romberg                (); break;
  case 17 : ar_use_integral_discrete      (); break;
  case 18 : ar_use_primitive              (); break;
  case 19 :                                   break;

  case 20 : ar_use_fourier_discrete       (); break;
  case 21 : ar_use_fourier_analytic       (); break;
  case 22 : ar_use_fourier_spectrum       (); break;
  case 23 : ar_use_fourier_synthesis      (); break;
  case 24 : ar_use_equadiff_11            (); break;
  case 25 : ar_use_equadiff_pc            (); break;
  case 26 : ar_use_equadiff_1n            (); break;
  case 27 : ar_use_equadiff_p1            (); break;
  case 28 :                                   break;
  case 29 : ar_list_buffer                (); break;
  case 30 : ar_read ("Number of buffer  : ",&i,AR_TINT);
            if (i <= AR_MAXBUFFER)
              ar_draw_buffer (ar_buff [i]);
                break;
```

```
      case 31 : ar_read ("Number of buffer to enter ? ", &i,
                         AR_TINT);
             if (i <= AR_MAXBUFFER)
                cin >> ar_buff [i];
                break;
      case 32 : ar_read ("Number of buffer to load ? ", &i,
                         AR_TINT);
              if (i <= AR_MAXBUFFER)
                 ar_buff [i].load ();
                 break;
      case 33 : ar_read ("Number of buffer to display ? ",
                         &i, AR_TINT);
              if (i <= AR_MAXBUFFER)
                cout << ar_buff [i];
                break;
      case 34 : ar_disp_graph ();
                break;
      case 35 : ar_read ("Number of buffer to save ? ", &i,
                         AR_TINT);
              if (i <= AR_MAXBUFFER)
                 ar_buff [i].save ();
                 break;
      case 36 : ar_read ("Number to evaluate : ",&r,AR_TDOU);
                cout << "The value of this number is : " << r
                     << ar_rational (r) << "\n";
                ar_pause ();
                break;
      case 37 : ar_erase_buffer ();

      default : break;
      }  /* switch */
   } while (choice);
}
```

The following module gives access to all of the algebra tools. It must be stored in the file ALGEBRA.CPP.

```
/*===========================================================
                        ALGEBRA.CPP:
           MATHEMATICAL SOFTWARE TOOLS IN C++
                        ALGEBRA TOOLS
===========================================================*/

#include <conio.h>
#include "armath.h"

#define  LINE  cout << setfill ('-') << setw (79) \
                    << " " << setfill (' ') << "\n";
```

```
void main ()
{
  int   choice;
  if (ar_init_math ()) exit (1);
  do {
    clrscr ();
    LINE
    cout << "  MATHEMATICAL SOFTWARE TOOLS IN C++ 2/2 ";
    cout << " - A.Reverchon and M.Ducamp, 1993" << "\n";
    LINE
    cout << " 1: Geometry : Surfaces                ";
    cout << "| 21: Fractions: Partial frac. decompos.\n";
    cout << " 2: Geometry : Arcs                    ";
    cout << "| 22: Matrices : Linear combination     \n";
    cout << " 3: Geometry : Conics Reduction        ";
    cout << "| 23: Matrices : Multiplication         \n";
    cout << " 4: Geometry : Conics determination    ";
    cout << "| 24: Matrices : Raising to power n     \n";
    cout << " 5: Geometry : Triangles               ";
    cout << "| 25: Matrices : Determinant            \n";
    cout << " 6: Polynom. : Evaluation at xo        ";
    cout << "| 26: Matrices : Inversion              \n";
    cout << " 7: Polynom. : Complex roots           ";
    cout << "| 27: Matrices : Eigen values           \n";
    cout << " 8: Polynom. : Multiplication          ";
    cout << "| 28: Matrices : Vector image V = M.U   \n";
    cout << " 9: Polynom. : Linear combination      ";
    cout << "| 29: Matrices : Linear systems M.U = V \n";
    cout << "10: Polynom. : Substitution P [Q]      ";
    cout << "| 30: Vectors  : Linear combination     \n";
    cout << "11: Polynom. : Euclidean division      ";
    cout << "| 31: Vectors  : Scalar products        \n";
    cout << "12: Polynom. : Incr. powers division   ";
    cout << "| 32: Vectors  : Vectorial products     \n";
    cout << "13: Polynom. : GCF - LCM               ";
    cout << "| 33: Vectors  : Mixed products         \n";
    cout << "14: Polynom. : n-th derivatives        ";
    cout << "| 34: Power series expansions : f X g   \n";
    cout << "15: Fractions: Simplification          ";
    cout << "| 35: Power series expansions : f / g   \n";
    cout << "16: Fractions: Evaluation at a point   ";
    cout << "| 36: Power series expansions : g [f]   \n";
    cout << "17: Fractions: Multiplication          ";
    cout << "| 37: Complexes: Second degree equations\n";
    cout << "18: Fractions: Linear combination      ";
    cout << "| 38: Complexes: Linear systems         \n";
    cout << "19: Fractions: Substitution            ";
    cout << "| 39: Complexes: Calculator             \n";
```

```
cout << "20: Fractions: n-th derivatives        ";
cout << "| 0 : EXIT                             \n";
LINE
ar_read ("Your choice : ", &choice, AR_TINT);
clrscr ();
switch (choice) {
  case  1 : ar_use_geo_surface              (); break;
  case  2 : ar_use_geo_circle               (); break;
  case  3 : ar_use_geo_reduc_conic          (); break;
  case  4 : ar_use_geo_find_conic           (); break;
  case  5 : ar_use_geo_triangle             (); break;
  case  6 : ar_use_pol_evaluation           (); break;
  case  7 : ar_use_bairstow                 (); break;
  case  8 : ar_use_pol_multiplication       (); break;
  case  9 : ar_use_pol_lincomb              (); break;
  case 10 : ar_use_pol_substitution         (); break;
  case 11 : ar_use_pol_division             (); break;
  case 12 : ar_use_pol_division_increasing (); break;
  case 13 : ar_use_pol_gcf                   (); break;
  case 14 : ar_use_pol_derivation           (); break;
  case 15 : ar_use_frac_simplification      (); break;
  case 16 : ar_use_frac_evaluation          (); break;
  case 17 : ar_use_frac_multiplication      (); break;
  case 18 : ar_use_frac_lincomb             (); break;
  case 19 : ar_use_frac_substitution        (); break;
  case 20 : ar_use_frac_derivation          (); break;
  case 21 : ar_use_frac_partial             (); break;
  case 22 : ar_use_combination_matrix       (); break;
  case 23 : ar_use_multiplication_matrix    (); break;
  case 24 : ar_use_raising_matrix           (); break;
  case 25 : ar_use_determinant_matrix       (); break;
  case 26 : ar_use_inversion_matrix         (); break;
  case 27 : ar_use_eigen_values             (); break;
  case 28 : ar_use_image_vector             (); break;
  case 29 : ar_use_linear_system            (); break;
  case 30 : ar_use_combination_vector       (); break;
  case 31 : ar_use_scalar_product           (); break;
  case 32 : ar_use_vectorial_product        (); break;
  case 33 : ar_use_mixed_product            (); break;
  case 34 : ar_use_pse_mul                  (); break;
  case 35 : ar_use_pse_div                  (); break;
  case 36 : ar_use_pse_comp                 (); break;
  case 37 : ar_use_complex_equation         (); break;
  case 38 : ar_use_complex_system           (); break;
  case 39 : ar_use_complex_calculator       (); break;
  }
} while (choice);
}
```

3
General Tools

In the preceding chapters, we discussed the utility of software tools and how to use them in the framework provided by this book. We will now present the general tools which are used throughout the text.

We start by describing the basic tools, particularly those which allow one to manipulate rational numbers with more precision than real numbers. Then we examine the role of a user interface. In addition, we show how to build such an interface using an elementary core, which we describe.

Then, we turn to the management of peripherals, especially in the domain of graphics. Finally, we illustrate how to build a structure for data exchange between different tools.

1 Basic Tools

The tool `ar_init_math` must contain all the initialisations necessary in order for the mathematical tools to function, in particular the memory allocation needed by the data entry module. Thus, this tool *must systematically be called upon* before any other mathematical tool is utilised.

The tool `ar_gcf (a, b)` gives the GCF of the two long integers *a* and *b*.

The tools `ar_pause` and `ar_stop_asked` respectively enable the user to control the display of results and to abort from long calculations.

The following module contains the general basic tools, and must be stored in the file `ARMATH.CPP`.

```
/*===========================================================
                        ARMATH.CPP:
                    GENERAL BASIC TOOLS
     Module to be systematically linked to a program using
            a C++ numerical tool from this book
===========================================================*/

#include <conio.h>
#include "armath.h"

char  ar_temp [80], ar_temp_2 [80];
int   ar_error;

int  ar_init_math ()
{
  int memerror = FALSE;

  if ((ar_ch = (AR_FIELD *) calloc
    (sizeof (AR_FIELD), AR_MAXFIELD)) == 0)
      memerror = TRUE;

  if (memerror)
    cerr << "Insufficient memory\n";

  cout << setw (30) << setprecision (12) << "\n";

  return (memerror);
}

void ar_pause ()
{
  cout << "\n\nPress any key : ";
  cout.flush ();
  getch  ();
  ar_nl;
}

int ar_stop_asked ()
{
  int cc;

  if (! kbhit ()) return (0);

  cc = getch ();

  return ((cc >= 0) && (cc <= 27));
}
```

```
int  ar_strfind (char *ch, char c)
{
  int   i = 0;

  do  {
    if (ch [i] == c)
      return (i);
  } while (ch [++i]);
  return (-1);
}

/* --------------------- RATIONAL APPROXIMATIONS */
void ar_calc_rational (ar_double r, long &p, long &q)
{
  ar_double  ab, ax;
  long        lastp , lastq, inter, ac;

  p = 0; q = 1;
  if (fabs (r) > 1E-8) {
    ax = fabs (r); ab = ax; ac = (long) ab; p = ac;
    lastp = 1; lastq = 0;
    while (1E7 * fabs (ax * q - p) > ax * q)  {
      ab = 1 / (ab - ac);
      ac = (long) ab;
      inter = ac * p + lastp; lastp = p; p = inter;
      inter = ac * q + lastq; lastq = q; q = inter;
      if ((q > 1E7) || (p * q > 1E9))  {
        p  = lastp / lastq; q  = 1;
        ax = p;
      }
    }
  }
  if (r < 0) p = -p;
}

/* --------------------- RATIONAL APPROX. DISPLAY */
char*  ar_rational (ar_double r)
{
  static char  res [30];
  long          p, q;

  ar_calc_rational (r, p, q);
  if ((q != 1) && (labs (p) < 32700) && (labs (q) < 32700))
    sprintf (res, "  # %ld / %ld", p, q);
  else
    sprintf (res, "                ");
  return res;
}
```

```
/*------------------------------ GCF CALCULATION */
long ar_gcf (long a, long b)
{
  long  r;

  a = labs (a);
  b = labs (b);
  if ((a == 0) || (b == 0))  return (1);
  if (a < b)  {
    r = a; a = b; b = r;
  }
  do {
    r = a % b; a = b; b = r;
  } while (r > 0);
  return (a);
}
```

2   The Rational Numbers

Calculations involving polynomials, or rational fractions with rational coefficients, systematically yield results with rational coefficients.

Because of this, and because we wished to avoid information loss due to the representation of rational numbers by decimals, we have defined the class `ar_number`. This class contains not only the real value representing the number, but also a boolean indicator and two long integers p and q.

The indicator differentiates between rational and real numbers. The integers p and q give the primary representation of the number if it is rational.

We have also defined tools which allow one to manipulate this new entity, and to accomplish the elementary calculations.

Most of these tools are implemented as the overload of the classical operators applied to real numbers (+, −, *, /, +=, −=, /=, *=, `cout` <<, `cin` >>, ==, !=). The class has two constructors. One is of the type `ar_number` (`long p, long q`), which allows one to create a class occurrence using the rational representation p/q. The other, of the form `ar_number` (`char *ch`), enables one to create a class occurrence using the character string representing the number.

To illustrate this, the elementary program below computes the sum of two numbers, whether they be rational or not, and then displays the result:

```
#include <armath.h>

main ()
```

```
{
  char       ch[20];
  ar_number n1, n2, n3;

  cout << "Input n1 : "; cin >> ch;
  n1 = ar_number (ch);
  cout << "Input n2 : "; cin >> ch;
  n2 = ar_number (ch);
  n3 = n1 + n2;
  cout << "n1 + n2 = " << n3 << "\n";
}
```

This program accepts rational or real numbers as input, and displays the result as real or rational, depending on which is most appropriate.

The class ar_number is an excellent example of the contribution which object-oriented mechanisms in C++ make to the programming of numerical calculation routines.

The following module must be stored in the file NUMBER.CPP.

```
/*==========================================================
                        NUMBER.CPP:
               CLASS DEFINITION AND MEMBERS
==========================================================*/

#include <string.h>
#include "armath.h"

/*------------------- Constructs a number from a string */
ar_number::ar_number (char *ch)
{
  int    j;
  long   r;
  char   chn [200];

  errno = 1;
  real  = FALSE;
  if (ch [strlen (ch) - 1] == '!') return;

//--------------------------- RATIONAL CASE
  if ((j = ar_strfind (ch, '/')) > -1)   {
    strncpy (chn, ch, j); chn [j] = 0;
    if (ch [j - 1] == '!') return;
    p = atol (chn); q = atol (&ch [j + 1]);
    if ((p == 0) || (q == 0)) return;
    r  = ar_gcf (p, q);
    p /= r; q /= r;
    value = (ar_double) p / (ar_double) q;
  }
```

```
  else  {
//---------------------------REAL CASE
    if ((value = atof (ch)) == 0)
      if (strcmp (ch, "0")) return;
    real = (ar_strfind(ch, '.') != -1) || (value > AR_LARGE);
//----------------------------INTEGER CASE
    if (! real)  {
      p = (long) value;
      q = 1;
    }
  }
  errno = 0;
}

//------------------- Constructs a number from two integers
ar_number::ar_number (long pp, long qq)
{
  real    = FALSE;
  p       = pp;
  q       = qq;
  value = (q == 1) ? (double) p : (double) p / (double) q;
}

ar_number N0, N1 (1);

//------------------- Overloading of binary operator -
ar_number ar_number::operator - ()
{
  ar_number  n = *this;
  n.p          = - p;
  n.value      = - value;
  return  n;
}

//------------------------ Overloading of operator ==
int operator == (ar_number &x, ar_number &y)
{
  return (x.value == y.value);
}

//------------------------ Overloading of operator !=
int operator != (ar_number &x, ar_number &y)
{
  return (x.value != y.value);
}

//----------------------- Overloading of operator *
ar_number operator * (ar_number x, ar_number y)
```

```
{
  ar_number   res;
  long        p1, q1, p2, q2, s;

  res.value = x.value * y.value;
  if (res.value == 0)   return N0;
  res.real = TRUE;
  if ((x.real) || (y.real)) return res;

  if (x.q > 1)   {
    s = ar_gcf (x.p, x.q);
    x.p /= s;
    x.q /= s;
  }

  if (y.q > 1)   {
    s = ar_gcf (y.p, y.q);
    y.p /= s;
    y.q /= s;
  }

  p1 = x.p; q1 = y.q;
  if (q1 > 1)   {
    s = ar_gcf (p1, q1);
    p1 /= s;
    q1 /= s;
  }

  p2 = y.p; q2 = x.q;
  if (q2 > 1)   {
    s = ar_gcf (p2, q2);
    p2 /= s;
    q2 /= s;
  }

  res.p = p1 * p2; if (res.p / p1 != p2) return res;
  res.q = q1 * q2; if (res.q / q1 != q2) return res;

  res.real = FALSE;
  return res;
}

//------------------------- Overloading of operator /
ar_number operator / (ar_number x, ar_number y)
{
  ar_number   n;

  if (y.zero ())   {
```

```
      cerr << "Division by zero\n"; errno = 1; return x;}
  n.real = y.real;
  n.p = (y.p < 0) ? -y.q : y.q;
  n.q = labs (y.p);
  n.value = 1 / y.value;
  return x * n;
}


//------------------------ Overloading of operator +
ar_number operator + (ar_number x, ar_number y)
{
  ar_number  res;
  double     r;
  long       s, t, dx, dy, pg;

  if (x.value == 0)
    res = y;
  else
    if (y.value == 0)
      res = x;
    else {
      res.value = x.value + y.value;
      res.real = TRUE;
      if ((x.real) || (y.real)) return res;
      if ((x.q == 1) || (y.q == 1))  {
        dx = x.q; dy = y.q;
      }
      else {
        pg = ar_gcf (x.q, y.q);
        dx = x.q / pg;
        dy = y.q / pg;
      }
      s = x.p * dy; if (s / dy != x.p)  return res;
      t = y.p * dx; if (t / dx != y.p)  return res;
      r = (double) s + t;
      if (fabs (r) > AR_MAXLONG)           return res;
      res.p = r;
      res.q = x.q * dy; if (res.q / dy != x.q)  return res;
      res.real = FALSE;
      if (res.q > 1)  {
        s   = ar_gcf (res.p, res.q);
        res.p /= s; res.q /= s;
      }
      res.value = (double) res.p / res.q;
      if (res.p == 0) res.q = 1;
    }
  return res;
}
```

```
//------------------------- Overloading of operator -
ar_number operator - (ar_number x, ar_number y)
{
  return x + (-y);
}

//------------------------- Overloading of operator +=
ar_number & ar_number::operator += (ar_number n)
{
  *this = *this + n;
  return *this;
}

//------------------------- Overloading of operator -=
ar_number & ar_number::operator -= (ar_number n)
{
  *this = *this - n;
  return *this;
}

//------------------------- Overloading of operator *=
ar_number & ar_number::operator *= (ar_number n)
{
  *this = *this * n;
  return *this;
}

//------------------------- Overloading of operator /=
ar_number & ar_number::operator /= (ar_number n)
{
  *this = *this / n;
  return *this;
}

//------------------------- Display of a number
ostream& operator << (ostream& s, ar_number& n)
{
  if (n.real)
    cout << n.value;
  else {
    cout << ((n.value > 0) ? "+ " : "- ");
    cout << labs (n.p);
    if (labs (n.q) != 1)
      cout << " / " << labs (n.q);
  }
  return s;
}
```

```
//------------------------ Test if a number is null
int ar_number::zero (void)
{
   return (value == 0);
}

//------------------------ Test if a number is positive
int ar_number::positive (void)
{
   return (value > 0);
}

//------------------------ Test if a number is small
int ar_number::small (void)
{
   return (real) ? (fabs (value) < AR_SMALL) : (p == 0);
}
```

3   User Interface

3.1 Need for a User Interface

First, let us define the concept of user interface in the context of resolution of numerical problems. One solves a numerical analysis problem in three steps:
- entry of the parameters;
- calculation;
- display of the results.

The diagram below illustrates how the information circulates:

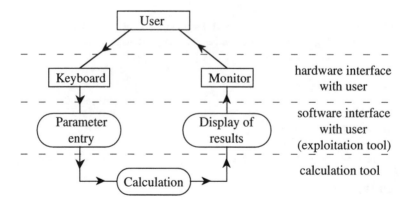

The user is in direct contact with the modules "Parameter Entry" and "Display of Results" which form the software user interface (which we call "exploitation tool" in this book).

The quality of this exploitation tool strongly influences how the user perceives the general functioning of the program. This is why, in general, the quality of the user interface is becoming more and more crucial to the subjective appreciation of software.

Unfortunately, the conception and construction of user interfaces represent a very important part (up to 80%) of the development of products, such as most spreadsheets or word processors available on the market.

Therefore, it is essential to turn to methods and tools which facilitate programming and reduce development time.

The elaboration of user interfaces is not the topic of this book. We will simply provide an approach which puts one on the right track concerning the building of a good interface.

The standard input/output functions in C++ are limited to rudimentary functions. It is absolutely indispensable to build tools around these basic functions in order to simplify the writing of the exploitation tools.

We distinguish between two levels of data entry tools:
- first, a low level tool (`ar_read`) which enables one to read a variable of a given type;
- then, other higher level tools, based on the previous tool, which allow one to simultaneously enter several parameters of different types, with the possibility of modifying prior input errors.

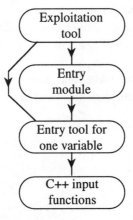

The diagram above summarises the different levels of data entry tools which we will use (an arrow from A to B means that tool A calls on tool B).

3.2 Input of a Variable

The tool `ar_read` allows one to enter a variable of a given type. It refuses invalid data (for example, a decimal point in an integer).

Its syntax is as follows: `ar_read (tx, vp, tp)` where:

– `tx` designates the message to display to tell the user to enter data ,

– `vp` must contain a pointer on the variable to fill.

– `tp` designates the type of variable:

      `AR_TSTR` : character string

      `AR_TINT` : simple integer (from -2^{15} to 2^{15})

      `AR_TLON` : long integer (from -2^{31} to 2^{31})

      `AR_TBOO` : boolean (`Y` or `N`)

      `AR_TDOU` : double real number

      `AR_TNUM` : number (real, or rational)

      `AR_TFUN` : user function with one variable

      `AR_TFYI` : user function with n variables

It is absolutely necessary to indicate the type of variable `tp`. The pointer `vp` points to a different object (type and length) depending on the case, and a function in C++ must know the type of this object in order to be able to manipulate it correctly.

In the output, the value of the function `ar_read` indicates the way the operation proceeded:

0: normal case, the data entry is complete

1: error (for example, character alpha in the middle of an integer variable)

2: return requested (the user typed "R")

No coherence verification is done (for example, extreme values). We will see that these verifications can be implemented at a higher level.

REMARK: the entry of a real number is a special case. It uses a special function, described in the next chapter, which converts a character string representing a number in symbolic form, "LOG (PI/2)" for example, into its real value in `double` type.

In an application for which the taking into account of the function interpreter, necessary for this particularity, is disproportionate compared to the increase in value it contributes, we can replace the following lines:

```
case AR_TDOU :
  if (strcmp (cc, "0") == 0)
    cd = 0;
  . . . . . .
  * (ar_double *) vp = cd;
  break;
```

with the lines:

```
case AR_TDOU :
  if (strcmp (cc, "0") == 0)
    * (ar_double *) vp = 0;
  else if ((cd = atof (cc)) == 0)
    bad = 1;
```

```
else
   * (ar_double *) vp = cd;
break;
```

3.3 Core of the Data Entry Module

Entering parameters means entering a certain number of variables. When this number becomes high, it is very bothersome not to be able to "go back" to correct erroneous data, resulting from a typographical error, for example.

One solution is to gather the data entry instructions in a loop, adding a boolean variable end which allows one to repeat the process if there is a mistake:

```
do  {
   ar_read ("Enter a ", &a, AR_TINT);
   ar_read (.....);

   ar_read (.....);
   ar_read (.....);
   ar_read ("Data Entry finished ? ", &end, AR_TBOO);
}  while (! end);
```

This solution would lead to the desired result. However, it would need to be implemented in all exploitation tools. The construction of a "data entry module" is closer to the philosophy of a structured language like C++.

One obtains access to the data entry module through three tools:

ar_init_entry	allows one to initialise a new data entry session and to specify the title to display at the beginning of input,
ar_fill_entry	allows one to define a data entry session by specifying the variables, their type, and their solicitation message one by one,
ar_do_entry	allows one to execute the current data entry session.

In the example below, a data entry session is defined and utilised:

```
ar_init_entry ("Title : example of data entry");
ar_fill_entry ("Enter a : ", &a, AR_TINT);
ar_fill_entry ("Enter b : ", &b, AR_TINT);
..............
ar_fill_entry (".........: ", ...........);
ar_do_entry   ();
```

Let us note that only the tool ar_do_entry does the entry on screen, waiting for the user to enter all of the information. The tools ar_init_entry and ar_fill_entry only serve to *define* the data entry session.

The data entry module permits one to just describe the data to be entered, without having to give information on the succession of operations necessary to carry out this data entry.

The module core presented here can be improved as much as desired, by incorporating new tasks into the tool `ar_do_entry`, and by adding parameters to the tool `ar_fill_entry` in order to specify each entry zone more precisely (coordinates on screen, default values, display formats, probability constraints, etc.).

One of the strong particularities of C++ can be used to make these improvements. In C++, it is possible to pass functions to other functions as parameters. For example, one can add an optional parameter "verification function" to the tool `ar_fill_entry`. Thus, at each variable entered for which the verification function pointer is not zero, the tool `ar_do_entry` will call on this verification function.

It is in this sense that the tool `ar_do_entry` developed here is but a core: the reader can improve it as desired by only questioning a minimum of external concepts.

3.4 Display of Results

In the same way as the data entry tool, as input `ar_read (tx, vr, tp)` allows one to homogenise and to simplify the exploitation tools where parameter entry is concerned. Now we will introduce a few output tools, which enable us to display the results in standard form.

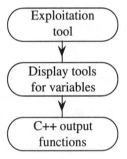

`ar_calc_rational (r, p, q)`
  provides the two long integers p and q which correspond to a rational, primary approximation to the nearest 10^{-9} of r. Usually, the display of a real number is in decimal form. Though this representation is not a problem for transcendent numbers or for simple rational numbers (it is obvious that 0.5 represents 1/2 and that 0.333333333333 represents 1/3), it is not very representative of rational numbers of average complexity. It is not clear whether 0.366666666667 represents 11/30 and that 0.368055556 represents 53/144. When the initial real parameter is a genuine rational number with average complexity, this tool recovers the exact primary representation of this number. In the other cases, however, the rational number provided is only an approximation.

`ar_rational (r)`
  allows one to calculate, then to display, the primary rational approximation of r.

The display operator `cout << ` is overloaded for the class `ar_number` so it can display the variable n of class `ar_number`, in the most appropriate form. This could be a real number, an integer, or the ratio of two integers.

The data entry module needs a prior memory allocation to be able to store information concerning the different input fields. This memory is allocated dynamically, just once, by the initialisation tool `ar_init_math`. This happens at the beginning of the execution of the main program.

In the version presented in this book, the tool `ar_init_math` makes only this memory allocation. More generally, however, this tool is intended to contain all of the initialisation instructions inherent to the mathematical tools. Thus, if you modify the global environment which we have chosen, remember to collect your initialisation sequences in the tool `ar_init_math`.

The printout of most of these output tools is in the basic tools module, `ARMATH.CPP`, presented in the preceding section.

3.5 Printout of the Data Entry Tool

The following module contains all of the data entry tools. It must be stored in the file `ENTRY.CPP`.

```
/*===========================================================
                          ENTRY.CPP:
                       DATA ENTRY TOOLS
===========================================================*/

#include "armath.h"

#define  AR_MAXTITLE   70

AR_FIELD    *ar_ch;

typedef struct  {
   char          title [AR_MAXTITLE];
   int        nb_champ;
   AR_FIELD  *champ;
   int      curf;
} AR_ENTRY;

static AR_ENTRY  sais;

static ar_double local_eval (int i)
{
   errno = 0; return (0);
}
```

```
static int local_anal (char *ch, int lc)
{
// Never a variable in a real-number string analyse

   return (-1);
}

/*=============================== Generic read function */
ar_read (char *msg, void *vp, int vt)
{
   ar_function  local_f (200);
   char         cc [80];
   int          i, j, k, bad, ci;
   long         cl;
   double       cd;
   ar_number    no;

   for (i = 0; i < 3; i++)  {
      bad = 0;
      cout << msg;
      cout.flush ();
      gets (cc);
      strupr (cc);
      if (strcmp (cc, "R") == 0)
         return (2);

      switch (vt)  {
         case AR_TSTR :
         strcpy ((char *) vp, cc);
         break;

         case AR_TINT :
         if (strcmp (cc, "0") == 0)
             * (int *) vp = 0;
         else if ((ci = atoi (cc)) == 0)
             bad = 1;
           else
             * (int *) vp = ci;
           break;

         case AR_TLON :
         if (strcmp (cc, "0") == 0)
           cl = 0;
         else
           if ((cl = atol (cc)) == 0)
             bad = 1;
         * (long *) vp = cl;
           break;
```

```
      case AR_TDOU :
      if (strcmp (cc, "0") == 0)
        cd = 0;
      else  {
          local_f.analyse (cc, local_anal);
          if (errno)
            bad = 1;
          else
            cd = local_f (local_eval);
      }
      * (ar_double *) vp = cd;
      break;

      case AR_TNUM :
      no = ar_number (cc);
      if (! errno)
        * (ar_number *) vp = no;
        else
        bad = 1;
      break;

      case AR_TBOO :
      j = strcmp (cc, "Y");
      k = strcmp (cc, "N");
      if (j * k != 0)
        bad = 1;
      else
        * (int *) vp = k;
        break;

      case AR_TFUN :
        (* (ar_function *) vp).anal_std_x (cc);
        bad = errno;
      break;

      case AR_TFYI :
        (* (ar_function *) vp).anal_std_xyi (cc);
        bad = errno;
      break;

    }  /* switch vt */
    if (! bad)
      return (0);
    ar_beep (300, 50);
  }  /* for */
  return (1);  /* bad */
}
```

```
/*============================== General initialisation */
void ar_init_entry (char *title)
{
  AR_ENTRY *s = &sais;
  AR_FIELD  *c = ar_ch;

  memset   ((char *)s, 0, sizeof (AR_ENTRY));
  strncpy (s->title, title, AR_MAXTITLE);
  s->champ    = c;
}

/*========================= Initialisation of an entry zone*/
int ar_fill_entry (char *txt, void *val, int ftype)
{
  AR_ENTRY *s = &sais;
  AR_FIELD *c;

  if (s->nb_champ >= AR_MAXFIELD)
    return (0);
  c = &s->champ [s->nb_champ++];
  strncpy (c->txt, txt, sizeof (c->txt));
  c->val     = val;
  c->ftype   = ftype;
  return (1);
}

/*========================= Data entry session */
int ar_do_entry ()
{
  AR_ENTRY   *s = &sais;
  AR_FIELD   *ch;
  int        fin = 0, modif;

  ar_nl;
  if (strcmp (s->title, "") != 0) cout << s->title << "\n";

  while (! fin)  {
    ch = &s->champ [s->curf];
    sprintf (ar_temp, "%-30s : ", ch->txt);
    switch (ar_read (ar_temp, ch->val, ch->ftype))  {
      case 1 :
      return (1);
      case 2 :
      if (s->curf > 0)
        --s->curf;
        else
        ar_beep (200, 50);
      break;
```

```
      case 0 :
      if (++s->curf == s->nb_champ) {
        ar_nl;
          ar_read ("Any change                          ? ", &modif,
                 AR_TBOO);
          if (modif)
          s->curf = 0;
        else
          fin = 1;
          ar_nl;
      }
      break;
    }  /* switch */
  }  /* while */
  return (0);
}
```

4 Using Peripherals

4.1 Graphics

Graphics are not standardised in C++. By using certain configurations (equipment, compiler), the management of graphics may even depend on which graphics card is used.

The module presented here is a set of tools developed for the Borland C++ version on a microcomputer. This configuration itself manages the differences between the graphics cards. It automatically refers to the graphics card that the hardware possesses, which makes using the card transparent for the user.

Adapting these tools to other work environments generally does not pose problems. It should be done by implementing the missing or different functions in the portability file GRAFPORT.CPP.

The global variables `ar_maxlig` and `ar_maxcol` respectively contain the number of lines and the number of columns in the graphics card. These variables are initialised automatically during the switch to graphic mode. However, they can be modified in the external programs in order to obtain graphics which take up only part of the screen.

The variable `ar_round` gives the rectangularity coefficient of the points. On certain cards, the pixels are much higher than they are long. This particularity must be taken into account in the drawing tools, especially so that circles are not ellipses on screen. This variable is also automatically initialised during the switch to graphic mode. To obtain round circles with the printer, in mode 39, one must re-establish the instruction `ar_round = 1` in the module `ar_init_graph`.

The module GRAPHICS.CPP contains the tools intended to facilitate the exploitation of graphism:
   – entering and leaving graphic mode;
   – saving and loading graphic images onto the disk;
   – copying from the screen onto a compatible Epson printer (10 modes);
   – copying from the screen onto a compatible Laser HP printer (with a memory of 1 MB minimum).

```cpp
/*==========================================================
                        GRAPHICS.CPP:
     GRAPHICAL TOOLS (PART INDEPENDENT OF THE COMPILER)
=========================================================*/

#include <conio.h>
#include <ctype.h>
#include <string.h>

#include "armath.h"

int        ar_maxlig = 200, ar_maxcol = 300;
ar_double  ar_round   = 1;

#ifdef _Windows
#error "Graphics not available under Windows"
#else
#include "grafport.cpp"
#endif

//------------------------- EXIT FROM A GRAPHICAL PROGRAM

void ar_close_graph ()
{
  char  name [63];
  int ch, mode, end = FALSE;

  while (! end)  {
    ar_erase_line (24);
    ar_grgotoxy (1, 24);
    ar_outtext ("P:Print - L:Laser print - S:Save - \
                E:Exit : ");

    ch = getch ();

    switch (toupper (ch))  {

      case 'P' :
      ar_erase_line (25);
```

```
        ar_grgotoxy (1, 25);
        ar_outtext ("PRINTING - Mode : ");
        ar_grread (name);
        mode = atoi (name);
        ar_hardcopy (mode);
        break;

        case 'L' :
        ar_erase_line (25);
        ar_grgotoxy (1, 25);
        ar_outtext ("LASER PRINTING - Enter title : ");
        ar_grread (name);
        ar_hardcopy_laser (name, 500, 500, 6);
        break;

        case 'S' :
        ar_erase_line (25);
        ar_grgotoxy (1, 25);
        ar_outtext ("SAVE - Filename : ");
        ar_grread (name);
        ar_save_graph (name);
        break;

        case 'E' :
        end = TRUE;
        ar_closegraph ();
        break;

        case 'R' :
        ar_erase_line (24);
        ar_erase_line (25);
        end = TRUE;
        break;

    } /* switch */
  } /* while */
}

/*============================================================
            HARDCOPY ON EPSON COMPATIBLE PRINTER
-------------------------------------------------------------
  0, 4, 5 : Modes without return
  1        : Double Density (120 dots per inch)
  2        : Double Density (120 dots per inch) high speed
  3        : Quadruple Density (240 dots per inch)
  6        : 90 dots per inch
  32, 33, 38, 39, 40 : 24 pins printers
============================================================*/
```

```
#define  build_byte(c, n)    \
    zmax = y + n + 7;  \
    if (zmax > ar_maxlig) zmax = ar_maxlig;  \
    for (c = 0, b = 128, z = y+n; z <= zmax; z++, b >>= 1)   \
      if (ar_getpixel (x, z))  \
        c |= b

void ar_hardcopy (int mode)
{
  unsigned char  nbpin = (mode < 7) ? 8 : 24;
  unsigned char  b, c1, c2, c3;
  int            i, x, y, z, zmax;

  fprintf (stdprn, "%c3%c", 27, 24);
  for (i = 0; i <= (ar_maxlig + 1) / nbpin; i++)   {
    if (mode == 1)
      fprintf (stdprn, "%cL", 27);
    else
      fprintf (stdprn, "%c*%c", 27, mode);
    fprintf (stdprn, "%c%c", (ar_maxcol + 1) & 255,
            (ar_maxcol + 1) >> 8);
    for (x = 0, y = nbpin * i; x <= ar_maxcol; x++)   {
      build_byte (c1, 0); if (c1 == 26) c1 = 24;
      fprintf (stdprn, "%c", c1);
      if (nbpin == 24)   {
      build_byte (c2, 8);  if (c2 == 26) c2 = 24;
      build_byte (c3, 16); if (c3 == 26) c3 = 24;
      fprintf (stdprn, "%c%c", c2, c3);
      }
    }
    if (mode != 4) fprintf (stdprn, "\n");
    if (ar_stop_asked ()) return;
  }
  fprintf (stdprn, "%c2", 27);
}

//--------------------------------- SAVE SCREEN IN A FILE
void  ar_save_graph (char *name)
{
  FILE    *f;
  int     size, i, lig;
  int     nblig = 1 + (ar_maxlig + 1) / 10;
  char    *buff;

  size = ar_imagesize (0, 0, ar_maxcol, nblig - 1);
  if ((buff = (char *) malloc (size)) == 0)   {
    ar_outtext ("Insufficient memory"); return;
  }
```

```
  if ((f = fopen (name, "wb")) == 0)
    ar_outtext ("Cannot open file");
  else {
    for (i = 0; i <= 9; i++)  {
      lig  = (i + 1) * nblig - 1;
      if (lig > ar_maxlig) lig = ar_maxlig;
      size = ar_imagesize (0, i * nblig, ar_maxcol, lig);
      ar_getimage (0, i * nblig, ar_maxcol, lig, buff);
      if (fwrite (buff, 1, size, f) != size)
      ar_outtext ("Disk problem");
    }
    fclose (f);
  }
  free (buff);
}

//--------------------------------LOAD FILE TO THE SCREEN
void ar_load_graph (char *name)
{
  FILE   *f;
  int    size, i, lig;
  int    nblig = 1 + (ar_maxlig + 1) / 10;
  char   *buff;

  size = ar_imagesize (0, 0, ar_maxcol, nblig - 1);

  if ((buff = (char *) malloc (size)) == 0)  {
    ar_outtext ("Insufficient memory");
    return;
  }

  if ((f = fopen (name, "rb")) == 0)
    ar_outtext ("Cannot open file");
  else {
    for (i = 0; i <= 9; i++)  {
      lig  = (i + 1) * nblig - 1;
      if (lig > ar_maxlig) lig = ar_maxlig;

      size = ar_imagesize (0, i * nblig, ar_maxcol, lig);
      if (fread (buff, 1, size, f) != size)
      ar_outtext ("Disk problem");
      ar_putimage (0, i * nblig, buff, 0);
    }
    fclose (f);
  }
  free (buff);
}
```

```
//----------------------------- Display user graphical file
void ar_disp_graph ()
{
  char  name [63];

  cout << "File name : ";
  cout.flush ();
  gets (name);
  ar_init_graph ();
  ar_load_graph  (name);
  ar_close_graph ();
}

//-------------------------- HARDCOPY ON HP LASER PRINTER
void ar_hardcopy_laser (char *title,int xo,int yo,int size)
{
  int  i, j, pix, lastpix;

  fprintf (stdprn, "%s  ", title);
  fprintf (stdprn, "%c%0B", 27);   // Enter HP-GL/2 mode
  fprintf (stdprn, "IN");          // Initialise HP-GL/2 mode
  fprintf (stdprn, "SP1;");        // Choose pencil 1
  fprintf (stdprn, "PW%5.3lf;", (double) size * 0.025);
                                   // Define size

  for (j = 0; j <= ar_maxcol; j ++)  {
    for (i = 0, lastpix = 0; i < ar_maxlig; i++)  {
      pix = (ar_getpixel (j, i) != 0);
      if (pix != lastpix) {
        if (lastpix)
          fprintf (stdprn, "PD%d,%d;", xo+size*i, yo+size*j);
        else
          fprintf (stdprn, "PU%d,%d;", xo+size*i, yo+size*j);
        lastpix = pix;
      }
    }
    if (lastpix)
      fprintf (stdprn, "PD%d,%d;", xo + size * ar_maxlig,
               yo + size * j);

    if (ar_stop_asked ()) return;
  }

  fprintf (stdprn, "%c%0A", 27);    // Returns to PCL mode
}
```

The module GRAFPORT.CPP contains all the graphic tools specific to the graphics environment used. For Borland C++, the file GRAFPORT.CPP should contain:

```
/*=========================================================
                     GRAFPORT.CPP:
          GRAPHICAL TOOLS SPECIFIC TO BORLAND C++
=====================================================*/

#include <graphics.h>

//--------------------------------- Enter graphics mode
void  ar_init_graph ()
{
  int   graph_mode   = 0;
  int   graph_driver = 0;
  int   xasp, yasp;

  initgraph (&graph_driver, &graph_mode, ".");

  if (graphresult ())   {
    cerr << "Graphics error : "
         << grapherrormsg (graph_driver);
    exit (1);
  }
  getaspectratio (&xasp, &yasp);

  ar_maxlig  = (23 * (getmaxy() + 1)) / 25 - 1;
  ar_maxcol  = getmaxx ();
  ar_round   = (double) yasp / (double) xasp;
  setcolor (getmaxcolor ());

//------ To get non ovals rounds ON PRINTER,
//       reactivate the following line
//   ar_round = 1;

}

//--------------------------------------- Set cursor

void ar_grgotoxy (int x, int y)
{
  moveto ((((x-1) * (getmaxx () + 1)) / 80,
         ((y-1) * (getmaxy () + 1)) / 25);
}

//------------------------------------- Erase character
void  ar_erase_character ()
{
  struct viewporttype v;
  int x = getx ();
  int y = gety ();
```

```
  getviewsettings (&v);
  setviewport (v.left + x, v.top + y,
               v.left + x + textwidth  (" ") - 1,
               v.top  + y + textheight (" ") - 1,
               1);
  clearviewport ();
  setviewport (v.left, v.top, v.right, v.bottom, v.clip);
  moveto (x, y);
}

//------------------------------------------- Erase line
void  ar_erase_line (int lig)
{
  struct viewporttype v;
  int deb = ((lig - 1) * (getmaxy () + 1)) / 25;
  getviewsettings (&v);
  setviewport (v.left, deb, v.right,
               deb + textheight (" ") - 1, 1);
  clearviewport ();
  setviewport (v.left, v.top, v.right, v.bottom, v.clip);
}

//------------------------------------------- Read string
void ar_grread (char *st)
{
  int    sl;
  char   ch;
  char   chs [2];

  st [0] = 0;
  do  {
    ch = toupper (getch ()); sl = strlen (st);
    switch (ch)  {
      case 8 :
      if (sl)  {
          st [sl - 1] = 0;
          moverel (- textwidth (" "), 0);
          ar_erase_character ();
        }
      break;
      case 13 :
        break;
      default :
        st [sl++] = ch; st [sl]   = 0;
        sprintf (chs, "%c", ch);
      ar_outtext (chs);
      break;
    }
```

```
  } while (ch != 13);
}

void   ar_line (int x1, int y1, int x2, int y2)
{
  line (x1, y1, x2, y2);
}

int  ar_getpixel (int x, int y)
{
  return getpixel (x, y);
}

void  ar_putpixel (int x, int y, int n)
{
  putpixel (x, y, n);
}

void  ar_outtext (char *ch)
{
  outtext (ch);
}

void  ar_setcolor (int c)
{
  setcolor (c);
}

int  ar_getmaxcolor (void)
{
  return getmaxcolor ();
}

unsigned  ar_imagesize (int x1, int y1, int x2, int y2)
{
  return imagesize (x1, y1, x2, y2);
}

void  ar_getimage (int left, int top, int right, int bottom,
                   char *bitmap)
{
  getimage (left, top, right, bottom, bitmap);
}

void  ar_putimage (int left, int top, char *bitmap, int op)
{
  putimage (left, top, bitmap, op);
}
```

```
void  ar_closegraph ()
{
   closegraph ();
}
```

For Microsoft C++, the graphics portability file is:

```
/*=======================================================
                      GRAFPORT.CPP :
       GRAPHICAL TOOLS SPECIFIC TO MICROSOFT C/C++
========================================================*/

#include <graph.h>

static        _videoconfig vc;

//----------------------------------- Enter graphics mode
void  ar_init_graph ()
{
   _setvideomoderows   (_MAXRESMODE, 25);
   _getvideoconfig     (&vc);

   ar_maxlig  = (23 * vc.numypixels) / 25 - 1;
   ar_maxcol  = vc.numxpixels - 1;
   ar_round   = 1;  // Tune depending on your graphics card
   // Leave 1 to get really round circles on the printer
}

//------------------------------------------- Set cursor
void ar_grgotoxy (int x, int y)
{
   int  y2 = (12 + vc.numtextrows * y) / 25;
   _settextposition (y2, x);
}

//------------------------------------------ Erase character
void ar_erase_char ()
{
   struct _rccoord  cur = _gettextposition ();

   _settextwindow (cur.row, cur.col, cur.row, cur.col);
   _clearscreen (_GWINDOW);
   _settextwindow (1, 1, vc.numtextrows, vc.numtextcols);
   _settextposition (cur.row, cur.col);
}

//------------------------------------------- Erase line
void  ar_erase_line (int lig)
```

```
{
  struct _rccoord  cur = _gettextposition ();
  int  lig2 = (12 + vc.numtextrows * lig) / 25;

  _settextwindow (lig2, 1, lig2, vc.numtextcols - 1);
  _clearscreen (_GWINDOW);
  _settextwindow (1, 1, vc.numtextrows, vc.numtextcols);
  _settextposition (cur.row, cur.col);
}

//--------------------------------------- Read string
void ar_grread (char *st)
{
  int    sl;
  char       ch, chs [2];
  struct _rccoord  cur;

  st [0] = 0;
  do  {
    ch = getch ();
    ch = toupper (ch);
    sl = strlen (st);
    switch (ch)   {
      case 8 :
      if (sl)   {
          st [sl - 1] = 0;
        cur = _gettextposition ();
        _settextposition (cur.row, cur.col - 1);
        ar_erase_char ();
        }
      break;
      case 13 :
        break;
      default :
        st [sl++] = ch; st [sl]    = 0;
        sprintf (chs, "%c", ch);
      ar_outtext (chs);
        break;
    }
  } while (ch != 13);
}

void   ar_line (int x1, int y1, int x2, int y2)
{
  _moveto (x1, y1);
  _lineto (x2, y2);
}
```

```
int  ar_getpixel (int x, int y)
{
  return  _getpixel (x, y);
}

void  ar_putpixel (int x, int y, int n)
{
  _setcolor ((n) ? vc.numcolors : 0);
  _setpixel (x, y);
}

void  ar_outtext (char *ch)
{
  _outtext (ch);
}

unsigned  ar_imagesize (int x1, int y1, int x2, int y2)
{
  return _imagesize (x1, y1, x2, y2);
}

void  ar_getimage (int left, int top, int right, int bottom,
                   char *bitmap)
{
  _getimage (left, top, right, bottom, bitmap);
}

void  ar_putimage (int left, int top, char *bitmap, int op)
{
  _putimage (left, top, bitmap, op);
}

void  ar_closegraph ()
{
  _setvideomode (_TEXTC80);
}

int  ar_getmaxcolor (void)
{
  return (vc.numcolors);
}

void  ar_setcolor (int col)
{
  _setcolor (col);
}
```

4.2 The Printer

On an IBM-PC compatible computer, one can always print out a page of text by using the screen print key (prtscr).

It is possible to print out the results continuously. In the case of the resolution of a differential equation with two variables at one hundred points, however, the result function needs 400 display lines. It is not practical to print out this result with 20 successive overlapping screen copies! The DOS continuous printing function can be activated by simultaneously holding down the keys CTRL, SHIFT and PRTSCR.

4.3 Disks

The disks (or the diskettes) may be used to memorize graphic images or data present in the "buffers," which are global data zones (see section 5 concerning this topic).

The saving and loading tools are:
– in the graphic module GRAPHICS.CPP for the images,
– in the module BUFFER.CPP for the data.

---

5   Data Exchange Between Tools

A buffer is a communication zone containing the following data:
– couples of real numbers,
– a title,
– index of the first active couple,
– index of the last active couple.

Implemented in the form of a class ar_buffer, this class allows large volumes of data to be communicated between different tools.

The exploitation tools in this book which manipulate large volumes of data systematically store their results in these buffers.

The dimension of a buffer is determined when it is opened. The dynamic memory necessary is freed by the member function close ().

The member functions of the class ar_buffer allow one to enter the data of a buffer, as well as to display, save, load, and erase a buffer.

The buffer management module must be stored in the file BUFFER.CPP.

```
/*=========================================================
                       BUFFER.CPP:
         THE CLASS AR_BUFFER AND ITS MEMBER FUNCTIONS
========================================================*/
```

```cpp
#include <conio.h>
#include "armath.h"

ar_buffer  ar_buff [AR_MAXBUFFER + 1];

// ----------------------------------------- OPEN A BUFFER
int  ar_buffer::open (char *tit, int bg, int ed)
{
  if (! empty) close ();
  x = (ar_double *) calloc (sizeof (ar_double), ed - bg + 1);
  y = (ar_double *) calloc (sizeof (ar_double), ed - bg + 1);
  empty = (x == NULL) || (y == NULL);
  if (empty)  {
    cerr << "Not enough memory\n";
    if (x) free (x);
    if (y) free (y);
    errno = TRUE;
    return FALSE;
  }
  start  = cur = bg;
  end    = ed;
  strcpy (title, tit);
  return TRUE;
}

// ----------------------------------------- CLOSE A BUFFER
void  ar_buffer::close (void)
{
  if (! empty)  {
    free (x); free (y);
    empty  = TRUE;
    start   = cur = end = 0;
    strcpy (title, "");
  }
}

// --------------------------- BUFFER NUMBER OF ELEMENTS
int  ar_buffer::nbelts (void)
{
  return ((empty) ? 0 : cur - start);
}

// ----------------------------------------- READ ABSCISSA i
ar_double  ar_buffer::readx (int i)
{
  return ((empty || (i<start) || (i>end)) ? 0 : x [i-start]);
}
```

```
// ------------------------------------ READ ORDINATE i
ar_double  ar_buffer::ready (int i)
{
   return ((empty || (i<start) || (i>end)) ? 0 : y [i-start]);
}

// ------------------------------------ WRITE ABSCISSA i
void  ar_buffer::writex (int i, ar_double r)
{
   if ((! empty) && (i >= start) && (i <= end))  {
     x [i - start] = r;
     if (i >= cur) cur = i + 1;
   }
}

// ------------------------------------ WRITE ORDINATE i
void  ar_buffer::writey (int i, ar_double r)
{
   if ((! empty) && (i >= start) && (i <= end))  {
     y [i - start] = r;
     if (i >= cur) cur = i + 1;
   }
}

// ------------------------------------ WRITE COUPLE i
void  ar_buffer::writecouple (int i,ar_double r,ar_double s)
{
   if ((! empty) && (i >= start) && (i <= end))  {
     x [i - start] = r;
     y [i - start] = s;
     if (i >= cur) cur = i + 1;
   }
}

// ------------------------------------ ADD COUPLE i
void  ar_buffer::addcouple (ar_double r, ar_double s)
{
   writecouple (cur, r, s);
}

// ------------------------------------ INPUT A BUFFER
istream& operator >> (istream& s, ar_buffer& t)
{
   char       tit [80];
   int        i, bg, ed;
   ar_double  r;

   cout << "INPUT BUFFER :\n\n";
```

```
    if (ar_read ("Title                 : ", tit, AR_TSTR))
        return s;
    if (ar_read ("Index of first point  : ", &bg, AR_TINT))
        return s;
    if (ar_read ("Index of last  point  : ", &ed, AR_TINT))
        return s;
    if (t.open (tit, bg, ed)) {
        for (i = bg; i <= ed; i++)  {
            sprintf (ar_temp, "x%d = ", i);
            ar_read  (ar_temp, &r, AR_TDOU);
            t.writex (i, r);
            sprintf (ar_temp, "y%d = ", i);
            ar_read  (ar_temp, &r, AR_TDOU);
            t.writey (i, r);
            ar_nl;
        }
    }
    cout << "Buffer entered\n"; ar_pause (); return s;
}

// -------------------------------------- DISPLAY A BUFFER
ostream& operator << (ostream& s, ar_buffer& t)
{
    int  i, bn, bm;

    cout << "BUFFER CONTENTS\n\n";
    if (t.nbelts () == 0)
        cout << "This buffer is empty\n";
    else {
        cout << "Begin index  : " << setw (3) << t.start << "\n"
             << "End   index  : " << setw (3) << t.end << "\n";
        ar_read  ("First display index : ", &bn, AR_TINT);
        ar_read  ("Last display index  : ", &bm, AR_TINT);
        for (i = max (bn, t.start); i <= min (bm, t.end); i++)   {
            cout << "\nCouple " << setw (3) << i << " :\n"
                 << " x = "  << t.readx (i)
                 << ar_rational (t.readx (i)) << "\n"
                 << " y = "  << t.ready (i) << "\n";
            if (kbhit ()) return s;
        }
    }
    ar_pause (); return s;
}

// ---------------------------------------- SAVE A BUFFER
void  ar_buffer::save (void)
{
    FILE     *f;
```

```
  char     nom [63];
  unsigned  nw, size = sizeof (*x) * (end - start + 1);

  cout << "SAVE A BUFFER\n\n";
  if (empty)
    cout << "This buffer is empty\n";
  else {
    cout << "File Name : "; cout.flush ();
    gets (nom);
    f = fopen (nom, "wb");
    nw =  fwrite (&start, sizeof (start), 1, f);
    nw += fwrite (&end,   sizeof (end),   1, f);
    nw += fwrite (title,  sizeof (title), 1, f);
    nw += fwrite (x,      size,           1, f);
    nw += fwrite (y,      size,           1, f);
    fclose (f);
    if (nw == 5)
      cout << "Buffer saved\n";
    else
      cerr << "Incomplete save\n";
  }
  ar_pause ();
}

// -------------------------------------- LOAD A BUFFER
void  ar_buffer::load (void)
{
  FILE  *f;
  char  nom [63]; cout << "LOAD A BUFFER\n\n";
  cout << "Name of the file to load : "; cout.flush ();
  gets (nom); errno = 0;
  f = fopen (nom, "rb");
  if (errno)
    cout << "Unknown file";
  else {
    close ();
    fread (&start, sizeof (start),  1, f);
    fread (&end,   sizeof (end),   1, f);
    fread (title,  sizeof (title), 1, f);
    if (open (title, start, end))  {
      fread (x, sizeof (*x), (end - start + 1), f);
      fread (y, sizeof (*x), (end - start + 1), f);
      cur = end; cout << "Correct loading\n";
    }
    fclose (f);
  }
  ar_pause ();
}
```

```
// -------------------------------------- ERASE A BUFFER
void  ar_erase_buffer (void)
{
  int  nt;

  cout << "ERASE A BUFFER\n\n";
  if (ar_read ("Number of buffer : ", &nt, AR_TINT)) return;
  if (nt > AR_MAXBUFFER) return;
  ar_buff [nt].close (); ar_pause ();
}

// ------------------------------- DIGITIZING A FUNCTION
int  ar_digitize_function (ar_double (*f) (ar_double),
      ar_buffer &t, ar_double a, ar_double b, int n,
      int disp)
{
  ar_double  s;
  int        i;

  if (! t.open ("Digitized function", 0, n)) return FALSE;
  for (i = 0; i <= n; i++)  {
    s = a + (b - a) * i / n; t.writecouple (i, s, f (s));
    if ((disp) && (! errno))
      cout << " x" << i << " = "  << setw (20) << t.readx (i)
           << " y" << i << " = "  << setw (20) << t.ready (i)
           << ar_rational (t.ready (i)) << "\n";
    if (ar_stop_asked ()) return FALSE;
  }
  return TRUE;
}

// ------------------------------------------- LIST BUFFERS
void  ar_list_buffer (void)
{
  int  i, nf = 0;

  for (i = 0; i <= AR_MAXBUFFER; i++)
    if (ar_buff [i].nbelts ())  {
      if (nf++ == 0)
        cout << "LIST OF NON-EMPTY BUFFERS\n\n";
      cout << "Buffer " << i << " : " << setw (40)
           << ar_buff [i].title << "  (From "
           << ar_buff [i].start << " To "
           << ar_buff [i].end << ")\n";
    }
  if (! nf) cout << "All the buffers are empty\n";
  ar_pause ();
}
```

4

Representation and Evaluation of Mathematical Functions

In this chapter, we describe the function interpreter, which is an essential part of this book. The function interpreter transcodes character chains representing mathematical functions into objects that the program can manipulate. However, this is the most complex part of this book in terms of programming. Mastery of C++ is absolutely necessary in order to understand how the different functions of these tools are articulated.

First, we describe the role of the function interpreter in detail. Second, we examine the way mathematical expressions are coded. Then we discuss the opposite transformation, how to determine the mathematical expression using its coded form. Lastly, we explain how the tools which evaluate a function for a given set of variable values operate.

1 The Role of a Function Interpreter

One of the main advantages of mathematical software tools is that they apply to different mathematical functions. They receive these mathematical functions in the form of functions in C++.

For example, the function $f(x) = \sin(x).e^{3x}$ is coded in the following manner:

```
ar_double  f_sinexp (ar_double x)
{
   return (sin (x) * exp (3 * x));
}
```

It can be integrated between 0 and π using Simpson's method applied over 1000 intervals through the call sequence:

```
result = ar_integral_simpson (f_sinexp, 0, PI, 1000);
```

You must use this type of calculation tool call when you integrate one or more mathematical tools in your personal software. It is both simple to use and quick.

However, this call sequence becomes inadequate when an exploitation tool calls up a calculation tool with a function as a parameter. In this case, the user enters a mathematical function in the form of a character chain. The latter changes with each utilisation.

We have created an artificial object, the class `ar_function`, so that the user need not program the mathematical function in C++ or recompile the program. This class represents the function in coded form (the next section discusses the code format which is used).

Thus, the data entry tool calls on the function interpreter when a mathematical expression is typed in. The function interpreter changes the character chain into a coded object of `ar_function` format. Then, when the exploitation tool calls on the calculation tool, it gives it the evaluation tool `ar_eval_f` as a parameter. The evaluation tool behaves as would the C++ function which corresponds to the entered mathematical function. In other words, it provides the value of the mathematical function applied to x when one gives it x as the parameter.

Coded representations of mathematical functions present an additional advantage: it is possible to transform or even to create mathematical functions. For example, we will examine the following formal derivation tool:

```
int ar_derive_function (ar_function *f, ar_function *g)
```

The tool uses the function f (in coded form) to create a function g (also coded) containing the derivative of f.

Entry of a Number in Symbolic Form

When we introduced the data entry tool, we saw that it is possible to enter real numbers in mathematical form, such as `SQRT(PI/2)`, or simply `11/30`.

This particularity exists because of the function interpreter. The latter considers these constant expressions as mathematical functions with 0 variables, and interprets and evaluates them as such.

Elaboration of a Spreadsheet

Like the data entry tool introduced in the preceding chapter, the manipulation environment of mathematical functions can be improved as desired. In particular, it can serve to create a spreadsheet, in which case the elaboration of formulas and of macro-functions is essential.

2 Internal Representation of a Function

The internal representation format which we use for mathematical functions comes from Polish notation. The major advantage of this representation lies in the simplicity and efficiency of the evaluation process. The evaluation can be done by examining the coded function from left to right, without backtracking. In this way, we can evaluate functions very rapidly.

Four classes of objects are identified separately in a mathematical expression:

- functions with two variables, or binary functions (addition, subtraction, multiplication, division, raising to a power);
- functions with one variable, or unary functions:
  . all mathematical functions (exp, log, sin, cos, ...);
  . abs, int, frac which yield respectively the absolute value, the integer portion and the decimal portion of a number;
  . the functions + and – used as unary operators (for example, +X or –Y);
  . the factorial function, symbolised by an exclamation point at the end of the operant (for example, the function $(x+3)$! is valid);
- the constants (3, 56.64, PI...);
- the variables $(x, y_1, y, ...)$.

Each object is represented by a letter indicating its class, followed by a certain number of bytes. These bytes encode the object itself. Thus:

– Binary functions are coded on two bytes, in the form Bx, x being a character which represents the relevant operation. Addition is coded as B+, multiplication as B*, and raising to a power as B^. The two representations of the operants of the function follow these two bytes.

– Unary functions are also coded on two bytes, in the form Ux, x being a character which represents the relevant operation. For example, sine is coded as UC, argument hyperbolic tangent as UN, and logarithm as UT. The representation of the operand of the function follows these two bytes.

– Constants are coded on nine bytes, in the form Cxxxxxxxx, the eight or sixteen bytes which follow the letter C contain the representation in double or long double format of the relevant constant.

– Variables are coded on three bytes (or five depending on the machine), in the form Vxx, the two (or four) bytes which follow the letter V contain the number, of type (int), of the relevant variable. In order to make the function interpreter flexible and usable in other contexts, we have not limited the manipulable variables to x and y_i.

The function interpreter calls on an external recognition function when it encounters a variable. This recognition function was passed to the function interpreter during the call. The return value of the recognition function is an integer which indicates the number of the variable on the list of valid variables. If the variable is not valid, the return value is –1.

Thus, the function `sin (3 * x) + 2` is coded in the following form:

```
B+UCB*CaaaaaaaaVbbCccccccc
```

where the letters `aaaaaaaa` contain the double representation of the number 3 and the letters `cccccccc` contain the double representation of the number 2. The letters `bb` contain the integer representation of the index of the variable, 1 in the case of a mono-variable system.

The tool `analyse`, a function belonging to the class `ar_function`, accepts as a parameter the character chain representing the mathematical expression. It also accepts a function in C++ which calculates the index of a variable.

We have built other tools which exploit the preceding tool. They facilitate its use in the restricted environment constituted by the programs in this book:

– the member function `anal_std_x` accepts only one parameter, the character chain representing the mathematical expression. In this case, the coding function of the variables in use is transparent. It recognizes two variables:

> x or t which is variable number 1
>
> y which is variable number 2

– the member function `anal_std_xyi`, also accepts only one parameter: the entered mathematical expression. This time the recognized variables are:

x	(variable number 0)
y	(variable number 1)
y_1 to y_n	(variables number 1 to n)
y'	(variable number 2)
y''	(variable number 3)
$y^{(n)}$	(variable number $n+1$)

3   Return to Mathematical Representation

The tool `ar_decompile_function`, a member function of the class `ar_function`, carries out the inverse transformation: using a coded function f, it reconstitutes the mathematical representation in the form of character chains.

To limit memory use, our tool truncates the reconstituted formulas at 255 characters. However, this constraint can easily be eliminated in the case of a more demanding project.

Parentheses are automatically generated around the operants of unary functions, so that the interpretation of the decompiled expression is unambiguous.

This "de-compilation" is particularly useful in the formal derivation tool. After calculating the derived function in coded form, one must be able to visualize the result in the form of a character chain representing the mathematical expression.

4 Evaluation of a Coded Function

The evaluation tool allows one to calculate the value of the function using its coded representation and a set of values of the variables.

The main tool, overflow of the evaluation operator ( ), is conceived in a way symmetrical to the interpretation tool. Its only parameter is a function that calculates the values of the variables.

Though this tool was conceived so as to be as flexible as possible in different applications, it is unable to satisfy our main objective: the emulation of a real function of a variable.

This explains why we built the tool `ar_eval_f`, which behaves like a real function with x as its only variable. This variable is copied into a variable (`ar_glob_x`) that is local to the function management module.

Then, a variable evaluation function in C++ which is also local to the module and is transparent for the user, takes on the utilisation of the variable `ar_glob_x`. As output, `ar_eval_f` gives the value of the function $f(x)$, f being the function coded in `ar_glob_f`.

Thus, the usual processing of a mathematical expression in a program will be as follows: entry of the expression using the data entry tool, with storage of the coded form in `ar_glob_f`, then utilisation of `ar_eval_f` instead of $f(x)$ during any reference to the function f.

Similar tools are developed for functions with two variables and with n variables. After reading the following printout and those concerning differential equations, one will understand their conception and utilisation.

This tool illustrates the power of the technique of recursivity. The evaluation of a binary function is accomplished by first evaluating the two operands, and then applying the binary operation to the two results. The complete evaluation tool is short. It is centered around the function `ar_evaluate`. If the reader wishes to familiarize himself with recursive technique, he should study this tool attentively.

5 Printout of Function Manipulation Tools

This group of tools is to be placed in the file `FUNCTION.CPP`.

```
/*==========================================================
                      FUNCTION.CPP:
          FUNCTION ANALYZE AND EVALUATION TOOLS
==========================================================*/
```

```
#include <string.h>
#include <ctype.h>
#include "armath.h"

ar_double   ar_glob_x, ar_glob_y, ar_glob_arr_y [10];
int         ar_glob_dim = 3;

ar_function  ar_glob_f (10000), ar_glob_g (10000);

//---------------------- OPEN A FUNCTION (ALLOCATE MEMORY)
void ar_function::open (int n)
{
  if (n >= 0)  {
    maxlen = n;
    start = new char [n];
    if (! start) {
      errno = TRUE;
      cerr << "Not enough memory";
    }
  }
  else  {
    maxlen = 0;
    start  = NULL;
  }
}

//----------------------------------------- COPY A FUNCTION
void ar_function::operator = (ar_function &f)
{
  int len = ar_funclen (f.start);

  if (len <= maxlen)
    memcpy (start, f.start, len);
  else
    errno = TRUE;
}

/*==========================================================
         EVALUATION OF A PRE-ANALYZED FUNCTION
----------------------------------------------------------
 Input parameters :
     f             : current pointer to analyzed function
     ar_val_var  : function giving a variable's value
                   from its coded number
----------------------------------------------------------
 Output parameters :
     f             : current pointer to analyzed function
     Func.value  : 'double' corresponding to the desired value
```

```
-------------------------------------------------------------
Technique :
    The core of this analysis is the RECURSIVE procedure
    evaluate, which has no parameters and only two local
    variables.
    The main variable used by this function is cur_form,
    current pointer is the formula to be evaluated.
    This pointer always progresses from left to right in
    the formula. It never goes back, which quickens the
    overall process. This advantage comes from the form
    chosen for the analyzed function
    =====================================================*/

/*-----------------------------------------------------------
      FUNCTION LOCAL VARIABLES, BUT DECLARED AS STATIC
    ------------------------------------------------------*/
ar_double (*ar_val_fn) (int);
char      *ar_cur_form;

static int    i, j;
static ar_double s;

/* WARNING : Using global variables in a recursive function
    allows one to increase the recursion depth for a given
    stack size, but necessitates great prudence: after each
    call to the function, one has to remember that those
    variables may have been changed.

/*-----------------------------------------------------------
                MAIN RECURSIVE PROCEDURE
    ------------------------------------------------------*/
ar_double ar_evaluate (void)
{
  ar_double  r;      // Those two variables (r and oper) must
  char       oper;   // be absolutely LOCAL
  switch (*(ar_cur_form++))  {
    //---------------------------------------- Constants
    case 'C' :
      r = * (ar_double *) ar_cur_form;
      ar_cur_form += sizeof (ar_double);
      return (r);

    //---------------------------------------- Variables
    case 'V' :
      r = (* ar_val_fn) (* (int *) ar_cur_form);
      if (errno) return (0);
      ar_cur_form += sizeof (int);
      return (r);
```

```
//-------------------------------- Binary operations
case 'B' :
  oper = * (ar_cur_form ++);
  r = ar_evaluate (); if (errno) return (0);
  switch (oper)  {
  case '+' : return (r + ar_evaluate ());
  case '-' : return (r - ar_evaluate ());
  case '*' : return (r * ar_evaluate ());
  case '/' : s = ar_evaluate ();
             if (fabs (s) < 1e-20) errno = TRUE;
             if (errno) return (0);
             return (r / s);
  case '^' : s = ar_evaluate (); if (errno) return (0);
             return (pow (r, s));
  default  : errno = TRUE;        // Invalid operation
             return (0);
  }

//-------------------------------- Unary operations
case 'U' :
  oper = * (ar_cur_form ++);
  r = ar_evaluate (); if (errno) return (0);

  switch (oper)  {
    case FMINUS  : return (- r);
  case FPLUS    : return (r);
  case FABS     : return (fabs (r));
  case FINT     : return (floor (r));
  case FFRAC    : return (r - floor (r));
  case FSQRT    : return (sqrt (r));
  case FEXP     : return (exp (r));
  case FLOG     : return (log (r));
  case FSIN     : return (sin (r));
  case FCOS     : return (cos (r));
  case FTAN     : return (tan (r));
  case FSH      : return (sinh (r));
  case FCH      : return (cosh (r));
  case FTH      : return (tanh (r));
  case FARCSIN  : return (asin (r));
  case FARCCOS  : return (acos (r));
  case FARCTAN  : return (atan (r));
  case FARGSH   : return (log (r + sqrt (1 + r * r)));
  case FARGCH   : return (log (r + sqrt (-1 + r * r)));
  case FARGTH   : return (log ((1 + r) / (1 - r)) / 2);
  case FFACT    : if (fabs (r) < 32)  {
                  for (s=1, i=1; i<=r; i++) s *= i;
                      return (s);
                  }
```

```
        default      : errno = TRUE;   // Invalid operation
                       return (0);
        } // switch oper

    //--------------------------------- Invalid operation
    case '\0' : return  (0);
    default   : errno = TRUE; return (0);

  }  // switch

}  // ar_evaluate ()

/*---------------------------------------------------------
             CALLING FUNCTIONS OF EVALUATION
-----------------------------------------------------------*/
ar_double ar_function::operator () (ar_double (*val) (int))
{
  ar_cur_form = start;
  ar_val_fn   = val;
  return (ar_evaluate ());
}

ar_double ar_eval_f (ar_double x)
{
  ar_glob_x   = x;
  return (ar_glob_f (ar_val_var));
}

ar_double ar_eval_g (ar_double x)
{
  ar_glob_x   = x;
  return (ar_glob_g (ar_val_var));
}

ar_double ar_eval_fxy (ar_double x, ar_double y)
{
  ar_glob_x   = x;
  ar_glob_y   = y;
  return (ar_glob_f (ar_val_var));
}

ar_double ar_eval_gxy (ar_double x, ar_double y)
{
  ar_glob_x   = x;
  ar_glob_y   = y;
  return (ar_glob_g (ar_val_var));
}
```

```
ar_double ar_eval_fyi (ar_double x, ar_double y [])
{
  int  i;

  ar_glob_x   = x;
  for (i = 0; i < ar_glob_dim; i++) ar_glob_arr_y[i] = y[i];
  return (ar_glob_f (ar_val_arr));
}

/*---------------------------------------------------------
                VARIABLE DECODING FUNCTIONS
---------------------------------------------------------*/
ar_double ar_val_var (int i)
{
  errno = FALSE;

  switch (i)  {
    case 0  : return (ar_glob_x);
    case 1  : return (ar_glob_y);
    default :
      errno = TRUE;
      return (0);
  }
}

ar_double ar_val_arr (int i)
{
  errno = FALSE;

  if (i == 0) return (ar_glob_x);
  if (i <= ar_glob_dim) return (ar_glob_arr_y [i - 1]);
  else  {
    errno = TRUE;
    return (0);
  }
}

/*---------------------------------------------------------
        PROGRESS TO THE END OF AN ANALYZED FUNCTION
---------------------------------------------------------*/
static void progress (void)
{
  switch (*(ar_cur_form++))  {
    case 'C' : ar_cur_form += sizeof (ar_double); break;
    case 'V' : ar_cur_form += sizeof (int); break;
    case 'U' : ar_cur_form++; progress (); break;
    case 'B' : ar_cur_form++; progress (); progress ();
      break;
```

```
         default  : break;
     }
}

/*--------------------------------------------------------
      CALCULATE LENGTH OF AN ANALYZED FUNCTION
--------------------------------------------------------*/
unsigned int ar_funclen (char *f)
{
  ar_cur_form = f;
  progress ();
  return ((unsigned int) (ar_cur_form - f));
}

/*=======================================================
                ANALYZE A USER FUNCTION (String)
  -----------------------------------------------------
  INPUT PARAMETERS :
      *f      : Current pointer to the function to be analyzed
      lm      : maximal length of the analyzed function
      (*isvar) () : function which makes it possible to know
                    if a string if a valid variable or not
  -----------------------------------------------------
  OUTPUT PARAMETERS :
      *form_ana : pointer to the analyzed formula
      lr : real length of the analyzed function
      value of the function : 0 if the syntax is correct
  -----------------------------------------------------
  PRINCIPLE :

      The core of this analysis is the RECURSIVE function
      analyse_string, which takes only two parameters,
      a string ch and its length lc.
      The other parameters are used as global variables,
      to avoid saturation of the stack.
      Thus, the role of analyse_function is :
          - Arranges the formula
          - Initialisation of global variables
          - Call the recursive function with the complete
            formula
=======================================================*/

/*=======================================================
  LOCAL VARIABLES (LOCAL TO FUNCTION, BUT DECLARED GLOBAL)
  =====================================================*/
static char ar_nom_op_unary [21] [7] =
      {"-", "+",
       "SIN","COS","TAN","ARCSIN","ARCCOS","ARCTAN",
```

```
            "SH",  "CH",  "TH",  "ARGSH",  "ARGCH",  "ARGTH",
            "ABS","INT","FRAC",  "FACT",  "EXP","LOG","SQRT"};

static int (*isv) (char*, int);        // Variables identifying
function
static int  lmax;        // Maximum length of the ANALYZED
formula
static char *f_ana;                 // ANALYZED formula (the
result)
static int  ana_cur;     // Current index in ANALYZED formula
static ar_double  r;
static int  res;
static char     forcte [30];

// WARNING : GLOBAL VARIABLES IN A RECURSIVE FUNCTION
//           SEE REMARK ABOVE (for function evaluation)

/*============================================================
                  LOCAL  FUNCTION  PROTOTYPES
 ============================================================*/
static skip_parentheses (char*, int*);
static ins_unary          (int);
static search            (char*, int, char, char);
static analyse_string     (char[], int);

/*============================================================
                    SKIP_PARENTHESES :
  The formula pointer points to an opening parenthesis:
  advances the formula pointer to the corresponding
  closing parenthesis, or the end of the string.
  'len' indicates the maximum number of characters
  At the output, it contains the number of characters jumped.
 ============================================================*/
static skip_parentheses (char *f, int *len)
{
  int  i = 0, np = 0;

  do  {
    switch (*f++)  {
      case '(' : np++; break;
      case ')' : np--; break;
    }
    i++;
  } while ((np) && (i < *len));
  f--;
  *len = i;
  return (! np);
}
```

```c
/*===========================================================
                      INS_UNARY :
  Puts in the result formula the unary operation detected.
  The result indicates if there was enough room for that.
  =========================================================*/
static ins_unary (int i)
{
  if (ana_cur + 2 >= lmax) return (0);
  f_ana [ana_cur++] = 'U';
  f_ana [ana_cur++] = (char) i;
  return (1);
}


/*===========================================================
                      SEARCH :
  At the output,the global variable 'res' indicates whether
  the search has been successful or not. The value TRUE
  indicates that something has been done, and that,
  therefore, the search must be aborted.
  =========================================================*/
static search (char *ch, int len, char c1, char c2)
{
  int np, i = len-1;

  do  {
    if (ch [i] == ')')  {
      np = 0;
      do switch (ch [i--])  {
      case '(' : np--; break;
      case ')' : np++; break;
      }       while ((np) && (i >= 0));
      i++;
      if (np)  {
      res = 0;
      return (1);
      }
    }
    else
      if (((ch[i]==c1) || (ch[i]==c2)) && (i>0) && (i<len-1))
      switch (ch [i-1])  {
        case '(': case 'E': case '+': case '-':
        case '*': case '/': case '^': break;
        default :
          if (ana_cur + 2 < lmax)  {
            f_ana [ana_cur++] = 'B';
            f_ana [ana_cur++] = ch [i];
            if (analyse_string (&ch [0], i))
            res = analyse_string (&ch[i+1], len-i-1);
```

```
          else
           res = 0;
          }
          else res = 0;
          return (1);
       } /* switch ch[i-1] */
   } while (--i >= 0);
   return (0);
}


/*=============================================================
            analyse_string : recursive procedure
   =========================================================*/
static analyse_string (char ch [], int lc)
{
  // WARNING - NO LOCAL VARIABLES -
  // SEE REMARK AT THE TOP OF THIS FILE

  //--------------------------------- 1 : Initializations
  if (lc == 0) return (1);

  //------------------ 2 : Searching for binary operations
  if (search (ch, lc, '-', '+')) return (res);
  if (search (ch, lc, '/', '*')) return (res);

  //---------------------- 3 : Searching for unary - and +
  if (ch [0] == '-')  {
    ins_unary (FMINUS);
    return (analyse_string (&ch[1], lc-1));
  }
  if (ch [0] == '+')
    return (analyse_string (&ch[1], lc-1));

  //------------------ 4 : Searching for the power function
  if (search (ch, lc, '^', '^')) return (res);

  //----------------------- 5 : Searching for parentheses
  if (ch [0] == '(')  {
    i = lc;
  if ((skip_parentheses (ch, &i)) && (i == lc))
    return (analyse_string (&ch[1], lc-2));
  else
    return (0);
  }

  //-------------------------- 6 : Searching for factorial
  if (ch [lc - 1] == '!')  {
    ins_unary (FFACT);
```

```
    return (analyse_string (&ch[0], lc-1));
  }

  //-------------------- 7 : Searching for unary functions
  for (i = (int) FSIN; i <= (int) FSQRT; i++)   {
    j = strlen (ar_nom_op_unary [i]);
    if (strncmp(ar_nom_op_unary [i], ch, j) == 0)   {
      res = 0;
     . if (ch [j] == '(')
      if (ins_unary (i))
        res = analyse_string (&ch[j], lc-j);
      return (res);
    }
  }

  //--------------------------- 8 : Searching for unknowns
  i = (*isv)(ch, lc);
  if (i >= 0)   {
    if (ana_cur + 1 + sizeof (int) >= lmax) return (0);
    f_ana [ana_cur++] = 'V';
    memcpy (&f_ana [ana_cur], (char *) &i, sizeof (int));
    ana_cur += sizeof(int);
    return (1);
  }

  //--------------------------- 9 : Searching for constants
  if (ana_cur + sizeof (ar_double) + 1 >= lmax) return (0);
  i = FALSE;
  strncpy (forcte, ch, lc);
  forcte [lc] = 0;
  if ((i = (strcmp (forcte, "0") == 0)) == TRUE)
    r = 0;
  if (i == FALSE)
    i = ((r = atof (forcte)) != 0);
  if (i == FALSE)
    if ((i = (strcmp (forcte, "PI") == 0)) == TRUE)
      r = AR_PI;
  if (i)   {
    f_ana [ana_cur++] = 'C';
    memcpy (&f_ana [ana_cur], (char *) &r,
            sizeof (ar_double));
    ana_cur += sizeof (ar_double);
    return (1);
  }

  return (0);     //------------- Nothing has been recognized
}
```

```
/*==============================================================
                AR_FUNCTION::ANALYSE : CALLING TOOL
  ============================================================*/
int ar_function::analyse (char *f,int (*isvar) (char *, int))
{
    int        i, j;
    char *fb;

    //------------------- Initialize global static variables
    isv              = isvar;
    lmax             = maxlen;
    f_ana    = start;
    ana_cur  = 0;

    //------------------------------- Normalizes the formula
    fb = (char *) malloc (strlen (f));
    if (fb == 0) return (0);
    for (i = 0, j = 0; i < strlen(f); i++)
        if (f[i] != ' ')
        fb [j++] = toupper (f[i]);

    //----------------------- Calls the recursive function
    errno = ! analyse_string (fb, j);
    free (fb);
    return (ana_cur);
}

static int num_vx (char *ch, int lc)
{
  if (lc == 1)
    switch (ch [0])   {
      case 'X':
      case 'T': return (0);
      default : return (-1);
    }
  return (-1);
}

static int num_vxyi (char *ch, int lc)
{
  int  i;

  if (lc == 1)
    switch (ch [0])   {
      case 'X':
      case 'T': return (0);
      case 'Y': return (1);
    }
```

```cpp
    if (lc < 1)           return (-1);
    if (ch [0] != 'Y') return (-1);

    if ((lc == 2) && (ch [1] > '0') && (ch [1] <= '9'))
      return (ch [1] - '0');

    for (i = 1; i < lc; i++)
      if (ch [i] != '\'') return (-1);
    return (lc);
}

void ar_function::anal_std_x (char *cc)
{
  analyse (cc, num_vx);
}

void ar_function::anal_std_xyi (char *cc)
{
  analyse (cc, num_vxyi);
}

/*-------------------------------------------------
            "DECOMPILE" A FUNCTION
------------------------------------------------*/
static char ar_nom_op [] [7] = {"-", "+",
     "SIN","COS","TAN","ARCSIN","ARCCOS","ARCTAN",
     "SH", "CH", "TH", "ARGSH", "ARGCH", "ARGTH",
     "ABS","INT","FRAC", "FACT", "EXP","LN","SQRT"};

static void ar_decompile_char (char *f, char *ch)
{
  char  ch1 [255], ch2 [255], *pv;

  switch (f [0])  {
    case 'C' :
      sprintf (ch2, "%30.15lf", * (ar_double *) & f[1]);
      pv = ch2; while (*(pv++) == ' ');   // eliminate spaces
      strcpy (ch, pv - 1);
      pv = ch + strlen (ch);
      while (*(--pv) == '0') *pv = 0;
      if (*pv == '.') *pv = 0;
      break;

    case 'V' :
      strcpy (ch, "X"); break;

    case 'U' :
      ar_decompile_char (&f [2], ch1);
```

```
    if (strlen (ch1) > 245) {errno = TRUE; return;}
    switch (f [1])  {
    case FMINUS :
      strcpy (ch, "- "); strcat (ch, ch1); break;
    case FPLUS   :
      strcpy (ch, ch1); break;
    default      :
      strcpy (ch, ar_nom_op [f [1]]);
      if (ch1 [0] == '(')  {
        strcat (ch, " "); strcat (ch, ch1);
      }
      else  {
        strcat (ch, " ("); strcat (ch, ch1);
        strcat (ch, ")");
      }
      break;
    }
   break;

  case 'B' :
    pv = &f [2 + ar_funclen (&f [2])];
    ar_decompile_char (&f [2], ch1);
    ar_decompile_char (pv, ch2);
    if (strlen (ch1) + strlen (ch2) > 245)
                                {errno = TRUE; return;}
    strcpy (ch, ch1);
    switch (f [1])  {
    case '+' : strcat (ch, " + "); strcat (ch, ch2); break;
    case '-' : strcat (ch, " - "); strcat (ch, ch2); break;
    case '*' : strcat (ch, " * "); strcat (ch, ch2); break;
    case '/' : strcat (ch, " / "); strcat (ch, ch2); break;
    case '^' : strcat (ch, " ^ "); strcat (ch, ch2); break;
    }
    strcpy (ch2, "("); strcat (ch2, ch);
    strcat (ch2, ")"); strcpy (ch, ch2);
    break;
  }
}

void ar_function::decompile (char *ch)
{
  ar_decompile_char (start, ch);
}
```

5

Geometry

In this chapter, we will study several algorithms used in geometrical calculations.

First, we will examine how to calculate a surface limited by a contour; then, we will move on to the calculation of arcs.

Subsequently, we will discuss conic sections. The first algorithm allows us to reduce a conic section; that is, to determine its nature and its reduction elements (centers, focuses, axes, and eccentricity). The second algorithm calculates the equation of the conic section which passes through five given points.

We conclude this chapter with the resolution of indefinite triangles; that is, the determination of three unknown parameters, three parameters being given.

The tools from this chapter can be found under the subdirectory GEO.

---

1 Calculation of a Surface

1.1 Principle

Let us consider any closed contour. We will look for an approximate value of its interior area.

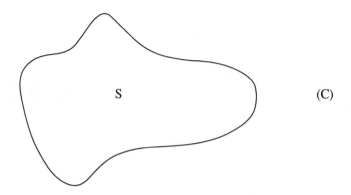

In order to do so, we approximate the contour (C) by a series of points belonging to (C) and interconnected by line segments:

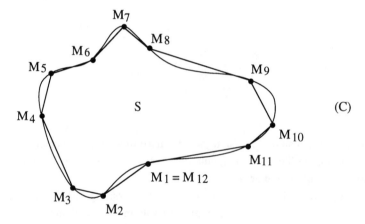

The polynomial defined by the points M_1, M_2, ..., $M_{12} = M_1$ is an approximation of the contour (C).

The surface of this polygon can be calculated by the program in a very simple way. We will then obtain an approximate value of the initial surface S. Of course, the higher the number of points on the contour, the higher the precision of the result.

1.2 Calculation Tool

The points which define the contour are submitted to the tool `ar_calc_surf` in the form of two double tables `x[]` and `y[]` and an integer n which indicates the number of points.

The origin of the orthonormal axes chosen to illustrate the coordinates does not affect the result. For example, the origin can be one of the points on the contour.

However, the points must be entered in the order in which they are situated on the contour. The last point must be the same as the first.

If the contour has double points (if it intersects itself at several points), one must choose a series of points which defines only one interior surface:

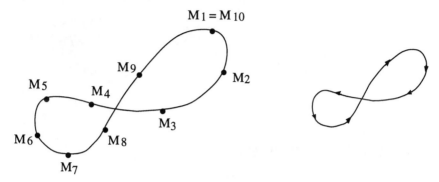

In the case shown above, the result given by the program will be incorrect, because the chosen contour does not define an interior surface. The points must be chosen in the following manner:

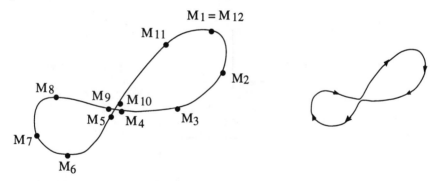

Thus, one must remember not to allow intersections to appear during the selection of the points which fix the boundaries of the contour.

In the above example, it is of course possible to calculate the surface of the two lobes separately, and to add them afterwards in order to obtain the total surface.

This tool is located in the file GEO\GEOSURF.CPP.

```
/*==============================================================
                        GEOSURF.CPP:
                    CALCULATE SURFACES
==============================================================*/

#include   "armath.h"
```

```
ar_number ar_calc_surf (ar_number x[], ar_number y[], int n)
{
  ar_number s = N0;
  int      i;

  for (i = 0; i <= n - 2; i++)
    s += (x [i] + x [i+1]) * (y [i] - y [i+1]);

  s /= ar_number (2);
  if (! s.positive ()) s = -s;

  return s;
}
```

1.3 Annotated Examples

Example 1

Let us consider the following polygon:

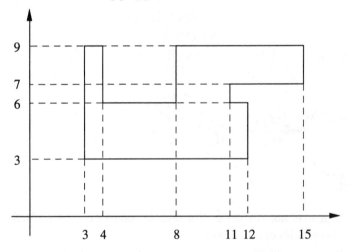

```
CALCULATION OF SURFACES

Number of points: 13
x0 = 3        y0 = 3
x1 = 12       y1 = 3
x2 = 12       y2 = 6
x3 = 11       y3 = 6
x4 = 11       y4 = 7
x5 = 15       y5 = 7
x6 = 15       y6 = 9
```

```
x7 = 8        y7 = 9
x8 = 8        y8 = 6
x9 = 4        y9 = 6
x10 = 4       y10 = 9
x11 = 3       y11 = 9
x12 = 3       y12 = 3
```

```
Value of the surface: + 47
```

The result 47 given by the program does indeed correspond to the number of square units contained in the contour.

Example 2

We will calculate an approximation of the value of *n*.

To this end, let us consider the circle with center 0 and radius 1, represent it graphically and make twenty measurements distributed along its circumference:

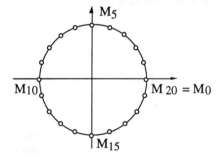

```
CALCULATION OF SURFACE
```

```
Number of points: 21
x0 = 1        y0 = 0
x1 = .95      y1 = .31
x2 = .81      y2 = .59
x3 = .59      y3 = .81
x4 = .31      y4 = .95
x5 = 0        y5 = 1
x6 = -.31     y6 = .95
x7 = -.59     y7 = .81
x8 = -.81     y8 = .59
x9 = -.95     y9 = .31
x10 = -1      y10 = 0
x11 = -.95    y11 = -.31
x12 = -.81    y12 = -.59
x13 = -.59    y13 = -.81
```

```
x14 = -.31    y14 = -.95
x15 = 0       y15 = -1
x16 = .31     y16 = -.95
x17 = .59     y17 = -.81
x18 = .81     y18 = -.59
x19 = .95     y19 = -.31
x20 = 1       y20 = 0

Value of the surface: 3.0936
```

The program gives $S = 3.0936$, which corresponds to an approximative value of π to the nearest 5.10^{-2}.

Naturally we would have obtained a better result if we had measured the points more precisely, or if we had used more points.

2 Calculation of Arcs

2.1 Principle

An arc can be characterised by four parameters:

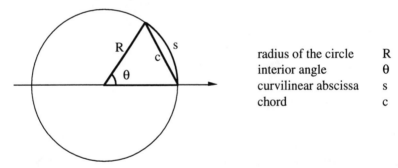

radius of the circle	R
interior angle	θ
curvilinear abscissa	s
chord	c

(R radius, s curvilinear abscissa, c chord, θ interior angle)

These four parameters are not independent; two are enough to define a given arc. The formulas are as follows:

$$\begin{cases} s = R.\theta \\ c = 2\,R\,\sin\left(\dfrac{\theta}{2}\right) \end{cases}$$

However, finding the missing parameters when s and c are given poses a problem. This is because we do not have an algebraic formula for R, R being the solution to the following equation:

$$2\,R\,\sin\left(\frac{s}{2R}\right) - c = 0$$

We will solve this equation using Newton's method (see chapter 10, Equations).

To this end, we let $x = 2R$ and start with $x_0 = c$ (minimum possible value for x). We then calculate:

$$x_{n+1} = x_n \left[\frac{c - s\,\cos\left(\frac{s}{x_n}\right)}{x_n\,\sin\left(\frac{s}{x_n}\right) - s\,\cos\left(\frac{s}{x_n}\right)} \right]$$

until we reach the maximum precision (10^{-8}). In this particular case, Newton's method allows us to find an accurate result very quickly.

2.2 Calculation Tool

The four parameters of the tool `ar_circle` are:
- r, the radius;
- s, the curvilinear abscissa;
- c, the chord;
- t, the angle.

Two parameters must be given; the two others need to be equal to zero. The angle must be expressed in radians.

The function calculates the two unknown parameters, and the two surfaces S_1 and S_2 where:

S_1 represents the surface of the sector:

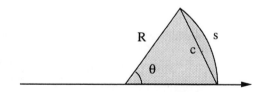

$$S_1 = \frac{s.R}{2}$$

and S_2 the portion between the chord and the circle:

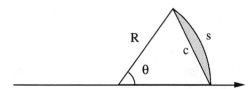

$$S_2 = S_1 - \frac{c.R}{2}\,\cos\left(\frac{\theta}{2}\right)$$

If no solution arc has been found, the variable `errno` is set to TRUE.

The exploitation tool, given at the end of the chapter, allows one to express the angle in a unit other than radians, through a conversion before and after the calculation tool.

The calculation tool is situated in the file GEO\ARC.CPP.

```
/*==========================================================
                        GEOARC.CPP:
                    CALCULATION OF ARCS
  =======================================================*/

#include   "armath.h"

void  ar_circle (
          ar_double &r, ar_double &s, ar_double &c,
          ar_double &t, ar_double &s1, ar_double &s2)
{
  int          nb_data = 0;
  ar_double    a, b, x, y, u;

  //--------------------- Check input data global coherence
  if (r != 0)  nb_data ++;
  if (s != 0)  nb_data ++;
  if (t != 0)  nb_data ++;
  if (c != 0)  nb_data ++;

  errno = TRUE;

  if ((nb_data != 2) || (t < 0) || (t > AR_PI)) return;
  if ((s > 0) && (c >= s))                      return;
  if ((c > 0) && (s > AR_PI / 2 * c)) return;
  if ((r > 0) && (s > AR_PI * r))       return;

  if (t > 0)
    if (r > 0)  {
      //--------------------- Case where t and r are known
      s = r * t;
      c = 2 * r * sin (t / 2);
    }
    else
      if (s > 0)  {
        //------------------- Case where t and s are known
        r = s / t;
        c = 2 * r * sin (t / 2);
      }
      else  {
        //------------------- Case where t and c are known
        r = c / 2 / sin (t / 2);
        s = r * t;
      }
```

```
   else
     if (c == 0)  {
       //---------------------- Case where r and s are known
       t = s / r; c = 2 * r * sin (t / 2);
     }
     else
       if (r > 0)  {
         //------------------- Case where r and c are known
         t = (c < 2 * r) ?
             2 * atan (c / sqrt (4 * r * r - c * c)) : AR_PI;
         s = r * t;
       }
       else  {
         //------------------- Case where s and c are known
         y = c;
         do  {
           x = y; u = s / x;
           a = s * cos (u); b = x * sin (u) - a;
           if ((c - a) * b <= 0) return;
           y = x * (c - a) / b;
         }  while (fabs (x - y) > AR_SMALL);
         r = y / 2; t = s / r;
       }

   //------------------------------------- Calculate surfaces
   s1 = s * r / 2;
   s2 = (s - c * cos (t / 2)) * r / 2;
   errno = FALSE;
}
```

2.3 Annotated Examples

Example 1

Let us consider the arc defined by:

$$\begin{cases} \theta = 1 \text{ rd} \\ c = 2 \end{cases}$$

```
CALCULATION OF ARCS

R                        : 0
S                        : 0
C                        : 2
Unit : Value of PI       : pi
T                        : 1
```

```
R   = 2.085829642933
S   = 2.085829642933
C   = 2
T   = 1
S1  = 2.17534264967
S2  = 0.344854927958
```

The program then gives:
$$\begin{cases} R = 2.085829642933 \\ s = 2.085829642933 \end{cases}$$
which is normal since $s = R.\theta$ and $\theta = 1$ rd.

Example 2

The parameters are:
$$\begin{cases} s = 2.5 \\ c = 2 \end{cases}$$

In this case, the radius must be calculated according to Newton's method.

```
CALCULATION OF ARCS

R                          : 0
S                          : 2.5
C                          : 2
Unit : Value of PI         : 180
T                          : 0

R   = 1.105116384541
S   = 2.5
C   = 2
T   = 129.614808708306
S1  = 1.381395480676
S2  = 0.9109890358
```

3   Reduction of Conic Sections

3.1 Review of Theory

A conic section is a curve whose cartesian equation has the following form:

$$ax^2 + 2bxy + cy^2 + 2dx + 2ey + f = 0$$

There are three main types of conic sections:
– hyperbola (including equilateral hyperbola);
– parabola;
– ellipse (including circles, in particular).
There are also degenerate conic sections: lines, the union of two lines, or a point.

The aim of the paragraph is to determine the type or family of a conic section and to identify its characteristics (center, foci, axes and eccentricity) using its cartesian equation. The discussion consists of a series of tests and calculations on the coefficients of the equation. This process is particularly well-suited to processing by a computer.

Here is the principle of this discussion. First we calculate the discriminant:

$$\Delta = b^2 - ac$$

If $\Delta = 0$, the conic section is a parabola.
If $\Delta < 0$, the conic section is an ellipse.
If $\Delta > 0$, the conic section is a hyperbola.

First case: $\Delta \neq 0$

The center Ω of the conic section, if it exists, has the following coordinates:

$$\Omega \quad \begin{cases} x_1 = \dfrac{dc-be}{\Delta} \\[2mm] y_1 = \dfrac{ae-bd}{\Delta} \end{cases}$$

and the equation of the conic section in the new coordinate system (Ω, i, j) is then:

$$aX^2 + 2bXY + cY^2 + f' = 0$$

with:

$$X = x-x_1 \qquad Y = y-y_1$$
$$f' = ax_1^2 + 2bx_1y_1 + cy_1^2 + 2dx_1 + 2ey_1 + f$$

If $f' = 0$:
If $\Delta < 0$, the conic section is reduced to the point Ω.
If $\Delta > 0$, the conic section is the union of two lines.
If $f' \neq 0$:
The quadratic matrix associated with the conic section is:

$$\begin{pmatrix} a & b \\ b & c \end{pmatrix}$$

of which the two eigenvalues are:

$$l = \frac{a+c-\sqrt{(a-c)^2+4b^2}}{2}$$

$$m = \frac{a+c+\sqrt{(a-c)^2+4b^2}}{2}$$

If $a = c$ and $b = 0$:

If $f.a > 0$, no solution.

If $f.a < 0$, the conic section is the circle with center Ω and radius $R = \sqrt{\frac{-f}{a}}$

If $a \neq c$ or $b \neq 0$:

We consider the following two new vectors:

$$\mathbf{I}\begin{pmatrix} \dfrac{b}{\sqrt{b^2+(1-a)^2}} \\ \dfrac{1-a}{\sqrt{b^2+(1-a)^2}} \end{pmatrix} \qquad \mathbf{J}\begin{pmatrix} \dfrac{-(1-a)}{\sqrt{b^2+(1-a)^2}} \\ \dfrac{b}{\sqrt{b^2+(1-a)^2}} \end{pmatrix}$$

The coordinate system basis (I, J) is orthonormal. The equation of the conic section in the coordinate system (Ω, I, J) is:

$$lX^2 + mY^2 + f = 0$$

If $\Delta < 0$:

If sgn (l) = sgn (f), no solution;

If sgn $(l) \neq$ sgn (f), the conic section is an ellipse with center Ω and axes (ΩX, ΩY).
Its foci are on the long axis, at the distance d $(\Omega, F) = \sqrt{a'^2+b'^2}$, where:

$$a' = \sqrt{\frac{-f}{l}} \qquad \text{and} \qquad b' = \sqrt{\frac{-f}{m}}$$

are the half-lengths of the axes.

The eccentricity of the ellipse is then $e = \dfrac{\sqrt{a'^2+b'^2}}{a'}$

If $\Delta > 0$:

The conic section is a hyperbola with center Ω and axes ΩX, ΩY.
It is equilateral if $a+c = 0$.
If $f > 0$:

$$a' = \sqrt{\frac{-|f|}{l}} \qquad\qquad b' = \sqrt{\frac{-|f|}{m}}$$

the transversal axis is ΩX.

If $f < 0$:

$$a' = \sqrt{\frac{-|f|}{m}} \qquad\qquad b' = \sqrt{\frac{-|f|}{l}}$$

the transversal axis is ΩY.

The eccentricity is $e = \dfrac{\sqrt{a'^2 + b'^2}}{a'}$.

The foci are on the transversal axis, at the distance $d(\Omega, F) = \sqrt{a'^2 + b'^2}$.
The vertices are on the transversal axis, at the distance $d(\Omega, S) = a'$.

Second case: $\Delta = 0$

If a, b and c are simultaneously null, the conic section is a line, or does not exist.
If a, b and c are not all null:
If $a = 0$ (therefore $b = 0$ and $c \neq 0$):
   – If $d = 0$:
The conic section is the union of two lines if $e^2 - cf \geq 0$, and does not exist if $e^2 - cf < 0$.
   – If $d \neq 0$:
The coordinates of the center are then:

$$\Omega \quad \begin{cases} x_1 = \dfrac{e^2 - cf}{2cd} \\[2ex] y_1 = -\dfrac{e}{c} \end{cases}$$

The equation of the conic section in the new coordinate system (Ω, i, j) is then:

$$Y^2 = -2\frac{d}{c}X$$

Therefore, it is a parabola with axis ΩX, and parameter $-\dfrac{d}{c}$.

The focus is on the parabola's axis, at the distance $-\dfrac{d}{2c}$ from the center.

If $a \neq 0$:
   We start by making a positive, by multiplying each coefficient by $\mathrm{sgn}(a)$. Then we set:

$$\mathbf{I} \begin{pmatrix} \dfrac{b}{\sqrt{a+c}} \\[2ex] \dfrac{-a}{\sqrt{a+c}} \end{pmatrix} \qquad\qquad \mathbf{J} \begin{pmatrix} \dfrac{a}{\sqrt{a+c}} \\[2ex] \dfrac{b}{\sqrt{a+c}} \end{pmatrix}$$

with:

$$\begin{cases} a = \sqrt{a} \\ b = \sqrt{c} \, \text{sgn}(b) \end{cases}$$

The equation of the conic section in the coordinate system (O, I, J) is then:

$$(a^2+b^2)^{3/2} \, Y^2 + (2db-2ea) \, X + (2da+2eb) \, Y + f \sqrt{a^2+b^2} = 0$$

This equation has the following form:

$$c'Y^2 + 2d'X + 2e'Y + f = 0$$

and thus we return to the case $a = 0$ with the new parameters c', d', e' and f.

If $d' \neq 0$, the center of the parabola is:

$$\Omega \quad \begin{cases} x_1 = \dfrac{e'^2-c'f}{2c'd'} \\ \\ y_1 = -\dfrac{e'}{c'} \end{cases}$$

and the equation of the parabola in the coordinate system (Ω, I, J) is:

$$Y = -\frac{2d'}{c'} X$$

3.2 Calculation Tool

The parameters to be entered for the tool `ar_conic_reduction` are the six coefficients of the cartesian equation:

$$ax^2 + 2bxy + cy^2 + 2dx + 2ey + f = 0$$

We must note that the coefficients to be fed into the program are not a, b, c, d, e, and f but a, $(2b)$, c, $(2d)$, $(2e)$ and f.

The output parameters are:

– tip: an integer which represents the type of conic section:

1: ellipse;

2: hyperbola;

3: parabola;

4: circle;

5: line;

6: the union of two lines;

7: a point;

8: the equation is not that of a conic section.

– ex: eccentricity, or parameter for a parabola;

– xc, yc: the coordinates of the center;

– la, lb: half-lengths for an ellipse, the radius for a circle;

– xf1, yf1, xf2, yf2: coordinates of the foci (only one focus for the parabola);

– xs1, ys1, xs2, ys2: coordinates of the vertices for a hyperbola;

– xv1, yv1, xv2, yv2: coordinates of the directive vectors.

This tool is in the file GEO\REDUCCON.CPP.

```cpp
/*=============================================================
                       REDUCCON.CPP :
                   REDUCTION OF CONICS
  =============================================================*/

#include   "armath.h"

static ar_double   delta, u, l, m, x2, y2;

static void parabola (
        ar_double a, ar_double b, ar_double c, ar_double d,
        ar_double e, ar_double f, int &tip, ar_double &ex,
        ar_double &xc,  ar_double &yc,  ar_double &xf1,
        ar_double &yf1, ar_double &xv1, ar_double &yv1)
{
  ar_double  x, y;

  tip = 3;
  if ((c == 0) && (a == 0))  {
    tip = ((d == 0) && (e == 0)) ? 8 : 5;
    return;
  }
  if (a == 0)  {
    x2 = 1; y2 = 0; l = 0; m = 1;
  }
  else  {
    if (a < 0)  {
      f = -f; e = -e; d = -d;
      c = -c; b = -b; a = -a;
    }
    l = sqrt (a);
    m = sqrt (c);
    if (b < 0)  m = -m;
    u = sqrt (a + c);
    x2 = m / u;
    y2 = - l / u;
    f = f * u;
    c = (a + c) * u;
    u = d * m - e * l;
```

```
      e = d * l + e * m;
      d = u;
    }
    if (d == 0)  {
      tip = (e * e < c * f) ? 8 : 6;
      return;
    }
    else  {
      x    = (e * e - c * f) / 2 / c / d;
      y    = -e / c;
      xc   = x * x2 - y * y2;
      yc   = y * x2 + x * y2;
      ex   = - d / c;
      xf1 = xc + ex * x2 / 2;
      yf1 = yc + ex * y2 / 2;
      xv1 = m;
      yv1 = -l;
    }
}

static void hyperbola (
        ar_double &f, int &tip, ar_double &ex, ar_double &xc,
        ar_double &yc, ar_double &la, ar_double &lb,
        ar_double &xf1, ar_double &yf1, ar_double &xf2,
        ar_double &yf2, ar_double &xs1, ar_double &ys1,
        ar_double &xs2, ar_double &ys2, ar_double &xv1,
        ar_double &yv1, ar_double &xv2, ar_double &yv2)
{
  tip = 2;
  la  = sqrt (- fabs (f) / l);
  lb  = sqrt (abs (f) / m);
  if (f < 0)  {
    u = la;   la  = lb;    lb  = u;
    u = x2;       x2  = -y2;       y2  = u;
    u = xv1; xv1 = -yv1; yv1 = u;
  }
  xv2 = -yv1; yv2 = xv1;
  u    = sqrt (la * la + lb * lb);
  xs1 = xc + x2 * la; ys1 = yc + y2 * la;
  xs2 = xc - x2 * la; ys2 = yc - y2 * la;
  xf1 = xc + x2 * u;  yf1 = yc + y2 * u;
  xf2 = xc - x2 * u;  yf2 = yc - y2 * u;
  ex  = u / la;
}

static void ellipse (
        ar_double &f, int &tip, ar_double &ex, ar_double &xc,
        ar_double &yc, ar_double &la, ar_double &lb,
```

```
        ar_double &xf1, ar_double &yf1, ar_double &xf2,
        ar_double &yf2, ar_double &xv1, ar_double &yv1,
        ar_double &xv2, ar_double &yv2)
{
  tip = 1;
  if (f * l > 0)  {
    tip = 8;
    return;
  }
  la = sqrt (- f / l);
  lb = sqrt (- f / m);
  if (l < 0)  {
    u = la;   la  = lb;    lb  = u;
    u = x2;   x2  = -y2;   y2  = u;
    u = xv1; xv1 = -yv1; yv1 = u;
  }
  xv2 = -yv1; yv2 = xv1;
  u    = sqrt (la * la - lb * lb);
  xf1 = xc + x2 * u; yf1 = yc + y2 * u;
  xf2 = xc - x2 * u; yf2 = yc - y2 * u;
  ex = u / la;
}

void ar_conic_reduction (
        ar_double a, ar_double b, ar_double c,
        ar_double d, ar_double e, ar_double f,
        int &tip, ar_double &ex, ar_double &xc,
        ar_double &yc, ar_double &la, ar_double &lb,
        ar_double &xf1, ar_double &yf1, ar_double &xf2,
        ar_double &yf2, ar_double &xs1, ar_double &ys1,
        ar_double &xs2, ar_double &ys2, ar_double &xv1,
        ar_double &yv1, ar_double &xv2, ar_double &yv2)
{
  b /= 2; d /= 2; e /= 2;
  delta = a * c - b * b;
  if (delta == 0)
    parabola (a,b,c,d,e,f,tip,ex,xc,yc,xf1,yf1,xv1,yv1);
  else  {
    xc = (b * e - d * c) / delta;
    yc = (b * d - a * e) / delta;
    f  = a * xc * xc + 2 * b * xc * yc + c * yc * yc +
         2 * d * xc + 2 * e * yc + f;
    if (f == 0)  {
      tip = (delta > 0) ? 7 : 6;
      return;
    }
    u = sqrt ((a - c) * (a - c) + 4 * b * b);
    l = (a + c - u) / 2;
```

```
m = (a + c + u) / 2;
if ((a == c) && (b == 0))
  if (f * a >= 0)   {
     tip = 8;
     return;
  }
  else  {
     tip = 4;
     la  = sqrt (- f / a);
     return;
  }
if ((a < c) && (b == 0))   {
  x2   = 1;
  y2   = 0;
  xv1 = 1;
  yv1 = 0;
}
else  {
  xv1 = b;
  yv1 = 1 - a;
  u    = sqrt (xv1 * xv1 + yv1 * yv1);
  x2   = xv1 / u;
  y2   = yv1 / u;
}
if (delta < 0)
  hyperbola (f, tip, ex, xc, yc, la, lb, xf1, yf1, xf2,
          yf2, xs1, ys1, xs2, ys2, xv1, yv1, xv2, yv2);
else
  ellipse    (f, tip, ex, xc, yc, la, lb, xf1, yf1, xf2,
          yf2, xv1, yv1, xv2, yv2);
  }
}
```

3.3 Annotated Examples

Example 1

Let us consider the following equation: $x^2 + y^2 + 2xy - 13x - 11y + 32 = 0$

```
REDUCTION OF CONIC SECTIONS

a = 1
b = 2
c = 1
d = -13
e = -11
f = 32
```

```
It is a parabola
    Center                    : x = 1
                                y = 5
    Vector symmetry axis      : x = 1
                                y = -1
    Focus                     : x = 1.125    # 9 / 8
                                y = 4.875    # 39 / 8
    Parameter                 :    0.353553390593  # 1189 / 3363
```

Thus, the proposed equation is that of a parabola with center Ω (1, 5), and whose symmetry axis has (i–j) as a directive vector.

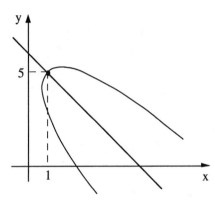

The coordinates of the focus are as follows:
$$\begin{cases} x_F = \dfrac{9}{8} \\[2mm] y_F = \dfrac{39}{8} \end{cases}$$

Example 2

Let us consider the equation: $9x^2 + 4y^2 - 18x + 16y - 11 = 0$

```
REDUCTION OF CONIC SECTIONS

a = 9
b = 0
c = 4
d = -18
e = 16
f = -11

It is an ellipse
    Center                    : x = 1
                                y = -2
    Vect.directive long axis  : x = 0
                                y = -5
```

```
Vect.directive short axis: x = 5
                           y = 0
Half-length long axis    :      3
Half-length short axis   :      2
First focus              : x = 1
                           y = -4.2360679775   # -5473 / 1292
Second focus             : x = 1
                           y = 0.2360679775    # 1292 / 5473
Eccentricity             :      0.7453559925   # 963 / 1292
```

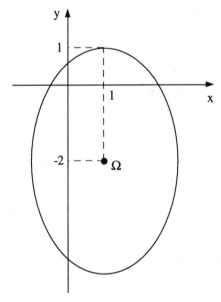

The proposed equation represents an ellipse with center Ω (1, –2), whose long axis has j for a direction vector. The half-lengths of the axes are 2 and 3, which allows us to draw the above ellipse easily.

Example 3

Let us consider the equation: $xy + 5x - y - 7 = 0$

```
REDUCTION OF CONIC SECTIONS

a = 0
b = 1
c = 0
d = 5
e = -1
f = -7.
```

```
It is an equilateral hyperbola
   Center                     : x = 1
                                y = -5

   Vect. direc. transv. axis: x = 0.5   # 1 / 2
                                y = 0.5   # 1 / 2
   Vect. direc. conjug. axis: x = -0.5   # -1 / 2
                                y = 0.5   # 1 / 2

   First vertex              : x = 2.414213562373  # 5741/2378
                                y = -3.585786437627 # -8527/2378
   Second vertex             : x = -0.414213562373 # -2378/5741
                                y = -6.414213562373 # -6318/985

   First focus               : x = 3
                                y = -3
   Second focus              : x = -1
                                y = -7

   Eccentricity              :       1.414213562373    # 3363/2378
```

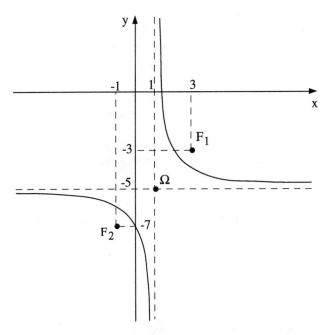

The proposed equation thus corresponds to an equilateral hyperbola with center Ω (1, −5), whose transversal axis is directed by $(i+j)$.

The foci are F_1 (3, −3) and F_2 (−1, −7); the eccentricity is $\sqrt{2}$.

4 Determining Conic Sections

In the preceding section, we examined how to use the cartesian equation to obtain the type and the parameters of the associated conic section.

Now we will approach the problem from a different point of view, and try to reconstitute the cartesian equation of a conic section passing through five given points.

One must note that for certain combinations of points, we will not find a non-degenerate conic section; for example, if the points are aligned, we will have a line.

4.1 Principle

We would like to find the cartesian equation:

$$ax^2 + bxy + cy^2 + dx + ey + f = 0$$

The unknown quantities are thus a, b, c, d, e et f. Since the equation can be multiplied by any number, the actual number of unknowns is five. That is why five given points allow us to determine the conic section perfectly; these points lead to a system of five homogenous equations with six unknowns.

The resolution proceeds by successive suppositions. Let us first suppose that $f \neq 0$; we can then set $f = 1$, and search for the other parameters by solving the following linear system of five equations with five unknowns:

$$\begin{cases} x_1^2\,a + x_1 y_1\,b + y_1^2\,c + x_1\,d + y_1\,e = -1 \\ x_2^2\,a + x_2 y_2\,b + y_2^2\,c + x_2\,d + y_2\,e = -1 \\ \text{...} \\ x_5^2\,a + x_5 y_5\,b + y_5^2\,c + x_5\,d + y_5\,e = -1 \end{cases}$$

The resolution of this system is accomplished using the Gauss-Jordan method. This method is explained in chapter 9, Matrices and Vectors.

If the system has a solution, the problem is solved; otherwise, we know that the hypothesis $f \neq 0$ was incorrect. We then suppose $e \neq 0$, and we attempt to solve:

$$\begin{cases} x_1^2\,a + x_1 y_1\,b + y_1^2\,c + x_1\,d + f = -y_1 \\ x_2^2\,a + x_2 y_2\,b + y_2^2\,c + x_2\,d + f = -y_2 \\ \text{...} \\ x_5^2\,a + x_5 y_5\,b + y_5^2\,c + x_5\,d + f = -y_5 \end{cases}$$

If it has a solution, the problem is solved. Otherwise, we continue with the hypotheses $(d \neq 0$, then $c \neq 0$, ...).

In the most unfavorable case, that is, if there is no non-degenerate conic section which corresponds to the problem, the program will have to solve six systems of degree 5. In the most common cases ($f \neq 0$ or $e \neq 0$), it will only solve one or two.

4.2 Calculation Tool

The parameters of the tool `ar_conic_find` are made up of two arrays of numbers containing the coordinates of the five points.

At the output, the boolean value of the function indicates if there is a conic section which corresponds to the desired specifications. If so, the array `coeff` contains the six coefficients of the conic section's equation.

The tool will be placed in the file GEO\FINDCON.CPP.

```
/*===========================================================
                        FINDCON.CPP :
    DETERMINATION OF THE CONIC PASSING THROUGH 5 POINTS
  =========================================================*/

#include   "armath.h"

int ar_conic_find (ar_number *x, ar_number *y,
                   ar_number *coeff)
{
  ar_matrix   m;
  ar_vector   u, v;
  ar_number   det, tm [5] [6];
  int         i, j, iter;

  for (i = 1; i < 5; i++)
    for (j = 0; j < i; j++)
      if ((x [i] == x [j]) && (y [i] == y [j]))
      return FALSE;

  if (! m.open (5, 5)) return FALSE;
  if (! u.open (5))    return FALSE;
  if (! v.open (5))    return FALSE;

  //------------------ Initialisation of disymmetric matrix
  for (i = 0; i < 5; i++)   {
    tm [i] [0] = x [i] * x [i];
    tm [i] [1] = x [i] * y [i];
    tm [i] [2] = y [i] * y [i];
    tm [i] [3] = x [i];
    tm [i] [4] = y [i];
    tm [i] [5] = 1;
  }
```

```
for (iter = 6; iter > 0; iter --)  {

  //-------------- Initialisation of matrix to be inverted
  for (i = 1; i <= 5; i++)  {
    for (j = 1; j < iter; j++)
    m.writecoeff (i, j, tm [i - 1] [j - 1]);
    for (j = iter; j <= 5; j++)
    m.writecoeff (i, j, tm [i - 1] [j]);
    v.writecoeff (i, - tm [i - 1] [iter - 1]);
  }
  u = ar_lin_sys (m, v, det);

  if ((errno == 0) && (! det.small ()))  {
    for (i = 0; i < iter - 1; i++)
      coeff [i] = u.readcoeff (i + 1);
    coeff [iter - 1] = N1;
    for (i = iter; i <= 5; i++)
      coeff [i] = u.readcoeff (i);
    return TRUE;
  }
}
return FALSE;
}
```

4.3 Annotated Examples

Example 1

Let us consider the following five points:
$$M_1 (0, 2); M_2 (1, 5); M_3 (5, 77); M_4 (-4, 50); M_5 (2, 14)$$
The program then looks for the equation of the conic section passing through these five points:

```
DETERMINATION OF CONICS

x1 = 0        y1 = 2
x2 = 1        y2 = 5
x3 = 5        y3 = 77
x4 = -4       y4 = 50
x5 = 2        y5 = 14

a = + 3 / 2
b = - 0
c = - 0
d = - 0
e = - 1 / 2
f = + 1
```

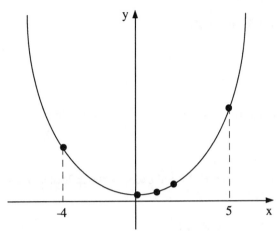

The equation is therefore $\frac{3}{2}x^2 - \frac{1}{2}y + 1 = 0$ or $y = 3x^2 + 2$, which is a parabola.

Example 2

Let us consider the following five points:

$$M_1 (0, 1); M_2 (0, -1); M_3 (1, 0); M_4 (-1, 0); M_5 (\frac{\sqrt{2}}{2}, \frac{\sqrt{2}}{2})$$

The conic section passing through these points is the circle with center 0 and radius 1.

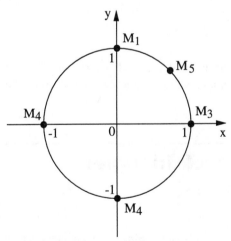

```
DETERMINATION OF CONICS

x1 = 0                       y1 = 1
x2 = 0                       y2 = -1
x3 = 1                       y3 = 0
x4 = -1                      y4 = 0
x5 = .707106781186548        y5 = .707106781186548
```

```
a = - 1
b = 2.6645352591e-15
c = - 1
d = - 0
e = - 0
f = + 1
```

The equation found by the program is $x^2 + y^2 = 1$, which is correct.

Example 3

Let us return to the above example, and examine the influence of uncertainty regarding one of the points, M_5. We set M_5 (0.7, 0.7).

```
SEARCH FOR CONIC SECTIONS

x1 = 0                    y1 = 1
x2 = 0                    y2 = -1
x3 = 1                    y3 = 0
x4 = -1                   y4 = 0
x5 = .7                   y5 = .7

a = - 1
b = - 0.040816326531
c = - 1
d = - 0
e = - 0
f = + 1
```

The equation we obtain is $x^2 + y^2 + 0.0408\, xy = 1$. The conic section we find is no longer the circle, but an ellipse whose eccentricity is a function of the imprecision regarding the coordinates of M_5.

---

5   Resolution of Triangles

5.1 Principle

One can describe an undefined triangle using six parameters: the lengths of its sides and the values of its angles. We will call the lengths of the sides a, b, and c, and the values of the angles t_a, t_b, and t_c (t_a is the value of the angle opposite the side a, and so forth).

We can define the triangle if we have three parameters, because the latter allow us to calculate the remaining three. This is not true if the three known parameters are the angles:

the sides cannot be determined because we do not know their unit of measurement. Therefore, we will examine how to use three known parameters of the triangle to determine the three others.

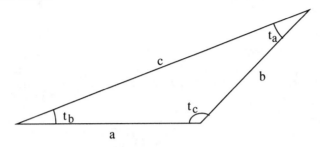

The formulas used for this are as follows:

$$t_a + t_b + t_c = 180°$$

$$c^2 = a^2 + b^2 - 2ab \cos(t_c)$$

$$\frac{a}{\sin(t_a)} = \frac{b}{\sin(t_b)} = \frac{c}{\sin(t_c)}$$

There are three possible cases, depending on the nature of the three given parameters:
– the three sides;
– two sides and the angle opposite the third side;
– two sides and the angle opposite one of these sides;
– one side and two angles.

If the three sides a, b and c are given:
The angles are then obtained using:

$$\begin{cases} t_c = \text{Arccos} \left[\dfrac{a^2+b^2-c^2}{2ab} \right] \\[2mm] t_b = \text{Arccos} \left[\dfrac{a^2+c^2-b^2}{2ac} \right] \\[2mm] t_a = \text{Arccos} \left[\dfrac{b^2+c^2-a^2}{2bc} \right] \end{cases}$$

If two sides and the angle opposite the third side are given:
For example, let us suppose that a, b and t_c are known. We then calculate:

$$c = \sqrt{a^2+b^2-2ab \cos(t_c)}$$

Now that we know the lengths of the three sides, we determine the two remaining angles as above.

If two sides and the angle opposite one of these sides are given:

For example, let us suppose that a, b and t_a are known. This is the most complicated case; depending on the parameters, we can have one solution triangle, two solution triangles, or no solution.

– If $t_a < 90°$

if $a \geq b$, one solution: $c = b \cos(t_a) + \sqrt{a^2 - b^2 \sin^2(t_a)}$

if $a < b$, two solutions: $c = b \cos(t_a) \pm \sqrt{a^2 - b^2 \sin^2(t_a)}$

– If $t_a \geq 90°$

if $a \leq b$, no solution.

if $a > b$, one solution: $c = b \cos(t_a) + \sqrt{a^2 - b^2 \sin^2(t_a)}$

After determining c, we have the three sides, and we calculate the unknown angles as above.

If one side and two angles are known:

We obtain the third angle using:

$$t_c = 180° - t_a - t_b$$

The two unknown sides are then calculated using:

$$b = a \frac{\sin(t_b)}{\sin(t_a)} \quad \text{and} \quad c = a \frac{\sin(t_c)}{\sin(t_a)}$$

In all cases, we can calculate the surface of the triangle using the formula:

$$S = \sqrt{h(h-a)(h-b)(h-c)}$$

with

$$h = \frac{a+b+c}{2}$$

5.2 Calculation Tool

The six parameters to be entered for the tool `ar_triangle` are:

– `a`, `b` and `c`, the lengths of the three sides;
– `ta`, `tb` and `tc`, the angles opposite each of these sides and less than $180°$;
– `two`, boolean described below, to be positioned at `FALSE` initially.

Only three parameters should be indicated; the three others should be zero.

As output, the tool has calculated the three unknown parameters and the surface S of the triangle.

In addition, if two triangles are solutions of the problem, the boolean two is positioned at `TRUE`. It is then possible to obtain the second solution triangle by calling on the tool `ar_triangle` for a second time with the parameter two positioned at `TRUE`.

The value of the function, boolean, indicates if a triangle fitting the entered specifications has been found.

The exploitation tool, given at the end of the chapter, allows one to express the angle in a unit other than radians by converting before and after the calculation tool.

The tool will be placed in the file GEO\TRIANGLE.CPP.

```cpp
/*=========================================================
                     TRIANGLE.CPP :
       DETERMINATION OF A TRIANGLE PARTIALLY KNOWN
=========================================================*/

#include  "armath.h"

static  ar_double  side [3], angle [3], r;
static  int        index [3];

static  void swap (int, int);
static  void calculate_angle (int);

static void swap (int i, int j)
{
  ar_double  r;
  int        n;

  n = index [i]; index [i] = index [j]; index [j] = n;
  r = angle [i]; angle [i] = angle [j]; angle [j] = r;
  r = side  [i]; side  [i] = side  [j]; side  [j] = r;
}

static void calculate_angle (int i)
{
  int  j = (i + 1) % 3;
  int  k = (i + 2) % 3;
  ar_double r = (side [j] * side [j] + side [k] * side [k]
          - side [i] * side [i]) / 2 / side [j] / side [k];
  angle [i] = AR_PI / 2 - atan (r / sqrt (1 - r * r));
}

void  ar_triangle (
            ar_double &a,   ar_double &b,   ar_double &c,
            ar_double &ta,  ar_double &tb,  ar_double &tc,
            ar_double &s,   int &two)
{
  int   i, nb_sides = 0, nb_angles = 0;

  //----------------------------- Prepare indexing arrays
  side [0] = a; angle [0] = ta;
```

```
side [1] = b; angle [1] = tb;
side [2] = c; angle [2] = tc;
for (i = 0; i < 3; i ++) index [i] = i;

//--------------------------- Check entry data coherence
for (i = 0; i < 3; i++)
  if ((angle [i] < 0) || (angle [i] > AR_PI)
    || (side [i] < 0)) return;
for (i = 0; i < 3; i++)
  if (side [i] > 0) nb_sides ++;
for (i = 0; i < 3; i++)
  if (angle [i] > 0) nb_angles ++;
if ((nb_sides == 0) || (nb_sides + nb_angles != 3) ||
  (angle [0] + angle [1] + angle [2] > AR_PI)) return;

switch (nb_sides)  {
  //----------------------- Case where one side is given
  case 1 :
    for (i = 0; i < 3; i++)
      if (angle [i] == 0)
        angle [i] = AR_PI - angle[0] - angle[1] - angle[2];
    if (side [1] > 0) swap (0, 1);
    if (side [2] > 0) swap (0, 2);
    side [1] = side [0] * sin (angle[1]) / sin (angle[0]);
    side [2] = side [0] * sin (angle[2]) / sin (angle[0]);
    break;
  //--------------------- Case where two sides are given
  case 2 :
    if (side [2] > 0)         // Put unkonwn side in 3
      swap ((side [0] > 0) ? 2 : 1, 3);
    if (angle [2] > 0)  {
      //------------------- Case where a, b, tc are given
      side [2] = sqrt (a*a + b*b - 2*a*b * cos (angle[2]));
      for (i = 0; i <= 1; i++) calculate_angle (i);
    }
    else  {
      //------------------- Case where a, b, ta are given
      if (angle [0] == 0) swap (0, 1);
      r = side [1] * sin (angle [0]);
      if (r > side [0])
        return;
      r = sqrt (side [0] * side [0] - r * r);
      if ((angle [0] >= AR_PI/2) && (side [0] <= side [1]))
        return;
      if ((angle [0] < AR_PI/2)  && (side [0] < side [1]))
        if (two)
          side [2] = side [1] * cos (angle [0]) - r;
        else  {
```

```
            side [2] = side [1] * cos (angle [0]) + r;
            two = TRUE;
        }
      else
      side [2] = side [1] * cos (angle [0]) + r;
      for (i = 1; i <= 2; i++) calculate_angle (i);
    }
    break;

  //---------------------- Case where a, b, c are given
  case 3 :
    if ((c <= fabs (a - b)) || (c >= a + b)) return;
    for (i = 0; i < 3; i++) calculate_angle (i);
    break;
}

//------------------------------------- Back index
a = side [index [0]]; ta = angle [index [0]];
b = side [index [1]]; tb = angle [index [1]];
c = side [index [2]]; tc = angle [index [2]];

//---------------------------- Calculate the surface
r = (a + b + c) / 2;
s = sqrt (r * (r - a) * (r - b) * (r - c));
errno = 0;
}
```

5.3 Annotated Examples

Example 1

Let us consider a triangle defined by its three sides:

```
RESOLUTION OF UNDEFINED TRIANGLES

A                                : 25
B                                : 40
C                                : 58
Unit angles : Value of PI   : 180
TA                               : 0
TB                               : 0
TC                               : 0

A   =              25
B   =              40
C   =              58
```

```
TA = 20.750954017709    # 16331 / 787
TB = 34.533679392623    # 6665 / 193
TC = 124.715366589668

S  = 410.995666035543
```

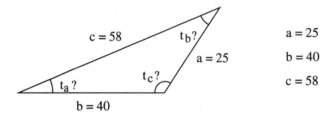

$c = 58$ t_b? $a = 25$

$a = 25$ $b = 40$

t_c? $c = 58$

t_a?

$b = 40$

The program then gives the three angles:

$$\begin{cases} t_a = 20.75° \\ t_b = 34.53° \\ t_c = 124.7° \end{cases}$$

and the surface:

$$S = 410.996$$

Example 2

Let us consider the following triangle, defined by one side and two angles:

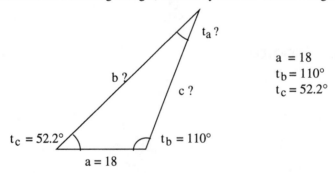

t_a?

b?

c?

$t_c = 52.2°$

$t_b = 110°$

$a = 18$

$a = 18$
$t_b = 110°$
$t_c = 52.2°$

```
RESOLUTION OF UNDEFINED TRIANGLES

A                              :  18
B                              :  0
C                              :  0
Unit angles : Value of PI      :  180
TA                             :  0
TB                             :  110
TC                             :  52,2
```

```
A   =                 18
B   = 55.331131684171
C   = 46.526034230323    # 25915 / 557
TA  =              17.8   # 89 / 5
TB  =               110
TC  =              52.2   # 261 / 5

S   = 393.481539366003
```

The program then gives the complementary parameters:

$$\begin{cases} b = 55.33 \\ c = 46.53 \\ t_a = 17.8° \end{cases} \qquad S = 393.48$$

Example 3

Lastly, let us analyse a triangle defined by two sides and an angle:

$$\begin{cases} a = 2\sqrt{3} \\ b = 5.6 \\ t_a = 15.5° \end{cases}$$

```
RESOLUTION OF UNDEFINED TRIANGLES

A                                 : 3.464101615137755
B                                 : 5.6
C                                 : 0
Unit  angles : Value of PI   : 180
TA                                : 15.5
TB                                : 0
TC                                : 0

A   =   3.464101615138    # 8733 / 2521
B   =                5.6   # 28 / 5
C   =   8.520491749399    # 2079 / 244
TA  =               15.5   # 31 / 2
TB  = 25.595341029567    # 12081 / 472
TC  = 138.904658970433

S   =   6.375606659793    # 9200 / 1443
There is a second solution triangle

A   =   3.464101615138    # 8733 / 2521
```

```
B  =                 5.6   # 28 / 5
C  =   2.272169326537     # 3331 / 1466


TA =               15.5   # 31 / 2
TB = 154.404658970433
TC = 10.095341029567     # 9318 / 923

S  =   1.700190354796     # 5359 / 3152
```

In this case, there are two solution triangles:

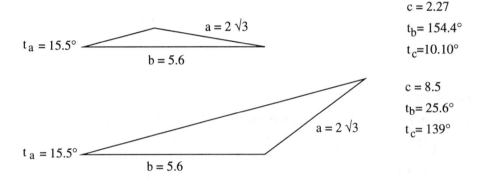

$c = 2.27$

$t_b = 154.4°$

$t_a = 15.5°$

$t_c = 10.10°$

$a = 2\sqrt{3}$

$b = 5.6$

$c = 8.5$

$t_b = 25.6°$

$a = 2\sqrt{3}$

$t_c = 139°$

$t_a = 15.5°$

$b = 5.6$

6 Exploitation Tools

The following tools allow the direct exploitation of the calculation tools.

The following tool will be placed in the file GEO\UGEOSURF.CPP:

```
/*===========================================================
                    UGEOSURF.CPP :
        CALCULATION OF SURFACES EXPLOITATION TOOL
========================================================*/

#include   "armath.h"

void  ar_use_geo_surface ()
{
  ar_number  x [50], y [50];
  int        i, n;

  cout << "CALCULATION OF SURFACES\n\n";
  if (ar_read ("Number of points : ", &n, AR_TINT)) return;
  if (n > 50) return;
```

```
  for (i = 0; i < n; i++)  {
    sprintf (ar_temp, "x%d = ", i);
    ar_read  (ar_temp, &x [i], AR_TNUM);
    sprintf (ar_temp, "y%d = ", i);
    ar_read  (ar_temp, &y [i], AR_TNUM);
  }

  cout << "\nValue of the surface : "
       << ar_calc_surf (x, y, n) << "\n";

  ar_pause ();
}
```

The following tool will be placed in the file `GEO\UARC.CPP`:

```
/*============================================================
                        UARC.CPP :
          CALCULATION OF ARCS EXPLOITATION TOOL
============================================================*/

#include  "armath.h"

void  ar_use_geo_circle ()
{
  ar_double  r, s, t, c, s1, s2, un;

  ar_init_entry ("CALCULATION OF ARCS");
  ar_fill_entry ("R", &r, AR_TDOU);
  ar_fill_entry ("S", &s, AR_TDOU);
  ar_fill_entry ("C", &c, AR_TDOU);
  ar_fill_entry ("Unit : Value of PI", &un, AR_TDOU);
  ar_fill_entry ("T", &t, AR_TDOU);
  if (ar_do_entry ()) return;
  t = (AR_PI / un) * t;

  ar_circle (r, s, c, t, s1, s2);

  if (! errno)
    cout << "R   = " << r << "\n"
         << "S   = " << s << "\n"
         << "C   = " << c << "\n"
         << "T   = " << t * (un / AR_PI) << "\n"
         << "S1  = " << s1 << "\n"
         << "S2  = " << s2 << "\n";
  else
    cerr << "Wrong data or no solution arc\n";
```

```
  ar_pause ();
}
```

The following tool will be placed in the file GEO\UREDUCCO.CPP:

```
/*==========================================================
                      UREDUCCO.CPP :
      REDUCTION OF CONICS SECTIONS EXPLOITATION TOOL
==========================================================*/

#include  "armath.h"

void ar_use_geo_reduc_conic ()
{
  ar_double  a, b, c, d, e, f, ex, xc, yc, la, lb, xf1, yf1,
        xf2, yf2, xs1, ys1, xs2, ys2, xv1, yv1, xv2, yv2;
  int        tp;

  ar_init_entry ("REDUCTION OF CONICS SECTION");
  ar_fill_entry ("a", &a, AR_TDOU);
  ar_fill_entry ("b", &b, AR_TDOU);
  ar_fill_entry ("c", &c, AR_TDOU);
  ar_fill_entry ("d", &d, AR_TDOU);
  ar_fill_entry ("e", &e, AR_TDOU);
  ar_fill_entry ("f", &f, AR_TDOU);
  if (ar_do_entry ()) return;

  ar_conic_reduction (a, b, c, d, e, f, tp, ex, xc, yc,
                     la, lb, xf1, yf1, xf2, yf2, xs1, ys1,
                     xs2, ys2, xv1, yv1, xv2, yv2);

  switch (tp) {

    case 1 :
      cout <<          "It is an ellipse\n";

      cout << "    Centre                     : x = "
           << xc << ar_rational (xc) << "\n";
      cout << "                               : y = "
           << yc << ar_rational (yc) << "\n";

      cout << "   Vect. directive long axis : x = "
           << xv1 << ar_rational (xv1) << "\n";
      cout << "                               : y = "
           << yv1 << ar_rational (yv1) << "\n";
      cout << "   Vect. directive short axis: x = "
           << xv2 << ar_rational (xv2) << "\n";
      cout << "                               : y = "
```

```
                << yv2 << ar_rational (yv2) << "\n";

     cout << "   Half-length long axis    :      "
          << la << ar_rational (la) << "\n";

     cout << "   Half-length short axis    :      "
          << lb << ar_rational (lb) << "\n";

     cout << "   First focus              : x = "
          << xf1 << ar_rational (xf1) << "\n";
     cout << "                            : y = "
          << yf1 << ar_rational (yf1) << "\n";

     cout << "   Second focus             : x = "
          << xf2 << ar_rational (xf2) << "\n";
     cout << "                            : y = "
          << yf2 << ar_rational (yf2) << "\n";

     cout << "   Eccentricity             :      "
          << ex << ar_rational (ex) << "\n";

     break;

case 2 :
   cout << "It is an ";
   if (a + c == 0) cout << "equilateral ";
   cout << "hyperbola\n";

   cout << "   Centre                   : x = "
        << xc << ar_rational (xc) << "\n";
   cout << "                            : y = "
        << yc << ar_rational (yc) << "\n";

   cout << "   Vect. direc. transv. axis : x = "
        << xv1 << ar_rational (xv1) << "\n";
   cout << "                            : y = "
        << yv1 << ar_rational (yv1) << "\n";

   cout << "   Vect. direc. conjug. axis : x = "
        << xv2 << ar_rational (xv2) << "\n";
   cout << "                            : y = "
        << yv2 << ar_rational (yv2) << "\n";

   cout << "   First vertex             : x = "
        << xs1 << ar_rational (xs1) << "\n";
   cout << "                            : y = "
        << ys1 << ar_rational (ys1) << "\n";
```

```
    cout << "   Second vertex              : x = "
         << xs2 << ar_rational (xs2) << "\n";
    cout << "                              : y = "
         << ys2 << ar_rational (ys2) << "\n";

    cout << "   First focus                : x = "
         << xf1 << ar_rational (xf1) << "\n";
    cout << "                              : y = "
         << yf1 << ar_rational (yf1) << "\n";

    cout << "   Second focus               : x = "
         << xf2 << ar_rational (xf2) << "\n";
    cout << "                              : y = "
         << yf2 << ar_rational (yf2) << "\n";

    cout << "   Eccentricity               :      "
         << ex << ar_rational (ex) << "\n";
    break;

case 3 :
    cout << "It is a parabola\n";

    cout << "   Centre                     : x = "
         << xc << ar_rational (xc) << "\n";
    cout << "                              : y = "
         << yc << ar_rational (yc) << "\n";

    cout << "   Vector symmetry axis       : x = "
         << xv1 << ar_rational (xv1) << "\n";
    cout << "                              : y = "
         << yv1 << ar_rational (yv1) << "\n";

    cout << "   Focus                      : x = "
         << xf1 << ar_rational (xf1) << "\n";
    cout << "                              : y = "
         << yf1 << ar_rational (yf1) << "\n";

    cout << "   Parameter                  :      "
         << ex << ar_rational (ex) << "\n";
    break;

case 4 :
    cout << "It is a circle       radius  :      "
         << la << ar_rational (la) << "\n";

    cout << "                     centre   : x = "
         << xc << ar_rational (xc) << "\n";
    cout << "                              : y = "
```

```
                   << yc << ar_rational (yc) << "\n";
        break;

     case 5 :
       cout << "It is a degenerated conic section: a line\n";
       break;

     case 6 :
       cout << "It is a degenerated conic section: a set of \
                 two lines\n";
       break;

     case 7 :
       cout << "It is a degenerated conic section: a point\n";
       break;

     case 8 :
       cout << "It is not a conic section\n";
       break;
   }

   ar_pause ();
}
```

The following tool will be placed in the file GEO\UFINDCON.CPP:

```
/*===========================================================
                      UFINDCON.CPP :
            CONICS DETERMINATION EXPLOITATION TOOL
===========================================================*/

#include  "armath.h"

void  ar_use_geo_find_conic ()
{
   ar_number  coeff [6], x [5], y [5];
   int        i;

   ar_init_entry ("SEARCH FOR CONIC SECTIONS");
   for (i = 0; i < 5; i++)  {
     sprintf (ar_temp, "x%d", i+1);
     ar_fill_entry (ar_temp, &x [i], AR_TNUM);
     sprintf (ar_temp, "y%d", i+1);
     ar_fill_entry (ar_temp, &y [i], AR_TNUM);
   }
   if (ar_do_entry ()) return;
   if (ar_conic_find (x, y, coeff))
     for (i = 0; i < 6; i++)
```

```
        cout << (char) ('a' + i) << " = " << coeff [i] << "\n";
   else
     cerr << "Wrong data or no solution conic\n";

   ar_pause ();
}
```

The following tool will be placed in the file GEO\UTRIANGL.CPP:

```
/*==========================================================
                    UTRIANGLE.CPP :
        CALCULATION OF TRIANGLES EXPLOITATION TOOL
 ==========================================================*/

#include  "armath.h"

static double  unit;

static  void  display_triangle (
        ar_double a, ar_double b, ar_double c, ar_double ta,
        ar_double tb, ar_double tc, int& two)
{
  ar_double  s;

  ar_triangle (a, b, c, ta, tb, tc, s, two);

  if (! errno)  {
    cout << "A   = " << setw (15) << a << ar_rational (a)
         << "\n";
    cout << "B   = " << setw (15) << b << ar_rational (b)
         << "\n";
    cout << "C   = " << setw (15) << c << ar_rational (c)
         << "\n\n";
    cout << "TA  = " << setw (15) << ta / unit
         << ar_rational (ta / unit) << "\n";
    cout << "TB  = " << setw (15) << tb / unit
         << ar_rational (tb / unit) << "\n";
    cout << "TC  = " << setw (15) << tc / unit
         << ar_rational (tc / unit) << "\n\n";
    cout << "S   = " << setw (15) << s << ar_rational (s)
         << "\n\n";
  }
  else
    cerr << "Wrong data or no solution triangle\n\n";
}
void ar_use_geo_triangle ()
{
  ar_double  a, b, c, ta, tb, tc;
```

```
int         two = FALSE;

ar_init_entry ("RESOLUTION OF UNDEFINED TRIANGLES");
ar_fill_entry ("A",  &a,  AR_TDOU);
ar_fill_entry ("B",  &b,  AR_TDOU);
ar_fill_entry ("C",  &c,  AR_TDOU);
ar_fill_entry ("Angles unit : Value of PI",&unit,AR_TDOU);
ar_fill_entry ("TA", &ta, AR_TDOU);
ar_fill_entry ("TB", &tb, AR_TDOU);
ar_fill_entry ("TC", &tc, AR_TDOU);
if (ar_do_entry ()) return;

unit = AR_PI / unit; ta *= unit; tb *= unit; tc *= unit;

display_triangle (a, b, c, ta, tb, tc, two);

if (two)  {
  cout << "There is a second solution triangle\n";
  ar_pause ();
  ar_nl;
  display_triangle (a, b, c, ta, tb, tc, two);
}
ar_pause ();
}
```

6

Complex Numbers

Complex numbers were first introduced by Italian mathematicians in the eighteenth century. They used them to solve equations of the third degree.

In reality, they allow one to do much more; for example, to solve equations of the type:

$$a_n x^n + a_{n-1} x^{n-1} + \dots + a_0 = 0$$

where the coefficients a_i are real numbers.

Physicists and technicians often use complex numbers. The latter make calculations easier by presenting them in a much more concise manner. For example, the Laplace transformation permits the study of the permanent sinusoidal functions associated with electrical and electronic systems. It uses a complex representation of tensions, intensities, and transfer functions.

In this chapter, we describe a tool which simulates a scientific calculator with reverse Polish notation, operating on complex numbers.

We also introduce two tools which solve linear systems of N equations with N unknowns, as well as equations of the second degree.

The tools for this chapter will be placed in the subdirectory COMPLEX.

Compared to calculations using polynomials or rational fractions, calculations with complex numbers yield rational results more rarely. Because of this, we have not separated here the processing of rational numbers from that of real numbers.

1 Calculations with Complex Numbers

1.1 Representation of Complex Numbers

Complex numbers are usually represented in two different ways: algebraic or rectangular notation, and polar notation.

Let us consider a complex number z. Its rectangular representation is then:

$$z = a + ib$$

in which a and b are real numbers, and i the complex number such that:

$$i^2 = -1$$

a is called the real part of z, and ib the imaginary part of z. If $b = 0$, the number z is real ; if $a = 0$, we call z a pure imaginary.

The polar representation of the number z is:

$$z = r\,(\cos\theta + i\sin\theta)$$

which we can also write as:

$$z = r\,e^{i\theta}$$

The real number r is called the modulus of the number z; it is usually written:

$$r = |z|$$

The real number θ is called the argument of z and is written:

$$\theta = \text{Arg}\,(z)$$

Naturally, there are relationships which allow one to convert rectangular coordinates into polar coordinates. In fact:

$$r = \sqrt{a^2 + b^2}$$

$$\theta = \text{Arctg}\left(\frac{b}{a}\right) \qquad \text{if } a \neq 0$$

$$\theta = \frac{\pi}{2} \qquad \text{if } a = 0 \text{ and } b > 0$$

$$\theta = -\frac{\pi}{2} \qquad \text{if } a = 0 \text{ and } b < 0$$

and the opposite conversion is given by:

$$a = r\cos\theta \qquad\qquad b = r\sin\theta$$

1.2 Reverse Polish Notation

This calculation method imitates the architecture of microprocessors. The operands are entered first, and then the operation code is specified.

For example, if one wishes to execute the multiplication 2 * 5, one enters:

2	(RETURN)
5	(RETURN)
*	(RETURN)

and the computer performs the operation.

The main advantage of this notation is that it facilitates calculation chains. It does this by eliminating the parentheses that are usually necessary to define the operations which have priority.

The data is entered and memorised in a structure called a stack: a group of four registers X, Y, Z and T, organized in the following manner:

```
T  [          ]
Z  [          ]
Y  [          ]
X  [          ]
```

The first operand entered is placed in the register X; if a second operand is entered, the register X is copied into Y, and the new number is stored in X. More generally, each time a number is entered, the stack shifts up one level:

$$N \rightarrow X \rightarrow Y \rightarrow Z \rightarrow T$$

Let us note that if the stack is full when N is entered, the value in T is lost.

If an operation code is entered, for example *, the computer calculates X * Y, shifts the stack down a level, and places the result in X. For example, let us consider the following calculation:

$$\sqrt{1+3\cos(0)}$$

The operations remaining to be done and the successive states of the stack are then:

```
1  (RETURN)    T  [          ]
               Z  [          ]
               Y  [          ]
               X  [        1 ]
```

3 (RETURN)	T	
	Z	
	Y	1
	X	3

0 (RETURN)	T	
	Z	1
	Y	3
	X	0

COS (RETURN)	T	
	Z	1
	Y	3
	X	1

* (RETURN)	T	
	Z	
	Y	1
	X	3

+ (RETURN)	T	
	Z	
	Y	
	X	4

SQRT (RETURN)	T	
	Z	
	Y	
	X	2

REMARK: when the stack is shifted down a level, the value of the register T is not modified.

1.3 Calculation Tools

Borland C++ has an extension which manages complex numbers. In particular, all the algebraic and mathematical operators are overloaded. This permits us to use the same notations as with the variables of the type `double`.

Only the functions argsh, argch, argth are not implemented in the C++ extension. We have added the corresponding three specific tools.

1.4 Calculator

The program presented here allows us to easily exploit the class `complex` and its overloaded operators, by simulating a scientific calculator with four registers and ten memories.

The screen permanently displays the contents of the registers and of the memories, in both algebraic and polar form. It also displays the list of valid operations. As a result, one can visualize the shifts of the stack according to the calculations. One can also preserve on screen the most important intermediate results contained in memory.

When an operation is finished, or at the beginning, the program awaits the next «operation to be executed».

The two categories of possible operations are the calculations, and the manipulation functions of the stack, the memory, and the screen.

Calculation Functions

They use the elementary operators of the class `complex` and operate on the two first registers X and Y of the stack (only X for unary operations). The result of the calculation overburdens the register X.

The call syntax for the calculation routines, continually present on screen, is:

```
+     -     *     /     1/X    X^2    SQRT    Y^X    EXP    LOG

SIN COS TAN SH CH TH   ARCSIN ARCCOS ARCTAN ARGCH ARGSH ARGTH
```

Stack, Memory, and Screen Exploitation Functions

The operations in this category are the following:

XA   Entry of a number in algebraic form. The program asks for its real part then for its imaginary part.

XP   Entry of a number in polar form. This time the program asks for its modulus, then its argument.

CLX   Erase the register X (and shift the stack down a level). This permits the correction of an entry error.

CLS   Erase the four registers of the stack.

^   Execute a rotation of the stack, that is:

$$\boxed{\;X \leftarrow Y \leftarrow Z \leftarrow T\;}$$

DECIxy Allows one to set the display format of the stack's registers. The integer x allows one to choose the register: 1 for X, 2 for Y, 3 for Z and 4 for T. The integer y indicates the number of decimal places desired. For example, the command DECI24 will display the register Y with four decimal places.

The three following functions manage the memories.

STOx x being an integer between 0 and 9, this function causes the register X to be copied to the memory number x.

RCLx Copies the memory number x to the register X, after having shifted the stack up one level.

CLM   Erases the contents of all memories.

The calculation tool is called ar_use_complex_calculator and it is stored in the file COMPLEX\UCOMPCAL.CPP.

```
/*============================================================
                       UCOMPCAL.CPP:
                 COMPLEX NUMBERS CALCULATOR
 ============================================================*/

#include   <conio.h>
#include   <string.h>
#include   "armath.h"

#define    NBSTACK     4
#define    NBMEM       9

static  complex    *cstack, *memory;
static  int        deci    [4] = {7, 7, 9, 9};

static  void   down_cstack      (int);
static  void   up_cstack        (void);
static  void   display_number   (char *, complex &);
static  void   calculate        (char *);
static  void   refresh_display  (void);

//---------------------------------------- Calculate 'ARGSH'
complex  ash  (complex &z)
{
  return (log (z + sqrt (complex (
              1 + real (z) * real (z) - imag (z) * imag (z),
              2 * real (z) * imag (z))))));
}
```

```
//---------------------------------- Calculate 'ARGCH'
complex  ach  (complex &z)
{
  return (log (z + sqrt (complex (-1 + real (z) * real (z)
          - imag (z) * imag (z), 2 * real (z) * imag (z)))));
}

//---------------------------------- Calculate 'ARGTH'
complex  ath  (complex &z)
{
  return (log (complex (1 + real (z), imag (z)) /
    complex (1 - real (z), - imag (z))) / complex (2, 0));
}

//---------------------------------- Moves cstack down
static void down_cstack (int n)
{
  memcpy (&cstack [n], &cstack [n + 1],
        sizeof (complex) * (NBSTACK - (n + 1)));
  memset (&cstack [NBSTACK - 1], 0, sizeof (complex));
}

//---------------------------------- Moves cstack up
static void up_cstack ()
{
  int  i;

  for (i = NBSTACK - 1; i > 0; i--)
    memcpy (&cstack [i], &cstack [i - 1], sizeof (complex));
  memset (&cstack [0], 0, sizeof (complex));
}

//-------------------------- Display a calculator number
static void display_number (char *msg, complex &z)
{
  cout << msg << setw (15) << setprecision (deci [0])
       << real (z);
  if (imag (z) != 0)
    cout << ((imag (z) > 0) ? " +" : " -") << " i "
         << setw (15) <<
         setprecision (deci [1]) << fabs (imag (z)) << " |";
  else
    cout << "                           |";
  if (norm (z) != 0)
    cout << setw (15) << setprecision (deci [2])
         << sqrt (norm (z)) << " ";
  else
    cout << "                     ";
```

```cpp
    if (arg (z) != 0)
      cout << ((arg (z) > 0) ? "EXP+" : "EXP-") << "i"
           << setw (15) <<
           setprecision (deci [3]) << fabs (arg (z)) << " |";
    else
      cout << "                        |";
    ar_nl;
}

//----------------------------------------- Global display
static void refresh_display ()
{
  int  i;

  clrscr ();
  cout << "                   CALCULATOR ON COMPLEX NUMBERS\n";
  for (i = 1; i <= 79; i++) cout << "|"; ar_nl;
  cout << "|  |           ALGEBRAIC FORM              ";
  cout << "|              POLAR FORM              |\n";
  for (i = 0; i < NBMEM; i++)  {
    sprintf (ar_temp, "|M%d|", i);
    display_number (ar_temp, memory [i]);
  }

  for (i = 1; i <= 79; i++) cout << "|"; ar_nl;
  display_number ("| T|", cstack [3]);
  display_number ("| Z|", cstack [2]);
  display_number ("| Y|", cstack [1]);
  display_number ("| X|", cstack [0]);
  for (i = 1; i <= 79; i++) cout << "|"; ar_nl;

  cout << "    +     -     *     /    1/X   X^2"
       << "        SQRT   Y^X    EXP     LOG\n"
       << " SIN  COS  TAN   SH   CH   TH  "
       << "ARCSIN ARCCOS ARCTAN ARGCH ARGSH ARGTH\n"
       << "   XA   XP  CLX  CLS  CLM  "
       << "   ^   DECIxy STOx  RCLx \n";
  for (i = 1; i <= 79; i++) cout << "|"; ar_nl;
}


//--------------------- Calculate - Calls elementary tools
static void calculate (char *oper)
{
  complex    inter;
  ar_double  x, y;
  int        i, j;
```

```
//-------------------------------------- Operator "XA"
if (strcmp (oper, "XA") == 0)   {
  up_cstack ();
  ar_read ("Real part          : ", &x, AR_TDOU);
  ar_read ("Imaginary part     : ", &y, AR_TDOU);
  cstack [0] = complex (x, y); return;
}
//-------------------------------------- Operator "XP"
if (strcmp (oper, "XP") == 0)   {
  up_cstack ();
  ar_read ("Modulus   : ", &x, AR_TDOU);
  ar_read ("Argument  : ", &y, AR_TDOU);
  cstack [0] = polar (x, y); return;
}
//-------------------------------------- Operator "CLX"
if (strcmp (oper, "CLX") == 0)   {
  down_cstack (1); return;
}
//-------------------------------------- Operator "CLS"
if (strcmp (oper, "CLS") == 0)   {
  memset (cstack, 0, NBSTACK * sizeof (complex)); return;
}
//-------------------------------------- Operator "CLM"
if (strcmp (oper, "CLM") == 0)   {
  memset (memory, 0, NBMEM * sizeof (complex));
  return;
}
//-------------------------------------- Operator "^"
if (strcmp (oper, "^") == 0)   {
  memcpy (&inter, &cstack [0], sizeof (complex));
  down_cstack (0);
  memcpy (&cstack [NBSTACK - 1], &inter, sizeof (complex));
  return;
}
//-------------------------------------- Operator "DECI"
if (strncmp (oper, "DECI", 4) == 0)   {
  i = oper [4] - '0';
  if ((i < 0) || (i > 3))
    ar_beep (300, 50);
  else {
    j = oper [5] - '0';
    if ((j < 0) || (j > 9))
      ar_beep (300, 50);
    else
    deci [i] = j;
  }
  return;
}
```

```
//----------------------------------------- Operator "STO"
if (strncmp (oper, "STO", 3) == 0)   {
  i = oper [3] - '0';
  if (i < NBMEM)
    memcpy (&memory [i], &cstack [0], sizeof (complex));
  else
    ar_beep (300, 50);
  return;
}
//----------------------------------------- Operator "RCL"
if (strncmp (oper, "RCL", 3) == 0)   {
  i = oper [3] - '0';
  up_cstack ();
  if (i < NBMEM)
    memcpy (&cstack [0], &memory [i], sizeof (complex));
  else
    ar_beep (300, 50);
  return;
}

if (strcmp (oper, "+") == 0)   {
  cstack [0] += cstack [1];
  if (errno) ar_beep (300, 50); else down_cstack (1);
  return;
}
if (strcmp (oper, "-") == 0)   {
  cstack [0] = cstack [1] - cstack [0];
  if (errno) ar_beep (300, 50); else down_cstack (1);
  return;
}
if (strcmp (oper, "*") == 0)   {
  cstack [0] *= cstack [1];
  if (errno) ar_beep (300, 50); else down_cstack (1);
  return;
}
if (strcmp (oper, "/") == 0)   {
  cstack [0] = cstack [1] / cstack [0];
  if (errno) ar_beep (300, 50); else down_cstack (1);
  return;
}
if (strcmp (oper, "Y^X") == 0)   {
  cstack [0] = exp (cstack [0] * log (cstack [1]));
  if (errno) ar_beep (300, 50); else down_cstack (1);
  return;
}

if      (strcmp (oper, "EXP") == 0)
  cstack [0] = exp   (cstack [0]);
```

```
  else if (strcmp (oper, "X^2") == 0)
    cstack [0] = cstack [0] * cstack [0];
  else if (strcmp (oper, "LOG") == 0)
    cstack [0] = log   (cstack [0]);
  else if (strcmp (oper, "1/X") == 0)
    cstack [0] = complex (1, 0) / cstack [0];
  else if (strcmp (oper, "SQRT") == 0)
    cstack [0] = sqrt (cstack [0]);
  else if (strcmp (oper, "SIN") == 0)
    cstack [0] = sin  (cstack [0]);
  else if (strcmp (oper, "COS") == 0)
    cstack [0] = cos  (cstack [0]);
  else if (strcmp (oper, "TAN") == 0)
    cstack [0] = tan  (cstack [0]);
  else if (strcmp (oper, "SH") == 0)
    cstack [0] = sinh (cstack [0]);
  else if (strcmp (oper, "CH") == 0)
    cstack [0] = cosh (cstack [0]);
  else if (strcmp (oper, "TH") == 0)
    cstack [0] = tanh (cstack [0]);
  else if (strcmp (oper, "ARCSIN") == 0)
    cstack [0] = asin (cstack [0]);
  else if (strcmp (oper, "ARCCOS") == 0)
    cstack [0] = acos (cstack [0]);
  else if (strcmp (oper, "ARCTAN") == 0)
    cstack [0] = atan (cstack [0]);
  else if (strcmp (oper, "ARGSH") == 0)
    cstack [0] = ash  (cstack [0]);
  else if (strcmp (oper, "ARGCH") == 0)
    cstack [0] = ach  (cstack [0]);
  else if (strcmp (oper, "ARGTH") == 0)
    cstack [0] = ath  (cstack [0]);
  else ar_beep (300, 50);

  if (errno)  ar_beep (300, 50);
}

void  ar_use_complex_calculator ()
{
  char  oper [10];

  cstack = (complex *) calloc (NBSTACK, sizeof (complex));
  memory = (complex *) calloc (NBMEM,  sizeof (complex));
  if ((cstack == NULL) || (memory == NULL)) return;
  do {
    refresh_display ();
    cout << "Next operator : "; cout.flush ();
    gets (oper); strupr (oper);
```

```
    if (strcmp (oper, "Q")) calculate (oper);
  } while (strcmp (oper, "Q"));
  free ((char *) cstack); free ((char *) memory);
}
```

1.5 Annotated Examples

Example 1

Let us consider the following calculation:

$$z = \sqrt{(5-i) \, \text{Log} \, (3+2i)}$$

We write it using the programming notation:

```
Z = SQRT ((5 - I) * LOG (3 + 2 * I))
```

Let us enter the two numbers 5–i and 3+2i in order, and store them in memories 0 and 1. Then we enter LOG to calculate the logarithm of 3+2i, and store the result in memory 2. Let us multiply (5–i) * LOG (3+2i) by entering *, and store the result in memory 3. Finally, let us take its square root by entering SQRT, and store the result in memory 4.

Below, we have reproduced the display on screen after the latter operation. Thus, we can check the intermediate results using the memories.

```
                 CALCULATOR ON COMPLEX NUMBERS
-------------------------------------------------------------------
|   |        ALGEBRIC FORM        |          POLAR FORM           |
|M0 |        5  - i            1  | 5.099019514 EXP-i  0.19739556 |
|M1 |        3  + i            2  | 3.605551275 EXP+i 0.588002604 |
|M2 | 1.2824747 + i 0.5880026     | 1.410846683 EXP+i 0.429892248 |
|M3 |  7.000376 + i 1.6575383     | 7.193934768 EXP+i 0.232496688 |
|M4 | 2.6640487 + i 0.3110939     | 2.682151146 EXP+i 0.116248344 |
|M5 |        0                    |                               |
|M6 |        0                    |                               |
|M7 |        0                    |                               |
|M8 |        0                    |                               |
-------------------------------------------------------------------
| T |        0                    |                               |
| Z |        0                    |                               |
| Y |        0                    |                               |
| X | 2.6640487 + i 0.3110939     | 2.682151146 EXP+i 0.116248344 |
-------------------------------------------------------------------
   +     -     *     /    1/X    X^2    SQRT    Y^X     EXP    LOG
  SIN COS TAN SH CH TH   ARCSIN ARCCOS ARCTAN ARGCH ARGSH ARGTH
  XA    XP    CLX   CLS    CLM    ^     DECIxy   STOx    RCLx
-------------------------------------------------------------------
Next operator:
```

Example 2

Let us calculate $z = \sin (2+3i)$.

Let us enter 2+3i, and store this value in memory 0. We then calculate its sine and store the result in memory 1.

Now let us execute the inverse function ARCSIN, and place the result in memory 2. The result obtained does not correspond to the first value 2+3i; this is because several complex numbers have the same sine, and because the function Arcsin only returns one determination. However, let us verify that:

$$\sin (1.14159265 - 3i) = 9.15449916 - 4.16890696i$$

Thus, let us calculate the sine of the value contained in X, and place the result in memory 3.

```
              CALCULATOR ON COMPLEX NUMBERS
------------------------------------------------------------------
|   |         ALGEBRIC FORM        |          POLAR FORM          |
|M0|          2 + i          3 | 3.605551275 EXP+i 0.982793723|
|M1| 9.1544991 - i  4.168907 |10.059057604 EXP-i 0.427330784|
|M2| 1.1415927 - i 3.0000000 | 3.209865073 EXP-i 1.207185501|
|M3| 9.1544991 - i 4.1689070 |10.059057604 EXP-i 0.427330784|
|M4|          0                |                              |
|M5|          0                |                              |
|M6|          0                |                              |
|M7|          0                |                              |
|M8|          0                |                              |
------------------------------------------------------------------
| T|          0                |                              |
| Z|          0                |                              |
| Y|          0                |                              |
| X| 9.1544991 - i 4.1689070 |10.059057604 EXP-i 0.427330784|
------------------------------------------------------------------
+      -     *     /     1/X   X^2    SQRT    Y^X    EXP   LOG
SIN COS TAN SH CH TH   ARCSIN ARCCOS ARCTAN ARGCH ARGSH ARGTH
XA    XP    CLX   CLS   CLM    ^     DECIxy   STOx   RCLx
------------------------------------------------------------------
Next operator:
```

Example 3

Finally, we calculate: $z = [\ (2+3i)\ (1-i) - \dfrac{3e^{5i}}{\sqrt{2-i}}\ ]\ (1/2 - 2i)$

First, let us enter the first two numbers, and store them in memories 0 and 1. Then let us calculate their product and store it in memory 2. Now we enter $3e^{5i}$ and 2–i, and store them in memories 3 and 4.

Let us take the square root of 2–i by entering SQRT, and save the result in memory 5. We divide $3e^{5i}$ by $\sqrt{2-i}$, and store the result in memory 6. Let us deduct this number from (2+3i) (1–i), and store the result in memory 7. We enter the exponent, and store it in memory 8. We raise to the power by entering the operator Y^X.

```
              CALCULATOR ON COMPLEX NUMBERS
-----------------------------------------------------------------
|  |        ALGEBRIC FORM        |           POLAR FORM          |
|M0|        2 + i          3 | 3.605551275 EXP+i 0.982793723|
|M1|        1 - i          1 | 1.414213562 EXP-i 0.785398163|
|M2|        5 + i          1 | 5.099019514 EXP+i  0.19739556|
|M3| 0.8509866 - i 2.8767728 |           3 EXP-i 1.283185307|
|M4|        2 - i          1 | 2.236067977 EXP-i 0.463647609|
|M5| 1.4553467 - i 0.3435607 | 1.495348781 EXP-i 0.231823805|
|M6| 0.9958672 - i 1.7416001 | 2.006220915 EXP-i 1.051361503|
|M7| 4.0041328 + i 2.7416001 | 4.852777642 EXP+i 0.600378494|
|M8|      0.5 - i          2 | 2.061552813 EXP-i 1.325817664|
-----------------------------------------------------------------
| T|        0               |                                  |
| Z|        0               |                                  |
| Y|        0               |                                  |
| X|-7.0289341 - i 2.0416068 | 7.319431115 EXP-i 2.858913254|
-----------------------------------------------------------------
+      -      *      /     1/X    X^2    SQRT    Y^X     EXP    LOG
SIN  COS  TAN SH  CH  TH    ARCSIN ARCCOS ARCTAN ARGCH ARGSH ARGTH
XA    XP    CLX    CLS    CLM     ^     DECIxy    STOx    RCLx
-----------------------------------------------------------------
Next operator:
```

---

2   Resolution of Complex Linear Systems

2.1 Principle

A linear system of N equations with N unknowns is a set of N equations of the form:

$$a_{11}z_1 + a_{12}z_2 + \dots + a_{1N}z_N = b_1$$

$$a_{21}z_1 + a_{22}z_2 + \dots + a_{2N}z_N = b_2$$

$$\dots\dots\dots\dots\dots\dots\dots\dots\dots\dots$$

$$a_{N1}z_1 + a_{N2}z_2 + \dots + a_{NN}z_N = b_N$$

where $z_1, \dots z_N$ are the N unknown complex numbers, and a_{ij} (i and j belong to [1,N]), b_i (i belongs to [1,N]) given complex numbers.

It is possible to represent this system in matrix form:

$$
\begin{pmatrix}
a_{11} & a_{12} & \cdots & a_{1N} \\
a_{21} & a_{22} & \cdots & a_{2N} \\
\cdots & \cdots & \cdots & \cdots \\
a_{N1} & a_{N2} & \cdots & a_{NN}
\end{pmatrix}
\begin{pmatrix}
z_1 \\ z_2 \\ \cdots \\ z_N
\end{pmatrix}
=
\begin{pmatrix}
b_1 \\ b_2 \\ \cdots \\ b_N
\end{pmatrix}
$$

We set:

$$z_k = x_k + iy_k$$

$$a_{kl} = c_{kl} + id_{kl}$$

$$b_k = e_k + if_k$$

where $x_k, y_k, c_{kl}, d_{kl}, e_k$ and f_k are real numbers.

The complex system is equivalent to the following real system of dimension $2N$:

$$
\begin{pmatrix}
c_{11} & -d_{11} & c_{12} & -d_{12} & \cdots & c_{1N} & -d_{1N} \\
d_{11} & c_{11} & d_{12} & c_{12} & \cdots & d_{1N} & c_{1N} \\
c_{21} & -d_{21} & c_{22} & -d_{22} & \cdots & c_{2N} & -d_{2N} \\
d_{21} & c_{21} & d_{22} & c_{22} & \cdots & d_{2N} & c_{2N} \\
\cdots & \cdots & \cdots & \cdots & \cdots & \cdots & \cdots \\
c_{N1} & -d_{N1} & c_{N2} & -d_{N2} & \cdots & c_{NN} & -d_{NN} \\
d_{N1} & c_{N1} & d_{N2} & c_{N2} & \cdots & d_{NN} & c_{NN}
\end{pmatrix}
\begin{pmatrix}
x_1 \\ y_1 \\ x_2 \\ y_2 \\ \cdots \\ x_N \\ y_N
\end{pmatrix}
=
\begin{pmatrix}
e_1 \\ f_1 \\ e_2 \\ f_2 \\ \cdots \\ e_N \\ f_N
\end{pmatrix}
$$

This system with real coefficients is then solved using the Gauss-Jordan method, which is explained in chapter 9, Matrices and Vectors.

2.2 Calculation Tool

The input parameters of the tool `ar_system_complex` are:
- XM, the matrix of the real parts of the coefficients a_{ij};
- YM, the matrix of the imaginary parts of the coefficients a_{ij};
- XV, the vector of the real parts of the coefficients b_i;
- YV, the vector of the imaginary parts of the coefficients b_i.

In the output, the value of the function, boolean, indicates if it was possible to solve the system (TRUE) or not, for example, if the determinant was zero (FALSE).

The vectors XU and YU then respectively contain the real parts and the imaginary parts of the solutions z_i.

REMARK: The concepts of vectors and matrices are explained in chapter 9.

This tool will be placed in the file COMPLEX\COMPSYST.CPP.

```
/*==========================================================
                   COMPSYST.CPP:
            SOLVING COMPLEX LINEAR SYSTEMS
 ========================================================*/

#include  "armath.h"

int  ar_system_complex (ar_matrix &xm, ar_matrix &ym,
                        ar_vector &xu, ar_vector &yu,
                        ar_vector &xv, ar_vector &yv)
{
  ar_matrix  m;
  ar_vector  u, v;
  ar_number  r, det;
  int        i, j, order, order2;

  //-------------------------------------------------- TESTS
  if ( (xm.col != xm.lig) || (ym.col != ym.lig) ||
       (xv.lig != yv.lig) || (ym.lig != xm.lig) ||
       (xv.lig != xm.lig) )
    return FALSE;
  order  = xm.lig; order2 = 2 * order;

  //--------------- INITIALISATION OF INTERMEDIATE MATRICES
  if (! m.open (order2, order2)) return FALSE;
  if (! u.open (order2))         return FALSE;
  if (! v.open (order2))         return FALSE;

  //---------------------------- FILL INTERMEDIATE VECTOR
  for (i = 1, j = 1; i <= order; i ++)  {
    v.writecoeff (j++, xv.readcoeff (i));
    v.writecoeff (j++, yv.readcoeff (i));
  }

  //---------------------------- FILL INTERMEDIATE MATRIX
  for (i = 1; i <= order; i ++)
    for (j = 1; j <= order; j ++)  {
      r = xm.readcoeff (i, j);
      m.writecoeff (2 * i - 1, 2 * j - 1, r);
      m.writecoeff (2 * i    , 2 * j    , r);
      r = ym.readcoeff (i, j);
      m.writecoeff (2 * i    , 2 * j - 1, r);
      m.writecoeff (2 * i - 1, 2 * j    , -r);
    }

  //-------------------------------- OVER-SYSTEM INVERSION
  u = ar_lin_sys (m, v, det); if (errno) return FALSE;
```

```
//------------------------- BUILD THE TWO RESULTS VECTORS
  for (i = 1, j = 1; i <= xu.lig; i++)  {
    xu.writecoeff (i, u.readcoeff (j++));
    yu.writecoeff (i, u.readcoeff (j++));
  }
 return TRUE;
}
```

2.3 Annotated Examples

Example 1

Let us consider the following system:

$$z_1 + z_2 + iz_3 = 5$$

$$z_1 + iz_2 + z_3 = -2i$$

$$iz_1 + z_2 + z_3 = 1$$

```
RESOLUTION OF A COMPLEX LINEAR SYSTEM

Dimension of the system: 3

Enter the matrix :
Re (M [1,1])            : 1
Im (M [1,1])            : 0
Re (M [1,2])            : 1
Im (M [1,2])            : 0
Re (M [1,3])            : 0
Im (M [1,3])            : 1

Re (M [2,1])            : 1
Im (M [2,1])            : 0
Re (M [2,2])            : 0
Im (M [2,2])            : 1
Re (M [2,3])            : 1
Im (M [2,3])            : 0

Re (M [3,1])            : 0
Im (M [3,1])            : 1
Re (M [3,2])            : 1
Im (M [3,2])            : 0
Re (M [3,3])            : 1
Im (M [3,3])            : 0

Any change             ? n
```

```
Enter the vector :
Re (V [1])                 : 5
Im (V [1])                 : 0
Re (V [2])                 : 0
Im (V [2])                 : -2
Re (V [3])                 : 1
Im (V [3])                 : 0

Any change                 ? n

U [ 1] = + 3 / 2   -  1 / 2   I
U [ 2] = + 1   +   1   I
U [ 3] = - 1 / 2   -  5 / 2   I
```

The program then yields the solution triplet:

$$z_1 = \frac{3}{2} - \frac{1}{2} i$$

$$z_2 = 1 + i$$

$$z_3 = -\frac{1}{2} - \frac{5}{2} i$$

Example 2

Consider the system with two unknowns:

$$(1-5i) z_1 + (8+2i) z_2 = 3i$$

$$-3 z_1 + (6+2i) z_2 = -7$$

The program then gives the solution:

```
RESOLUTION OF A COMPLEX LINEAR SYSTEM

Dimension of the system: 2

Enter the matrix :
Re (M [1,1])               : 1
Im (M [1,1])               : -5
Re (M [1,2])               : 8
Im (M [1,2])               : 2

Re (M [2,1])               : -3
Im (M [2,1])               : 0
Re (M [2,2])               : 6
Im (M [2,2])               : 2
```

```
Enter the vector :
Re (V [1])              : 0
Im (V [1])              : 3
Re (V [2])              : -7
Im (V [2])              : 0

Any change              ? n

U [ 1] = + 324 / 521   + 595 / 521   I
U [ 2] = - 312 / 521   + 803 / 1042   I
```

---

3   Equations of the Second Degree

3.1 Principle

An equation of the second degree with complex coefficients is of the type:

$$az^2 + bz + c = 0 \qquad \text{with } a \neq 0$$

where a, b and c are complex numbers.

Unlike equations with real numbers, this equation always has two solutions (distinct or not), given by:

$$z' = \frac{-b - \sqrt{b^2 - 4ac}}{2a}$$

$$z'' = \frac{-b + \sqrt{b^2 - 4ac}}{2a}$$

3.2 Calculation Tool

The input parameters of the tool `ar_equation_complex` are the three complex numbers a, b and c.

In the output, s1 and s2 contain the two solutions of the corresponding equation.

The tool will be placed in the file COMPLEXE\COMPEQUA.CPP.

```
/*============================================================
                        COMPEQUA.CPP:
        RESOLUTION OF A COMPLEX EQUATION OF DEGREE 2
==============================================================*/

#include   "armath.h"
```

```
void  ar_equation_complex (complex &a, complex &b,
            complex &c, complex &s1, complex &s2)
{
  complex  u, v, w;
  double   r;

  u = complex (real (b) * real (b) - imag (b) * imag (b)
      - 4 * real (a) * real (c) + 4 * imag (a) * imag (c),
        2 * real (b) * imag (b) - 4 * real (a) * imag (c)
      - 4 * imag (a) * real (c));

  r = sqrt (real (u) * real (u) + imag (u) * imag (u));

  v = complex (sqrt ((r + real (u)) / 2),
              (imag (u) < 0) ?
              - sqrt ((r - real (u)) / 2) :
              sqrt ((r - real (u)) / 2));

  w = complex ((- real (b) - real (v)) / 2,
              (- imag (b) - imag (v)) / 2);

  u = complex ((- real (b) + real (v)) / 2,
              (- imag (b) + imag (v)) / 2);

  r = real (a) * real (a) + imag (a) * imag (a);

  s1 = complex ((real(a) * real(w) + imag(a) * imag(w)) / r,
               (real(a) * imag(w) - imag(a) * real(w)) / r);

  s2 = complex ((real(a) * real(u) + imag(a) * imag(u)) / r,
               (real(a) * imag(u) - imag(a) * real(u)) / r);
}
```

3.3 Annotated Examples

Example 1

Let us consider the following equation:

$$(-4+i)\, z^2 + (2-3i)\, z + (5-i) = 0$$

```
RESOLUTION OF A COMPLEX EQUATION OF THE SECOND DEGREE

a : Real part          : -4
a : Imaginary part     : 1
b : Real part          : 2
b : Imaginary part     : -3
```

```
c : Real part           : 5
c : Imaginary part      : -1

Modifications           ? n

Solution 1 : 1.4446445 - 0.352759213 i
Solution 2 : -0.797585676 - 0.235476081 i
```

Example 2

Let us consider the following equation, whose solutions are the three cubic roots of the unit:

$$z^3 = 1$$

and which can be factorised in the form:

$$(z-1)(z^2+z+1) = 0$$

The value 1 is of course a solution, and the two other roots are solutions of the equation:

$$z^2+z+1 = 0$$

It is an equation with real coefficients. As a result, its solutions are conjugated, which means that if z' is a solution, then:

$$z'' = z'^* \qquad \text{(with if } z' = a+ib, z'^* = a-ib)$$

is also a solution. The exact roots are:

$$z' = -\frac{1}{2} - i\frac{\sqrt{3}}{2}$$

$$z'' = -\frac{1}{2} + i\frac{\sqrt{3}}{2}$$

The program obtains them with maximum precision:

```
RESOLUTION OF A COMPLEX EQUATION OF THE SECOND DEGREE

a : Real part           : 1
a : Imaginary part      : 0
b : Real part           : 1
b : Imaginary part      : 0
c : Real part           : 1
c : Imaginary part      : 0

Modifications           ? n

Solution 1 : -0.5 - 0.866025404 i
Solution 2 : -0.5 + 0.866025404 i
```

4 Exploitation Tools

The following tools allow the direct exploitation of the preceding tools.

The following tool is to be placed in the file COMPLEX\UCOMPSYS.CPP:

```
/*===========================================================
                        UCOMPSYS.CPP:
          COMPLEX LINEAR SYSTEMS EXPLOITATION TOOL
 ===========================================================*/

#include  "armath.h"

void ar_use_complex_system ()
{
  ar_matrix  xm, ym;
  ar_vector  xu, xv, yu, yv;
  ar_number  *tn;
  int        i, j, k, dim;

  cout << "RESOLUTION OF A COMPLEX LINEAR SYSTEM\n\n";

  ar_read ("Dimension of the system: ", &dim, AR_TINT);
  if (dim <= 0) return;
  tn = new ar_number [2 * dim * dim];

  //--------------------------- OPEN INTERMEDIATE MATRICES
  xm.open (dim, dim); ym.open (dim, dim);
  xu.open (dim);        yu.open (dim);
  xv.open (dim);        yv.open (dim);

  if ((errno) || (tn == NULL))  {
    cerr << "Not enough memory\n";
    exit;
  }

  //----------------------------------------- ENTER MATRIX
  ar_init_entry ("Enter the matrix :");
  for (i = 1, k = 0; i <= dim; i++)
    for (j = 1; j <= dim; j++)  {
      sprintf (ar_temp, "Re (M [%d, %d])", i, j);
      ar_fill_entry (ar_temp, &tn [k++], AR_TNUM);
      sprintf (ar_temp, "Im (M [%d, %d])", i, j);
      ar_fill_entry (ar_temp, &tn [k++], AR_TNUM);
    }
  ar_do_entry ();
  ar_nl;
```

```
  for (i = 1, k = 0; i <= dim; i++)
    for (j = 1; j <= dim; j++)   {
      xm.writecoeff (i, j, tn [k++]);
      ym.writecoeff (i, j, tn [k++]);
    }

  //----------------------------------------- ENTER VECTOR
  ar_init_entry ("Enter the vector :");
  for (j = 1, k = 0; j <= dim; j++)   {
    sprintf (ar_temp, "Re (V [%d])", j);
    ar_fill_entry (ar_temp, &tn [k++], AR_TNUM);
    sprintf (ar_temp, "Im (V [%d])", j);
    ar_fill_entry (ar_temp, &tn [k++], AR_TNUM);
  }
  ar_do_entry ();
  ar_nl;
  for (j = 1, k = 0; j <= dim; j++)   {
    xv.writecoeff (j, tn [k++]);
    yv.writecoeff (j, tn [k++]);
  }

  //------------------------------- SOLVING AND DISPLAY
  if (ar_system_complex (xm, ym, xu, yu, xv, yv))
    for (i = 1; i <= dim; i++)   {
      cout << "U [" << i << "] = " <<
           xu.readcoeff (i) << "   ";
      if (! yu.readcoeff (i).zero ())
        cout << yu.readcoeff (i) << "  I";
      ar_nl;
    }
  else
    cerr << "Impossible solving\n";
  ar_pause ();
}
```

The following tool is to be placed in the file COMPLEX\UCOMEQUA.CPP:

```
/*===========================================================
                     UCOMEQUA.CPP:
        COMPLEX EQUATIONS SOLVING EXPLOITATION TOOL
   =========================================================*/

#include  "armath.h"

void ar_use_complex_equation ()
{
  complex     a, b, c, s1, s2;
  ar_double   x1, y1, x2, y2, x3, y3;
```

```
ar_init_entry ("RESOLUTION OF A COMPLEX EQUATION OF THE \
               SECOND DEGREE");

ar_fill_entry ("a : Real part",       &x1, AR_TDOU);
ar_fill_entry ("a : Imaginary part", &y1, AR_TDOU);
ar_fill_entry ("b : Real part",       &x2, AR_TDOU);
ar_fill_entry ("b : Imaginary part", &y2, AR_TDOU);
ar_fill_entry ("c : Real part",       &x3, AR_TDOU);
ar_fill_entry ("c : Imaginary part", &y3, AR_TDOU);
if (ar_do_entry ()) return;
ar_nl;

a = complex (x1, y1);
b = complex (x2, y2);
c = complex (x3, y3);

ar_equation_complex (a, b, c, s1, s2);

cout << "Solution 1 : " << real (s1)
     << ((imag (s1) > 0) ? " + " : " - ")
     << fabs (imag (s1)) << " i\n";

cout << "Solution 2 : " << real (s2)
     << ((imag (s2) > 0) ? " + " : " - ")
     << fabs (imag (s2)) << " i\n";

ar_nl;
ar_pause ();
}
```

7

Polynomials

Polynomial functions are of particular interest to the programmer, because calculations using these functions are relatively easy to program.

As a reminder, we note that a polynomial function generally has the following format:

$$P(x) = a_0 + a_1 x + a_2 x^2 + \dots + a_p x^p = \sum_{i=0}^{p} a_i x^i$$

in which the real numbers a_i ($i \in [0, p]$) are the coefficients of the polynomial. The highest exponent of a term in the polynomial is called the degree of the polynomial. The smallest power of a term in the polynomial (the term must be different from zero) is its valuation.

Calculations made using polynomials are not complicated from a theoretical standpoint, but they are long, especially when the degree of the polynomial is high.

The class `ar_polynomial` and the associated tools studied in this chapter will allow us to calculate the value of a polynomial at a certain point. They will also allow us to find the complex roots of a polynomial; to add, multiply, or compose two polynomials; to divide a polynomial by another using two different methods (Euclidean division and division by increasing powers); to determine the LCM and GCF (Least Common Multiple and Greatest Common Factor); and lastly, to calculate the successive derivatives of a polynomial.

All the tools for this chapter will be placed in the subdirectory POL.

1 The class ar_polynomial and its members

The class `ar_polynomial` is a perfect example of the contribution of object-oriented programming to the programming of numerical analysis tools.

Programs perceive polynomials, which they manipulate in a purely conceptual manner, as sèts of numbers which represent the coefficients attributed to each monomial.

After one "opens" a polynomial using the function `open(maxdegree)`, which reserves the memory necessary for the new polynomial, the coefficients of this polynomial will be manipulated exclusively through the public variable `degree` and by the two member functions `readcoeff` and `writecoeff`.

The physical representation of the polynomial is known only by the elementary member functions `open`, `close`, `readcoeff`, and `writecoeff`, as well as by the constructor and destructor of the class.

The physical implementation that we have programmed is a dense representation, which means it is formed by a contiguous memory zone able to contain `maxdegree + 1` objects of the type `ar_number`.

The advantage of this representation, other than its simplicity, is to provide direct access to any of the polynomial's coefficients. It is inapplicable, however, to polynomials with a high degree, such as ($x^{10000} + 3$).

The appropriate representation would then be the "hollow" representation, which memorizes the polynomial in the form of a table, or better yet, in that of a chained list of monomials including the degree and the associated coefficients. The above polynomial would then be memorised very simply:

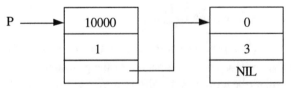

If the reader wishes to implement this physical representation, he can do so by modifying only the elementary member functions `open ()`, `close ()`, `readcoeff ()`, `writecoeff ()`, `operator =`, `clear ()`.

The member function `reduce ()` allows one to eliminate the coefficients of the terms of highest degree if they are infinitely small (this situation may arise after a long and complicated calculation which creates numerical errors).

The operators `==` and `!=` are overloaded in order to test the equality or inequality of two polynomials using the classical notation of C.

The source code which corresponds to the implementation of all of the member functions belonging to the class `ar_polynomial` is grouped in the file POL\POL.CPP.

```
/*===========================================================
                         POL.CPP:
        CLASS AR_POLYNOMIAL AND ITS MEMBER FUNCTIONS
 ==========================================================*/

#include  "armath.h"

int ar_polynomial::open (int maxdeg)
{
  if (!empty) close ();
  if (maxdeg < 0) maxdeg = 0;
  ptcoeff = new ar_number [maxdeg + 1];
  if (ptcoeff == NULL) {
    errno = 1; cerr << "Insufficient memory\n";
    return FALSE;
  }
  else  {
    maxdegree = maxdeg; degree = 0;
    ptcoeff [0] = N0;  empty  = FALSE;
    return TRUE;
  }
}

void ar_polynomial::close (void)
{
  if (!empty) delete[]ptcoeff; empty = TRUE;
}

ar_number & ar_polynomial::readcoeff  (int i)
{
  if ((i < 0) || (i > degree)) return N0;
  else return ptcoeff [i];
}

void ar_polynomial::writecoeff (int i, ar_number &n)
{
  if ((i >= 0) && (i <= maxdegree))  {
    ptcoeff [i] = n;
    if ((! n.zero ()) && (i > degree)) degree = i;
  }
}

int ar_polynomial::zero (void)
{
  int res = FALSE;
  if (degree == 0) res = readcoeff (0).zero ();
  return res;
}
```

```
void ar_polynomial::clear (void)
{
  int i;
  if (empty) return;
  for (i = 0; i<= maxdegree; i++) writecoeff (i, N0);
  degree = 0;
}

void ar_polynomial::reduce (void)
{
  while (readcoeff (degree).small ())   {
    writecoeff (degree, N0);
    if (degree > 0) degree --; else return;
  }
}

void ar_polynomial::operator = (ar_polynomial &p)
{
  close ();
  if (! open  (p.degree)) {errno = 1; return;}
  memcpy (ptcoeff, p.ptcoeff,
          sizeof (ar_number) * (p.degree + 1));
  degree = p.degree;
}

int operator == (ar_polynomial &p, ar_polynomial &q)
{
  int  i;
  if (p.degree != q.degree) return (FALSE);
  for (i = 0; i <= p.degree; i++)
    if (p.readcoeff (i) != q.readcoeff (i)) return (FALSE);
  return (TRUE);
}

int operator != (ar_polynomial &p, ar_polynomial &q)
{
  return (! (p == q));
}

ar_number ar_polynomial::operator () (ar_number &x)
{
  int        i;
  ar_number  n;

  for (i = degree; i >= 0; i--)
    n = n * x + readcoeff (i);
  return n;
}
```

2 Entry and Display of Polynomials

2.1 Entry

The simplest method involves entering first the degree of the polynomial, then each of its coefficients. It is then extremely tedious to enter a polynomial of the form $(x^{100} - 1)$ because it calls for the entry of 102 numbers.

A more refined method consists of entering each monomial using two numbers, its degree and its coefficient. One marks the end of an entry by, for example, entering a negative degree.

We have developed here a tool which permits us to enter polynomials in symbolic form; that is, the way they are usually manipulated. Thus, the polynomial:

$$x^5 + \frac{3}{5} x^4 - 12 x^2 + 8x - \frac{1}{4}$$

will be entered as the following chain of characters:

```
X5 +3/5X4 -12X2 +8X -1/4
```

REMARK: *The blanks preceding the + and – signs separate the different monomials and are mandatory*. It is not necessary to write the polynomial in order, and two monomials can have the same degree: the entry tool will then add the corresponding coefficients. Lowercase characters are automatically converted into uppercase. The operator >> is overloaded for the class `ar_polynomial` by our specific polynomial entry tool. Thus, the instruction `cin >> p` will permit the entry of the polynomial p.

This tool will be placed in the file POL\POLENTRY.CPP.

```
/*===========================================================
                      POLENTRY.CPP:
              SYMBOLIC FORM POLYNOMIAL ENTRY
   =========================================================*/

#define   AR_MAXPOLINPUT   1000

#include   <string.h>
#include   "armath.h"

static int ar_extract_monom (char *ch, ar_polynomial & p)
{
   ar_number   coeff;
   char        chn [200];

   int         degree, xpos, sppos, signe;
```

```
//--------------- Suppression of superfluous spaces
while (ch [0] == ' ') strcpy (ch, &ch [1]);
if (! ch [0]) return FALSE;
signe = (ch [0] == '-') ? -1 : 1;
if ((ch [0] == '+') || (ch [0] == '-'))
  if (ch [1])
    strcpy (ch, &ch [1]);
while (ch [0] == ' ') strcpy (ch, &ch [1]);
if (! ch [0]) return FALSE;

//--------------- Looking for X
if ((xpos = ar_strfind (ch, 'X')) == -1)  {
  degree = 0; coeff = ar_number (ch);
  if (errno) return FALSE;
  ch [0] = 0;
}
else {
  if (xpos == 0)
    strcpy (chn, "1");
  else {
    strncpy (chn, ch, xpos); chn [xpos] = 0;
  }
  coeff = ar_number (chn); if (errno) return FALSE;

  //-------------- Looking for space
  if ((sppos = ar_strfind (ch, ' ')) == -1)
    sppos = strlen (ch);
  if (xpos == sppos - 1) degree = 1;
  else {
    strncpy (chn, &ch [xpos + 1], sppos - xpos - 1);
    chn [sppos - xpos - 1] = 0; degree = atoi (chn);
  }
  if (degree > AR_MAXPOLINPUT)  {
    errno = TRUE; return FALSE;
  }
  if (sppos >= strlen (ch))
    strcpy (ch, "");
  else
    strcpy (ch, &ch [sppos + 1]);
}
if (signe == -1) coeff = - coeff;
coeff += p.readcoeff (degree);
p.writecoeff (degree, coeff); if (errno) return FALSE;
{
  if (degree > p.degree) p.degree = degree;
}
  return TRUE;
}
```

```
istream& operator >> (istream& s, ar_polynomial& p)
{
   int            j;
   char           *ch = new char [200];
   ar_polynomial  np;

   if (! np.open (AR_MAXPOLINPUT)) return s;

   cout.flush (); gets (ch); strupr (ch);

   while  ((ch [0]) && (ar_extract_monom (ch, np)));
   if ((ch [0] == 0) && (! errno))  {
      if (p.open (np.degree)) {
         for (j = 0; j <= np.degree; j++)
         p.writecoeff (j, np.readcoeff (j));
      }
   }
   else  {
      errno = 1;
      cerr << "This expression does not stand for a
               polynomial\n";
      ar_pause ();
   }
   return s;
}
```

2.2 Display

The tool presented here controls the display of the symbolic representation of a polynomial on the screen. It is accessible through the overload of the operator <<. Thus, the instruction cout << p will produce the display of the polynomial *p*. The terms with zero as a coefficient do not appear, and rational coefficients appear in the form *p/q*.

The tool will be placed in the file POL\POLDISP.CPP.

```
/*===========================================================
                       POLDISP.CPP:
               POLYNOMIAL SYMBOLIC DISPLAY
   =========================================================*/

#include   "armath.h"

ostream& operator << (ostream& s, ar_polynomial& p)
{
   int        i;
   long       lp, lq;
   ar_number  n;
```

```
if (p.zero ())
   cout << "0";
else
   for (i = p.degree; i >= 0; i--)  {
      n = p. readcoeff (i);
      if (fabs (n.value) > AR_SMALL)  {
         cout << ((n.value < 0) ? "- " : "+ ");
         if (n.real) cout << fabs (n.value);
         else  {
            lp = labs (n.p); lq = labs (n.q);
            if ((lp != 1) || (lq != 1) || (i == 0))
               cout << lp;
            if (lq != 1)
               cout << "/" << lq;
         }
         if (i > 0) cout << " X";
         if (i > 1) cout << i;
         cout << " ";
      }
   }
ar_nl;
return s;
}
```

---

3   Evaluation of a Polynomial at a Point

3.1 Principle

Let us consider the following polynomial P:

$$P(x) = a_0 + a_1 x + a_2 x^2 + ... + a_p x^p$$

We wish to calculate the value of the polynomial at a given point x_0; the calculation is very simple, since the answer is given by the formula:

$$P(x_0) = a_0 + a_1 x_0 + a_2 x_0^2 + ... + a_p x_0^p$$

However, we prefer the following formula, called Horner's formula, when attempting to increase the precision and speed of the calculation:

$$P(x_0) = ((...((a_p x_0 + a_{p-1}) x_0 + a_{p-2}) x_0 + ...) x_0 + a_1) x_0 + a_0$$

In this formula, only additions and multiplications are performed, whereas the first formula calls for the power function. In a computer, the process of raising to a power is long and relatively imprecise. It is thus preferable to avoid it.

3.2 Calculation Tool

The calculation tool consists of an overload of the operator ( ). The only parameter of this tool is the number x, at which P must be evaluated. The output contains the number $P(x)$.

This tool is placed at the end of the file POL\POL.CPP (see section 1).

3.3 Annotated Examples

The exploitation tool allows one to calculate the value of the polynomial at several points. The calculation for $x_0 = 0$ ends the program.

Example 1

```
EVALUATION OF A POLYNOMIAL AT A POINT (P(xo))

P(X) = X3 - 5X2 + 7X + 4

+   X3 - 5 X2 + 7 X + 4

Value of xo : 1
P (xo) = + 7
Value of xo : 10
P (xo) = + 574
Value of xo : -5/2
P (xo) = - 483/8
Value of xo : 1/3
P (xo) = + 157/27
Value of xo : 0
P (xo) = + 4
```

Example 2

```
EVALUATION OF A POLYNOMIAL AT A POINT (P(xo))

P(X) = X16

+   X16

Value of xo : 2
P (xo) = + 65536
Value of xo : 3
P (xo) = + 43046721
Value of xo : 1/2
P (xo) = + 1/65536
```

```
Value of xo : 1/2
P (xo) = + 1/65536
Value of xo : 1/3
P (xo) = + 1/43046721
Value of xo : 0
P (xo) = - 0
```

4 Calculation of the Complex Roots of a Polynomial

4.1 Introduction

This method permits the approximation of all of the roots of a polynomial of degree n:

$$P(x) = a_0 x^n + a_1 x^{n-1} + ... + a_{n-1} x + a_n = 0$$

As we recall, a polynomial of degree n always has n roots, either real or complex. The complex roots of a polynomial with real coefficients form couples of conjugated numbers.

4.2 Principle

The method calls for the decomposition of the polynomial P into the product of simpler polynomials, of degree 2 or perhaps 1.

The first step consists of determining 2 values p and q such that:

$$P(x) = (x^2 + px + q) . Q(x)$$

The roots of $P(x)$ are then solutions of $x^2 + px + q = 0$ which we are perfectly able to determine, and also solutions of $Q(x)$, which is a polynomial of degree $n-2$. We repeat the process for $Q(x)$, and continue until all of the roots have been determined.

The difficulty lies in the determination of the coefficients p and q; therefore, we resort to an iterative method.

Let p_0 and q_0 be given. There is no particular reason for $x^2 + p_0 x + q_0$ to divide the polynomial $P(x)$; thus, we have the general relationship:

$$P(x) = (x^2 + p_0 x + q_0) . B(x) + (R_0 x + S_0)$$

where R_0 and S_0 are two real numbers.

Bairstow's method allows us to calculate two values p_1 and q_1 such that:

$$P(x) = (x^2 + p_1 x + q_1) . B(x) + (R_1 x + S_1)$$

with:

$$|R_1| < |R_0| \qquad \text{and} \qquad |S_1| < |S_0|$$

We will confine ourselves to providing the transformation which permits one to progress from the values (p_n, q_n) to the values (p_{n+1}, q_{n+1}); the determination of this transformation goes beyond the domain of this book.

Using the coefficients (a_i) of the polynomial P, we calculate:

– *the coefficients (b_i):*

$$b_0 = a_0$$
$$b_1 = a_1 - pb_0$$
$$b_2 = a_2 - pb_1 - qb_0$$

$$\dots\dots\dots\dots\dots\dots$$

$$b_{n-1} = a_{n-1} \quad - pb_{n-2} - qb_{n-3}$$
$$b_n \quad = a_n \quad\quad - pb_{n-1} - qb_{n-2}$$

These coefficients are those of the polynomial B, the quotient of the division of P by (x^2+px+q).

– *the array of (c_i):*

$$c_0 = b_0$$
$$c_1 = b_1 - pc_0$$
$$c_2 = b_2 - pc_1 - qc_0$$

$$\dots\dots\dots\dots\dots\dots$$

$$c_{n-2} \quad = b_{n-2} \quad - pc_{n-3} - qc_{n-4}$$
$$c_{n-1} \quad = 0 \quad\quad - pc_{n-2} - qc_{n-3}$$

We then calculate:

$$D = c_{n-2}^2 - c_{n-1} \cdot c_{n-3}$$
$$U = b_{n-1} \cdot c_{n-2} - b_n \cdot c_{n-3}$$
$$V = b_n \cdot c_{n-2} - b_{n-1} \cdot c_{n-1}$$

and then:

$$p_{n+1} = p_n + \frac{U}{D} \qquad\qquad q_{n+1} = q_n + \frac{V}{D}$$

4.3 Calculation Tool

The input parameters of the tool `ar_bairstow` are:

- `pol`, the polynomial whose roots we are looking for;
- `sol`, a table of complex numbers of sufficient dimension (> degree of the polynomial) which will contain the roots as output;
- `p` and `q`, the two initial research parameters (the couple (0, 0) generally leads to the answer);
- `prec`, the desired precision, which corresponds to the maximum difference $|p_{n+1}-p_n|$ and $|q_{n+1}-q_n|$. The iterations will stop when this difference is reached.

The value of the function indicates the number of *detected* roots.

The tool is placed in the file `POL\BAIRSTOW.CPP`.

```
/*============================================================
                        BAIRSTOW.CPP:
        DETERMINATION OF THE ROOTS OF A POLYNOMIAL
==============================================================*/

#include "armath.h"

#define  MAXITER    100
#define  MB1         AR_MAXBAIRSTOW + 1

int  ar_bairstow (ar_polynomial &pol, complex sol [],
     ar_double prec, ar_double p, ar_double q)
{
  ar_double  a [MB1], b [MB1], c [MB1];
  ar_double  d, u, v, y, z, delta;
  ar_number  n;
  int        iter, i, k, found = 0,
             deg = pol.degree, d1, d2, d3;

  if (deg > AR_MAXBAIRSTOW) {errno = 1; return 0;}

  n = pol.readcoeff (deg); u = n.value;

  for (i = 1; i <= deg; i++)  {
    n = pol.readcoeff (deg - i);
    a [i] = n.value / u;
  }

  a [0] = 1;
  while (deg > 1)  {
    if (deg == 2)  {
      p = a [1];
      q = a [2];
    }
    else  {
      iter  = 0;
      do  {
        iter++;
        if (iter >= MAXITER) {errno = 1; return found;}
        b [0] = a [0];
        b [1] = a [1] - p * b [0];
        for (k = 2; k <= deg; k++)
          b [k] = a [k] - p * b [k-1] - q * b [k-2];
        c [0] = b [0];
        c [1] = b [1] - p * c [0];
        if (deg > 3)
          for (k = 2; k <= deg - 2; k++)
            c [k] = b [k] - p * c [k-1] - q * c [k-2];
```

```
      d1 = deg - 1; d2 = deg - 2; d3 = deg - 3;
        c [d1] = - p * c [d2]   - q * c [d3];
      d = pow (c [d2], (double) 2) - c [d1] * c [d3];
        u = b [d1] * c [d2]      - b [deg] * c [d3];
        v = b [deg] * c [d2] - b [d1] * c [d1];
        if (d == 0) {errno = 1; return found;}
        y = u / d;
        z = v / d;
        p += y;
        q += z;
      } while ((fabs (y) + fabs (z)) > prec);
    }   /* else */

    /*------------------------- Resolution of X2 + px + q */
    delta = p * p - 4 * q;
    if (delta >= 0)  {
      sol [found++] = complex ((- p - sqrt (delta)) / 2, 0);
      sol [found++] = complex ((- p + sqrt (delta)) / 2, 0);
    }
    else  {
      sol [found++] = complex (-p / 2, - sqrt (- delta) / 2);
      sol [found++] = complex (-p / 2,   sqrt (- delta) / 2);
   }
    deg -= 2;
    for (i = 1; i <= deg; i++)
      a [i] = b [i];
  } /* while */

  if (deg == 1)
    sol [found++] = complex (- a [1] / a [0], 0);

  return found;
}
```

4.4 Annotated Examples

Example 1

SEARCH FOR COMPLEX ROOTS OF A POLYNOMIAL

P (X) = X4 + 4X3 - 164X2 - 336X + 5760

Precision	:	1e-10
p	:	0
q	:	0

```
Real solutions :
x 0 = -8
x 1 = 6
x 2 = -12
x 3 = 10

Complex solutions :
```

Example 2

```
SEARCH FOR COMPLEX ROOTS OF A POLYNOMIAL

P(X) = 2X7 - 13X6 - 49X5 + 385X4 - 77X3 - 1652X2 + 684X + 720

Precision           : 1e-10
p                   : 0
q                   : 0

Real solutions :
x 0 = -0.5
x 1 = 1
x 2 = -2
x 3 = 3
x 4 = -5
x 5 = 6
x 6 = 4

Complex solutions :
```

The roots of the two equations:

$$x^4 + 4x^3 - 164x^2 - 336x + 5760 = 0$$

$$2x^7 - 13x^6 - 49x^5 + 385x^4 - 77x^3 - 1652x^2 + 684x + 720 = 0$$

are obtained with excellent precision.

Example 3

```
SEARCH FOR COMPLEX ROOTS OF A POLYNOMIAL

P (X) = X6 - 7X5 - 21X4 + 203X3 - 140X2 - 756X + 720

Precision           : 1e-10
p                   : 0
q                   : 0
```

```
Real solutions :
x 0 = -2
x 1 = 3
x 2 = 4
x 3 = 6
x 4 = -5
x 5 = 1

Complex solutions :
```

The roots of:

$$x^6 - 7x^5 - 21x^4 + 203x^3 - 140x^2 - 756x + 720 = 0$$

are very satisfactory.

Example 4

```
SEARCH FOR COMPLEX ROOTS OF A POLYNOMIAL

P (X) = X4 - 2X3 + 30X2 - 50X + 125

Precision              : 1e-10
p                      : 0
q                      : 0

Real solutions :

Complex solutions :
x 0 = 1 + -2 i
x 1 = 1 + 2 i
x 2 = 0 + -5 i
x 3 = 0 + 5 i
```

The polynomial:

$$x^4 - 2x^3 + 30x^2 - 50x + 125 = 0$$

has the roots:

$$z_1 = 1+2i \qquad z_2 = 1-2i \qquad z_3 = +5i \qquad z_4 = -5i$$

Example 5

Let us return to the equation of example 3. This time we will ask for a higher precision level of 10^{-15}.

```
SEARCH FOR COMPLEX ROOTS OF A POLYNOMIAL

P (X) = X6 - 7X5 - 21X4 + 203X3 - 140X2 - 756X + 720

Precision            : 1e-15
p                    : 0
q                    : 0

Unadapted method or too many iterations
```

The program cannot find the roots, because the desired precision is too high.

This is a very important remark, and it is applicable to all programs which ask for a precision level. The program will almost always function abnormally when an excessively high precision level is specified.

We may then proceed in the following manner: first, we perform a search using average precision (10^{-1} or 10^{-2}) in order to locate the roots. Then, we repeat the calculation with improved precision (10^{-9} or 10^{-10}).

Example 6

Multiple Roots

Let us consider the following equation:

$$x^6 - 4x^5 - 6x^4 + 32x^3 + x^2 - 60x + 36 = 0$$

which has 1, −2 and 3 as double roots.

```
SEARCH FOR COMPLEX ROOTS OF A POLYNOMIAL

P (X) = X6 - 4X5 - 6X4 + 32X3 + X2 - 60X + 36

Precision            : 1e-5
p                    : 0
q                    : 0

Real solutions:
x 0 = 0.999997130351
x 1 = 3.00000264142
x 2 = 1.000005739318
x 3 = 2.999994717238
x 4 = -2.000003438648
x 5 = -1.999996561346

Complex solutions :
```

The results are relatively imprecise. Let us explain why, intuitively.

When a function has a multiple root x_0, its graphical representation in the proximity of x_0 has a "flattened" shape. Thus, when one moves along the curve, a weak variation of y corresponds to a large variation of x. The higher the multiplicity of the root, the more this phenomenon is marked.

In a more rigorous manner, let us consider Taylor's power series expansion representing the function f in proximity to x_0:

$$f(x_0 + h) = f(x_0) + \frac{h}{1!} f'(x_0) + \frac{h^2}{2!} f''(x_0) + ... + \frac{h^n}{n!} f^{(n)}(x_0) + h^n \, \varepsilon(h)$$

If x_0 is a root of f, then $f(x_0)=0$. If x_0 is a double root of f, then $f(x_0)=0$ and $f'(x_0)=0$.

More generally, if x_0 is a root of multiplicity m, all the derivatives of order equal to or lesser than $(m-1)$ are zero at x_0; thus the development of order m of f is reduced to:

$$f(x_0 + h) = \frac{h^m}{m!} f^{(m)}(x_0) + h^m \, \varepsilon(h)$$

For example, let us imagine a function with a root of multiplicity 4, and let us set $h = 0.01$.

$$f(x_0 + 0{,}01) \approx \frac{10^{-8}}{24} f^{(4)}(x_0) < 4.10^{-10} f^{(4)}(x_0)$$

If the derivative $f^{(4)}(x_0)$ is not too large, a high variation of x (0.01) has little effect on the value of the function.

Example 7

Let us consider the following equation:

$$x^7 + 7x^6 + 21x^5 + 35x^4 + 35x^3 + 21x^2 + 7x + 1 = 0$$

of which -1 is the only root of multiplicity 7.

```
SEARCH FOR COMPLEX ROOTS OF A POLYNOMIAL

P (X) = X7 + 7X6 + 21X5 + 35X4 + 35X3 + 21X2 + 7X + 1

Precision          : 1e-3
p                  : 0
q                  : 0

Real solutions :
x 6 = -1.006721526978

Complex solutions :
x 0 = -0.994908459538   + -0.002435944505 i
x 1 = -0.994908459538   + 0.002435944505 i
```

```
x 1 = -0.994908459538   + 0.002435944505 i
x 2 = -0.997889144923   + -0.005772132398 i
x 3 = -0.997889144923   + 0.005772132398 i
x 4 = -1.00382475088    + -0.005301987416 i
x 5 = -1.00382475088    + 0.005301987416 i
```

Even though the specified precision is low, the program displays the answers with a precision of only 0.7% , which is hardly satisfactory!

· Thus, it is fitting to remain very wary of the results given by the program in the case of multiple roots, and to settle for an approximate value.

---

5   Product of Polynomials

5.1 Principle

Let us consider the following two polynomials P and Q:

$$P(x) = a_0 + a_1x + a_2x^2 + ... + a_px^p$$

$$Q(x) = b_0 + b_1x + b_2x^2 + ... + b_qx^q$$

The product of these two polynomials is then:

$$R(x) = [P.Q](x) = P(x) . Q(x)$$

$$= c_0 + c_1x + c_2x^2 + ... + c_rx^r$$

with:

$$r = p + q$$

$$c_n = \sum_{(i,j)} a_i b_j$$

the summation being applicable to all terms (i, j) such that:

$$i + j = n \qquad\qquad i \in [0, p] \qquad\qquad j \in [0, q]$$

5.2 Calculation Tool

The calculation tool consists of an overload of the operator * applied to two polynomials. Thus, if p, q and r are polynomials and if p and q are correctly initialized, the instruction r = p * q will produce the calculation of the product of the two polynomials. This answer is stored in a static zone within the tool. The operator = then produces the duplication of this result in the object r.

REMARK: Let us keep the limitations of the tool in mind. The result of the product of two polynomials is always stored in the same internal static variable. Its lifespan ends at the next calculation of a product of polynomials. Unless it is transferred into a target polynomial, this result will be lost.

This is why an instruction of the type r = p1 * q1 + p2 * q2 is forbidden. The compiler's call mechanism calls on the sum of polynomials operator, transmitting to it the results of the calculations p1 * q1 and p2 * q2. Unfortunately, the answer to the calculation p2 * q2 has replaced that of p1 * q1 and the final result obtained is then (p2 * q2)^2.

The use of a dynamic memory allocation mechanism within the tools would have avoided this problem, but would have had the disadvantage of continually increasing the occupied memory without being able to free it.

This tool will be placed in the file POL\POLMUL.CPP.

```
/*===========================================================
                        POLMUL.CPP:
                POLYNOMIALS MULTIPLICATION
 ===========================================================*/

#include   "armath.h"

//--------------------- MULTIPLICATION OF TWO POLYNOMIALS

ar_polynomial & operator * (ar_polynomial & p,
                            ar_polynomial & q)
{
  static ar_polynomial  u;
  ar_number             res;
  int                   i, n, deg = p.degree + q.degree;

  if (p.zero () || q.zero ()) deg = 0;
  if (! u.open (deg)) {errno = 1; return u;}
  for (n = 0; n <= deg; n++)  {
    for (res = N0, i = max(0, n - q.degree);
         i <= min (n, p.degree); i++) {
      res += p.readcoeff (i) * q.readcoeff (n - i);
      if (errno) return u;
    }
    u.writecoeff (n, res);
  }
  return u;
}

//------------- MULTIPLICATION OF A NUMBER BY A POLYNOMIAL

ar_polynomial & operator * (ar_number & a, ar_polynomial & p)
```

```
{
  static  ar_polynomial u;
  int     i, deg = p.degree;

  if (a.zero ()) deg = 0;
  if (! u.open (deg)) {errno = 1; return u;}
  for (i = 0; i <= deg; i++)
    u.writecoeff (i, a * p.readcoeff (i));

  return u;
}

//------------------------ OVERLOADING OF OPERATOR *=

ar_polynomial & ar_polynomial::operator *= (ar_polynomial &p)
{
  *this = *this * p; return *this;
}

ar_polynomial &  ar_polynomial::operator *= (ar_number &n)
{
  *this = n * *this; return *this;
}
```

5.3 Annotated Example

```
MULTIPLICATION OF TWO POLYNOMIALS

P(X) = X - 1
Q(X) = 2X + 3

+ 2 X2 +  X - 3

MULTIPLICATION OF TWO POLYNOMIALS

P(X) = X3 - 6X + 7
Q(X) = 5X5 - 3X4 + X2 - 3

+ 5 X8 - 3 X7 - 30 X6 + 54 X5 - 21 X4 - 9 X3 + 7X2 + 18X - 21

MULTIPLICATION OF TWO POLYNOMIALS

P(X) = 3/5X + 2
Q(X) = X2 + 5/4

+ 3/5 X3 + 2 X2 + 3/4 X + 5/2
```

We indeed find:

$$(x-1)(2x+3) = 2x^2+x-3$$

$$(x^3-6x+7)(5x^5- 3x^4 +x^2 - 3) = 5x^8 - 3x^7 - 30x^6 +54x^5 - 21x^4 - 9x^3 +7x^2 +18x - 21$$

$$(\tfrac{3}{5}x + 2)(x^2 + \tfrac{5}{4}) = \tfrac{3}{5}x^3 + 2x^2 + \tfrac{3}{4}x + \tfrac{5}{2}$$

---

6   Linear Combination of Polynomials

6.1 Principle

Let us consider the following two polynomials P and Q:

$$P(X) = a_0 + a_1X + a_2X^2 + ... + a_pX^p$$

$$Q(x) = b_0 + b_1x + b_2x^2 + ... + b_qx^q$$

and two numbers λ and μ.

We will form the following linear combination:

$$R(X) = \lambda P(X) + \mu Q(x)$$

The generic coefficient of the polynomial R is:

$$c_i = \lambda . a_i + \mu . b_i$$

REMARK: The addition, subtraction, and multiplication by a coefficient are special cases in linear combination, which correspond to the following couples (λ, μ) respectively:

$$(1, 1); (1, -1); (\lambda, 0).$$

6.2 Calculation Tools

Six tools are overloaded:

- the operator +, addition of two polynomials;
- the operator −, subtraction of two polynomials;
- the operators += and −=.

These four tools are placed in the file POL\POLSUM.CPP.

- the operator * applied to a number and to a polynomial;
- the corresponding *= operator .

These two tools are integrated with the multiplication tools in the file POL\POLMUL.CPP.

The remark concerning the multiplication of two polynomials (preceding section) is also valid for addition, subtraction, or scalar multiplication.

Thus, the following expressions are invalid:

```
(p1 + p2) * (p3 + p4)
(p1 - p2) * (p3 - p4)
(l * p1) + (m * p2)
```

However, the following expression is valid:

$$\lambda * (p1 + p2) * (p3 - p4)$$

The four operators used are different and each uses its "static" polynomial. In short, any expression which calls on a given operator more than once is invalid.

The exploitation tool allows one to enter the two numbers λ and μ in order to perform the entire calculation. It is placed in the file UPOLLC.CPP.

The four addition and substraction tools will be placed in the file POL\POLSUM.CPP.

```
/*==========================================================
                      POLSUM.CPP:
       ADDITION AND SUBTRACTION OF TWO POLYNOMIALS
  ========================================================*/

#include  "armath.h"

ar_polynomial & operator + (ar_polynomial &p,
                            ar_polynomial &q)
{
  static ar_polynomial  u;
  ar_number             a, b;
  int                   i, deg = max (p.degree, q.degree);

  if (! u.open (deg)) {errno = 1; return u;}
  for (i = 0; i <= deg; i++)  {
     a = (i <= p.degree) ? p.readcoeff (i)  : N0;
     b = (i <= q.degree) ? q.readcoeff (i)  : N0;
     u.writecoeff (i, a + b);
  }
  u.reduce (); return u;
}

//------------------- OVERLOADING OF OPERATOR -
ar_polynomial & operator - (ar_polynomial &p,
                            ar_polynomial &q)
{
  static ar_polynomial u;
  ar_number   a, b;

  int         i, deg = max (p.degree, q.degree);
  if (! u.open (deg)) {errno = 1; return u;}
```

```
for (i = 0; i <= deg; i++)  {
   a = (i <= p.degree) ? p.readcoeff (i) : NO;
   b = (i <= q.degree) ? q.readcoeff (i) : NO;
   u.writecoeff (i, a - b);
}
u.reduce (); return u;
}


//------------------ OVERLOADING OF OPERATOR +=
ar_polynomial & ar_polynomial::operator += (ar_polynomial &p)
{
   *this = *this + p; return *this;
}


//------------------ OVERLOADING OF OPERATOR -=
ar_polynomial & ar_polynomial::operator -= (ar_polynomial &p)
{
   *this = *this - p; return *this;
}
```

6.3 Annotated Example

Let:

$$P\ (x) = x^3 + \frac{5}{4}x^2 - 8 \qquad Q\ (x) = 2x^2 - \frac{1}{7} \qquad \lambda = \frac{1}{2} \qquad \mu = -\frac{1}{3}$$

```
LINEAR COMBINATION OF TWO POLYNOMIALS (aP + bQ)

Coefficient a : 1/2
P(X) = x3 + 5/4x2 - 8
Coefficient b : -1/3
Q(X) = 2x2 - 1/7

+ 1/2 X3  - 1/24 X2  - 83/21
```

---

7   Composition of Polynomials

7.1 Principle

Let us consider the two following polynomials P and Q:

$$P\ (X) = a_0 + a_1X + a_2X^2 + \ldots + a_pX^p$$

$$Q\ (x) = b_0 + b_1x + b_2x^2 + \ldots + b_qx^q$$

We form the composite polynomial $R(x) = P[Q(x)]$ by replacing X with $Q(x)$ in the expression $P(X)$. For example, with:

$$P(X) = X^2 - 3$$

$$Q(x) = x + 1$$

we obtain:

$$P[Q(x)] = (x + 1)^2 - 3$$

$$= x^2 + 2x - 2$$

Generally, the degree of the substituted polynomial $R(x)$ is equal to the product of the degrees of P and of Q:

$$r = p.q$$

REMARK: The raising of a polynomial $Q(x)$ to a power k is a special case corresponding to:

$$P(X) = X^k$$

7.2 Calculation Tool

The tool `ar_subst_pol` works exactly like the multiplication tool.
The tool will be placed in the file `POL\POLSUBST.CPP`.

```
/*===========================================================
                      POLSUBST.CPP:
                POLYNOMIALS SUBSTITUTION
  =========================================================*/

#include "armath.h"

ar_polynomial& ar_subst_pol (ar_polynomial &p,
                             ar_polynomial &q)
{
    static ar_polynomial   u;
    ar_polynomial          v;
    int                    i, deg = p.degree * q.degree;

    if (! u.open (deg)) return u;
    if (! v.open (deg)) return u;

    u.writecoeff (0, p.readcoeff (0));
    v.writecoeff (0, N1);
```

```
for (i = 1; i <= p.degree; i++)  {
    v = v * q;
    u += p.readcoeff (i) * v;
    if (errno) return u;
}
return u;
}
```

7.3 Annotated Examples

Example 1

Let: $P(X) = -5X^2 + 3$ $Q(x) = 2x^3 - x + 5$

```
SUBSTITUTION OF TWO POLYNOMIALS

P(X)  =  -5X2 + 3
Q(X)  =  2X3 - X + 5

- 20 X6 + 20 X4 - 100 X3 - 5 X2 + 50 X - 122
```

The program provides the correct answer:

$$P[Q(x)] = -20x^6 + 20x^4 - 100x^3 - 5x^2 + 50x - 122$$

Example 2

The program also allows one to raise a polynomial to any power.
For example, we wish to calculate:

$$R(x) = (2x^2 - 3)^4$$

We set:

$$P(X) = X^4 \qquad Q(x) = 2x^2 - 3$$

The program then gives:

$$R(x) = P[Q(x)] = (2x^2 - 3)^4$$

```
SUBSTITUTION OF TWO POLYNOMIALS

P(X)  =  X4
Q(X)  =  2X2 - 3

+ 16 X8 - 96 X6 + 216 X4 - 216 X2 + 81
```

8 Euclidean Division

There are two types of divisions among polynomials: Euclidean division and division by increasing powers. Euclidean division is the most common.

8.1 Principle

If two polynomials P and Q are given, there is a unique couple of polynomials (H, R) such that:

$$P = Q . H + R \qquad \text{with } d° (R) < d° (Q)$$

($d° (R)$ and $d° (Q)$ are the degrees of the polynomials R and Q). H and R are respectively the quotient and the remainder of the Euclidean division of P by Q.

Let, for example:

$$P (x) = 2x^5 + 2x^3 - x^2 + 2x - 1$$

$$Q (x) = x^3 - 1$$

The manual disposition of the calculation is as follows:

$$
\begin{array}{ll|l}
2x^5 + 2x^3 - x^2 + 2x - 1 & & x^3 - 1 \\
\hline
2x^2 . Q(x) \rightarrow \quad 2x^5 \qquad - 2x^2 & & 2x^2 \quad + \quad 2 \\
\hline
\qquad \qquad 2x^3 + x^2 + 2x - 1 & & (= \dfrac{2x^5}{x^3}) \quad (= \dfrac{2x^3}{x^3}) \\
2 . Q(x) \rightarrow \qquad 2x^3 \qquad \qquad - 2 & & \\
\hline
\qquad \qquad x^2 + 2x + 1 & &
\end{array}
$$

The quotient is then:

$$H (x) = 2x^2 + 2$$

and the remainder:

$$R (x) = x^2 + 2x + 1$$

Thus, we have the relationship:

$$(2x^5 + 2x^3 - x^2 + 2x - 1) = (x^3 - 1) (2x^2 + 2) + (x^2 + 2x + 1)$$

$$\qquad P (x) \qquad\qquad\quad Q (x) \quad H (x) \qquad\quad R (x)$$

and we indeed have:

$$d^\circ (R) < d^\circ (Q)$$

This division is sometimes called "division by decreasing powers" because during the division, the polynomials are classified according to the decreasing powers of the variable.

8.2 Calculation Tool

The following tool simulates manual calculation, and proceeds in the same manner.

The parameters of the tool `ar_div_pol` are the two polynomials P and Q to be divided and an empty polynomial in which the tool will store the remainder R. The return value of the tool is the polynomial H.

If the remainder is not useful, the operator `/` is overloaded. This allows one to write `h = p / q`. The remainder generated by the division tool is then destroyed automatically.

The tool will be placed in the file `POL\POLDIV.CPP`.

```
/*============================================================
                        POLDIV.CPP:
            EUCLIDEAN DIVISION OF TWO POLYNOMIALS
  ==========================================================*/

#include "armath.h"

ar_polynomial & ar_div_pol (ar_polynomial &p,
                ar_polynomial &q, ar_polynomial &r)
{
  static ar_polynomial  nh;
  ar_polynomial         nr;
  int                   i, j, deg = p.degree - q.degree;
  if (q.zero ())        {errno = 1; return nh;}
  if (! nh.open (deg))  {errno = 1; return nh;}
  nr = p;
  for (i = deg; i >= 0; i--)   {
    nh.writecoeff (i, nr.readcoeff (nr.degree) /
                      q.readcoeff (q.degree));
    for (j = i; j <= nr.degree; j++)   {
      nr.writecoeff (j, nr.readcoeff (j) -
      nh.readcoeff (i) * q.readcoeff (j - i));
      if (errno) return nh;
    }
    if (nr.degree > 0) nr.degree --;
    if (errno) return nh;
  }
  nr.reduce (); r = nr; return nh;
}
```

```
//------------------------ OVERLOADING OF OPERATOR /

ar_polynomial& operator / (ar_polynomial &p,ar_polynomial &q)
{
   ar_polynomial  r;
   return ar_div_pol (p, q, r);
}

//------------------------ OVERLOADING OF OPERATOR /=

ar_polynomial&  ar_polynomial::operator /= (ar_polynomial &p)
{
   *this = *this / p; return *this;
}
```

8.3 Annotated Examples

Example 1

Let us return to the result of the previous example:

$$P(x) = 2x^5 + 2x^3 - x^2 + 2x - 1$$

$$Q(x) = x^3 - 1$$

```
EUCLIDEAN DIVISION OF TWO POLYNOMIALS

P(X)  = 2X5 + 2X3 - X2 + 2X - 1
Q(X)  = X3 - 1

Quotient :
+ 2 X2 + 2

Remainder :
+ X2 + 2 X + 1
```

Example 2

Let us consider the two polynomials:

$$P(x) = x^{10} - 1$$

$$Q(x) = x - 1$$

Since the polynomial P is divisible by the polynomial Q, the remainder of the division is zero.

EUCLIDEAN DIVISION OF TWO POLYNOMIALS

```
P(X)  =  X10 - 1
Q(X)  =  X - 1
```

Quotient :
+ X9 +   X8 +   X7 +   X6 +   X5 +   X4 +   X3 +   X2 +   X + 1

Remainder :
0

Example 3

The results obtained with rational coefficients are correct.

EUCLIDEAN DIVISION OF TWO POLYNOMIALS

```
P(X)  =  5X3 + 29/3X2 - 43/36X + 1
Q(X)  =  3X2 - 1/2X + 1/3
```

Quotient :

+ 5/3 X + 7/2

Remainder :

- 1/6

9 Division by Increasing Powers

9.1 Principle

Let us return to the practical disposition of Euclidean division, this time ranking the polynomials according to the increasing powers of the variable.

$$
\begin{array}{l|l}
-1 + 2x - x^2 + 2x^3 + 2x^5 & -1 + x^3 \\
-1 \qquad\qquad\quad + x^3 & \\
\hline
\qquad 2x - x^2 + \ x^3 + 2x^5 & -1 \\
\end{array}
$$

If one performs the division, one notes that it is possible, if P is not a multiple of Q, to prolong the calculation indefinitely. This is not the case with Euclidean division, which inevitably yields a unique solution couple.

Furthermore, one notes that at each stage of the calculation, it is possible to factor a monomial x^k out of the remainder. k increases with each stage.

The polynomials P and Q are not enough to solve the problem completely; we then set an integer k, and stop the division when x^k can be factorised in the remainder.

We have then performed the division according to the increasing powers of P by Q to the degree k.

Thus, the theorem is written:

Given two polynomials P and Q, with $Q(0) \neq 0$, and an integer k, there is a unique couple of polynomials (H, R) such as:

$$P = Q \cdot H + x^k \cdot R \qquad\qquad \text{with } d^\circ (H) < k$$

REMARK: The polynomial Q must have a valuation of zero, which means that $Q(0)$ must be other than zero. The first elementary division must be done with the monomial of degree 0 of the polynomial Q. If the latter is zero, the division is impossible.

9.2 Calculation Tool

The following tool simulates the manual calculation, and works in the same way.

The parameters of the tool `ar_dcr_pol` are the two polynomials P and Q, the order k of the division, and an empty polynomial in which the tool will store the remainder R. The return value of the function is the quotient polynomial H.

The tool will be placed in the file POL\POLDIVIP.CPP.

```
/*=============================================================
                    POLDIVIP.CPP:
              DIVISION BY INCREASING POWERS
  =============================================================*/

#include "armath.h"

ar_polynomial &  ar_dcr_pol (ar_polynomial& p,
               ar_polynomial& q, int k, ar_polynomial& r)

{
   static ar_polynomial   nh;
   ar_polynomial          nr, nq;
   ar_number              u;
   int            i, j, mx = max (p.degree, q.degree + k - 1);

   if ((k <= 0) || (q.readcoeff (0).zero ()))
      {errno = 1; return nh;}
```

```
if (! nh.open (mx)) {errno = 1; return nh;}
if (! nr.open (mx)) {errno = 1; return nh;}
if (! nq.open (mx)) {errno = 1; return nh;}

for (i = 0; i <= p.degree; i++)
  nr.writecoeff (i, p.readcoeff (i));

for (i = 0; i <= q.degree; i++)
  nq.writecoeff (i, q.readcoeff (i));

for (i = 0; i < k; i++)   {
  u = nr.readcoeff (i) / nq.readcoeff (0);
  nh.writecoeff (i, u);

  for (j = i; j <= mx; j++)   {
    nr.writecoeff (j, nr.readcoeff (j) -
                   u * nq.readcoeff (j - i));
    if (errno) return nh;
  }
}
nh.reduce ();

if (! r.open (mx - k)) {errno = 1; return nh;}
for (i = 0; i <= mx - k; i++)
  r.writecoeff (i, nr.readcoeff (i + k));
r.reduce ();

return nh;
}
```

9.3 Annotated Examples

Example 1

Let us consider the following two polynomials P and Q:

$$P(x) = x + 2x^2$$

$$Q(x) = 1 - x^2 + x^3$$

Let us now perform the division to the fourth order. We get the following result:

$$(x + 2x^2) = (1 - x^2 + x^3)(x + 2x^2 + x^3) + x^4(1 - x - x^2)$$

$$\quad P(x) \qquad\quad Q(x) \qquad\quad H(x) \qquad\qquad\quad R(x)$$

The relationship $d°(H) < k$ is verified.

$$
\begin{array}{ll|l}
x \;+\; 2x^2 & & 1 \;-\; x^2 \;+\; x^3 \\[4pt]
\quad x \qquad\qquad -\,x^3 \;+\; x^4 & & \rule{0pt}{1.4em} \\[-2pt]
\hline
\qquad 2x^2 +\; x^3 -\; x^4 & & x \;+\; 2x^2 \;+\; x^3 \\[4pt]
\qquad 2x^2 \qquad\quad -\,2x^4 +\; 2x^5 & & \\[2pt]
\hline
\qquad\quad x^3 +\; x^4 -\; 2x^5 & & \\[4pt]
\qquad\quad x^3 \qquad\quad -\,x^5 +\; x^6 & & \\[2pt]
\hline
\qquad\qquad x^4 -\; x^5 -\; x^6 & &
\end{array}
$$

Let us make this calculation using the program:

```
DIVISION OF TWO POLYNOMIALS BY INCREASING POWERS

P(X)  = 2X2 + X
Q(X)  = X3 - X2 + 1
Order : 4

Quotient :
+ X3 + 2 X2 +   X

Remainder :
- X2 -   X + 1
```

Let us repeat the calculation, this time specifying a division of order 6:

```
DIVISION OF TWO POLYNOMIALS BY INCREASING POWERS

P(X)  = 2X2 + X
Q(X)  = X3 - X2 + 1
Order : 6

Quotient :
- X5 +   X4 +   X3 + 2 X2 +   X

Remainder :
+ X2 - 2 X
```

The quotient has been completed by the term $x^4 - x^5$. We note that it is possible to factorize x in the remainder: the quotient of the division at order 7 is the same as for the division at order 6. The equalities which correspond to the two divisions are then:

$$(x + 2x^2) = (1 - x^2 + x^3) (x + 2x^2 + x^3 + x^4 - x^5) + x^6 (-2x + x^2) \quad \text{order 6}$$
$$(x + 2x^2) = (1 - x^2 + x^3) (x + 2x^2 + x^3 + x^4 - x^5) + x^7 (-2 + x) \quad \text{order 7}$$

The program confirms this result:

```
DIVISION OF TWO POLYNOMIALS BY INCREASING POWERS

P(X) = 2X2 + X
Q(X) = X3 - X2 + 1
Order : 7

Quotient :
- X5 +   X4 +   X3 + 2 X2 +   X

Remainder :

+ X - 2
```

REMARK: Initially, x can be factored out in P; the division at order one of P by Q does not call for any calculations:

$$(x + 2x^2) = (1 - x^2 + x^3) . 0 + x^1 (1 + 2x)$$

therefore:

$$H(x) = 0 \qquad R(x) = 1 + 2x$$

```
DIVISION OF TWO POLYNOMIALS BY INCREASING POWERS

P(X) = 2X2 + X
Q(X) = X3 - X2 + 1
Order : 1

Quotient :
0

Remainder :
+ 2 X + 1
```

Example 2

Of course, it is possible to use rational coefficients:

```
DIVISION OF TWO POLYNOMIALS BY INCREASING POWERS

P(X) = 3/5X3 + 2X - 4
Q(X) = X2 - 5/4
Order : 1
```

```
Quotient :
+ 16/5

Remainder :
+ 3/5 X2 - 16/5 X + 2

DIVISION OF TWO POLYNOMIALS BY INCREASING POWERS

P(X) = 3/5X3 + 2X - 4
Q(X) = X2 - 5/4
Order : 5

Quotient :
+ 256/125 X4 - 44/25 X3 + 64/25 X2 - 8/5 X + 16/5

Remainder :
- 256/125 X + 44/25

DIVISION OF TWO POLYNOMIALS BY INCREASING POWERS

P(X) = 3/5X3 + 2X - 4
Q(X) = X2 - 5/4
Order : 9

Quotient :
+ 4096/3125 X8 - 704/625 X7 + 1024/625 X6 - 176/125 X5
+ 256/125 X4 - 44/25 X3 + 64/25 X2 - 8/5 X + 16/5

Remainder :
- 4096/3125 X + 704/625
```

10 Calculation of GCF and LCM

10.1 Principle

Let us consider two polynomials P and Q. We will call the set of factors of P, D_P, and call the set of factors of Q, D_Q. These are two sets of polynomials.

Let us define an ordinal relationship between these polynomials: P_1 and P_2 are two elements of D_P. P_1 is greater than P_2 if and only if:

$$d^{\circ}(P_1) > d^{\circ}(P_2)$$

This relationship is a partially ordinal relationship because two polynomials of equal degree are not comparable.

Now let us consider the set $D = D_P \cap D_Q$ made up of the factors that P and Q have in common. One cannot designate *the* greatest element of D: because the ordinal relationship is partial, there is in fact a set of maximum polynomials. It can be proven that all polynomials in this set are proportionate. Thus, the GCF of P and Q is a polynomial defined "to the nearest coefficient." If R is among the greatest elements of D, all the others will be of the type λR with $\lambda \in R$.

For example, the GCF of:

$$P\,(x) = (x - 1)\,(x - 2)$$

$$Q\,(x) = (x - 1)\,(x - 3)$$

is $\lambda\,(x{-}1)$: $(x{-}1)$ is acceptable, but so are $(2x{-}2)$ and $(-3x{+}3)$.

The LCM can be obtained from the GCF through the relationship:

$$P\,(x) \,.\, Q\,(x) = \text{GCF}\,(P, Q) \,.\, \text{LCM}\,(P, Q)$$

Thus, it is also defined to the nearest coefficient.

10.2 Practical Calculation

It is based on Euclid's algorithm. After permuting P and Q if $d°\,(P) < d°\,(Q)$, we execute the Euclidean division of P by Q:

$$P = Q \,.\, H_1 + R_1$$

If the remainder R_1 is not zero, we divide Q by R_1:

$$Q = R_1 \,.\, H_2 + R_2$$

We reiterate the process until we obtain a remainder of zero. The previous remainder is then a GCF of the polynomials P and Q.

10.3 Calculation Tool

The parameters of the tool `ar_gcf_pol` are the two polynomials P and Q.

The return value of the function contains the GCF of the two polynomials.

The tool will be placed in the file `POL\POLGCF.CPP`.

```
/*==============================================================
                        POLGCF.CPP:
                  GCF OF TWO POLYNOMIALS
================================================================*/

#include "armath.h"

ar_polynomial & ar_gcf_pol (ar_polynomial &p,
                            ar_polynomial &q)
```

```
{
  static ar_polynomial   nr;
  ar_polynomial          nh, np, nq;
  ar_number              z;
  long                   pg, pp;
  int                    i;

  if ((p.zero ()) || q.zero ()) {
    errno = 1;
    cerr << "One of the two polynomials is null\n";
    return nr;
  }
  if (p.degree > q.degree)   {np = p; nq = q;}
  else                       {nq = p; np = q;}
  nr = nq; if (errno) return nr;
  while (nr.degree > 0)   {
    nh = ar_div_pol (np, nq, nr); if (errno) return nr;
    if (nr.degree == 0)   {
      if (! nr.zero ()) nq.clear ();
    }
    else  {
      np = nq;
      nq = nr;
    }
    for (i = 0, z = nq.readcoeff (nq.degree); i < nq.degree;
         i++)
      nq.writecoeff (i, nq.readcoeff (i) / z);
    nq.writecoeff (nq.degree, N1);
  }
  nr = nq;
  if (nq.zero ())
    nr.writecoeff (0, N1);
  else {
    for (pg = 0, i = 0; i <= nr.degree; i++)  {
      z = nr.readcoeff (i);
      if (! z.real) pg = (pg) ? ar_gcf (pg, z.p) : z.p;
    }
    for (pp = 0, i = 0; i <= nr.degree; i++)  {
      z = nr.readcoeff (i);
      if (! z.real)
        pp = (pp) ? (pp * z.q) / ar_gcf (pp, z.q) : z.q;
    }
    if (pg)
      for (i = 0; i <= nr.degree; i++)
      nr.writecoeff (i,nr.readcoeff (i) * ar_number (pp,pg));
  }
  return nr;
}
```

The following tool `ar_lcm_pol` calculates the LCM of two polynomials. It works the same way as the previous tool.

It will be placed in the file `POL\POLLCM.CPP`.

```
/* =============================================================
                        POLLCM.CPP:
                  LCM OF TWO POLYNOMIALS
   ===========================================================*/

#include "armath.h"

ar_polynomial & ar_lcm_pol (ar_polynomial &p,
                            ar_polynomial &q)

{
  ar_polynomial         u, v;
  static ar_polynomial  w;

  u = ar_gcf_pol (p, q);

  v = p * q;
  w = v / u;

  return w;
}
```

10.4 Annotated Examples

Example 1

We wish to calculate the GCF of:

$$P(x) = x^5 + 5x^4 + 7x^3 + 5x^2 + x - 1$$

$$Q(x) = x^4 + 4x^3 - 7x + 2$$

```
CALCULATION OF THE GCF AND LCM OF TWO POLYNOMIALS

P(X) = X5 + 5X4 + 7X3 + 5X2 + X - 1
Q(X) = X4 + 4X3 - 7X + 2

GCF (P,Q) = + X2 + 3 X - 1

LCM (P,Q) = + X7 + 6 X6 + 10 X5 + 2 X4 - 8 X3 - 10X2 - 3X + 2
```

The GCF of P and of Q is $\lambda(x^2 + 3x - 1)$.

Example 2

Now let us consider the polynomials with rational coefficients:

$$P(x) = \frac{4}{3}x^2 + \frac{35}{18}x + \frac{1}{2} = (\frac{4}{3}x + \frac{3}{2})(x + \frac{1}{3})$$

$$Q(x) = \frac{8}{3}x^2 + \frac{4}{3}x - \frac{15}{8} = (\frac{4}{3}x + \frac{3}{2})(2x - \frac{5}{4})$$

Their GCF is $R(x) = \lambda(\frac{4}{3}x + \frac{3}{2})$.

```
CALCULATION OF THE GCF OF TWO POLYNOMIALS

P(X)  =  4/3X2 + 35/18X + 1/2
Q(X)  =  8/3X2 + 4/3X - 15/8

GCF (P, Q)  = + 8 X  + 9

LCM (P, Q)  = + 4/9 X3 + 10/27 X2 - 103/432 X - 5/48
```

The GCF is: $R(x) = 8x + 9$

Example 3

Consider the following example:

$$P(x) = -12 + (15 + 4\sqrt{2})x - 5\sqrt{2}x^2$$

$$Q(x) = -3 + (\sqrt{2} - 6)x + 2\sqrt{2}x^2$$

The GCF of these two polynomials is $\lambda(-3 + \sqrt{2}x)$.

```
CALCULATION OF THE GCF OF TWO POLYNOMIALS

P(X)  =  -7.071067810X2 + 20.656854248X - 12
Q(X)  =  2.828427124X2 - 4.585786438X - 3

GCF (P, Q)  = +   X - 2.121320344119

LCM (P, Q)  = - 19.999999989447 X3 + 48.426406856834 X2
              - 4.727922062221 X - 16.970562744
```

REMARK 1: If the polynomials have high degrees, the program may not find the exact GCF; it would then indicate that the polynomials are prime relative to each other. This is because the algorithm does successive divisions among polynomials, and the error is amplified with each stage.

The program considers that any coefficient of a remainder less than 10^{-10} is zero; this security, however, can prove insufficient. In particular, one must be sure to enter real numbers such as $\sqrt{2}$, with the maximum number of significant digits allowed by the compiler (16 places with doubles, 32 with long doubles).

REMARK 2: As with integers, one can extend the definition of the GCF to several polynomials. Thus, the calculation of the GCF of:

$$P_1(x) = x^3 - 3x^2 - 10x + 24$$

$$P_2(x) = x^3 + 5x^2 - 2x - 24$$

$$P_3(x) = x^3 - x^2 - x - 2$$

can be done by first finding the GCF of P_1 and P_2 (for example):

$$\text{GCF}(P_1, P_2) = x^2 + x + 6$$

and then finding the GCF of $x^2 + x + 6$ with P_3:

$$\text{GCF}(P_1, P_2, P_3) = x - 2$$

One can also define polynomials which are prime relative to each other within their sets or prime two by two.

11   Successive Derivatives of a Polynomial

11.1 Principle

By definition, a polynomial is written in the form of a sum of monomials:

$$P(x) = \sum_{k=0}^{p} a_k x^k \qquad \text{(where p is the degree of P)}$$

Since the derivative of x^k is $k\,x^{k-1}$, the derivative of a monomial $a_k x^k$ is $k\,a_k x^{k-1}$. We then obtain:

$$P'(x) = \sum_{k=1}^{p} k\,a_k x^{k-1}$$

which we can also write in the following manner, showing the fact that P' is of degree $p-1$:

$$P'(x) = \sum_{k=0}^{p-1} (k+1)\,a_{k+1} x^k$$

By reiterating the calculation n times, we obtain the n-th derivative of P:

$$P^{(n)}(x) = \sum_{k=0}^{p-n} (k+1)(k+2)...(k+n) \, a_{k+n} \, x^k$$

or:

$$P^{(n)}(x) = \sum_{k=0}^{p-n} \frac{(k+n)!}{k!} a_{k+n} \, x^k$$

The degree of $P^{(n)}$ is equal to $p-n$: if $n>p$, the polynomial $P^{(n)}$ is zero.

11.2 Calculation Tool

The parameters of the tool `ar_der_pol` are the polynomial P and the order n of the derivation. The return value of the function contains the n-th derivative of P.

This tool will be placed in the file `POL\POLDERIV.CPP`.

```
/*=============================================================
                        POLDERIV.CPP:
                  POLYNOMIAL N-TH DERIVATIVE
   =============================================================*/

#include "armath.h"

ar_polynomial & ar_der_pol (ar_polynomial &p, int n)
{
   static ar_polynomial   nq;
   ar_number              u;
   int                    i, j, deg = max (0, p.degree - n);


   if (! nq.open (deg)) {errno = 1; return nq;}

   nq.degree = deg;

   if (n <= p.degree)
      for (i = 0; i <= deg; i++)  {
         for (j = 1, u = 1; j <= n; j++) u *= ar_number (i + j);
         nq.writecoeff (i, u * p.readcoeff (i + n));
         if (errno) return nq;
      }

   return nq;
}
```

11.3 Annotated Examples

Example 1

Let us consider the monomial $P(x) = x^8$.

```
N-TH DERIVATIVE OF A POLYNOMIAL

P(X) = X8
Order of the derivative : 1
+ 8 X7

N-TH DERIVATIVE OF A POLYNOMIAL

P(X) = X8
Order of the derivative : 3
+ 336 X5

N-TH DERIVATIVE OF A POLYNOMIAL

P(X) = X8
Order of the derivative : 8
+ 40320

N-TH DERIVATIVE OF A POLYNOMIAL

P(X) = X8
Order of the derivative : 12
0
```

We indeed obtain:

$$P'(x) \quad = 8\,x^7$$
$$P^{(3)}(x) \quad = 336\,x^5$$
$$P^{(8)}(x) \quad = 40320$$
$$P^{(12)}(x) \quad = 0$$

Example 2

Similarly, for derivatives of the first and second order of the polynomial:

$$P(x) = 4\,x^5 - \frac{3}{5}x^3 + x^2 - \frac{7}{2}x + 11$$

```
N-TH DERIVATIVE OF A POLYNOMIAL

P(X) = 4X5 - 3/5X3 + X2 - 7/2X + 11
Order of the derivative: 1
+ 20 X4 - 9/5 X2 + 2 X - 7/2

N-TH DERIVATIVE OF A POLYNOMIAL

P(X) = 4X5 - 3/5X3 + X2 - 7/2X + 11
Order of the derivative: 3
+ 240 X2 - 18/5
```

12   Exploitation Tools

The following tools permit the direct exploitation of the calculation tools.

The following tool is to be placed in the file POL\UPOLEVAL.CPP:

```
/*============================================================
                         UPOLEVAL.CPP:
            EXPLOITATION OF POLYNOMIALS EVALUATION
  ============================================================*/

#include  "armath.h"

void ar_use_pol_evaluation ()
{
  ar_polynomial  p;
  ar_number      a, b;

  cout << "EVALUATION OF A POLYNOMIAL AT A POINT \
          (P(xo))\n\n";
  cout << "P(x) = "; cin >> p; if (errno) return;
  cout << p;
  do  {
    ar_nl;
    ar_read ("Value of xo : ", &a, AR_TNUM);
    cout << "P (xo) = ";
    b = p (a);
    if (! errno)
      cout << b;
    else
      cerr << "Impossible calculation\n";
  } while (! a.zero ());
  ar_pause ();
}
```

The following tool is to be placed in the file `POL\UBAIRSTO.CPP`:

```
/*===========================================================
                       UBAIRSTO.CPP:
            EXPLOITATION TOOL OF BAIRSTOW'S METHOD
=============================================================*/

#include   "armath.h"

void ar_use_bairstow ()
{
  ar_polynomial  pol;
  complex        sol [AR_MAXBAIRSTOW];
  ar_double      p, q, prec;
  int            i, found;

  cout << "SEARCH FOR COMPLEX ROOTS OF A POLYNOMIAL\n\n";
  cout << "P (X) = "; cin >> pol; if (errno) return;

  ar_init_entry ("");
  ar_fill_entry ("Precision", &prec,  AR_TDOU);
  ar_fill_entry ("p        ", &p,     AR_TDOU);
  ar_fill_entry ("q        ", &q,     AR_TDOU);

  if (ar_do_entry ()) return;

  found = ar_bairstow (pol, sol, prec, p, q);

  if ((errno) || (found == 0))
    cerr << "\nUnadapted method or too many iterations\n";

  else {
    cout << "\nReal solutions      :\n";
    for (i = 0; i < found; i++)
      if (imag (sol [i]) == 0)
        cout << "X" << setw (2) << i << " = "
             << real (sol [i]) << "\n";

    cout << "\nComplex solutions :\n";
    for (i = 0; i < found; i++)
      if (imag (sol [i]) != 0)
        cout << "X" << setw(2) << i << " = "
             << real (sol [i]) << " + "
             << imag (sol [i]) << " i\n";
  }
  ar_pause ();
}
```

The following tool is to be placed in the file POL\UPOLMUL.CPP:

```
/*============================================================
                        UPOLMUL.CPP:
          EXPLOITATION OF POLYNOMIALS MULTIPLICATION
==============================================================*/

#include  "armath.h"

void  ar_use_pol_multiplication ()
{
  ar_polynomial  p, q, r;

  cout << "MULTIPLICATION OF TWO POLYNOMIALS\n\n";
  cout << "P(X) = "; cin >> p; if (errno) return;
  cout << "Q(X) = "; cin >> q; if (errno) return;
  ar_nl;

  r = p * q;

  if (errno)
    cerr << "Impossible multiplication\n";
  else
    cout << r;

  ar_pause ();
}
```

The following tool is to be placed in the file POL\UPOLLC.CPP:

```
/*============================================================
                        UPOLLC.CPP:
        EXPLOITATION OF POLYNOMIALS LINEAR COMBINATION
==============================================================*/

#include  "armath.h"

void ar_use_pol_lincomb ()
{
  ar_polynomial  p, q, r;
  ar_number      a, b;

  cout << "LINEAR COMBINATION OF TWO POLYNOMIALS \
          (aP + bQ)\n\n";

  ar_read ("Coefficient a : ", &a, AR_TNUM);
  cout << "P (X) = "; cin >> p; if (errno) return;
  ar_read ("Coefficient b : ", &b, AR_TNUM);
```

```
  cout << "Q (X) = "; cin >> q; if (errno) return;

  p = a * p;
  q = b * q;
  r = p + q;

  if (! errno)
    cout << r;
  else
    cerr << "Impossible calculation\n";

  ar_pause ();
}
```

The following tool is to be placed in the file POL\UPOLSUBS.CPP:

```
/*===========================================================
                      UPOLSUBS.CPP:
         EXPLOITATION OF POLYNOMIALS SUBSTITUTION
=========================================================*/

#include  "armath.h"

void ar_use_pol_substitution ()
{
  ar_polynomial  p, q, r;

  cout << "SUBSTITUTION OF TWO POLYNOMIALS\n\n";
  cout << "P (X) = "; cin >> p; if (errno) return;
  cout << "Q (X) = "; cin >> q; if (errno) return;
  ar_nl;

  r = ar_subst_pol (p, q);
  if (! errno)
    cout << r;
  else
    cerr << "Impossible substitution\n";

  ar_pause ();
}
```

The following tool is to be placed in the file POL\UPOLDIV.CPP:

```
/*===========================================================
                      UPOLDIV.CPP:
       EXPLOITATION OF POLYNOMIALS EUCLIDEAN DIVISION
=========================================================*/
#include  "armath.h"
```

```
void  ar_use_pol_division ()
{
  ar_polynomial  p, q, h, r;

  cout << "EUCLIDEAN DIVISION OF TWO POLYNOMIALS\n\n";
  cout << "P (X) = "; cin >> p; if (errno) return;
  cout << "Q (X) = "; cin >> q; if (errno) return;
  ar_nl;

  h = ar_div_pol (p, q, r);

  if (! errno)  {
    cout << "\nQuotient  :\n" << h;
    cout << "\n\nRemainder :\n"  << r;
  }
  else
    cerr << "Impossible division\n";
  ar_pause ();
}
```

The following tool is to be placed in the file POL\UPOLDIVI.CPP:

```
/*==========================================================
                    UPOLDIVI.CPP:
              EXPLOITATION OF POLYNOMIALS
              DIVISION BY INCREASING POWERS
==========================================================*/

#include   "armath.h"

void  ar_use_pol_division_increasing ()
{
  ar_polynomial  p, q, h, r;
  int            k;

  cout << "DIVISION OF TWO POLYNOMIALS BY INCREASING \
          POWERS\n\n";
  cout << "P (X) = "; cin >> p; if (errno) return;
  cout << "Q (X) = "; cin >> q; if (errno) return;
  ar_read ("Order : ", &k, AR_TINT);
  ar_nl;
  h = ar_dcr_pol (p, q, k, r);
  if (! errno)  {
    cout << "\nQuotient  :\n" << h;
    cout << "\n\nRemainder :\n"  << r;
  }
  else
```

```
      cerr << "Impossible division\n";
    ar_pause ();
}
```

The following tool is to be placed in the file POL\UPOLGCF.CPP:

```
/*===========================================================
                    UPOLGCF.CPP:
   EXPLOITATION OF POLYNOMIALS GCF AND LCM CALCULATION
============================================================*/

#include  "armath.h"

void ar_use_pol_gcf ()
{
  ar_polynomial  p, q, r;

  cout << "CALCULATION OF THE GCF AND LCM OF TWO \
          POLYNOMIALS\n\n";
  cout << "P (X) = "; cin >> p; if (errno) return;
  cout << "Q (X) = "; cin >> q; if (errno) return;

  cout << "\nGCF (P, Q) = ";

  r = ar_gcf_pol (p, q);
  if (! errno)
    cout << r;
  else
    cerr << "Impossible calculation\n";
  cout << "\nLCM (P, Q) = ";
  r = ar_lcm_pol (p, q);

  if (! errno)
    cout << r;
  else
    cerr << "Impossible calculation\n";

  ar_pause ();
}
```

The following tool is to be placed in the file POL\UPOLDERI.CPP:

```
/*===========================================================
                    UPOLDERI.CPP:
   EXPLOITATION TOOL OF DERIVATIVES OF POLYNOMIALS
============================================================*/

#include  "armath.h"
```

```
void  ar_use_pol_derivation ()
{
  ar_polynomial  p, q;
  int            n;

  cout << "N-TH DERIVATIVE OF A POLYNOMIAL\n\n";
  cout << "P (X) = "; cin >> p; if (errno) return;
  ar_read ("Order of the derivative: ", &n, AR_TINT);

  q = ar_der_pol (p, n);

  if (! errno)
    cout << q;
  else
    cerr << "Impossible calculation\n";

  ar_pause ();
}
```

8

Rational Fractions

The set composed of all polynomials, subject to the laws of addition and multiplication, has the structure of a commutative ring. The main insufficiency of this structure lies in the fact that polynomials of degree 1 or higher do not have a symmetrical polynomial for the multiplication law.

We define a rational fraction as the ratio of two polynomials:

$$R(x) = \frac{P(x)}{Q(x)} \qquad \text{with } Q(x) \neq 0$$

The polynomial P is called the numerator of the rational fraction. The polynomial Q, which must not be equal to zero, is the denominator.

Of course, the set of polynomials is included in the set of rational fractions; the latter has the structure of a commutative body.

If R is a rational fraction different from the fraction zero, its reciprocal is also a rational fraction:

$$R = \frac{P}{Q} \quad \Rightarrow \quad \frac{1}{R} = R^{-1} = \frac{Q}{P} \qquad \text{with } R \neq 0$$

Rational fractions are frequently used in signal treatment or the analysis of linear systems, during Laplace or Z transformations, to name just a few.

The tools for this chapter will be placed under the subdirectory FRAC.

1 The Class ar_fraction and its Elements

A rational fraction is entirely determined by the two given polynomials P and Q such that:

$$F = \frac{P}{Q}$$

Although this couple of polynomials (P, Q) is not unique, and is only a representation of the rational fraction, we call P the numerator of F and Q its denominator. In fact, it would be more correct to call them the associated numerator and denominator.

The class `ar_polynomial` and the associated tools presented in the previous chapter will prove extremely useful during calculations involving rational fractions.

This illustrates the advantage of object oriented programming, which allows one to build complex processing systems with autonomous tools that execute simple calculations. In this way, object oriented programming reduces error and effort.

1.1 Entry of a Fraction

One enters a rational fraction in two steps. First one enters the numerator, then the denominator.

The entry of these polynomials is identical to the entry process described in the previous chapter. The operator `>>` is overloaded, which lets us write `cin >> f` to summon the fraction entry tool.

This tool will be placed in the file FRAC\FRACENTR.CPP.

```
/*===========================================================
                      FRACENTR.CPP:
          ENTRY OF A FRACTION IN SYMBOLIC FORM
==========================================================*/

#include   "armath.h"

istream&  operator >> (istream& s, ar_fraction& f)
{
    f.clear ();

    cout << "Numerator    : "; cin >> f.numer;

    if (! errno)
      cout << "Denominator : "; cin >> f.denom;

    ar_nl;
    return s;
}
```

1.2 Fraction Display

The fraction is displayed in the form of two polynomials, separated by a horizontal line. The operator << is overloaded, which lets us write cout << f to display the fraction f.

This tool will be placed in the file FRAC\FRACDISP.CPP.

```
/*===========================================================
                    FRACDISP.CPP:
            DISPLAY OF A FRACTION IN SYMBOLIC FORM
=========================================================*/

#include  "armath.h"

ostream& operator << (ostream& s, ar_fraction& f)
{
   cout << f.numer;

   if ((f.denom.degree > 0) || (f.denom.readcoeff (0) != N1))
{
      cout << setfill ('-') << setw (20) << " " << "\n";
      cout << setfill (' ') << f.denom;
   }

   return s;
}
```

---

2   Simplification of Rational Fractions

2.1 Fraction Entry

Among all the representations $\dfrac{P}{Q}$ of a fraction F, there is one class called primary representations. $\dfrac{P_0}{Q_0}$ is a primary representation of F if:

$$\forall\,(P, Q) \in P^2[X] \text{ such that } F = \frac{P}{Q}$$

then $d° P > d° P_0$

$d° Q > d° Q_0$

or $P = \lambda P_0$

$Q = \lambda Q_0$ with $\lambda \in R.$

In other words, this means that P_0 and Q_0 are the polynomials of *minimum* degree which represent F. For example, a primary representation of:

$$F = \frac{x^2+4x-5}{x^2-1} = \frac{(x-1)\,(x+5)}{(x-1)\,(x+1)} \qquad \text{is} \qquad \frac{(x+5)}{(x+1)}$$

But $\dfrac{3x+15}{3x+3}$ is also a primary representation.

In order to find the primary representation of a rational function, one divides the numerator and the denominator by a GCF of these two polynomials.

2.2 Calculation Tool

The tool presented here does not simply seek a primary representation of F. Rather, it attempts to optimise its legibility by converting as many rational coefficients as possible into integers. In order to do this, it multiplies the numerator and denominator of the fraction by an appropriate rational number.

This improvement in presentation is optimal. It forms the only boolean parameter of the member function simp ().

This tool will be placed in the file FRAC\FRACSIMP.CPP.

```
/*==========================================================
                    FRACSIMP.CPP:
          SIMPLIFICATION OF A RATIONAL FRACTION
==========================================================*/

#include   "armath.h"

void ar_fraction::simp (int intcoeff)
{
    ar_polynomial   p;
    ar_number       z;
    long            pg, pp1, pp2;
    int             i;

    p = ar_gcf_pol (numer, denom);

    numer = numer / p; denom = denom / p;
    if (intcoeff)   {
        for (pg=0, pp1=0, i=0; i <= numer.degree; i++) {
            z = numer.readcoeff (i);
            if (! z.real)   {
                pg  = (pg)  ? ar_gcf (pg, z.p) : z.p;
                pp1 = (pp1) ? pp1 * z.q / ar_gcf (pp1, z.q) : z.q;
            }
        }
    }
```

```
for (pp2=0, i=0; i <= denom.degree; i++)  {
  z = denom.readcoeff (i);

  if (! z.real)  {
    pg  = (pg)  ? ar_gcf (pg, z.p) : z.p;
    pp2 = (pp2) ? pp2 * z.q / ar_gcf (pp2, z.q) : z.q;
  }
}

if (pg)  {
  z = ar_number (pp1 * pp2 / ar_gcf (pp1, pp2), pg);

  for (i = 0; i <= numer.degree; i++)
    numer.writecoeff (i, z * numer.readcoeff (i));

  for (i = 0; i <= denom.degree; i++)
    denom.writecoeff (i, z * denom.readcoeff (i));
  }
 }
}
```

2.3 Annotated Examples

Example 1

Let us consider the following fraction:

$$F(x) = \frac{2x^3-7x^2+12x-7}{6x^4-6x^3-5x^2+3x+2}$$

```
SIMPLIFICATION OF A FRACTION

Numerator    : 2X3 - 7X2 + 12X - 7
Denominator : 6X4 - 6X3 - 5X2 + 3X + 2
Do you want integer coeff ? n

+ 2 X2 - 5 X + 7
----------------
+ 6 X3 - 5 X - 2
```

The program has simplified the fraction by $(x-1)$, and provides:

$$F(x) = \frac{2x^2-5x+7}{6x^3-5x-2}$$

Example 2

Let us consider the following rational fraction:

$$F(x) = \frac{\frac{5}{3}x^2 + \frac{73}{18}x + \frac{7}{6}}{\frac{10}{3}x^2 + \frac{59}{12}x - \frac{35}{8}}$$

First we ask for the primary representation.

```
SIMPLIFICATION OF A FRACTION

Numerator    : 5/3X2 + 73/18X + 7/6
Denominator : 10/3X2 + 59/12X - 35/8
Do you want integer coeff ? n

+ 1/6 X + 1/18
--------------
+ 1/3 X - 5/24
```

Now we ask for a further simplification of the rational coefficients :

```
SIMPLIFICATION OF A FRACTION

Numerator    : 5/3X2 + 73/18X + 7/6
Denominator : 10/3X2 + 59/12X - 35/8
Do you want integer coeff ? y

+ 12 X + 4
----------
+ 24 X - 15
```

The program then gives $F(x) = \dfrac{12x+4}{24x-15}$.

3 Evaluation of a Fraction at a Point

3.1 Principle

One calculates the value of a fraction at a particular point by applying Horner's method to both numerator and denominator. This method is described in the preceding chapter.

If the denominator is zero, the fraction is undefined at x_0.

3.2 Calculation Tool

One evaluates a fraction at a particular point through the overloaded operator `()`. The only parameter of this function is x, the number for which F must be evaluated.

The function's return value contains the value of the fraction at x_0, if the fraction is defined (denominator is not zero). If not, the variable `errno` will be positioned at 1.

The tool is placed in the file `FRAC\FRAC.CPP`.

```
/*=========================================================
                      FRAC.CPP:
       CLASS AR_FRACTION AND ITS MEMBERS FUNCTIONS
=========================================================*/

#include  "armath.h"

int ar_fraction::zero (void)
{
   return numer.zero ();
}

void ar_fraction::clear (void)
{
   numer.clear ();
}

void ar_fraction::operator = (ar_fraction &f)
{
   numer = f.numer;
   denom = f.denom;
}

int operator == (ar_fraction &f1, ar_fraction &f2)
{
   if (! (f1.numer == f2.numer)) return FALSE;
   if (! (f1.denom == f2.denom)) return FALSE;
   return TRUE;
}

int operator != (ar_fraction &f1, ar_fraction &f2)
{
   return (! (f1 == f2));
}

ar_number ar_fraction::operator () (ar_number &x)
{
   return numer (x) / denom (x);
}
```

```
ar_fraction& operator~ (ar_fraction &f)
{
    static ar_fraction nf;
    nf.numer = f.denom; nf.denom = f.numer;
    return nf;
}
```

3.3 Annotated Example

We would like to determine the value of $F(x) = \dfrac{x^3 - 5x + 2}{x^2 - 1}$ at the points -2, $\dfrac{1}{2}$ and 2.

```
EVALUATION OF A FRACTION AT A POINT (F(xo))

Numerator    : X3 - 5X + 2
Denominator  : X2 - 1

+   X3 - 5 X + 2
---------------
+   X2 - 1

Value of xo : -2
F (xo) = + 4 / 3
Value of xo : 1/2
F (xo) = + 1 / 2
Value of xo : 2
F (xo) = - 0
Value of xo : 0
F (xo) = - 2
```

---

4 Inversion of a Rational Fraction

4.1 Principle

This calculation is simple, because if $\dfrac{P}{Q}$ is a representation of a fraction F, $\dfrac{Q}{P}$ is a representation of the function $\dfrac{1}{F}$. In addition, if $\dfrac{P}{Q}$ is primary, $\dfrac{Q}{P}$ is as well. The main advantage of this tool is that it allows one to transform a division of two fractions into a multiplication. This is accomplished by writing:

$$\frac{F_1}{F_2} = F_1 \cdot \left(\frac{1}{F_2}\right)$$

4.2 Calculation Tool

The overloaded operator $\sim$ has only one parameter, the fraction to be inverted. It returns the fraction $1/F$ as output.

This tool is placed in the file FRAC\FRAC.CPP (see section 1).

---

5 Multiplication of Two Rational Fractions

5.1 Principle

Let $F1 = \dfrac{P_1}{Q_1}$ and $F2 = \dfrac{P_2}{Q_2}$ two rational fractions.

The simplest way of calculating $F = \dfrac{P}{Q} = F_1.F_2$ is to calculate $P = P_1.P_2$ and $Q = Q_1.Q_2$, and then to simplify the resulting fraction. We will not use this method, because to do so one must calculate the GCF of two polynomials of high degree.

The following method is more efficient:

– simplify F_1 and F_2 separately at $F'_1 = \dfrac{P'_1}{Q'_1}$ and $F'_2 = \dfrac{P'_2}{Q'_2}$

– form the intermediate fractions $F_3 = \dfrac{P'_1}{Q'_2}$ and $F_4 = \dfrac{P'_2}{Q'_1}$

– simplify F_3 and F_4 at $F'_3 = \dfrac{P'_3}{Q'_3}$ and $F'_4 = \dfrac{P'_4}{Q'_4}$

– F_1F_2 is then equal to $\dfrac{P'_3.P'_4}{Q'_3.Q'_4}$, and does not need to be simplified further.

In short, one must simplify before multiplying, and not the contrary.

5.2 Calculation Tool

The operator * is overloaded, so that one may write F = F1 * F2 in order to multiply the fractions F1 and F2. The result is stored in F.

The operator *= is also overloaded, which allows us to write F *= F1 instead of F = F * F1.

Remarks concerning the multiplication of polynomials are also valid for rational fractions; one cannot write:

        F1 * F2 * F3

nor can one write:

        (F1 * F2) + (F3 * F4).

The tool will be placed in the file FRAC\FRACMUL.CPP.

```
/*=========================================================
                      FRACMUL.CPP:
            MULTIPLICATION OF TWO FRACTIONS
==========================================================*/

#include   "armath.h"

//---------------------------- OVERLOADING OF OPERATOR *

ar_fraction& operator *  (ar_fraction& f1, ar_fraction& f2)
{
  static ar_fraction  f;
  ar_fraction         nf1, nf2;

  f1.simp (FALSE); f2.simp (FALSE);

  nf1.numer = f2.numer; nf1.denom = f1.denom;
  nf2.numer = f1.numer; nf2.denom = f2.denom;
  nf1.simp (FALSE); nf2.simp (FALSE);

  f.numer = nf1.numer * nf2.numer;
  f.denom = nf1.denom * nf2.denom;
  return f;
}

ar_fraction& operator *  (ar_number& n,  ar_fraction& f1)
{
  static ar_fraction f;

  f.numer = n * f1.numer;
  f.denom = f1.denom;
  f.simp (FALSE);
  return f;
}

//---------------------------- OVERLOADING OF OPERATOR *=

ar_fraction &  ar_fraction::operator *= (ar_fraction &f)
{
  *this = *this * f;
  return *this;
}

ar_fraction &  ar_fraction::operator *= (ar_number &n)
{
  *this = n * *this;
  return *this;
}
```

5.3 Annotated example

Consider the two fractions:

$$F1(x) = \frac{x-1}{x^2+5x-7} \qquad F2(x) = \frac{x+3}{x^2-1}$$

The product $F1.F2$ corresponds to:

$$F(x) = F1(x).F2(x) = \frac{(x-1)\ (x+3)}{(x^2+5x-7)\ (x^2-1)}$$

The program simplifies the fraction by $(x-1)$ and yields the result:

$$F(x) = \frac{x+3}{(x^2+5x-7)\ (x+1)} = \frac{x+3}{x^3+6x^2-2x-7}$$

```
MULTIPLICATION OF TWO FRACTIONS

F1 :
Numerator    : X - 1
Denominator : X2 + 5X - 7

F2 :
Numerator    : X + 3
Denominator : X2 - 1

+   X + 3
--------
+   X3 + 6 X2 - 2 X - 7
```

6 Linear Combination of Two Fractions

6.1 Principle

Let us consider the two fractions $F_1 = \dfrac{P_1}{Q_1}$ and $F_2 = \dfrac{P_2}{Q_2}$ as well as two numbers a and b.

We wish to calculate the following linear combination:

$$F = a\,F_1 + b\,F_2 = \frac{a\,P_1.Q_2 + b\,P_2.Q_1}{Q_1.Q_2}$$

However, the previous section shows that it is preferable to simplify before calculating. Here it is apparent that the common denominator will not be Q_1Q_2, but rather LCM (Q_1, Q_2) or else Q_1Q_2 / GCF (Q_1, Q_2).

Therefore, we calculate the representation of F with the following formulas:

$$P = \frac{a\,P_1Q_2 + b\,P_2Q_1}{\text{PGCF}\,(Q_1, Q_2)}$$

$$Q = \frac{Q_1Q_2}{\text{PGCF}\,(Q_1, Q_2)}$$

REMARK: The representation obtained is not necessarily primary as a result of the addition. One should simplify it further.

6.2 Calculation Tool

The operators $+$ and $-$ are overloaded, which allows us to write $F1 + F2$ or $F1 - F2$ in order to add or subtract two fractions.

The overloaded $*$ operator applied to a couple (number, polynomial) takes care of the multiplication of a fraction by a scalar quantity.

The corresponding combined operators $+=$, $*=$, $-=$ are also overloaded.

The tools concerning $+$, $-$, $+=$, $-=$ are stored in the file FRACSUM.CPP, and those concerning $*$ and $*=$ in FRACMUL.CPP.

The tool ar_use_frac_comlin, stored in the file UFRALC.CPP allows one to enter the two numbers a and b which are necessary for the calculation of the linear combination.

The four addition and subtraction tools will be placed in the file FRAC\FRACSUM.CPP.

```
/*==========================================================
                        FRACSUM.CPP:
                    SUM OF TWO FRACTIONS
   ======================================================*/

#include   "armath.h"

ar_fraction & operator + (ar_fraction &f1, ar_fraction &f2)

{
   static ar_fraction    nf;
   ar_polynomial         p, q, r;

   p = ar_gcf_pol (f1.denom, f2.denom);
   q = f1.numer * f2.denom;
   r = f2.numer * f1.denom;

   nf.numer = (q + r) / p;
   nf.denom = (f1.denom * f2.denom) / p;
   nf.simp (FALSE);
   return nf;
}
```

```
/*---------------------- SUBTRACTION OF TWO FRACTIONS   */
ar_fraction & operator - (ar_fraction &f1, ar_fraction &f2)
{
  static ar_fraction  nf;
  ar_polynomial         p, q, r;

  p = ar_gcf_pol (f1.denom, f2.denom);
  q = f1.numer * f2.denom;
  r = f2.numer * f1.denom;

  nf.numer = (q - r) / p;
  nf.denom = (f1.denom * f2.denom) / p;

  nf.simp (FALSE);
  return nf;
}
```

6.3 Annotated Example

Addition is the simplest case of linear combination among fractions. It corresponds to:

$$a = b = 1$$

Let us calculate the sum of:

$$F1(x) = \frac{2x+3}{x-1} \qquad F2(x) = \frac{-5x+1}{x^2-1}$$

```
LINEAR COMBINATION OF TWO FRACTIONS (aF1 + bF2)

Coefficient a : 1
F1 :
Numerator    : 2X + 3
Denominator : X - 1

Coefficient b : 1
F2 :
Numerator    : -5X + 1
Denominator : X2 - 1

+ 2 X2 + 4
----------
+   X2 - 1
```

The sum fraction is then:

$$F(x) = F1(x) + F2(x) = \frac{(2x+3)\,(x+1) - 5x+1}{x^2-1} = \frac{2x^2+4}{x^2-1}$$

7. Substitution of Fractions

7.1 Principle

We have seen in polynomial substitution that the notation $R(x) = P[Q(x)]$ indicates the replacement of x with $Q(x)$ in the expression P. We will define a substituted fraction in the same way.

Suppose $F1 = \dfrac{P_1}{Q_1}$ and $F2 = \dfrac{P_2}{Q_2}$ are two rational fractions. The notation:

$$F = F1\ [F2(x)]$$

indicates that we replace x with $F2(x)$ in the expression $F1$. Let us write F as a function of the polynomials P_1, Q_1, P_2 and Q_2:

$$F(x) = \frac{P_1[\frac{P_2}{Q_2}]}{Q_1[\frac{P_2}{Q_2}]} = \frac{a_0 + a_1[\frac{P_2}{Q_2}] + \ldots + a_{p_1}[\frac{P_2}{Q_2}]^{p_1}}{b_0 + b_1[\frac{P_2}{Q_2}] + \ldots + b_{q_1}[\frac{P_2}{Q_2}]^{q_1}}$$

where (a_i) are the coefficients of the polynomial P_1 of degree p_1, and (b_i) are the coefficients of the polynomial Q_1 of degree q_1. This expression can also be written:

$$F(x) = \frac{a_0Q_2^{p_1} + a_1P_2Q_2^{p_1-1} + a_2P_2^2Q_2^{p_1-2} + \ldots + a_{p_1}P_2^{p_1}\quad Q_2^{q_1}}{b_0Q_2^{q_1} + b_1P_2Q_2^{q_1-1} + b_2P_2^2Q_2^{q_1-2} + \ldots + b_{q_1}P_2^{q_1}\quad Q_2^{p_1}}$$

The numerator and the denominator are actually polynomials at P_2 with polynomial coefficients. In the program, they are calculated through a generalisation of Horner's method.

7.2 Calculation Tool

The input parameters of the tool `ar_subst_frac` are the two fractions $F1$ and $F2$. In the output, the value of the function contains `F1 [F2]`.

The tool will be placed in the file `FRAC\FRACSUBS.CPP`.

```
/*=============================================================
                    FRACSUBS.CPP:
            SUBSTITUTION OF TWO FRACTIONS
=============================================================*/

#include   "armath.h"

ar_fraction & ar_subst_frac (ar_fraction &f1,ar_fraction &f2)
{
```

```
static ar_fraction   nf;
ar_polynomial        p, q;
int                  delta, i;

if (! p.open (0)) {errno = 1; return nf;}
if (! q.open (0)) {errno = 1; return nf;}

q.writecoeff (0, N1);
for (i = f1.numer.degree; i >= 0; i--)  {
  p *= f2.numer;
  p += f1.numer.readcoeff (i) * q;
  q *= f2.denom;
}
nf.numer = p;

p.clear ();
q.clear (); q.writecoeff (0, N1);
for (i = f1.denom.degree; i >= 0; i--)  {
  p *= f2.numer;
  p += f1.denom.readcoeff (i) * q;
  q *= f2.denom;
}

nf.denom = p;
if ((delta = f1.denom.degree - f1.numer.degree) > 0)
  for (i = 1; i <= delta; i++)
    nf.numer *= f2.denom;
if (delta < 0)
  for (i = 1; i <= - delta; i++)
    nf.denom *= f2.denom;

nf.simp (FALSE);

return nf;
}
```

7.3 Annotated Examples

Example 1

Let us consider the two rational fractions $F1(X) = \dfrac{X-2}{4X+3}$ and $F2(x) = \dfrac{x-1}{x+1}$.

We then obtain:

$$F(x) = F1[F2(x)] = \frac{\dfrac{x-1}{x+1} - 2}{4\left(\dfrac{x-1}{x+1}\right) + 3} = \frac{-x-3}{7x-1}$$

```
SUBSTITUTION OF TWO FRACTIONS

F1 :
Numerator ` : X - 2
Denominator : 4X + 3
F2 :
Numerator   : X - 1
Denominator : X + 1

-   X - 3
--------
+ 7 X - 1
```

Example 2

The remarks concerning the substitution of polynomials remain pertinent. In particular, it is possible to raise the fraction $F2$ to the power n. In order to do this, one sets:

$$F1\ (X) = X^n \qquad \text{then:} \qquad F1[F2(x)] = [F2(x)]^n$$

For example, let us calculate $F(x) = [\dfrac{\frac{1}{2}x}{x^2-5}]^3:$

```
SUBSTITUTION OF TWO FRACTIONS

F1 :
Numerator    : X3
Denominator  : 1
F2 :
Numerator    : 1/2X
Denominator  : X2 - 5

+ 1/8 X3
--------
+   X6 - 15 X4 + 75 X2 - 125
```

---

8 Successive Derivatives of a Fraction

8.1 Principle

Our aim is to determine the expression of the nth derivative of the rational fraction:

$$F1 = \frac{P_0}{Q_0}$$

The first derivative of $F1$ is:

$$F1' = \frac{P_0'Q_0 - P_0 Q_0'}{Q_0{}^2} = \frac{P_1}{Q_1}$$

To obtain the second derivative, we derive $F1'$:

$$F1'' = (F1')' = \frac{P_1' Q_1 - P_1 Q_1'}{Q_1{}^2} = \frac{P_2}{Q_2}$$

Generally, if $F1^{(n)} = \dfrac{P_n}{Q_n}$, we find $F1^{(n+1)}$ using:

$$F1^{(n+1)} = \frac{P_n' Q_n - P_n Q_n'}{Q_n{}^2}$$

8.2 Calculation Tool

The input parameters of the tool ar_der_frac are the fraction F to be derived, and n, the order of the desired derivation.

The return value of the function contains a primary representation of $(F)^{(n)}$.

The tool will be placed in the file FRAC\FRACDER.CPP.

```
/*===========================================================
                     FRACDER.CPP:
              N-TH DERIVATIVE OF A FRACTION
   =========================================================*/

#include   "armath.h"

ar_fraction & ar_der_frac (ar_fraction &f, int n)
{
  static ar_fraction  nf;
  ar_polynomial       p, q;
  int                 i;

  for (i = 1, nf = f; i <= n; i++)   {
    p = ar_der_pol (nf.numer, 1) * nf.denom;
    q = ar_der_pol (nf.denom, 1) * nf.numer;
    nf.numer = p - q;
    nf.denom = nf.denom * nf.denom; nf.simp (TRUE);
  }

  return nf;
}
```

8.3 Annotated Examples

Example 1

The derivative of the function:

$$F1(x) = \frac{3x^2+2x+1}{4x^2+5x+56}$$

is equal to:

$$F1'(x) = \frac{7x^2+328x+107}{16x^4+40x^3+473x^2+560x+3136}$$

The program confirms this result:

```
N-TH DERIVATIVE OF A FRACTION

Numerator    : 3X2 + 2X + 1
Denominator : 4X2 + 5X + 56
Order of the derivative : 1

+ 7 X2 + 328 X + 107
--------------------
+ 16 X4 + 40 X3 + 473 X2 + 560 X + 3136
```

Example 2

Here is an example of how to calculate the fifth derivative:

```
N-TH DERIVATIVE OF A FRACTION

Numerator    : X - 1
Denominator : X + 1
Order of the derivative : 5

+ 240
-----
+   X6 + 6 X5 + 15 X4 + 20 X3 + 15 X2 + 6 X + 1
```

Thus, a representation of the fifth derivative of:

$$f(x) = \frac{x-1}{x+1}$$

is:

$$f^{(5)}(x) = \frac{240}{x^6+6x^5+15x^4+20x^3+15x^2+6x+1}$$

9   Partial fractions decomposition

9.1 Principle and Theoretical Review

Let us consider a rational fraction $F = \dfrac{P}{Q}$. Its denominator is written in the form of a product of primary polynomials.

We recall that a polynomial with primary real coefficients is either of degree 1 or of degree 2. In neither case does it have a real root. Thus, the polynomial $Q(x)$ must have the following form:

$$Q(x) = [H_1(x)]^{\alpha_1} \cdot [H_2(x)]^{\alpha_2} \ldots [H_f(x)]^{\alpha_f}$$

where the polynomials $H_i(x)$ are primary and different by pairs.

We can then prove that there is one unique decomposition of the fraction F, of the following form:

$$F(x) = E(x) + B_1(x) + B_2(x) + \ldots + B_f(x)$$

where $E(x)$ is a polynomial called integer portion of $F(x)$ and the terms $B_i(x)$ have the form:

$$B_i(x) = \sum_{j=1}^{\alpha_i} \frac{L_{ij}(x)}{[H_i(x)]^j}$$

where the polynomials $L_{ij}(x)$ have degrees strictly smaller than that of H_i.

Thus, for the elements "of type one", that is, the polynomials of degree 1, $L_{ij}(x)$ must be a scalar quantity a_{ij}.

For the elements of "type two," $L_{ij}(x)$ is a polynomial with a degree less than or equal to 1. This polynomial is written as $a_{ij} + b_{ij}x$.

For example, let us consider the fraction:

$$F(x) = \frac{2x^9 + 1}{x^3(x^2 + x + 1)^2}$$

The primary polynomials are:

$$H_1(x) = x \qquad\qquad (\alpha_1 = 3)$$
$$H_2(x) = x^2 + x + 1 \qquad\qquad (\alpha_2 = 2)$$

Theory permits us to state that the fraction can be written in a unique manner as:

$$F(x) = E(x) \; + \; \underbrace{\frac{a_{11}}{x} + \frac{a_{12}}{x^2} + \frac{a_{13}}{x^3}}_{[\qquad B_1(x) \qquad]} \; + \; \underbrace{\frac{a_{21} + b_{21}x}{x^2 + x + 1} + \frac{a_{22} + b_{22}x}{(x^2 + x + 1)^2}}_{[\qquad B_2(x) \qquad]}$$

To decompose the fraction $F(x)$ into simple elements means finding the integer portion $E(x)$. It also means finding the group of coefficients a_{ij} and b_{ij} which correspond to the different factors.

9.2 Calculation Tool

The fraction to be decomposed is not provided in the form of a variable resembling `ar_fraction`. The program asks for the following three input parameters:
  – `numer`, the polynomial representing the numerator of the fraction;
  – `nb_factor`, the number of factors of the denominator;
  – `factor`, vector of variables of the type `ar_factor`.
We have defined the type `ar_factor`, in ARMATH.H, as follows:

```
class ar_factor {
   public :
      ar_number a, b, c;
      int       power;
}
```

where a, b, c are the coefficients of the polynomial $H_i(x) = ax^2 + bx + c$ of the considered factor (a is zero if the factor is of degree 1). `power` is the power attributed to this factor, thus α_i.

The output parameters of the tool `ar_partial_fraction` are:
  – `intportion`, polynomial which provides the integer portion of the decomposition;
  – `V`, vector (type defined in chapter 9) which contains the list of all the coefficients a_{ij} and b_{ij}, *in the order in which they appear in the previous theoretical decomposition*;
The result of the function is a Boolean which indicates if the calculation could be completed (`TRUE`) or not (`FALSE`).

The computer first checks the validity of the entered data (in particular the irreducibility of the fraction), and may display an appropriate error message.

If the input parameters are correct, it assimilates the initial fraction to the sum of the simple elements which must be obtained. It does this for several values of x. Thus, it creates a linear system of several equations. We will solve this system using the Gauss-Jordan method, which is described in chapter 9, Matrices and Vectors.

The tool `ar_use_frac_partial`, introduced at the end of the chapter, allows one to enter the numerator of the fraction, as well as each of the factors (one enters the power 0 after entering the last factor).

After using the calculation tool, it displays the integer portion, and the coefficients associated with each factor.

The calculation tool will be placed in the file FRAC\FRACPART.CPP.

```
/*===========================================================
                    FRACPART.CPP:
          PARTIAL FRACTION DECOMPOSITION
  =========================================================*/

#include   "armath.h"

#define  STEP    ar_number (1, 4)

int  ar_partial_fraction (ar_polynomial& numer,
        int nb_factor, ar_factor factor [],
        ar_polynomial& intportion, ar_vector& u)
{
  ar_matrix      m;
  ar_vector      v;
  ar_polynomial  inter, denom, r;
  ar_number      x, y, z, t, w;
  int            i, j, k, h, ok, dim;

  /*---------------------------------------------------------
            Check irreducibility of each factor
  ---------------------------------------------------------*/
  if ((nb_factor < 1) || (nb_factor > AR_MAXFACT))
    return FALSE;

  for (i = 0; i < nb_factor; i++)
    if (! factor [i].a.zero ())   {
      y = factor [i].b * factor [i].b - ar_number (4) *
          factor [i].a * factor [i].c;
      if ((y.positive ()) || (y.zero ()))   {
        cerr << "One of the factors is not irreducible\n";
        return FALSE;
      }
    }


  /*---------------------------------------------------------
            Check all factors are different
  ---------------------------------------------------------*/
  for (i = 0; i < nb_factor; i++)
    for (j = 0; j < i; j++)
      if ((factor [i].a == factor [j].a)
      && (factor [i].b == factor [j].b)
      && (factor [i].c == factor [j].c))   {
        cerr << "At least two factors are identical\n";
        return FALSE;
      }
```

```
/*----------------------------------------------------------
                Calculate system dimension
   ----------------------------------------------------*/
for (i = 0, dim = 0; i < nb_factor; i++)   {
  dim += factor [i].power;
  if (! factor [i].a.zero ()) dim += factor [i].power;
}


/*----------------------------------------------------------
          Memory allocation and initializations
   ----------------------------------------------------*/
if (! m.open (dim, dim)) {errno = 1;  return FALSE;}
if (! v.open (dim))        {errno = 1;  return FALSE;}
if (! denom.open (2))      {errno = 1;  return FALSE;}


/*----------------------------------------------------------
            Check irreducibility of fraction
   ----------------------------------------------------*/
for (i = 0; i < nb_factor; i++)   {
  denom.writecoeff (0, factor [i].c);
  denom.writecoeff (1, factor [i].b);
  denom.writecoeff (2, factor [i].a);
  inter = ar_div_pol (numer, denom, r);
  if (r.zero ())   {
    cerr << "The fraction is not irreducible\n";
    return FALSE;
  }
}


/*----------------------------------------------------------
        Calculation of denominator's polynomial
   ----------------------------------------------------*/
denom.clear ();
denom.writecoeff (0, N1);
if (! inter.open (2))     {errno = 1;  return FALSE;}

for (i = 0; i < nb_factor; i++)   {
  inter.writecoeff (0, factor [i].c);
  inter.writecoeff (1, factor [i].b);
  inter.writecoeff (2, factor [i].a);
  for (j = 0; j < factor [i].power; j++)
    denom *= inter;
}


/*----------------------------------------------------------
                Calculate integer portion
   ----------------------------------------------------*/
intportion = ar_div_pol (numer, denom, r);
```

```
/*----------------------------------------------------------
                Fills system to be inverted
----------------------------------------------------------*/
x = - STEP * ar_number (2 + dim, 2);

for (i = 1; i <= dim; i++)  {
  //-- Eliminate an x which would make the denominator null
  do  {
    x += STEP; ok = TRUE;
    for (k = 0; k < nb_factor; k++)
      if ((factor [k].c + x * (factor [k].b +
          x * factor [k].a)).small ())
        ok = FALSE;
  } while (! ok);
  //-------------- Fills line i of matrix
  for (j = 0, k = 0; k < nb_factor; k++)  {
    z = denom (x);
    t = factor[k].c + x * (factor[k].b + factor[k].a * x);
    for (h = 0; h < factor [k].power; h++)  {
      z /= t;
      m.writecoeff (i, ++j, z);
      if (! factor [k].a.zero ())
        m.writecoeff (i, ++j, z * x);
    }
  }
  v.writecoeff (i, r (x));
}

/*----------------------------------------------------------
                  Linear system solving
----------------------------------------------------------*/
u = ar_lin_sys (m, v, z);

return (! errno);
}
```

9.3 Annotated Examples

Example 1

Let us consider the decomposition:

$$\frac{1}{(x-1)\,(x+1)} = \frac{\frac{1}{2}}{x-1} + \frac{-\frac{1}{2}}{x+1}.$$

In this example, the integer portion is zero.

```
PARTIAL FRACTION DECOMPOSITION

Numerator : 1

Entry of factor 1 :
Power (or 0 to exit) : 1
Coeff. of X2 : 0
Coeff. of X  : 1
Constant     : -1

Entry of factor 2 :
Power (or 0 to exit) : 1
Coeff. of X2 : 0
Coeff. of X  : 1
Constant     : 1

Entry of factor 3 :
Power (or 0 to exit) : 0

Integer portion :
0

Factor related terms 1
A [1, 1] = + 1 / 2

Factor related terms 2
A [2, 1] = - 1 / 2
```

Example 2

Let us return to the fraction in the previous section:

$$F(x) = \frac{2x^9 + 1}{x^3 \, (x^2 + x + 1)^2}$$

```
PARTIAL FRACTION DECOMPOSITION

Numerator : 2X9 + 1

Entry of factor 1 :
Power (or 0 to exit) : 3
Coeff. of X2 : 0
Coeff. of X  : 1
Constant     : 0

Entry of factor 2 :
Power (or 0 to exit) : 2
```

```
Coeff. of X2 : 1
Coeff. of X  : 1
Constant     : 1

Entry of factor 3 :
Power (or 0 to exit) : 0

Integer portion :
+ 2 X2 - 4 X + 2

Factor related terms 1
A [1, 1] = 1
A [1, 2] = -2
A [1, 3] = 1

Factor related terms 2
A [2, 1] = -3
B [2, 1] = 3
A [2, 2] = 3
B [2, 2] = -2.687405853408e-13
```

Thus, the decomposition of F(x) is as follows:

$$F(x) = [2x^2{-}4x{+}2] + [\frac{1}{x} + \frac{(-2)}{x^2} + \frac{1}{x^3}] + [\frac{(-3)+3x}{x^2+x+1} + \frac{3+0x,}{(x^2+x+1)^2}]$$

    integer portion   portion related   portion related

                   to the first factor   to the second factor

Example 3

```
PARTIAL FRACTION DECOMPOSITION

Numerator : 2X4 - 4X3 - 4X2 - 4X + 3

Entry of factor 1 :
Power (or 0 to exit) : 1
Coeff. of X2 : 0
Coeff. of X  : 1
Constant     : -3

Entry of factor 2 :
Power (or 0 to exit) : 1
Coeff. of X2 : 1
Coeff. of X  : 1
Constant     : 1
```

```
Entry of factor 3 :
Power (or 0 to exit) : 0

Integer portion :
+ 2 X

Factor related terms 1
A [1, 1] = + 9 / 13

Factor related terms 2
A [2, 1] = - 10 / 13
B [2, 1] = - 9 / 13
```

Thus, the fraction is written as:

$$\frac{3-4x-4x^2-4x^3+2x^4}{(x-3)(x^2+x+1)} = 2x + \frac{\frac{9}{13}}{x-3} + \frac{(-\frac{10}{13}) + (-\frac{9}{13})x}{x^2+x+1}$$

We obtain the coefficients with maximum precision. The degrees of the linear systems solved by the program are 2, 7 and 3 respectively.

In fact, the degree of the system is equal to the sum of the highest powers of x in the denominator. As long as the latter remains less than 10, the precision generally remains very good.

Let us examine the following example, in which the system degree is 18:

$$F(x) = \frac{x+2}{(x^2+x+1)^9}$$

The theoretical coefficients are all zero, except $a_{1,9} = 2$ and $b_{1,9} = 1$. Here are the results given by the program.

```
PARTIAL FRACTION DECOMPOSITION

Numerator : X + 2

Entry of factor 1 :
Power (or 0 to exit) : 9
Coeff. of X2 : 1
Coeff. of X  : 1
Constant     : 1

Entry of factor 2 :
Power (or 0 to exit) : 0

Integer portion :
0
```

```
Factor related terms 1
A [1, 1] = 2.982976185506e-09
B [1, 1] = -6.94585303336e-10
A [1, 2] = -4.595278851882e-08
B [1, 2] = 6.203762871471e-09
A [1, 3] = 2.984781399817e-07
B [1, 3] = -6.431315535682e-09
A [1, 4] = -1.068355071965e-06
B [1, 4] = -1.138014283364e-07
A [1, 5] = 2.306942304742e-06
B [1, 5] = 5.690132023339e-07
A [1, 6] = -3.080432669833e-06
B [1, 6] = -1.216153187933e-06
A [1, 7] = 2.486236329702e-06
B [1, 7] = 1.357152241255e-06
A [1, 8] = -1.109799669052e-06
B [1, 8] = -7.707812210711e-07
A [1, 9] = 2.000000209901
B [1, 9] = 1.000000175493
```

The average precision is on the order of 10^{-6}.

We have limited the degree of the system to be solved to 20. In this way, we can maintain an acceptable precision level. If one tries to enter an overly complicated fraction, the program will refuse it and display the message, "the denominator occupies too much space." However, it is still possible to modify the system's maximum degree: one must then be extremely cautious in interpreting the results.

One may increase precision significantly during fraction decompositions which create systems of high degree. To do this, it is necessary to adjust the constant HX. In general, reducing HX improves precision (HX = 0,1 for example).

10 Numerical Errors and Precision of the Results

In this chapter, we have presented a wide range of tools. These tools are used in the execution, and especially the verification, of the most common calculations involving rational fractions.

When the fractions have high degrees, the calculations are abundant (the execution can take several seconds). Generally, however, the execution remains much faster and more reliable than by hand! The main difficulty is the need to reduce the fraction to its primary representation. We have seen that this involves the calculation of the GCF of polynomials. Furthermore, GCF calculation is relatively imprecise. Nevertheless, the precision of the coefficients themselves remains excellent in most cases.

11 Exploitation Tools

The following tools allow the direct utilisation of the tools described above.

The following tool is to be placed in the file `FRAC\UFRASIMP.CPP`:

```
/*===========================================================
                        UFRASIMP.CPP:
          UTILISATION OF SIMPLIFICATION OF FRACTIONS
=========================================================*/

#include  "armath.h"

void ar_use_frac_simplification ()
{
  ar_fraction  f;
  int          intcoeff;

  cout << "SIMPLIFICATION OF A FRACTION\n\n";

  cin >> f; if (errno) return;
  ar_read ("Do you want integer coeff ? : ", &intcoeff,
          AR_TBOO);

  f.simp (intcoeff);

  if (! errno)
    cout << f;
  else
    cerr << "Impossible calculation\n";

  ar_pause ();
}
```

The following tool is to be placed in the file `FRAC\UFRAEVAL.CPP`:

```
/*===========================================================
                        UFRAEVAL.CPP:
            UTILISATION OF EVALUATION OF FRACTIONS
=========================================================*/

#include  "armath.h"

void ar_use_frac_evaluation ()
{
  ar_fraction  f;
  ar_number    a, b;
```

```
  cout << "EVALUATION OF A FRACTION AT A POINT (F (xo))\n\n";
  cin  >> f; if (errno) return;
  cout << f;

  do  {
     ar_nl;
     ar_read ("Value of xo : ", &a, AR_TNUM);
     cout <<  "F (xo) = ";

     b = f (a);

     if (! errno)
        cout << b;
     else
        cerr << "Impossible calculation\n";

  } while (! a.zero ());

  ar_pause ();
}
```

The following tool is to be placed in the file FRAC\UFRAMUL.CPP:

```
/*============================================================
                     UFRAMUL.CPP:
     UTILISATION OF MULTIPLICATION OF TWO FRACTIONS
============================================================*/

#include  "armath.h"

void  ar_use_frac_multiplication ()
{
  ar_fraction  f, f1, f2;

  cout << "MULTIPLICATION OF TWO FRACTIONS\n\n";

  cout << "F1 : \n"; cin >> f1; if (errno) return;
  cout << "F2 : \n"; cin >> f2; if (errno) return;

  f = f1 * f2;

  if (! errno)
    cout << f;
  else
    cerr << "Impossible multiplication\n";

  ar_pause ();
}
```

The following tool is to be placed in the file FRAC\UFRAINV.CPP:

```
/*============================================================
                      UFRAINV.CPP:
          UTILISATION OF INVERSION OF FRACTIONS
   =========================================================*/

#include  "armath.h"

void ar_use_frac_inversion ()
{
  ar_fraction  f;

  cout << "INVERSION OF A FRACTION\n\n";

  cout << "Fraction to invert :\n";
  cin  >> f; if (errno) return;

  f = ~f;

  if (! errno)
    cout << "1 / f : \n" << f;
  else
    cerr << "Impossible calculation\n";

  ar_pause ();
}
```

The following tool is to be placed in the file FRAC\UFRALC.CPP:

```
/*============================================================
                      UFRALC.CPP:
   UTILISATION OF LINEAR COMBINATION OF TWO FRACTIONS
   =========================================================*/

#include  "armath.h"

void ar_use_frac_lincomb ()
{
  ar_fraction  f, f1, f2;
  ar_number    a, b;

  cout << "LINEAR COMBINATION OF TWO FRACTIONS
            (aF1 + bF2)\n\n";
  ar_read ("Coefficient a : ", &a, AR_TNUM);
  cout << "F1 : \n"; cin >> f1; if (errno) return;
  ar_read ("Coefficient b : ", &b, AR_TNUM);
  cout << "F2 : \n"; cin >> f2; if (errno) return;
```

```
  f1 *= a ; f2 *= b; f = f1 + f2;

  if (! errno)
    cout << f;
  else
    cerr << "Impossible calculation\n";
  ar_pause ();
}
```

The following tool is to be placed in the file FRAC\UFRASUBS.CPP:

```
/*===========================================================
                      UFRASUBS.CPP:
       UTILISATION OF SUBSTITUTION OF TWO FRACTIONS
=========================================================*/

#include  "armath.h"

void  ar_use_frac_substitution ()
{
  ar_fraction  f, f1, f2;

  cout << "SUBSTITUTION OF TWO FRACTIONS\n\n";
  cout << "F1 : \n"; cin >> f1; if (errno) return;
  cout << "F2 : \n"; cin >> f2; if (errno) return;

  f = ar_subst_frac (f1, f2);

  if (! errno)
    cout << f;
  else
    cerr << "Impossible substitution\n";
  ar_pause ();
}
```

The following tool is to be placed in the file FRAC\UFRADER.CPP:

```
/*===========================================================
                      UFRADER.CPP:
        UTILISATION OF N-TH DERIVATION OF FRACTIONS
=========================================================*/

#include  "armath.h"

void  ar_use_frac_derivation ()
{
  int          n;
  ar_fraction  f1, f2;
```

```
   cout << "N-TH DIFFERENTIATION OF A FRACTION\n\n";
   cin >> f1; if (errno) return;
   ar_read ("Order of the derivative : ", &n, AR_TINT);

   f2 = ar_der_frac (f1, n);

   if (! errno)
     cout << f2;
   else
     cerr << "Impossible calculation\n";

   ar_pause ();
}
```

The following tool is to be placed in the file FRAC\UFRAPART.CPP:

```
/*============================================================
                       UFRAPART.CPP:
      UTILISATION OF PARTIAL FRACTION DECOMPOSITION
  ============================================================*/

#include   "armath.h"

void  ar_use_frac_partial ()
{
  ar_polynomial   numer, intportion;
  ar_factor       factor [AR_MAXFACT];
  ar_vector       u;
  int             nb_factor, i, j ,k;

  cout << "PARTIAL FRACTION DECOMPOSITION\n\n";

  cout << "Numerator : "; cin >> numer; if (errno) return;
  ar_nl;

  i = 0;
  do  {
    cout << "Entry of factor " << (i + 1) << " : \n";
    ar_read ("Power (or 0 to exit) :  ",
          &factor [i].power, AR_TINT);

    if (factor [i].power)  {
      ar_read ("Coeff. of X2 :  ", &factor [i].a, AR_TNUM);
      ar_read ("Coeff. of X  :  ", &factor [i].b, AR_TNUM);
      ar_read ("Constant     :  ", &factor [i].c, AR_TNUM);
    }
    i ++; ar_nl;
  } while ((i < AR_MAXFACT / 2) && (factor [i - 1].power));
```

```
  nb_factor = i - 1;
  ar_nl;

  if (ar_partial_fraction (numer, nb_factor, factor,
                           intportion, u))  {

    cout << "\n\nInteger portion : \n" << intportion;

    for (j = 0, i = 0; i < nb_factor; i++)  {
      cout << "\nTerms relatives to factor " << (i + 1)
           << "\n";
      for (k = 0; k < factor [i].power; k ++)  {
        cout << "A [" << (i+1) << ", " << (k+1) << " ] = "
             << u.readcoeff (++j) << "\n";
        if (! factor [i].a.zero ())  {
        cout << "B [" << (i+1) << ", " << (k+1) << " ] = "
             << u.readcoeff (++j) << "\n";
        }
      }
    }
  }
  else
    cerr << "Impossible calculation\n";

  ar_pause ();
}
```

9

Matrices and Vectors

Calculations of matrices and vectors are extremely frequent in all the fields of physics. Many problems in optics, in mechanics, or in electromagnetism lead to linear systems or to a search for eigenvalues, and most of the time their solution can be found numerically (let us take as an example the method of the finite elements, very often used in aeronautics for the calculation of flows and pressures).

The tools shown in this chapter will make it possible to do elementary operations on vectors (linear combinations, scalar products, mixed and vectorial) and on matrices (linear combinations, product, calculation of the trace) but also operations of a more complex nature such as the calculation of the determinant, of the rank, of the eigenvalues and of the inverse of a matrix, not to forget the calculation of its raising to the power N.

We will also study in detail how to solve linear systems and how to calculate the image of a vector with the help of a linear application, defined by its matrix.

1 The Classes ar_matrix and ar_vector

The approach decided on for the definition of classes `ar_matrix` and `ar_vector` is similar to that of the class `ar_polynomial`.

The matrix is initialized by a elementary constructor, which makes it possible if wanted to give a name to it. Then, the matrix will be "opened" by the intermediary of the member-function `open (lig, col)`, which allocates the memory necessary to the new matrix.

The elements of this matrix will be exclusively manipulated by the intermediary of the two member functions readcoeff (i, j) and writecoeff (i, j, n).

The physical representation of the matrix is only perceived by the elementary member functions: open (), close (), readcoeff (), writecoeff (), operator = (duplication).

The physical implementation that we have programmed is a dense representation, that is, made up of a contiguous memory area which can contain lig * col numbers.

If the reader wants to adopt another physical representation, a sparse representation for example, which makes it possible to deal with cases of very important matrices whose coefficients are for the most part equal to 0, or to deal with a mixed representation modified automatically (and in a totally transparent way) according to the size and the contents of the matrix, he will be able to do so by exclusively modifying the elementary member functions open (), close (), readcoeff (), writecoeff (), operator = (duplication).

The implementation of the functions which deals only with matricial calculations (sum, multiplication, determinant, calculation of eigenvalues) is totally independent of the physical representation.

The class ar_vector is built on the same model as that of the class ar_matrix. It is created, manipulated and destroyed by the basic member functions open (), close (), readcoeff (i), writecoeff (i, x) and the operator =. The physical representation decided on here is again a dense representation.

The following module groups together the elementary member functions of the class ar_matrix. It must be placed in the file MAT\MAT.CPP.

```
/*==========================================================
                        MAT.CPP:
        THE CLASS AR_MATRIX AND ITS MEMBER FUNCTIONS
=========================================================*/

#include   "armath.h"

/*==========================================================
             OPEN A MATRIX (MEMORY ALLOCATION)
 ========================================================*/
int ar_matrix::open (int li, int co)
{
  if (!empty) close ();

  if (li < 1) li = 1;
  if (co < 1) co = 1;
  ptcoeff = new ar_number [li * co];
  if (ptcoeff == NULL) {
    errno = 1;
    cerr << "Insufficient memory\n";
```

```
      return FALSE;
    }
  else  {
    empty = FALSE;
    lig  = li;
    col  = co;
    clear ();
    return TRUE;
  }
}

/*==============================================================
                     CLOSE A MATRIX
  ============================================================*/
void ar_matrix::close (void)
{
  if (!empty) delete[]ptcoeff;
  empty = TRUE;
}

/*==============================================================
                 READ A MATRIX'S ELEMENT
  ============================================================*/
ar_number & ar_matrix::readcoeff  (int i, int j)
{
  if ((i < 1) || (i > lig) || (j < 1) || (j > col))
    return N0;
  else return ptcoeff [col * (i - 1) + (j - 1)];
}

/*==============================================================
                 WRITE A MATRIX'S ELEMENT
  ============================================================*/
void ar_matrix::writecoeff (int i, int j, ar_number &n)
{
  if ((i >= 1) && (i <= lig) && (j >= 1) && (j <= col))
    ptcoeff [col * (i - 1) + (j - 1)] = n;
}

/*==============================================================
                     CLEAR A MATRIX
  ============================================================*/
void ar_matrix::clear (void)
{
  int i, j;

  if (empty) return;
  for (i = 1; i <= lig; i++)
```

```
    for (j = 1; j <= col; j++)
      writecoeff (i, j, N0);
}

/*============================================================
            OVERLOADING OF OPERATOR = FOR A MATRIX
  ==========================================================*/
void ar_matrix::operator = (ar_matrix &m)
{
  close ();
  if (! open  (m.lig, m.col)) {errno = 1; return;}
  memcpy (ptcoeff, m.ptcoeff,
          sizeof (ar_number) * m.lig * m.col);
  lig = m.lig; col = m.col;
}

/*============================================================
            OVERLOADING OF OPERATOR == FOR A MATRIX
  ==========================================================*/
int operator == (ar_matrix &m1, ar_matrix &m2)
{
  if ((m1.lig != m2.lig) || (m1.col != m2.col))
    return (FALSE);
  return (! memcmp (m1.ptcoeff, m2.ptcoeff,
          sizeof (ar_number) * m1.lig * m1.col));
}

/*============================================================
            OVERLOADING OF OPERATOR != FOR A MATRIX
  ==========================================================*/
int operator != (ar_matrix &m1, ar_matrix &m2)
{
  return (! (m1 == m2));
}
```

The following module groups together the elementary member functions of the class `ar_vector`. It must be placed in the file MAT\VEC.CPP.

```
/*============================================================
                        VEC.CPP:
        THE CLASS AR_VECTOR AND ITS MEMBER FUNCTIONS
  ==========================================================*/

#include  "armath.h"

/*============================================================
              OPEN A VECTOR (ALLOCATE MEMORY)
  ==========================================================*/
```

```
int ar_vector::open (int li)
{
  if (!empty) close ();
  if (li < 1) li = 1;
  ptcoeff = new ar_number [li];
  if (ptcoeff == NULL) {
    errno = 1;
    cerr << "Not enough memory\n";
    return FALSE;
  }
  else  {
    lig   = li; empty  = FALSE; clear ();
    return TRUE;
  }
}

/*==========================================================
                    CLOSE A VECTOR
  ======================================================*/
void ar_vector::close (void)
{
  if (!empty) delete[]ptcoeff;
  empty = TRUE;
}

/*==========================================================
                 READ A VECTOR'S ELEMENT
  ======================================================*/
ar_number & ar_vector::readcoeff  (int i)
{
  if ((i < 1) || (i > lig)) return N0;
  else return ptcoeff [i - 1];
}

/*==========================================================
                 WRITE A VECTOR'S ELEMENT
  ======================================================*/
void ar_vector::writecoeff (int i, ar_number &n)
{
  if ((i >= 1) && (i <= lig)) ptcoeff [i - 1] = n;
}

/*==========================================================
                    CLEAR A VECTOR
  ======================================================*/
void ar_vector::clear (void)
{
  int i;
```

```
    if (empty) return;
    for (i = 1; i <= lig; i++)
        writecoeff (i, N0);
}

/*=============================================================
            OVERLOADING OF OPERATOR = FOR A VECTOR
   ==========================================================*/
void ar_vector::operator = (ar_vector &v)
{
    close ();
    if (! open  (v.lig)) {errno = 1; return;}
    memcpy (ptcoeff, v.ptcoeff, sizeof (ar_number) * v.lig);
    lig = v.lig;
}

/*=============================================================
            OVERLOADING OF OPERATOR == FOR A VECTOR
   ==========================================================*/
int operator == (ar_vector &v1, ar_vector &v2)
{
    if (v1.lig != v2.lig) return FALSE;
    return (! memcmp (v1.ptcoeff, v2.ptcoeff,
            sizeof (ar_number) * v1.lig));
}

/*=============================================================
            OVERLOADING OF OPERATOR != FOR A VECTOR
   ==========================================================*/
int operator != (ar_vector &v1, ar_vector &v2)
{
    return (! (v1 == v2));
}
```

2 Creation of an Application Program

Let us suppose that we want to write a program which asks for the value of a number x and does the multiplication of the following matrices:

$$M1: \begin{pmatrix} n & 2 & 3 & 4 & \ldots & 1000 \\ 1 & 0 & 1 & 0 & \ldots & 0 \end{pmatrix} \quad \text{and} \quad M2: \begin{pmatrix} 1 & n \\ 2 & 1 \\ 3 & 1 \\ \ldots & \ldots \\ 1000 & 1 \end{pmatrix}$$

We would write:

```
#include <armath.h>

main()
{
  ar_matrix   m1 ("M1"), m2 ("M2");
  ar_number   n;
  int         i;

  if (! m1.open (2, 1000)) return;
  if (! m2.open (1000, 2)) return;
  ar_read ("Input a number : ", &n, AR_TNOM);

  m1.writecoeff (1, 1, n);
  m1.writecoeff (2, 1, N1);
  m2.writecoeff (1, 1, N1);
  m2.writecoeff (1, 2, n);

  for (i = 2; i <= 1000; i++) {
    m1.writecoeff (1, i, n);
    m2.writecoeff (i, 1, n);
    m1.writecoeff (2, i, ((i%2) ? 0 : 1));
    m2.writecoeff (i, 2, N1);
  }
  m1 *= m2  // the matrix m1 has been replaced by m1 * m2
  if (errno) return;
  cout << m1; ar_pause ()
}
```

3 Entry and Display of Matrices and Vectors

The two following tools are user-interface tools, making possible the entry and display of matrices, by overloading the stream operators cout << and cin >>. They have to be placed just after the ones we have previously seen, in the file MAT\MAT.CPP.

```
/*===========================================================
                    DISPLAY A MATRIX
  =========================================================*/
ostream& operator << (ostream& s, ar_matrix& m)
{
  ar_number   r;
  int         i, j;
```

```
for (i = 1; i <= m.lig; i++)  {
  ar_nl;
  for (j = 1; j <= m.col; j++)  {
    r = m.readcoeff (i, j);
    if (m.col < 6)  {
      cout << setw (15) << r;
      if (j == m.col) ar_nl;
    }
    else
      cout << m.title << " [" << i << ", " << j
           << "] = " << r << "\n";
  }
}
ar_nl;
return s;
}


/*===========================================================
                   ENTRY  OF  A  MATRIX
 ===========================================================*/
istream& operator >> (istream& s, ar_matrix& m)
{
  int        i, j, k, li, co;
  ar_number  *n;

  cout << "\nEntry of matrix " << m.title << " : \n\n";
  if (ar_read ("Number of lines    : ", &li, AR_TINT))
    {errno = 1; return s;}
  if (ar_read ("Number of columns : ", &co, AR_TINT))
    {errno = 1; return s;}
  if (! m.open (li, co)) {errno = 1; return s;}
  n = new ar_number [li * co];
  if (n == NULL) {errno = 1; return s;}

  ar_init_entry ("");

  for (i = 1, k = 0; i <= li; i++)
    for (j = 1; j <= co; j++)  {
      sprintf (ar_temp, "%s [%d, %d]", m.title, i, j);
      ar_fill_entry (ar_temp, &n [k++], AR_TNUM);
    }
  if (! ar_do_entry ())
    for (i = 1, k = 0; i <= li; i++)
      for (j = 1; j <= co; j++)
        m.writecoeff (i, j, n [k++]);
  delete[]n;
  return s;
}
```

In the same way, two tools making possible the display and the input of vectors have to be placed at the end of the file MAT\VEC.CPP.

```cpp
/*============================================================
                    DISPLAY  OF  A  VECTOR
  ==========================================================*/
ostream& operator << (ostream& s, ar_vector& v)
{
  int          i;

  ar_nl;

  for (i = 1; i <= v.lig; i++)
    cout << v.title << " [" << i << "] = "
         << v.readcoeff (i) << "\n";

  ar_nl;
  return s;
}


/*============================================================
                    ENTRY  OF  A  VECTOR
  ==========================================================*/
istream& operator >> (istream& s, ar_vector& v)
{
  int          i, k, li, ret;
  ar_number    *n;

  cout << "\nEntry of vector " << v.title << " : \n\n";
  if (ar_read ("Number of lines    : ", &li, AR_TINT))
    {errno = 1; return s;}
  if (! v.open (li))  {errno = 1; return s;}

  n = new ar_number [li];
  if (n == NULL)  {errno = 1; return s;}

  ar_init_entry ("");
  for (i = 1, k = 0; i <= v.lig; i++)  {
      sprintf (ar_temp, "%s [%d]", v.title, i);
      ar_fill_entry (ar_temp, &n [k++], AR_TNUM);
    }
  ret = ! ar_do_entry ();
  if (ret)
    for (i = 1, k = 0; i <= v.lig; i++)
      v.writecoeff (i, n [k++]);
  delete[]n;
  return s;
}
```

---

4   Vector Analysis

4.1 Theoretical Points

Let us consider a vectorial space E of dimension n, with U and V two vectors belonging to that vectorial space.

Let us consider K_1 and K_2 two real numbers; vector W defined by:

$$W = K_1.U + K_2.V$$

is called linear combination of U and V. In the case of U and V not being collinear, W belongs to the vectorial plane generated by U and V.

Scalar Product

We call scalar product a symmetrical and bilinear form defined as positive of ExE in R, that is, an application f of ExE in R establishing the following properties:

$$f(U, V) = U.V \ \in R$$

$$f(\lambda U + \mu U', V) = \lambda f(U, V) + \mu f(U', V) \qquad \text{(bilinearity properties)}$$
$$f(U, \lambda'V + \mu'V') = \lambda' f(U, V) + \mu' f(U, V')$$

$$f(U, V) = f(V, U)$$

$$f(U, U) = 0 \Rightarrow U = 0$$

$$\forall \ U \neq 0, \ f(U, U) > 0$$

this $\forall \ \lambda \in R, \ \forall \ \lambda' \in R, \ \forall \ \mu \in R, \ \forall \ \mu' \in R, \ \forall \ U \in E, \ \forall \ U' \in E, \ \forall \ V \in E, \ \forall \ V' \in E.$

From a misuse of language, we call the scalar product of U and V the real number $U.V$. When the scalar product $U.V$ is equal to 0, we can say that the vectors U and V are orthogonal.

By definition, we call the norm of a vector U the real number $\| U \|$ given by the relation:

$$\| U \| = \sqrt{U.U}$$

We call the orthonormal basis of the vectorial space E of dimension n, a basis of E whose vectors $(a_i)_{i \in [1,n]}$ establish the relations:

$$\forall \ (i, j) \in [1, n]^2 \text{ and } i \neq j \qquad a_i.a_j = 0$$

$$\forall \ i \in [1, n] \qquad a_i.a_i = 1$$

This amounts to saying that the vectors of the basis are orthogonal to one another and that they all have a norm equal to 1. Let us therefore try to express the scalar product of the vectors U and V on such an orthonormal basis of the vectorial space E.

The vectors U and V can be written according to the vectors of the base:

$$U = \sum_{i=1}^{n} u_i\, a_i \qquad\qquad V = \sum_{j=1}^{n} v_j\, a_j \qquad\qquad u_i \in \mathbb{R} \quad v_j \in \mathbb{R}$$

The scalar product can then be written as follows:

$$U.V = (\sum_{i=1}^{n} u_i\, a_i) \,.\, (\sum_{j=1}^{n} v_j\, a_j) \;=\; \sum_{i=1}^{n}\sum_{j=1}^{n} (u_i\, a_i)\,.\,(v_j\, a_j) \;=\; \sum_{i=1}^{n}\sum_{j=1}^{n} u_i\, v_j\,.\,(a_i.a_j)$$

The vectors a_i being normed and orthogonal from one another, we finally obtain:

$$U.V = \sum_{i=1}^{n} u_i\, v_i$$

For example, in a space of dimension 3, if the vectors U and V have on an orthonormal basis the following coordinates, we can obtain:

$$U \begin{pmatrix} x \\ y \\ z \end{pmatrix} \qquad V \begin{pmatrix} x' \\ y' \\ z' \end{pmatrix} \qquad U.V = xx' + yy' + zz'$$

Let us now place ourselves in a Euclidean vectorial space (that is, one which has a scalar product) which is oriented, of dimension 3 related to a direct orthonormal basis.

Vectorial Product

We call vectorial product of two vectors U and V the vector $W = U \wedge V$ defined by:
  – if U and V are collinear, $W = 0$;
  – if U and V are not collinear:
    – W is orthogonal to the plan generated by U and V;
    – (U, V, W) make a direct base;
    – the norm of W is given by: $\qquad \| W \| = \| U \| \,.\, \| V \| \,.\, |\sin (U, V)|$
If the vectors U and V have the following coordinates, we obtain:

$$U \begin{pmatrix} x \\ y \\ z \end{pmatrix} \qquad V \begin{pmatrix} x' \\ y' \\ z' \end{pmatrix} \qquad W \begin{pmatrix} yz'-zy' \\ zx'-xz' \\ xy'-yx' \end{pmatrix}$$

Mixed Product

We call mixed product of three vectors U, V, W the determinant of these vectors:

$$PM = \det (U, V, W)$$

The mixed product is linked to the scalar product and to the vectorial product by the relations:

$$\det (U, V, W) = (U \wedge V) \cdot W = U \cdot (V \wedge W)$$

4.2 Calculation Tools

The following tools make it possible to calculate linear combinations, scalar products, vectorial products and mixed products of vectors.

Linear combination

The operators +, – applied to a couple of vectors are overloaded for us to be able to use traditional notations.

The first two tools must be placed in the file MAT\VECSUM.CPP.

```
/*=========================================================
                       VECSUM.CPP:
                    SUM OF TWO VECTORS
=========================================================*/

#include  "armath.h"

ar_vector & operator + (ar_vector &v1, ar_vector &v2)
{
   static ar_vector  nv;
   int               i;

   if (v1.lig != v2.lig)
      {nv.close (); errno = 1; return nv;}

   if (! nv.open (v1.lig))
     {errno = 1; return nv;}

   for (i = 1; i <= v1.lig; i++)
     nv.writecoeff (i,
       v1.readcoeff (i) + v2.readcoeff (i));

   return nv;
}

//----------------------------- SUBTRACTION OF TWO VECTORS
ar_vector & operator - (ar_vector &v1, ar_vector &v2)
{
   static ar_vector  nv;
   int               i;
```

```
  if (v1.lig != v2.lig)
     {nv.close (); errno = 1; return nv;}

  if (! nv.open (v1.lig))
    {errno = 1; return nv;}

  for (i = 1; i <= v1.lig; i++)
    nv.writecoeff (i,
      v1.readcoeff (i) - v2.readcoeff (i));

  return nv;
}

//--------------------------- OVERLOADING OF OPERATOR +=
ar_vector &  ar_vector::operator += (ar_vector &v)
{
  *this = *this + v;
  return *this;
}

//--------------------------- OVERLOADING OF OPERATOR -=
ar_vector &  ar_vector::operator -= (ar_vector &v)
{
  *this = *this - v;
  return *this;
}
```

Scalar product

The scalar product of two vectors is implemented through the overloading of operator *. Thus, r = u * v will put the scalar product of u and v in r.

This tool, as well as the two following ones and the overloading of operator * applied to a couple (number, vector), must be placed in the file MAT\VECMUL.CPP.

```
/*==========================================================
                      VECMUL.CPP:
                 MULTIPLICATION OF VECTORS
==========================================================*/

#include  "armath.h"

/*==========================================================
            PRODUCT OF A VECTOR BY A SCALAR
 =========================================================*/

ar_vector & operator * (ar_number &n, ar_vector &v)
{
```

```
    static ar_vector   nv;
    int                i;

    if (! nv.open (v.lig)) {errno = 1; return nv;}

    for (i = 1; i <= v.lig; i++)
      nv.writecoeff (i, n * v.readcoeff (i));

    return nv;
}

ar_vector &  ar_vector::operator *= (ar_number &n)
{
    *this = n * *this;
    return *this;
}


/*============================================================
                SCALAR PRODUCT OF TWO VECTORS
  ==========================================================*/

ar_number operator * (ar_vector &v1, ar_vector &v2)
{
    ar_number  ret = N0;
    int        i;

    if (v1.lig != v2.lig) {errno = 21; return ret;}

    for (i = 1; i <= v1.lig; i++)
      ret += v1.readcoeff (i) * v2.readcoeff (i);

    return ret;
}
```

Vectorial product

The vectorial product can be obtained through the overloading of operator ^.

```
/*============================================================
               VECTORIAL PRODUCT OF TWO VECTORS
  ==========================================================*/

ar_vector & operator ^ (ar_vector &v1, ar_vector &v2)
{
    static ar_vector  nv;

    if ((v1.lig != 3) || (v2.lig != 3))
      {errno = 1; nv.close (); return nv;}
```

```
if (! nv.open (3)) {errno = 1; return nv;}

nv.writecoeff (1, v1.readcoeff (2) * v2.readcoeff (3)
                - v1.readcoeff (3) * v2.readcoeff (2));
nv.writecoeff (2, v1.readcoeff (3) * v2.readcoeff (1)
                - v1.readcoeff (1) * v2.readcoeff (3));
nv.writecoeff (3, v1.readcoeff (1) * v2.readcoeff (2)
                - v1.readcoeff (2) * v2.readcoeff (1));

return nv;
}
```

Mixed product

The input parameters are the three vectors to be multiplied U, V and W. On output, the value of the function is equal to the mixed product of the three vectors.

REMARK: in the same way as for polynomials and rational fractions, it is forbidden to use the same operator more than once in a given expression.

```
/*==============================================================
              MIXED PRODUCT OF THREE VECTORS
  ============================================================*/
ar_number ar_mix_vec (ar_vector &u,ar_vector &v,ar_vector &w)
{
  if ((u.lig != 3) || (v.lig != 3) || (w.lig != 3))
     {errno = 1; return N0;}

  ar_number x1 = u.readcoeff (1);
  ar_number x2 = u.readcoeff (2);
  ar_number x3 = u.readcoeff (3);

  ar_number y1 = v.readcoeff (1);
  ar_number y2 = v.readcoeff (2);
  ar_number y3 = v.readcoeff (3);

  ar_number z1 = w.readcoeff (1);
  ar_number z2 = w.readcoeff (2);
  ar_number z3 = w.readcoeff (3);

  ar_number t1 =   x1 * (y2 * z3 - y3 * z2);
  ar_number t2 = - y1 * (x2 * z3 - x3 * z2);
  ar_number t3 =   z1 * (x2 * y3 - x3 * y2);

  return (t1 + t2 + t3);
}
```

4.3 Annotated Examples

Example 1

Let us calculate the linear combination $V = 2\,U_1 - 4\,U_2$ as well as the scalar product $U_1.U_2$ of the two following vectors, belonging to a space of dimension 5:

$$U_1 \begin{pmatrix} 2 \\ -5 \\ 7/2 \\ 0 \\ 6 \end{pmatrix} \qquad U_2 \begin{pmatrix} 2 \\ -7 \\ 0 \\ 3/5 \\ 1 \end{pmatrix}$$

```
LINEAR COMBINATION OF TWO VECTORS V = a.V1 + b.V2

Input scalar a : 2
Input scalar b : -4
Entry of vector V1 :          Entry of vector V2 :
Number of lines : 5           Number of lines : 5
V1 [1] = 2                    U2 [1] = 2
V1 [2] = -5                   U2 [2] = -7
V1 [3] = 7/2                  U2 [3] = 0
V1 [4] = 0                    U2 [4] = 3/5
V1 [5] = 6                    U2 [5] = 1

Vector V (a.V1 + b.V2)
V [1] = - 4
V [2] = + 18
V [3] = + 7
V [4] = - 12 / 5
V [5] = + 8


SCALAR PRODUCT OF TWO VECTORS : U.V

Entry of vector U :           Entry of vector V :
Number of lines : 5           Number of lines : 5
U [1] = 2                     V [1] = 2
U [2] = -5                    V [2] = -7
U [3] = 7/2                   V [3] = 0
U [4] = 0                     V [4] = 3/5
U [5] = 6                     V [5] = 1

U.V = + 45
```

Example 2

Let us calculate the scalar product and the vectorial product of the vectors of dimension 3:

$$U \begin{pmatrix} 2 \\ -5 \\ 6 \end{pmatrix} \qquad V \begin{pmatrix} 1 \\ 7 \\ 5/2 \end{pmatrix}$$

```
SCALAR PRODUCT OF TWO VECTORS : U.V

Entry of vector U :              Entry of vector V :
Number of lines : 3              Number of lines : 3
U [1] = 2                        V [1] = 1
U [2] = -5                       V [2] = 7
U [3] = 6                        V [3] = 5/2

U.V = - 18


VECTORIAL PRODUCT OF TWO VECTORS (U ^ V)

Entry of vector U :              Entry of vector V :
Number of lines : 3              Number of lines : 3
U [1] = 2                        V [1] = 1
U [2] = -5                       V [2] = 7
U [3] = 6                        V [3] = 5/2

W [1] = - 109 / 2
W [2] = + 1
W [3] = + 19
```

Example 3

Still in a space of dimension 3, let us search for the mixed product of vectors:

$$U \begin{pmatrix} 2 \\ 5 \\ 0 \end{pmatrix} \qquad V \begin{pmatrix} -4 \\ 2/5 \\ 3/2 \end{pmatrix} \qquad W \begin{pmatrix} 4 \\ -1/5 \\ 3/2 \end{pmatrix}$$

```
MIXED PRODUCT OF THREE VECTORS : det (U, V, W)

Entry of vector U :              Entry of vector V :
Number of lines : 3              Number of lines : 3
U [1] = 2                        V [1] = -4
U [2] = 5                        V [2] = 2/5
U [3] = 0                        V [3] = 3/2
```

```
Entry of vector W :
Number of lines : 3
W [1] = 4
W [2] = -1/5
W [3] = 3/2

The mixed product is : + 309 / 5
```

5   Linear Combination of Matrices

5.1 Calculation Tools

Two operators are overloaded:
    – the multiplication of a matrix by a scalar;
    – the sum of two matrices (M_1 and M_2 must have the same dimensions).

The first tool will be placed in the file MAT\MATMUL.CPP. The second tool will be placed in the file MAT\MATSUM.CPP.

```
/*===========================================================
                       MATSUM.CPP:
                    SUM OF TWO MATRICES
=========================================================*/

#include   "armath.h"

//---------------------------- OVERLOADING OF OPERATOR +

ar_matrix & operator + (ar_matrix &m1, ar_matrix &m2)
{
  static ar_matrix  np;
  int               i, j;

  if ((m1.col != m2.col) || (m1.lig != m2.lig))
     {np.close (); errno = 1; return np;}
  if (! np.open (m1.lig, m1.col))
    {errno = 1; return np;}

  for (i = 1; i <= m1.lig; i++)
    for (j = 1; j <= m1.col; j++)
      np.writecoeff (i, j,
        m1.readcoeff (i, j) + m2.readcoeff (i, j));

  return np;
}
```

```
//--------------------------------- OVERLOADING OF OPERATOR -

ar_matrix & operator - (ar_matrix &m1, ar_matrix &m2)
{
   static ar_matrix   np;
   int                i, j;

   if ((m1.col != m2.col) || (m1.lig != m2.lig))
      {np.close (); errno = 1; return np;}
   if (! np.open (m1.lig, m1.col))
      {errno = 1; return np;}

   for (i = 1; i <= m1.lig; i++)
      for (j = 1; j <= m1.col; j++)
         np.writecoeff (i, j,
            m1.readcoeff (i, j) - m2.readcoeff (i, j));

   return np;
}

//--------------------------- OVERLOADING OF OPERATOR +=

ar_matrix &  ar_matrix::operator += (ar_matrix &m)
{
   *this = *this + m;
   return *this;
}

//--------------------------- OVERLOADING OF OPERATOR -=

ar_matrix &  ar_matrix::operator -= (ar_matrix &m)
{
   *this = *this - m;
   return *this;
}
```

The exploitation tool `ar_use_combination_matrix ()` given at the end of the chapter makes it possible to enter M and N, the two matrices to be combined, as well as the two scalars a and b. It calculates and displays the linear combination.

5.2 Annotated Example

Let us consider the two matrices:

$$M_1 = \begin{pmatrix} 2 & -1 & 1/5 \\ 3/5 & 0 & 6 \end{pmatrix} \qquad M_2 = \begin{pmatrix} 1 & 2 & 5 \\ -7 & 3 & 0 \end{pmatrix}$$

Let us calculate $M = 5.M_1 + M_1$:

```
LINEAR COMBINATION OF MATRICES M = a.M1 + b.M2

Input scalar a : 5              Input scalar b : 1
Entry of matrix M1 :            Entry of matrix M2 :
Number of lines      : 2        Number of lines      : 2
Number of columns    : 3        Number of columns    : 3

M1 [1,1] = 2                    M2 [1,1] = 1
M1 [1,2] = -1                   M2 [1,2] = 2
M1 [1,3] = 1/5                  M2 [1,3] = 5
M1 [2,1] = 3/5                  M2 [2,1] = -7
M1 [2,2] = 0                    M2 [2,2] = 3
M1 [2,3] = 6                    M2 [2,3] = 0

    + 11          - 3        + 6
    - 4           + 3       + 30
```

The result is therefore:

$$M = \begin{pmatrix} 11 & -3 & 6 \\ -4 & 3 & 30 \end{pmatrix}$$

6 Multiplication of Two Matrices

6.1 Principle

Let us consider two matrices $A = (a_{ij})$ and $B = (b_{ij})$.

We are going to calculate their product $C = A.B = (c_{ij})$. The latter exists only if the number of columns of A is equal to the number of lines of B and this number is n. The coefficients c_{ij} are then given by:

$$c_{ij} = \sum_{k=1}^{n} a_{ik} \cdot b_{kj}$$

The product matrix C has the same number of lines as A, and the same number of columns as B. Let us remind ourselves that the multiplication of matrices is not commutative (the matrices AB and BA cannot exist simultaneously unless A and B are square matrices of the same dimension).

6.2 Calculation Tool

The operator * is overloaded, which allows us to use the notation M1 * M2.

The remark made for the product of polynomials is equally valid for matrices: it is forbidden to use more than once in the same expression the operator * applied to two matrices (see the technical explanation in the section on the multiplication of polynomials).

This tool will be placed in the file MAT\MATMUL.CPP.

```cpp
/*============================================================
                        MATMUL.CPP:
                 MULTIPLICATION OF MATRICES
============================================================*/

#include  "armath.h"

//----------------------------- OVERLOADING OF OPERATOR *
ar_matrix & operator * (ar_matrix &m1, ar_matrix &m2)
{
  static ar_matrix  np;
  ar_number         res;
  int               i, j, k;

  if (m1.col != m2.lig) {errno = 1; np.close (); return np;}
  if (! np.open (m1.lig, m2.col)) {errno = 1; return np;}
  for (i = 1; i <= np.lig; i++)
    for (j = 1; j <= np.col; j++)   {
      for (k = 1, res = N0; k <= m1.col; k++)
        res += m1.readcoeff (i, k) * m2.readcoeff (k, j);
      np.writecoeff (i, j, res);
    }
  return np;
}

ar_matrix & operator * (ar_number &n, ar_matrix &m)
{
  static ar_matrix  np;
  int               i, j;

  if (! np.open (m.lig, m.col))
    {errno = 1; return np;}
  for (i = 1; i <= m.lig; i++)
    for (j = 1; j <= m.col; j++)
      np.writecoeff (i, j, n * m.readcoeff (i, j));
  return np;
}
```

```
//---------------------------- OVERLOADING OF OPERATOR *=

ar_matrix &  ar_matrix::operator *= (ar_matrix &m)
{
   *this = *this * m; return *this;
}

ar_matrix &  ar_matrix::operator *= (ar_number &n)
{
   *this = n * *this; return *this;
}
```

6.3 Annotated Example

Let us consider the two following matrices A and B and their product C:

$$A = \begin{pmatrix} 3 & 1 & -7 \\ 2 & 4 & 1 \end{pmatrix} \qquad B = \begin{pmatrix} 1/4 & 2 \\ 6 & 0 \\ 1 & -3 \end{pmatrix} \qquad C = \begin{pmatrix} -1/4 & 27 \\ 51/2 & 1 \end{pmatrix}$$

```
MULTIPLICATION OF TWO MATRICES M = M1.M2

Entry of matrix M1 :            Entry of matrix M2 :
Number of lines    : 2          Number of lines    : 3
Number of columns  : 3          Number of columns  : 2

M1 [1,1] = 3                    M2 [1,1] = 1/4
M1 [1,2] = 1                    M2 [1,2] = 2
M1 [1,3] = -7                   M2 [2,1] = 6
M1 [2,1] = 2                    M2 [2,2] = 0
M1 [2,2] = 4                    M2 [3,1] = 1
M1 [2,3] = 1                    M2 [3,2] = -3

     - 1 / 4          + 27
     + 51 / 2         + 1
```

7 The Raising to a Power *N*

7.1 Principle

It would be possible, in order to raise matrix A (which must be square) to the power N, to do $N-1$ successive multiplications due to the previous program.

This method has two drawbacks when N is high:
– a lot of operations are needed, which lowers the accuracy;
– the time of calculation is proportionate to $N-1$ and rapidly increases.

Legendre's method that we are going to use leads to a time of calculation proportionate to $\log_2 N$, and is therefore much more efficient when N is high.

The principle of the method lies in the following observation: in order to calculate A^{2p}, it is sufficient to know A^p and to multiply it by itself. Let us use an auxiliary matrix D, and let us initialise the matrices C and D thus:

$$C = I \qquad\qquad D = A$$

The algorithm is then as follows:
– if N is even, we divide N by 2 and we square D;
– if N is odd, we take away one unit from N and we multiply C by D.
The operation is repeated until N is equal to 0; C then contains A^N.

Let us consider the following example, where $N = 14$. We initially have:

$$C = I \qquad\qquad D = A \qquad N = 14$$

N is even; let us divide it by 2 and let us square D:

$$C = I \qquad\qquad D = A^2 \qquad N = 7$$

N is odd; let us decrement N and multiply C by D:

$$C = I \,.\, A^2 = A^2 \qquad D = A^2 \qquad N = 6$$

In the same way we obtain successively:

$$C = A^2 \qquad\qquad D = A^4 \qquad N = 3$$
$$C = A^2 .\, A^4 = A^6 \qquad D = A^4 \qquad N = 2$$
$$C = A^6 \qquad\qquad D = A^8 \qquad N = 1$$
$$C = A^6 .\, A^8 = A^{14} \qquad D = A^8 \qquad N = 0$$

We have done 6 multiplications, instead of 13 with the method of successive multiplications. The difference is all the more obvious as N increases:
– if $N = 100$, only 9 multiplications are necessary;
– if $N = 1000$, only 15 multiplications are necessary.

7.2 Calculation Tool

The operator $^\wedge$ is overloaded which makes it possible to write P = M $^\wedge$ n, where M is the matrix to be used as the exponent and n the long integer containing the power.

It will have to be placed in the file MAT\MATRAIS.CPP.

```
/*===========================================================
                      MATRAIS.CPP:
            RAISING OF A MATRIX TO A POWER N
===========================================================*/
```

```
#include  "armath.h"

ar_matrix & operator ^ (ar_matrix &m, long n)
{
  static ar_matrix  np;
  ar_matrix         p;
  int               i, j;

  ·if ((m.col != m.lig) || (! np.open (m.lig, m.col)))
    {np.close(); errno = 1; return np;}
  p = m;
  for (i = 1; i <= np.lig; i++)
    for (j = 1; j <= np.col; j++)
      np.writecoeff (i, j, (j == i) ? N1 : N0);
  while (n)
    if (n % 2)  {
      n--;
      np *= p;
    }
    else  {
      n /= 2;
      p *= p;
    }

  return np;
}
```

7.3 Annotated Example

```
RAISING A MATRIX TO THE POWER n : P = M^n

Entry of matrix M :
Number of lines    : 4
Number of columns  : 4

M [1,1] = 1    M [1,2] = 0    M [1,3] = 2    M [1,4] = 1
M [2,1] = 0    M [2,2] = -3   M [2,3] = 0    M [2,4] = -5
M [3,1] = 2    M [3,2] = -5   M [3,3] = 0    M [3,4] = 2
M [4,1] = 0    M [4,2] = 9    M [4,3] = 0    M [4,4] = 0

n = 5

    + 65         - 1425        + 58          + 255
       0         - 13608          0          - 4455
    + 58          - 157        + 36          + 8993
       0         + 8019           0          - 10935
```

We therefore obtain:

$$
\begin{pmatrix}
1 & 0 & 2 & 1 \\
0 & -3 & 0 & -5 \\
2 & -5 & 0 & 2 \\
0 & 9 & 0 & 0
\end{pmatrix}^5
=
\begin{pmatrix}
65 & -1425 & 58 & 255 \\
0 & -13608 & 0 & -4455 \\
58 & -157 & 36 & 8993 \\
0 & 8019 & 0 & -10935
\end{pmatrix}
$$

8 Calculation of the Determinant

8.1 Principle

We are trying here to calculate the determinant of a matrix A.

This result is in fact a sub-product of the inversion of a matrix by the Gauss-Jordan method, that we are going to see in detail in the following section.

The algorithm consisting of bringing the calculation of a determinant of order N to N determinants of order $N-1$, then $N(N-1)$ determinants of order $N-2$..., is not used since the time of calculation is proportionate to $N!$, whereas that of the algorithm of Gauss-Jordan is proportionate to N^3.

8.2 Exploitation Tool

The tool `ar_use_determinant_matrix`, shown at the end of the chapter, allows one to enter the matrix, calls the tool of inversion which exploits the algorithm of Gauss-Jordan, and displays the determinant of A.

8.3 Annotated Examples

Example 1

```
CALCULATION OF THE DETERMINANT OF A MATRIX M

Entry of matrix M :
Number of lines    : 4
Number of columns  : 4

M [1,1] = 2     M [1,2] = 1     M [1,3] = 1     M [1,4] = 4
M [2,1] = 0     M [2,2] = 1     M [2,3] = 3     M [2,4] = 2
M [3,1] = 3     M [3,2] = 1     M [3,3] = 2     M [3,4] = 1
M [4,1] = 1     M [4,2] = 1     M [4,3] = 0     M [4,4] = 3
The determinant is :  - 16
```

We have therefore:

$$
\begin{vmatrix}
2 & 1 & 1 & 4 \\
0 & 1 & 3 & 2 \\
3 & 1 & 2 & 1 \\
1 & 1 & 0 & 3
\end{vmatrix} = -16
$$

Example 2

```
CALCULATION OF THE DETERMINANT OF A MATRIX M

Entry of matrix M :
Number of lines    : 3
Number of columns  : 3

M [1,1] = -1    M [1,2] = 2    M [1,3] = 5
M [2,1] = 2     M [2,2] = 4    M [2,3] = 3
M [3,1] = 4     M [3,2] = 0    M [3,3] = -7

The determinant is : - 0
```

9   Calculation of the Inverse

9.1 Principle

The inverse matrix A^{-1} of the matrix A establishes the equality:

$$A \cdot A^{-1} = I \qquad (1)$$

We are going to calculate the matrix A^{-1} by solving linear systems, that is, by successively calculating all the columns A^{-1}. For this let us call X_j the column vector representing the jth column of the matrix A^{-1}. The equality (1) then leads to:

$$
A \cdot X_j = \begin{pmatrix}
0 \\
\cdots \\
0 \\
1 \\
0 \\
\cdots \\
0
\end{pmatrix}
$$

This column vector contains 1 at the *j*th coordinate, and 0 everywhere else.

We will see, in the section dealing with solving linear systems, that the Gauss-Jordan method makes it possible to solve simultaneously several linear systems based on the same matrix *A*. Thus, inverting matrix *A* amounts to trying to find the *n* solution-vectors of *n* systems of the type:

$$A \cdot X_j = \begin{pmatrix} 0 \\ \cdots \\ 0 \\ 1 \\ 0 \\ \cdots \\ 0 \end{pmatrix} \qquad\qquad j \in [1, n]$$

The vectors X_j obtained are then the columns of matrix A^{-1}.

9.2 Calculation Tool

The input parameter is the matrix M to be inverted.

At the output, the value of the function contains the inverse matrix, rank contains its rank and det its determinant. If det is equal to zero, the inversion is impossible, and the returned matrix is not significant.

The tool must be placed in the file MAT\MATINV.CPP.

The tool ar_use_inversion_matrix shown at the end of the chapter makes it possible to multiply the coefficients by the determinant, in order to obtain the matrix with whole coefficients if the initial matrix was itself with whole coefficients.

```
/*==========================================================
                        MATINV.CPP:
      INVERSION OF A MATRIX WITH GAUSS-JORDAN'S METHOD
 ==========================================================*/

#include   "armath.h"

ar_matrix & ar_inv_mat (ar_matrix& m, int& rang,
                        ar_number& det)
{
  ar_matrix          m1;
  static ar_matrix   m2;
  ar_number          r, pivot;
  int                i, j, n = m.lig, ligpivot, ligcour;

  det = N1; rang = n; m2.close ();
  if (m.col != m.lig) {errno = 1; return m2;}
  m1 = m; if (errno) return m2;
```

```
//---------------------- Initialisation of result matrix
if (! m2.open (n, n)) {errno = 1; return m2;}
for (i = 1; i <= m2.lig; i++)
  for (j = 1; j <= m2.col; j++)
    m2.writecoeff (i, j, (j == i) ? N1 : N0);

for (ligcour = 1; ligcour <= n; ligcour ++)  {
  ligpivot = ligcour;
  //----------- Determination of the first non-zero pivot
  r = m1.readcoeff (ligpivot, ligcour);
  while (r.small () && (ligpivot < n))  {
    ligpivot ++;
    det = - det;
    r = m1.readcoeff (ligpivot, ligcour);
  }
  if (r.small () && (ligpivot == n))  {
      det  = N0;
      rang --;
  }
  else  {
    //----------------- Swap current line with pivot line
    for (j = 1; j <= n; j++)  {
      r = m1.readcoeff (ligcour,   j);
      m1.writecoeff (ligcour,j,m1.readcoeff (ligpivot,j));
      m1.writecoeff (ligpivot, j, r);
      r = m2.readcoeff (ligcour,   j);
      m2.writecoeff (ligcour,j,m2.readcoeff (ligpivot,j));
      m2.writecoeff (ligpivot, j, r);
    }
    pivot = m1.readcoeff (ligcour, ligcour);

    //------------- Divide current line elements by pivot
    for (j = ligcour + 1; j <= n; j++)
    m1.writecoeff (ligcour, j,
        m1.readcoeff (ligcour, j) / pivot);

    for (j = 1; j <= n; j++)
    m2.writecoeff (ligcour, j,
        m2.readcoeff (ligcour, j) / pivot);

    det *= pivot;
    m1.writecoeff (ligcour, ligcour, N1);

    //------------------------------- Update other lines
    for (i = 1; i <= n; i++)
      if (i != ligcour)  {
          r = m1.readcoeff (i, ligcour);
          for (j = ligcour + 1; j <= n; j++)
```

```
            m1.writecoeff (i, j, m1.readcoeff (i, j)
                                  - r * m1.readcoeff (ligcour, j));
            for (j = 1; j <= n; j++)
            m2.writecoeff (i, j,
                    m2.readcoeff (i, j) -
                r * m2.readcoeff (ligcour, j));
            m1.writecoeff (i, ligcour, N0);
        }
    }
}
return m2;
}
```

9.3 Annotated Example

Let us consider the matrix:

$$A = \begin{pmatrix} 3 & -1 & 2 \\ 1 & 0 & 3 \\ 4 & 0 & 2 \end{pmatrix}$$

whose determinant is equal to det $(A) = -10$.

```
INVERSION OF MATRIX M

Entry of matrix M :
Number of lines   : 3
Number of columns : 3

M [1,1] = 3    M [1,2] = -1    M [1,3] = 2
M [2,1] = 1    M [2,2] = 0     M [2,3] = 3
M [3,1] = 4    M [3,2] = 0     M [3,3] = 2

Multiplication by the determinant ? n
The determinant is :  - 10
Inverse matrix :

        0             - 1 / 5           + 3 / 10
      - 1             + 1 / 5           + 7 / 10
        0             + 2 / 5           - 1 / 10


INVERSION OF MATRIX M

Entry of matrix M :
Number of lines   : 3
Number of columns : 3
```

```
M [1,1] = 3      M [1,2] = -1      M [1,3] = 2
M [2,1] = 1      M [2,2] = 0       M [2,3] = 3
M [3,1] = 4      M [3,2] = 0       M [3,3] = 2
```

Multiplication by the determinant ? y
The determinant is : - 10
Inverse matrix :

```
       0             + 2             - 3
    + 10             - 2             - 7
       0             - 4             + 1
```

We therefore obtain $A^{-1} = \begin{pmatrix} 0 & -1/5 & 3/10 \\ -1 & 1/5 & 7/10 \\ 0 & 2/5 & -1/10 \end{pmatrix} = \frac{1}{(-10)} \begin{pmatrix} 0 & 2 & -3 \\ 10 & -2 & -7 \\ 0 & 4 & 1 \end{pmatrix}.$

10 The Trace of a Matrix

10.1 Principle

Let us consider a square matrix A, of dimension n. We call the trace of matrix A the real number:

$$\mathrm{tr}(A) = \sum_{i=1}^{n} a_{ii}$$

The calculation of the trace of a matrix is used in the calculation of the eigenvalues, described in the following section.

10.2 Calculation Tool

The return value of the function `trace`, member of the class `ar_matrix`, is the trace of the matrix.

This tool will be placed in the file MAT\MATTRACE.CPP.

```
/*================================================================
                      MATTRACE.CPP:
             CALCULATE THE TRACE OF A MATRIX
================================================================*/

#include   "armath.h"

ar_number ar_matrix::trace (void)
```

```
{
  ar_number  res;
  int        i;

  for (i = 1, res = N0; i <= lig; i++)
    res += readcoeff (i, i);

  return (res);
}
```

---

11   Search for Eigenvalues

11.1 Principle

Let us consider a square matrix A, of dimention n.

A vector X is called the eigenvector of A associated with the eigenvalue λ only if the following relation is established:

$$A . X = \lambda X$$

Vector X is not unique, but belongs to a sub-vectorial space of R^n. This relation can also be written as follows:

$$(A - \lambda I) . X = 0$$

where I is the identity matrix.

This homogeneous system admits solutions for X other than the trivial solution if it is degenerate, that is if:

$$\det(A - \lambda I) = 0$$

which can also be written as follows:

$$\begin{vmatrix} a_{11}-\lambda & a_{12} & \dots & a_{1n} \\ a_{21} & a_{22}-\lambda & \dots & a_{2n} \\ \dots & \dots & \dots & \dots \\ a_{n1} & a_{n2} & \dots & a_{nn}-\lambda \end{vmatrix} = 0$$

This determinant is a polynomial in λ of degree n, called the characteristic polynomial of A. The eigenvalues are the roots of this polynomial. There are therefore n of them, and they can be complex or mixed.

The determination will be done in two stages: determination of the characteristic polynomial of A, then a search for the complex roots of this polynomial.

Determination of the characteristic polynomial

We are going to use Souriau's method. Let us call $(c_i)_{i \in [0,n]}$ the $(n+1)$ coefficients characteristic polynomial:

$$P(A) = c_0 \lambda^n + c_1 \lambda^{n-1} + \dots + c_{n-1} \lambda + c_n$$

We then define a series of matrices (A_k) by the recurrence relation:

$$k \in [1, n] \qquad \begin{cases} A_0 = 0 \\ A_k = (A_{k-1} + c_{k-1}\, I)\,.\,A \end{cases} \qquad \begin{cases} c_0 = 1 \\ c_k = -\dfrac{1}{k}\,\mathrm{tr}(A_k) \end{cases}$$

where $\mathrm{tr}(A_k)$ designates the trace of the matrix A_k, that is, the sum of its diagonal elements. The $(c_k)_{k \in [0,n]}$ are then obtained step by step.

Solving the characteristic equation

The search for the n zeros of the polynomial obtained is done with Bairstow's method, which is shown in chapter 10, dedicated to methods of solving equations.

11.2 Calculation Tool

The function `ar_valeurs_propres` accepts as parameters:
  – matrix M whose eigenvalues we have to find;
  – the three parameters p, q and `prec` initializing Bairstow's method.
(The couple (0,0) generally leads to the result.)

At the output, the value of the function, boolean, indicates if the calculation has been possible, and the array of complex numbers `sol` contains the eigenvalues.

The tool will be placed in the file `MAT\EIGENVAL.CPP`.

```
/*==============================================================
                        EIGENVAL.CPP:
            DETERMINATION OF MATRIX M EIGEN VALUES
  ============================================================*/

#include   "armath.h"

#define   MAXITER   100

int   ar_eigen_values (ar_matrix &m, complex sol [],
            ar_double prec, ar_double p, ar_double q)
{
    ar_matrix       m1;
    ar_polynomial   pol;
    ar_number       r;

    int             i, k;
```

```
if (m.col != m.lig)        {errno = 1; return 0;}
if (! pol.open (m.lig))    {errno = 1; return 0;}

m1 = m;                     if (errno) return 0;

pol.writecoeff (m.lig, N1);
pol.writecoeff (m.lig - 1, - m1.trace ());

for (k = 2; k <= m.lig; k++)   {

   for (i = 1; i <= m.lig; i++)   {
     r = pol.readcoeff (m.lig - k + 1);
     m1.writecoeff (i, i, m1.readcoeff (i, i) + r);
   }

   m1 = m * m1;   if (errno) return 0;

   pol.writecoeff (m.lig - k, - m1.trace () / ar_number(k));
}

return  ar_bairstow (pol, sol, prec, p, q);
}
```

11.3 Annotated Examples

Example 1

Let us consider the following matrix A:

$$A = \begin{pmatrix} 17 & 24 & 30 & 17 \\ 8 & 13 & 20 & 7 \\ 2 & 10 & 8 & 6 \\ -23 & -43 & -54 & -26 \end{pmatrix}$$

whose four proper values are $7, 2, -1, 4$.

```
DETERMINATION OF THE EIGENVALUES OF A MATRIX

Entry of matrix M :
Number of lines    : 4
Number of columns  : 4

M [1,1] = 17     M [1,2] = 24     M [1,3] = 30     M [1,4] = 17
M [2,1] = 8      M [2,2] = 13     M [2,3] = 20     M [2,4] = 7
M [3,1] = 2      M [3,2] = 10     M [3,3] = 8      M [3,4] = 6
M [4,1] = -23    M [4,2] = -43    M [4,3] = -54    M [4,4] = -26
```

```
p          : 0
q          : 0
Precision : 1e-10

E.V. 1 = -1 + 0 I
E.V. 2 = 2 + 0 I
E.V. 3 = 4 + 0 I
E.V. 4 = 7 + 0 I
```

Example 2

```
DETERMINATION OF THE EIGENVALUES OF A MATRIX

Entry of matrix M :
Number of lines   : 3
Number of columns : 3

M [1,1] = 0    M [1,2] = -73    M [1,3] = 25
M [2,1] = 1    M [2,2] = 39     M [2,3] = -13
M [3,1] = 3    M [3,2] = 103    M [3,3] = -34

p          : 0
q          : 0
Precision : 1e-10

E.V. 1 = 1 + -2 I
E.V. 2 = 1 + 2 I
E.V. 3 = 3 + 0 I
```

Matrix *A* has in this case two complex-conjugated eigenvalues, 1+2i and 1–2i.

Example 3

Let us consider the matrix:

$$A = \begin{pmatrix} 1 & 3 & -9 \\ 2 & 1 & 6 \\ 2 & 2 & 1 \end{pmatrix}$$

The eigenvalue 1 is triple root of the characteristic polynomial.

```
DETERMINATION OF THE EIGENVALUES OF A MATRIX

Entry of matrix M :
Number of lines   : 3
Number of columns : 3
```

```
M [1,1] = 1     M [1,2] = 3     M [1,3] = -9
M [2,1] = 2     M [2,2] = 1     M [2,3] = 6
M [3,1] = 2     M [3,2] = 2     M [3,3] = 1

p           : 0
q           : 0
Precision : 1e-8

E.V. 1 = 0.999999885 + -1.98666899e-07 I
E.V. 2 = 0.999999885 + 1.98666899e-07 I
E.V. 3 = 1.00000023 + 0 I
```

We realize that the precision of the triple root is only moderate: we meet here again the phenomenon seen in the search for multiple roots (see chapter 10).

There exist other methods of searching eigenvalues, but they all have the particularity of giving only approximate results for multiple roots.

---

12 Image of a Vector by a Matrix

12.1 Principle

Let us consider a matrix M and a vector U, such as the number of columns of M is equal to the dimension of U.

We therefore call the image of the vector U by the matrix M the vector V defined by the relation:

$V = M . U$

The dimension of V is equal to the number of lines of the matrix M.

12.2 Calculation Tool

The operator [ ] is overloaded for the couple (matrix, vector) which makes it possible to write:

```
V = M[U];
```

It must be placed in the file MAT\VECIM.CPP.

```
/*==============================================================
                        VECIM.CPP:
              PRODUCT OF A VECTOR BY A MATRIX
==========================================================*/

#include  "armath.h"
```

```
ar_vector &  ar_matrix::operator [] (ar_vector &u)
{
   static ar_vector  v1;
   ar_number          res;
   int                i, j;

   if  (u.lig != col)      {errno = 1; v1.close (); return v1;}
   if (! v1.open (lig))    {errno = 1; return v1;}

   for (v1.lig = lig, i = 1; i <= lig; i++)   {
      for (res = N0, j = 1; j <= col; j++)
         res += readcoeff (i, j) * u.readcoeff (j);
      v1.writecoeff (i, res);
   }

   return v1;
}
```

12.3 Annotated Example

Let us consider the matrix M and the following vector U:

$$M = \begin{pmatrix} 5 & -1/2 & 1 \\ -2 & 4 & 0 \\ 0 & 5/2 & 3 \\ -1 & 6 & 9 \end{pmatrix} \qquad U = \begin{pmatrix} 2 \\ -1 \\ 1/2 \end{pmatrix}$$

Vector V obtained is of dimension 4.

```
IMAGE OF A VECTOR BY A MATRIX V = M.U

Entry of matrix M :
Number of lines    : 4
Number of columns  : 3

M [1,1] = 5       M [1,2] = -1/2     M [1,3] = 1
M [2,1] = -2      M [2,2] = 4        M [2,3] = 0
M [3,1] = 0       M [3,2] = 5/2      M [3,3] = 3
M [4,1] = -1      M [4,2] = 6        M [4,3] = 9

Entry of vector U :
Number of lines    : 3

U [1] = 2
U [2] = -1
U [3] = 1/2
```

```
V [1]  =  +  11
V [2]  =  -  8
V [3]  =  -  1
V [4]  =  -  7 / 2
```

---

13 Solving a Linear System

13.1 Principle

Let us consider a square matrix M and a vector V of dimension n.

Solving the linear system $MU = V$ is to find the set of vectors U establishing this matricial relationship. When the matrix M cannot be inverted, the system is degenerate; the set of solutions is either infinite or empty. In contrast, when the matrix M can be inverted, the solution vector U is unique:

$$U = M^{-1} V$$

The linear system can be written as follows:

$$
\begin{pmatrix}
m_{11} & m_{12} & \cdots & m_{1n} \\
m_{21} & m_{22} & \cdots & m_{2n} \\
\cdots & \cdots & \cdots & \cdots \\
m_{n1} & m_{n2} & \cdots & m_{nn}
\end{pmatrix}
\begin{pmatrix}
u_1 \\
u_2 \\
\cdots \\
u_n
\end{pmatrix}
=
\begin{pmatrix}
v_1 \\
v_2 \\
\cdots \\
v_n
\end{pmatrix}
$$

We are going to solve it by the Gauss-Jordan method, whose algorithm depends on the following properties:

- we can multiply a line of the system by any number not equal to 0 without changing its solutions;
- in the same way we can add one line to another;
- finally, we can permute two lines.

REMARK: a line of the system is made up of the line of the matrix as well as the corresponding component v_i .

The Gauss-Jordan method consists in transforming the initial system by using these properties, until matrix M is replaced by the identity matrix I; the system then only amounts to $I \cdot U = V'$; vector V' contains the solution to the initial system.

This algorithm makes it possible to simultaneously solve several systems all using the same matrix M. Indeed let us suppose that we have the p following systems to solve:

$$
\begin{cases}
MU = V_1 \\
MU = V_2 \\
\quad \cdots \\
MU = V_p
\end{cases}
$$

By grouping the systems V_j, we obtain the following condensed form:

$$
\begin{pmatrix}
m_{11} & m_{12} & \cdots & m_{1n} \\
m_{21} & m_{22} & \cdots & m_{2n} \\
\cdots & \cdots & \cdots & \cdots \\
m_{n1} & m_{n2} & \cdots & m_{nn}
\end{pmatrix}
\begin{pmatrix}
u_1 \\
u_2 \\
\cdots \\
u_n
\end{pmatrix}
=
\begin{pmatrix}
v_1^1 \\
v_2^1 \\
\cdots \\
v_n^1
\end{pmatrix}
\begin{pmatrix}
v_1^2 \\
v_2^2 \\
\cdots \\
v_n^2
\end{pmatrix}
\cdots
\begin{pmatrix}
v_1^p \\
v_2^p \\
\cdots \\
v_n^p
\end{pmatrix}
$$

$$
\quad M \qquad\qquad U \qquad V_1 \qquad V_2 \qquad V_p
$$

Solving those p systems is therefore done in the same way as for only one system, but this time having as the line of the system the line of matrix M followed by all the ith components of the vectors V_j. We have used the multiple solving in the program of inversion of matrices; the n vectors V_j were:

$$
V_1 \begin{pmatrix} 1 \\ 0 \\ 0 \\ \cdots \\ 0 \end{pmatrix}
\qquad
V_2 \begin{pmatrix} 0 \\ 1 \\ 0 \\ \cdots \\ 0 \end{pmatrix}
\qquad \cdots \qquad
V_p \begin{pmatrix} 0 \\ \cdots \\ 0 \\ 0 \\ 1 \end{pmatrix}
$$

13.2 Algorithm of Gauss-Jordan

Let us consider the term m_{11} of the matrix. If it is equal to 0, let us interchange line 1 with another in order to obtain a term which is not equal to 0. We call this term a pivot, which explains the term "pivot method" sometimes given to this algorithm.

Let us therefore divide all the first line by m_{11}; we then obtain:

$$
\begin{pmatrix}
1 & \dfrac{m_{12}}{m_{11}} & \cdots & \dfrac{m_{1n}}{m_{11}} \\
m_{21} & m_{22} & \cdots & m_{2n} \\
\cdots & \cdots & \cdots & \cdots \\
m_{n1} & m_{n2} & \cdots & m_{nn}
\end{pmatrix}
\begin{pmatrix}
u_1 \\
u_2 \\
\cdots \\
u_n
\end{pmatrix}
=
\begin{pmatrix}
\dfrac{v_1}{m_{11}} \\
v_2 \\
\cdots \\
v_n
\end{pmatrix}
$$

Let us then subtract from each of the lines j ($j \neq 1$) line 1 multiplied by m_{j1}; this operation results in having zeros in all the rest of the first column.

Let us go on with the calculation with pivot m_{22}, then m_{kk} ($k < n$).

If sometimes it is impossible to find a pivot which is not equal to 0, the system cannot be inverted, and the line where this pivot occurs gives the rank of the matrix M, up to one unit.

13.3 Calculation Tool

The input parameters of this tool are the matrix M and the vector V representing the system.

On output, vector U contains the result, and det is the determinant of the matrix.

It must be placed in the file MAT\SYSTLIN.CPP.

```
/*=========================================================
                        SYSTLIN.CPP:
           DETERMINATION OF LINEAR SYSTEM SOLUTION SET
                  THROUGH GAUSS-JORDAN'S METHOD
  =======================================================*/

#include  "armath.h"

ar_vector & ar_lin_sys (ar_matrix &m, ar_vector &v,
                        ar_number &det)
{
   static ar_vector  v1;
   ar_matrix         m1;
   ar_number         r, pivot;
   int               i, j, n = m.lig, ligpivot, ligcour;

   //--------------------------------------------------- TESTS
   det = N1; v1.close ();
   if ((m.col != m.lig)  || (v.lig != n))
     {errno = 1; return v1;}


   //---------------------- INITIALISATION OF RESULT MATRIX
   m1 = m; v1 = v; if (errno) return v1;

   for (ligcour = 1; ligcour <= n; ligcour ++)  {
     ligpivot = ligcour;

     //----------- Determination of the first non-null pivot
     while ((m1.readcoeff (ligpivot, ligcour).small ()) &&
            (ligpivot < n))  {
       ligpivot ++;
       det = -det;
     }
     if (ligpivot == n)
       if (m1.readcoeff (ligpivot, ligcour).small ())
         {errno = 1; return v1;}

     //-------------------- Swap current line and pivot line
     for (j = 1; j <= n; j++)  {
       r = m1.readcoeff (ligcour, j);
```

```
        m1.writecoeff (ligcour, j, m1.readcoeff (ligpivot, j));
        m1.writecoeff (ligpivot, j, r);
    }
    r = v1.readcoeff (ligcour);
    v1.writecoeff (ligcour, v1.readcoeff (ligpivot));
    v1.writecoeff (ligpivot, r);
    pivot = m1.readcoeff (ligcour, ligcour);

    //--------------- Divide current line elements by pivot
    for (j = ligcour + 1; j <= n; j++)
      m1.writecoeff (ligcour, j,
         m1.readcoeff (ligcour, j) / pivot);
    v1.writecoeff (ligcour,
         v1.readcoeff (ligcour) / pivot);
    det *= pivot;
    m1.writecoeff (ligcour, ligcour, N1);

    //------------------------------- Update other lines
    for (i = 1; i <= n; i++)
      if (i != ligcour)  {
          r = m1.readcoeff (i, ligcour);
          for (j = ligcour + 1; j <= n; j++)
            m1.writecoeff (i, j,
                 m1.readcoeff (i, j) -
               r * m1.readcoeff (ligcour, j));
          v1.writecoeff (i,
                 v1.readcoeff (i) -
               r * v1.readcoeff (ligcour));
          m1.writecoeff (i, ligcour, N0);
      }
  }
  return v1;
}
```

13.4 Annotated Example

```
DETERMINATION OF A LINEAR SYSTEM SOLUTION M.U = V

Entry of matrix M :
Number of lines   : 3
Number of columns : 3

M [1,1] = 2    M [1,2] = -1    M [1,3] = 1
M [2,1] = 1    M [2,2] = 5     M [2,3] = -2
M [3,1] = 3    M [3,2] = -2    M [3,3] = 3
```

```
Entry of vector V :
Number of lines    : 3
V [1] = 5
V [2] = 1
V [3] = 3

U [1] = + 47 / 14
U [2] = - 27 / 14
U [3] = - 51 / 14
```

The solution of the system:

$$\begin{pmatrix} 2 & -1 & 1 \\ 1 & 5 & -2 \\ 3 & -2 & 3 \end{pmatrix} \begin{pmatrix} u_1 \\ u_2 \\ u_3 \end{pmatrix} = \begin{pmatrix} 5 \\ 1 \\ 3 \end{pmatrix}$$

is:

$$U = \begin{pmatrix} 47/14 \\ -27/14 \\ -51/14 \end{pmatrix}$$

14 Speed and Accuracy of the Calculations

When the order of the matrices does not go beyond 10, the calculations are generally very precise and very fast (a few seconds).

The precision remains satisfactory when the dimensions increase for simple operations (linear combination, multiplication, raising to a power).

However, the results of inversion, of solving systems or of searching for eigenvalues can become inadequate.

In particular, numerical errors can become very important if the initial matrix is not well "conditioned" (a matrix which is not well conditioned can be characterized by the dispersion of its coefficients).

15 Exploitation Tools

The following tools make possible the direct exploitation of the calculation tools shown in this chapter.

The following tool must be placed in the file MAT\UVECLC.CPP:

```
/*============================================================
                        UVECLC.CPP:
     EXPLOITATION OF LINEAR COMBINATION OF TWO VECTORS
============================================================*/

#include   "armath.h"

void  ar_use_combination_vector ()
{
  ar_vector   v1 ("V1"), v2 ("V2"), v ("V");
  ar_number   a, b;

  cout << "LINEAR COMBINATION OF TWO VECTORS
             V = a.V1 + b.V2\n\n";

  ar_read ("Input scalar a  : ", &a, AR_TNUM);
  ar_read ("Input scalar b  : ", &b, AR_TNUM);

  cin >> v1; if (errno) return;
  cin >> v2; if (errno) return;

  v = a * v1;
  v += b * v2;
// Warning : never v = a * v1 + b * v2 - See book

  if (! errno)
    cout << "\nVector V (a.V1 + b.V2) :\n" << v;
  else
    cerr << "\nImpossible calculation\n";

  ar_pause ();
}
```

The following tools must be placed in the file MAT\UVECMUL.CPP:

```
/*============================================================
                       UVECMUL.CPP:
              EXPLOITATION OF VECTOR PRODUCTS
============================================================*/

#include   "armath.h"

//----------------------------------------- Scalar product
void ar_use_scalar_product ()
{
  ar_vector   u ("U"), v ("V");

  cout << "SCALAR PRODUCT OF TWO VECTORS : U.V\n\n";
```

```
  cin >> u; if (errno) return;
  cin >> v; if (errno) return;

  cout << "\nU.V = " << u * v << "\n";

  ar_pause ();
}

//----------------------------------- Vectorial product
void  ar_use_vectorial_product ()
{
  ar_vector  u ("U"), v ("V"), w ("W");

  cout << "VECTORIAL PRODUCT OF TWO VECTORS (U ^ V)\n\n";

  cin >> u; if (errno) return;
  cin >> v; if (errno) return;

  if ((u.lig == 3) && (v.lig == 3))  {
    w = u ^ v;
    cout << "\n U ^ V :\n" << w;
  }
  else
    cerr << "Incorrect dimensions\n";

  ar_pause ();
}

//------------------------------------------ Mixed product
void  ar_use_mixed_product ()
{
  ar_vector  u ("U"), v ("V"), w ("W");

  cout << "MIXED PRODUCT OF THREE VECTORS: det (U,V,W)\n\n";

  cin >> u; if (errno) return;
  cin >> v; if (errno) return;
  cin >> w; if (errno) return;

  if ((u.lig == 3) && (v.lig == 3) && (w.lig == 3))
    cout << "\nThe mixed product is : "
         << ar_mix_vec (u, v, w) << "\n";
  else
    cerr << "\nIncorrect dimensions\n";

  ar_pause ();
}
```

The following tool must be placed in the file MAT\UMATLC.CPP.

```
/*===========================================================
                        UMATLC.CPP:
          UTILISATION OF MATRICES LINEAR COMBINATION
===========================================================*/

#include  "armath.h"

void  ar_use_combination_matrix ()
{
  ar_matrix  m1 ("M1"), m2 ("M2"), m ("M");
  ar_number  a, b;

  cout << "LINEAR COMBINATION OF MATRICES M = a.M1+b.M2\n\n";

  ar_read ("Input scalar a  : ", &a, AR_TNUM);
  ar_read ("Input scalar b  : ", &b, AR_TNUM);

  cin >> m1; if (errno) return;
  cin >> m2; if (errno) return;

  m = a * m1; m += b * m2;
// Warning : never m = a * m1 + b * m2 - See text

  if (! errno)
    cout <<  m;
  else
    cerr << "Impossible calculation\n";

  ar_pause ();
}
```

The following tool must be placed in the file MAT\UMATMUL.CPP:

```
/*===========================================================
                        UMATMUL.CPP:
          UTILISATION OF MATRICES MULTIPLICATION
===========================================================*/

#include  "armath.h"

void  ar_use_multiplication_matrix ()
{
  ar_matrix  m1 ("M1"), m2 ("M2"), m ("M");

  cout << "MULTIPLICATION OF TWO MATRICES M = M1.M2\n\n";
```

```
  cin >> m1; if (errno) return;
  cin >> m2; if (errno) return;

  m = m1 * m2;

  if (! errno)
    cout << m;
  else
    cerr << "Impossible multiplication\n";

  ar_pause ();
}
```

The following tool must be placed in the file `MAT\UMATRAIS.CPP`:

```
/*===========================================================
                    UMATRAIS.CPP:
        UTILISATION OF MATRIX RAISING TO POWER N
===========================================================*/

#include  "armath.h"

void  ar_use_raising_matrix ()
{
  ar_matrix  m ("M"), p ("P");
  long       n;

  cout << "RAISING A MATRIX TO THE POWER n : P = M^n\n\n";

  cin >> m; if (errno) return;

  ar_read ("n = ", &n, AR_TLON);

  p = m ^ n;
  if (! errno)
    cout << p;
  else
    cerr << "Impossible calculation\n";

  ar_pause ();
}
```

The following tool must be placed in the file `MAT\UDETER.CPP`:

```
/*===========================================================
                    UDETER.CPP:
      UTILISATION OF MATRIX DETERMINANT DETERMINATION
===========================================================*/
```

```
#include   "armath.h"

void  ar_use_determinant_matrix ()
{
  ar_matrix   m ("M"), n;
  ar_number   det;
  int         rang;

  cout << "CALCULATION OF THE DETERMINANT OF A MATRIX M\n\n";

  cin  >> m; if (errno) return;

  n = ar_inv_mat (m, rang, det);

  if (! errno)
    cout << "The determinant is : " << det << "\n";
  else
    cerr << "Insufficient memory\n";

  ar_pause ();
}
```

The following tool must be placed in the file MAT\UMATINV.CPP:

```
/*===========================================================
                      UMATINV.CPP:
            UTILISATION OF MATRICES INVERSION
=============================================================*/

#include   "armath.h"

void  ar_use_inversion_matrix ()
{
  ar_matrix   m ("M"), n ("N");
  ar_number   det;
  int         rang, i, j, b;

  cout << "INVERSION OF MATRIX M\n\n";

  cin  >> m; if (errno) return;

  ar_read ("Multiplication by the determinant ? ", &b,
           AR_TBOO);

  n = ar_inv_mat (m, rang, det);

  if ((! errno) && (! det.zero ()))  {
      cout << "The determinant is : " << det << "\n";
```

```
        if (b)
          for (i = 1; i <= n.lig; i++)
            for (j = 1; j <= n.col; j++)
              n.writecoeff (i, j, det * n.readcoeff (i, j));
        cout << "Inverse matrix :\n" << n;
    }
    else
      cerr << "Imposisible inversion - The rank of the " <<
              "matrix is : " << rang << "\n";

    ar_pause ();
}
```

The following tool must be placed in the file MAT\UMATTRAC.CPP:

```
/*==========================================================
                      UMATTRAC.CPP:
          UTILISATION OF MATRIX TRACE CALCULATION
==========================================================*/

#include  "armath.h"

void  ar_use_trace_matrix ()
{
  ar_matrix  m ("M");
  ar_number  n;

  cout << "CALCULATION OF THE TRACE OF THE MATRIX M\n\n";

  cin  >> m;

  n = m.trace ();

  if (! errno)
    cout << "The trace is : " << n << "\n";

  ar_pause ();
}
```

The following tool must be placed in the file MAT\UEIGENVA.CPP:

```
/*==========================================================
                      UEIGENVA.CPP:
          UTILISATION OF EIGENVALUES DETERMINATION
==========================================================*/

#include  "armath.h"
```

```
void  ar_use_eigen_values ()
{
  ar_matrix  m ("M");
  complex    *sol;
  ar_double  p, q, prec;
  int        i;

  cout << "DETERMINATION OF THE EIGENVALUES OF A MATRIX\n\n";

  cin  >> m; if ((errno) || (m.lig != m.col)) return;

  sol = (complex *) calloc (m.lig, sizeof (complex));

  if (sol && (! errno))  {
    ar_read ("p                       : ", &p,      AR_TDOU);
    ar_read ("q                       : ", &q,      AR_TDOU);
    ar_read ("Precision               : ", &prec,   AR_TDOU);
    ar_nl;

    if (ar_eigen_values (m, sol, prec, p, q))
      for (i = 0; i < m.lig; i++)
      cout << "E.V. " << (i + 1) << " =  " <<
              real (sol [i]) << "  +  "   <<
              imag (sol [i]) << "I\n";
    else
      cerr << "Impossible calculation with those \
              parameters\n";
  }
  else
    cerr << "Insufficient memory\n";

  ar_pause ();
}
```

The following tool must be placed in the file `MAT\UVECIM.CPP`:

```
/*============================================================
                       UVECIM.CPP:
            UTILISATION OF VECTOR MATRIX IMAGES
============================================================*/

#include  "armath.h"

void  ar_use_image_vector ()
{
  ar_matrix  m ("M");
  ar_vector  u ("U"), v ("V");
```

```
  cout << "IMAGE OF A VECTOR BY A MATRIX V = M.U\n\n";

  cin  >> m;  if (errno) return;
  cin  >> u;  if (errno) return;

  v = m [u];

  if (! errno)
    cout << "Vector V :\n" << v;
  else
    cerr << "Impossible calculation\n";

  ar_pause ();
}
```

The following tool must be placed in the file MAT\USYSTLIN.CPP:

```
/*============================================================
                      USYSTLIN.CPP:
         UTILISATION OF LINEAR SYSTEM SOLVING
============================================================*/

#include  "armath.h"

void  ar_use_linear_system ()
{
  ar_matrix  m ("M");
  ar_vector  u ("U"), v ("V");
  ar_number  det;

  cout << "DETERMINATION OF A LINEAR SYSTEM SOLUTION \
           M.U = V\n\n";

  cin  >> m;  if (errno) return;
  cin  >> v;  if (errno) return;

  u = ar_lin_sys (m, v, det);

  if (! errno)
    cout << "Vector U :\n" << u;
  else
    cerr << "Impossible resolution\n";

  ar_pause ();
}
```

10
Equations

Solving equations is very important in numerical analysis. However, only a few particular cases can be solved in an exact way: usually one can only obtain approximate values of the roots.

There exists exact algebraic formulas giving the roots of the polynomial equations of degree less than 5 and the mathematician Evariste Gallois showed that this exact solution was no longer possible for the polynomials of degree greater than or equal to 5.

The systematic search for the roots of these polynomials can however be approximated through Bairstow's method. The non-polynomial equations can also be solved through several methods of approximation. We will study the method of dichotomies and Newton's method. Finally we will study a method of solving systems of non-linear equations with two unknowns.

The tools used in this chapter will be placed in the subdirectory EQUATION.

1 Method of Bisection

The simplest method of search for an approximation to the zeros of any function is the bisection method.

1.1 Principle

Let us consider a given function f; we are going to try to determine its zeros over a fixed interval $[x_{min}, x_{max}]$.

Let us suppose that we know an interval $[a, b]$ over which the function changes sign, that is, such as $f(a).f(b) < 0$. If the function f is continuous, we know that this interval then contains a root of f.

Let us divide the interval in two by writing:

$$c = \frac{a+b}{2}$$

Two cases are possible:
– if $f(c)$ is of the sign of $f(a)$, the root belongs to the interval $[c, b]$.
– if $f(c)$ is of the opposite sign to $f(a)$, the root belongs to $[a, c]$.

We have therefore surrounded the root with an interval twice as small. One has only to repeat the process until the required precision is reached.

1.2 Calculation Tool

The bisection method has two major drawbacks: one has to know beforehand an interval $[a, b]$ on which the function changes sign, and only one root can be found on that interval.

The tool suggested doesn't have those two drawbacks. The interval $[x_{min}, x_{max}]$ is broken up into n subintervals. On each of those subintervals, the program sees if the function changes sign; if that is the case, the bisection method can be applied. By choosing n high enough, we can obtain all the roots.

The parameters of the tool `ar_dichotomies` are the following:
– `f`, function with one variable describing the equation;
– `xi` and `xf`, extremes of the interval to be studied;
– `n`, number of subintervals;
– `prec`, precision wanted.

On output, the tool puts in buffer `t` all the roots found, and it also gives the number of roots found. The boolean `errno` indicates if the function has not been defined at one point or another.

REMARK: The standard version of the tool is limited to the first 50 roots. The constant `MAXSOL` should be changed to increase this limit.

The tool will be placed in the file `EQUATION\DICHO.CPP`.

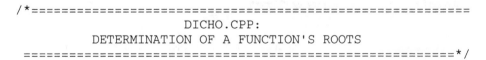

```
/*=============================================================
                        DICHO.CPP:
           DETERMINATION OF A FUNCTION'S ROOTS
 ===========================================================*/
```

```
#include "armath.h"

#define  MAXSOL  50

void ar_dichotomies (
     ar_double (*f) (ar_double), ar_double xi, ar_double xf,
     int n, ar_double prec, ar_buffer &res)
{
  ar_double  x, y, z, p, q, pas = (xf - xi) / n;
  int        i;

  if (! res.open ("Roots of an equation (bisection \
                  method)",
      1, MAXSOL))  {errno = TRUE; return;}
  for (i = 0; i < n; i++)  {
    x = xi + i * pas;
    z = f (x);             if (errno)  return;
    y = f (x + pas);  if (errno)  return;
    if (z == 0)
      res.addcouple (x, 0);
    if (z * y < 0)  {
      p = x; q = x + pas;
      do  {
        x = (p + q) / 2; y = f (x); if (errno)  return;
        if (y * z > 0) p = x;
        else q = x;
      } while ((y != 0) && (fabs (q - p) > prec));
      res.addcouple (x, 0);
    }
  }
  if (y == 0) res.addcouple (xf, 0);
}
```

1.3 Annotated Examples

Example 1

```
EQUATIONS : BISECTION METHOD

Function studied     : x + 4 * log (x) - 5
Enter xmin           : 1
Enter xmax           : 10
Enter precision      : 1e-10
Enter n              : 10

Solution 1 : 2.076761384861  # 1975 / 951
```

Example 2

```
EQUATIONS : BISECTION METHOD

Function studied      : 4 * sin (x) - x + 1
Enter xmin            : -3
Enter xmax            : 3
Enter precision       : 1e-10
Enter n               : 6

Solution 1 : -2.210083944083   # -263 / 119
Solution 2 : -0.342185052868   # -3273 / 9565
Solution 3 : 2.702061373333    # 4326 / 1601
```

The roots of the equations $4 \sin x + 1 - x = 0$ can be found instantaneously up to 10^{-10} (the precision is effectively of 10^{-10} when the root is not multiple).

Example 3

```
EQUATIONS : BISECTION METHOD

Function sudied       : -2*x^4 + 4*x^3 + 90*x^2 + 68*x - 160
Enter xmin            : -10
Enter xmax            : 10
Enter precision       : 1e-10
Enter n               : 4

Solution 1 : - 5
Solution 2 : 0.999999999985
Solution 3 : 7.999999999956
```

With four subintervals, the program finds only three roots, whereas the four roots are obtained with 20 subintervals:

```
EQUATIONS : BISECTION METHOD

Function studied      : -2*x^4 + 4*x^3 + 90*x^2 + 68*x - 160
Enter xmin            : -10
Enter xmax            : 10
Enter precision       : 1e-10
Enter n               : 20

Solution 1 : - 5
Solution 2 : - 2
Solution 3 : 1
Solution 4 : 8
```

When we know neither the number nor the approximate position of the roots, we can adopt the following process: a first search with a low precision and an important number of subintervals making possible a speedy location of all the roots, then a second search with a high precision and a limited number of subintervals leading then to precise values.

2 Newton's Method

2.1 Principle

We are once more going to consider an equation of the type $f(x) = 0$.

Newton's method consists in the calculation of a series of values (x_n) converging towards the root α of the equation. From a point x_0, we can successively calculate:

$$x_1 = x_0 - \frac{f(x_0)}{f'(x_0)}$$

$$x_2 = x_1 - \frac{f(x_1)}{f'(x_1)}$$

. . . .

$$x_n = x_{n-1} - \frac{f(x_{n-1})}{f'(x_{n-1})}$$

The process stops when the difference $|x_n - x_{n-1}|$ becomes less than the maximal error which has been fixed: x_n is then an approximate value of α.

The method can be applied on the following double condition: it must be possible for the function to be differentiated and the derivative must not cancel itself at the neighborhood of α. In particular, the method cannot be used for the determination of multiple roots.

2.2 Calculation Tool

The parameters of the tool `ar_newton` are the following:
  - `f`, function with one variable representing the equation to be solved;
  - `xo`, initial point of search;
  - `prec`, precision.

The value of the function is the root found. If the tool `ar_newton` doesn't find any root, or if the function cannot be defined at one point, then the boolean `errno` is positioned on TRUE.

The derivative of the function is calculated in an approximate way by the program by the formula:

$$f'(x) = \frac{f(x+h) - f(x-h)}{2h} \qquad \text{with } h = 0.01.$$

The tool must be placed in the file EQUATION\NEWTON.CPP.

```
/*===========================================================
                       NEWTON.CPP:
   SEARCH FOR THE ROOTS OF A FUNCTION (Newton's method)
=============================================================*/

#include "armath.h"

#define  H        0.01
#define  MAXITER  100

ar_double  ar_newton (ar_double  (*f) (ar_double),
                      ar_double xo, ar_double prec)
{
  int        iter = 1;
  ar_double  x, y, z;

  errno = FALSE;

  for (x = xo; iter < MAXITER; iter++)  {
    y = f (x - H);                     if (errno)  return 0;
    z = (f (x + H) - y) / 2 / H;  if (errno)  return 0;
    if (z == 0)
      break;
    y  = f (x) / z;                    if (errno)  return 0;
    x -= y;
    if (fabs (y) < prec) return x;
  }

  errno = TRUE;
  return 0;
}
```

2.3 Annotated Examples

Example 1

```
EQUATIONS : NEWTON'S METHOD

Function studied    : 4 * sin (x) - x + 1
Input xo            : -3
Input precision     : 1e-10

Solution :          -2.210083944093  # -263 / 119
```

```
EQUATIONS : NEWTON'S METHOD

Function studied       : 4 * sin (x) - x + 1
Enter xo               : 0
Enter precision        : 1e-10

Solution :                -0.342185052924   # -3273 / 9565
```

According to the initial value x_0, the detected roots are not the same. The precision of the values obtained is 10^{-10}; we will be able to compare theses values to the results given through the bisection method.

Example 2

```
EQUATIONS : NEWTON'S METHOD

Function studied       : x + 4 * log (x) - 5
Enter xo               : 1
Enter precision        : 1e-10

Solution :                2.076761384869   # 1975 / 951
```

The root obtained differs from the value given through the bisection method by less than 10^{-10}.

2.4 Which Method is to be Used ?

Newton's method is very quick; in general, a few iterations are enough in order to obtain the root with maximal precision.

However, we have a marked preference for the bisection method because the latter makes possible the simultaneous seach of several roots, and has a condition of application which is very wide (it is sufficient for the function to be continuous); furthermore, the saving of time brought by Newton's method is not really tangible, in most cases.

3 Systems of Two Equations With Two Unknowns

The problem is as follows; one has to determine a solution (α, β) of the system:

$$\begin{cases} f(x,y) = 0 \\ g(x,y) = 0 \end{cases}$$

3.1 Principle

Here, we are going to use a generalization of Newton's method, called linearisation.

We are therefore going to form at the initial point (x_0, y_0), two series (x_n) and (y_n) converging towards (α, β).

The relation of definition of the series is the following relation of recurrence:

$$x_{k+1} = x_k - \frac{f \cdot g'_y - g \cdot f'_y}{\Delta}$$

$$y_{k+1} = y_k - \frac{g \cdot f'_x - f \cdot g'_x}{\Delta} \qquad \text{with} \qquad \Delta = f'_x \cdot g'_y - f'_y \cdot g'_x$$

The notations adopted for the partial derivatives are the following:

$$f'_x = \frac{\partial f}{\partial x} \qquad f'_y = \frac{\partial f}{\partial y}$$

$$g'_x = \frac{\partial g}{\partial x} \qquad g'_y = \frac{\partial g}{\partial y}$$

The program stops when the quantity $|x_n - x_{n-1}| + |y_n - y_{n-1}|$ is less than the maximal error which has been fixed; (x_n, y_n) then constitutes an approximate solution of the system.

3.2 Calculation Tool

The parameters of the tool `ar_non_linear_system` are:
- `f` and `g`, the functions of x et y describing the system;
- `xo` and `yo`, coordinates of the initial point;
- `prec`, precision.

On output, x and y contain the solution found. The variable `errno` is not equal to 0 if the method does not converge, or if an error is made during evaluation of the function. The program calculates the approximate values of the different partial derivatives by the following formulas:

$$f'_x (x, y) \;=\; \frac{f(x+h,y) - f(x-h,y)}{2h}$$

$$f'_y (x, y) \;=\; \frac{f(x,y+h) - f(x,y-h)}{2h}$$

$$g'_x (x, y) \;=\; \frac{g(x+h,y) - g(x-h,y)}{2h}$$

$$g'_y (x, y) \;=\; \frac{g(x,y+h) - g(x,y-h)}{2h}$$

The tool must be placed in the file EQUATION\SYSTEMS.CPP.

```
/*==========================================================
                      SYSTEMS.CPP:
        SOLVING NON-LINEAR SYSTEMS WITH 2 VARIABLES
   ========================================================*/

#include "armath.h"

#define   MAXITER  100
#define   H        0.01
#define   H2       2 * H

void  ar_non_linear_system (
      ar_double (*f) (ar_double, ar_double),
      ar_double (*g) (ar_double, ar_double),
      ar_double xo, ar_double yo, ar_double prec,
      ar_double &x, ar_double &y)
{
  int        iter = 0;
  ar_double  a, b, c, d, delta, m, n, p, q;

  x  = xo; y = yo;

  do {
    if (++iter > MAXITER)  {errno = TRUE; return;}
    a  = f (x + H, y);
    if (errno) return;
    b  = g (x + H, y); if (errno) return;
    a -= f (x - H, y); if (errno) return;
    b -= g (x - H, y); if (errno) return;
    c  = f (x, y + H); if (errno) return;
    d  = g (x, y + H); if (errno) return;
    c -= f (x, y - H); if (errno) return;
    d -= g (x, y - H); if (errno) return;
    a /= H2; b /= H2;
    c /= H2; d /= H2;
    if ((delta = a * d - b * c) == 0)  {
      errno = 1;
      return;
    }
    m = f (x, y);        if (errno) return;
    n = g (x, y);        if (errno) return;
    p = (m * d - n * c) / delta;
    q = (n * a - m * b) / delta;
    x -= p;
    y -= q;
  } while (fabs (p) + fabs (q) > prec);
  errno = FALSE;
}
```

3.3 Annotated Examples

Example 1

```
SOLVING NON-LINEAR SYSTEMS

Enter f (x, y)          : x^2 + y^2 + 2*(x+y) - 23
Enter g (x, y)          : x^2 + y^2 + x*y - 19
xo                      : -1
yo                      : 1
Precision               : 1e-10

x =             -5
y =              2
```

If we choose the point $(0, 0)$, the program indicates that the method is inadequate: this is due to the fact that all the derivatives are equal to 0 at the origin.

Example 2

```
SOLVING NON-LINEAR SYSTEMS

Enter f (x, y)          : 8*x - y - 3
Enter g (x, y)          : x^2 + 4*x*y - 5*y*y + 12*x + 92
xo                      : 0
yo                      : 0
Precision               : 1e-10

x =          -0.163763066202   # -47 / 287
y =          -4.310104529617   # -1237 / 287

SOLVING NON-LINEAR SYSTEMS

Enter f (x, y)          : 8*x - y - 3
Enter g (x, y)          : x^2 + 4*x*y - 5*y*y + 12*x + 92
xo                      : 1
yo                      : 1
Precision               : 1e-10

x =              1
y =              5
```

Here both solutions of the system are found in an exact way.
The first couple is effectively $(\frac{-47}{287}, \frac{-1237}{287})$.

Example 3

This method also makes it possible to determine the complex zeros of a complex function. Let us try to find the roots of the equation:

$$z^2 + z + 1 = 0$$

Let us write:

$$z = x + iy$$

The equation becomes after substituting:

$$(x + iy)^2 + (x + iy) + 1 = 0$$

$$(x^2 - y^2 + x + 1) + i(2xy + y) = 0$$

This equation can be verified if the real part and the imaginary part are equal to 0; therefore x and y are two solutions of the system:

$$\begin{cases} x^2 - y^2 + x + 1 = 0 \\ 2xy + y = 0 \end{cases}$$

```
SOLVING NON-LINEAR SYSTEMS

Enter f (x, y)          : x^2 - y^2 + x + 1
Enter g (x, y)          : 2*x*y + y
xo                      : 1
yo                      : 1
Precision               : 1e-10

x =                     -0.5        # -1 / 2
y =            0.866025403784       # 2521 / 2911

SOLVING NON-LINEAR SYSTEMS

Enter f (x, y)          : x^2 - y^2 + x + 1
Enter g (x, y)          : 2*x*y + y
xo                      : -1
yo                      : -1
Precision               : 1e-10

x =                     -0.5        # -1 / 2
y =           -0.866025403784       # -2521 / 2911
```

The program effectively finds the two roots of $z^2 + z + 1 = 0$, that is:

$$j = -\frac{1}{2} + \frac{\sqrt{3}}{2} i \qquad j^2 = -\frac{1}{2} - \frac{\sqrt{3}}{2} i$$

4 Exploitation Tools

The following tools makes possible the direct exploitation of the previous calculation tools.
This one must be placed in the file EQUATION\UDICHO.CPP:

```
/*============================================================
                       UDICHO.CPP:
              UTILISATION OF DICHOTOMIZING METHOD
============================================================*/

#include "armath.h"

void ar_use_dichotomies ()
{
  int         i, n;
  ar_double   xmin, xmax, prec;

  ar_init_entry ("EQUATIONS : DICHOTOMIZING METHOD");
  ar_fill_entry ("Function studied", &ar_glob_f, AR_TFUN);
  ar_fill_entry ("Enter xmin",       &xmin, AR_TDOU);
  ar_fill_entry ("Enter xmax",       &xmax, AR_TDOU);
  ar_fill_entry ("Enter precision",  &prec, AR_TDOU);
  ar_fill_entry ("Enter n",          &n,    AR_TINT);
  if (ar_do_entry ()) return;

  ar_dichotomies (ar_eval_f, xmin,xmax, n, prec, ar_buff[1]);

  if (ar_buff [1].nbelts () == 0)
    cout << "No solutions\n";
  else
    for (i = 1; i <= ar_buff [1].nbelts (); i++)
      cout << "Solution " << setw (3) << i << " : " <<
              ar_buff [1].readx (i) <<
              ar_rational (ar_buff [1].readx (i)) << "\n";

  ar_pause ();
}
```

The following tool must be placed in the file EQUATION\UNEWTON.CPP:

```
/*============================================================
                       UNEWTON.CPP:
                UTILISATION OF NEWTON'S METHOD
============================================================*/

#include "armath.h"
```

```
void ar_use_newton ()
{
  ar_double   r, xo, prec;

  ar_init_entry ("EQUATIONS : NEWTON'S METHOD");
  ar_fill_entry ("Function studied", &ar_glob_f, AR_TFUN);
  ar_fill_entry ("Enter xo",    &xo,    AR_TDOU);
  ar_fill_entry ("Enter prec", &prec, AR_TDOU);
  if (ar_do_entry ()) return;

  r = ar_newton (ar_eval_f, xo, prec);

  if (errno)
    cerr << "No solution or non-adapted method\n";
  else
    cout << "Solution : " << r << ar_rational (r) << "\n";

  ar_pause ();
}
```

The following tool must be placed in the file EQUATION\USYSTEM.CPP:

```
/*===========================================================
                        USYSTEM.CPP:
         USING THE SOLVING OF NON-LINEAR SYSTEMS
===========================================================*/

#include "armath.h"

void  ar_use_non_linear_syst ()
{
  ar_double   xo, yo, x, y, prec;

  ar_init_entry ("SOLVING NON-LINEAR SYSTEMS");
  ar_fill_entry ("Enter f (x, y)", &ar_glob_f, AR_TFYI);
  ar_fill_entry ("Enter g (x, y)", &ar_glob_g, AR_TFYI);
  ar_fill_entry ("xo", &xo, AR_TDOU);
  ar_fill_entry ("yo", &yo, AR_TDOU);
  ar_fill_entry ("Precision", &prec, AR_TDOU);
  ar_do_entry ();

  ar_non_linear_system (ar_eval_fxy, ar_eval_gxy, xo, yo,
                        prec, x, y);
  if (errno)
    cerr << "Undefined functions or inadapted method\n";
  else  {
    cout << "x = " << setw (25) << x << ar_rational (x)
         << "\n";
```

```
    cout << "y = " << setw (25) << y << ar_rational (y)
        << "\n";
}

ar_pause ();
}
```

11

Graphical Representations

In this chapter, we will exploit the graphical characteristics of personal computers in order to display the graphical representations of several types of functions.

We will be able to draw the analytical curves, of equation $y = f(x)$, the discrete curves, given by a series of points: for example the parametric curves, the cycloidal curves and the curves with a polar equation.

The tools used in this chapter will be placed in the subdirectory CURVE.

---

1 Drawing of Axes

1.1 Principle

A special tool will be used for the preparation of the drawing of a curve:

– it calculates the scale on each axis, the coordinates of the center of the orthogonal coordinates system (which has to appear on the screen), and the multiplying coefficients which make it possible to convert the values of x and y into a number of points on the screen;

– it draws graduated axes and a "grid", which in fact constitutes a square pattern of dotted lines on the screen making it possible to locate certain points.

The values of the graduations, calculated by the program in order to optimise the readability, are whole powers of 10 (for example 0.01, 1, 10). These values will be displayed at the bottom of the screen (*PX* on the axis of the abcissas, and *PY* on the axis of the ordinates). In fact it is possible to have an orthonormal coordinates system which corresponds to the case where *PX = PY*.

1.2 The Tool for Drawing

The parameters of input of the tool `ar_draw_axes` are the following:
- xn and xm: scale of the abscissas (minimal and maximal value of *x*);
- yn and ym: scale of the ordinates (minimal and maximal value of *y*);
- axes: boolean making possible the effective drawing of the axes;
- grid: boolean making possible the effective drawing of the grid;
- ortho: boolean making it possible to obtain an orthonormal coordinates system.
At the output, the tool gives:
- xa and ya, coordinates on the screen of the center of the coordinates system;
- ex and ey, the multiplying coefficients which make it possible to obtain a number of pixels from the real values of *x* and *y*.

This tool will be placed in the file `CURVES\AXES.CPP`. It is used by the majority of graphical tools.

```
/*==========================================================
                       AXES.CPP :
       TOOL FOR DRAWING AXES, GRADUATIONS AND THE GRID
   ========================================================*/

#include "armath.h"

void ar_draw_axes (ar_double &xn, ar_double &xm,
 ar_double &yn, ar_double &ym, ar_double &ex, ar_double &ey,
 int &xa, int &ya, int axes, int ortho, int grid)
{
  ar_double   xx, yy, ll, px, py, u, r;
  int         i, j, k, hx, hy, x, y;
  int         col4 = ar_maxcol - 4;
  int         lig4 = ar_maxlig - 4;

  if (xn > 0)   xn = 0;
  if (xm < 0)   xm = 0;
  if (yn > 0)   yn = 0;
  if (ym < 0)   ym = 0;
  if (xm == xn)   {
   xn = -1; xm = 1;
  }
```

```
if (ym == yn)  {
 yn = -1;
 ym = 1;
}
xx = xm - xn;
yy = ym - yn;

if (ortho)  {
  r  = (double) col4 / (double) lig4 / ar_round;
  ll = yy * r;
  if (xx > ll)  ll = xx;
  py = px = pow10 (floor (log10 (ll / 4)));
  u  = col4 / floor (ll / px + 1.5);
  hx = floor (u);
  hy = floor (u / ar_round);
  u  = xx - r * yy;
  xa = (u < 0) ? 2 + col4 * (0.5 + (-xn - xx/2)/r/yy) :
               2 + col4 * (-xn)/xx;
  ya = (u > 0) ? 2 + lig4 * (0.5 + (ym - yy/2)*r/xx) :
               2 + lig4 * ym / yy;
}
else  {
  px  = pow10 (floor (log10 (xx / 4)));
  py  = pow10 (floor (log10 (yy / 4)));
  hx  = floor (col4 / floor (xx / px + 1.5));
  hy  = floor (lig4 / floor (yy / py + 1.5));
  xa = 2 + col4 * (-xn) / xx;
  ya = 2 + lig4 * ym / yy;
}
ex = hx / px;
ey = hy / py;

if (axes)  {
  ar_line (0, ya, ar_maxcol, ya);
  ar_line (xa, 0, xa, ar_maxlig);

  ar_erase_line (25);
  ar_grgotoxy (1, 25);
  ar_outtext   ("SCALE :  ");
  sprintf      (ar_temp, "(DX = %10.5lf  ", px);
  ar_outtext   (ar_temp);
  sprintf      (ar_temp, "DY = %10.5lf)", py);
  ar_outtext   (ar_temp);

  for (i = -xa / hx; i <= (ar_maxcol - xa) / hx; i++)  {
    x = xa + i * hx;
    ar_line (x, ya-2, x, ya+2);
    if (i %  5 == 0) ar_line (x, ya-3, x, ya+3);
```

```
        if (i % 10 == 0) ar_line (x, ya-4, x, ya+4);
      }
    for (i = -ya / hy; i <= (ar_maxlig - ya) / hy; i++)   {
      y = ya + i * hy;
      ar_line (xa-2, y, xa+2, y);
      if (i %  5 == 0) ar_line (xa-3, y, xa+3, y);
      if (i % 10 == 0) ar_line (xa-4, y, xa+4, y);
    }
  }

  if (axes && grid)   {
    for (i = -xa / hx; i <= (ar_maxcol - xa) / hx; i++)   {
      x = xa + i * hx;
      k = (i % 5 == 0) ? 2 : 4;
      for (j = 0; j < ar_maxlig; j += k)
      ar_putpixel (x, j, 1);
    }
    for (i = -ya / hy; i <= (ar_maxlig - ya) / hy; i++)   {
      y = ya + i * hy;
      k = (i % 5 == 0) ? 4 : 8;
      for (j = 0; j < ar_maxcol; j += k)
        ar_putpixel (j, y, 1);
    }
  }
}
```

2 Analytical Curves

2.1 Method

The method used is very simple; the horizontal axis being that of the abscissa x, we are going to associate to each x the corresponding value $f(x)$ and we are going to draw a straight segment between the point $(x, f(x))$ and the previous point.

The choice of the scale on the vertical axis can be manual, one just has to feed the wanted minimal and maximal values into the computer. It can also be automatic. In this case, the program calculates the extremes of the function, and represents it by using all the height of the screen.

Both possibilities have advantages: the fact of choosing the scale makes it possible, for example, to center the axes on the screen and to maintain a constant scale, which allows for a direct comparison between different functions. The automatic scale makes it possible to draw the curve without knowing its extremes, and uses all the screen for the drawing.

2.2 Drawing Tool

The tool `ar_curve_yfx` has the following parameters:
- `f`, the function to be represented;
- `xn` and `xm`, extremes of the interval on which the graphical representation will be done;
- `yn` and `ym`, extremes on the vertical axis (if the extremes are equal to each other then it is interpreted as an appeal for the automatic calculation of the scale);
- `axes`, `grid` and `ortho`: booleans passed on to the procedure of drawing of axes.

The tool will be placed in the file CURVES\YFX.CPP.

```
/*========================================================
                        YFX.CPP :
         DRAWING OF ANALYTICAL CURVES (Y = F(X))
 ========================================================*/

#include "armath.h"

void ar_curve_yfx (ar_double (*f) (ar_double),
           ar_double xn, ar_double xm,
           ar_double yn, ar_double ym,
           int axes, int ortho, int grid)
{
  ar_double  x, r, ex, ey;
  int        i, j, k, xa, ya, imin, imax, valid;
  if (yn == ym)  {
    ym = yn = f (xn); x  = (xm - xn) / 200;
    for (i = 1; i <= 200; i++)  {
      r = f (xn + i * x);
      if (r > ym)  ym = r; if (r < yn)  yn = r;
    }
  }
  ar_init_graph ();
  ar_draw_axes (xn, xm, yn, ym, ex, ey, xa, ya, axes,
                ortho, grid);
  imax = (int) (xm * ex + xa); x = (imax - xa) / ex;
  if (x > xm)  imax++;
  imin = (int) (xn * ex + xa); x = (imin - xa) / ex;
  if (x < xn)  imin++;
  valid = FALSE;
  for (i = imin; i <= imax; i++)  {
    errno = 0;
    j  = ya - (int) (ey * (*f) ((i - xa) / ex));
    if (valid)  {
      if ((j > ar_maxlig) || (j < 0) || (errno))
        valid = FALSE;
```

```
      else
      ar_line (i-1, k, i, j);
    }
    else
      if ((j <= ar_maxlig) && (j >= 0) && (errno == 0)) {
        valid = TRUE;
        ar_putpixel (i, j, 1);
      }
    k = j;
  }
}
```

2.3 Examples

Example 1

Let us represent the curve of equation:

$$y = \frac{5x}{1+x^2} \text{ (cubical serpentine)} \qquad \text{for } x \in [-10; 10]$$

The drawing reveals two extremes of the function situated approximately at the points:

(−1; −2.5)   which corresponds to the minimum,
(1; 2.5)   which corresponds to the maximum.

The calculation of the zeros of the derivative of f confirms the result.

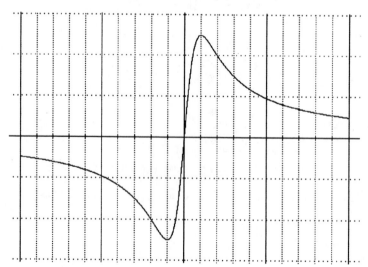

The interest of the grid is obvious in this example: it makes it possible to read the value of the extremes on the representation much more easily.

Example 2

Let us consider the equation of gaussian:

$$y = e^{-x^2} \qquad \text{for } x \in [-3, 3]$$

This curve decreases very rapidly from part to part of the axis Oy and ends up joining the axis Ox.

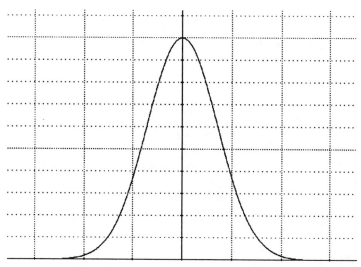

Example 3

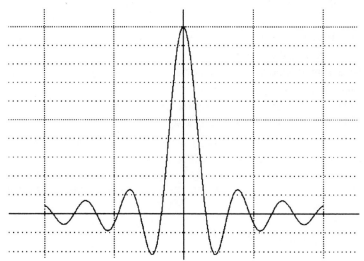

The equation of the previous curve is:

$$y = \frac{\sin x}{x} \qquad \text{for } x \in [-20, 20].$$

The graduations correspond to 10 units on the axis of the abcissas, a tenth of a unit on the axis of the ordinates.

---

3   Discrete Curves

3.1 Principle

In contrast to the previous program when the curve was defined by its cartesian equation, this program makes it possible to represent curves only known through the values taken by the function at a finite number of points. These functions are called discrete functions.

The principle concerning drawing is very simple: we are going to link two consecutive points of the curve by a straight segment.

The aspect of the discrete curve will therefore be a succession of straight segments; to obtain a precise representation, it will be better to use a large number of points.

3.2 Drawing Tool

The points which we have to represent, describing the discrete function, will generally come from another program (derivatives, primitives, differential equations...) and will therefore be found in a buffer.

The parameters of input of the tool `ar_curve_discrete` are the following:
- `t`, buffer containing the function;
- `xn` and `xm`, scale on the axis of the abscissas
  (automatically calculated if `xn = xm`);
- `yn` and `ym`, scale on the axis of the ordinates
  (automatically calculated if `yn = ym`);
- `axes`, `ortho`, `grid`: booleans passed on to the tool for drawing axes.

This tool will be placed in the file `CURVES\DISCRETE.CPP`.

```
/*===========================================================
                    DISCRETE.CPP :
               DRAWING OF DISCRETE CURVES
=============================================================*/

#include "armath.h"
```

```
void ar_curve_discrete (ar_buffer &t, ar_double xn,
              ar_double xm, ar_double yn, ar_double ym,
              int axes, int ortho, int grid)
{
  int        i, xa, ya, valid, newvalid, x, y, xp, yp;
  ar_double  r, ex, ey;

  if (xn == xm)  {
    xm = xn = 0;
    for (i = t.start; i <= t.end; i++)  {
      r = t.readx (i);
      if (r > xm)   xm = r;
      if (r < xn)   xn = r;
    }
  }
  if (yn == ym)  {
    ym = yn = 0;
    for (i = t.start; i <= t.end; i++)  {
      r = t.ready (i);
      if (r > ym)   ym = r;
      if (r < yn)   yn = r;
    }
  }

  ar_init_graph ();

  ar_draw_axes (xn, xm, yn, ym, ex, ey, xa, ya, axes,
                ortho, grid);

  valid = FALSE;

  for (i = t.start; i <= t.end; i++)  {
    x = xa + ex * t.readx (i);
    y = ya - ey * t.ready (i);

    newvalid = (y >= 0) && (y <= ar_maxlig) && (x >= 0)
                        && (x <= ar_maxcol);
    if (valid && newvalid)
      ar_line (xp, yp, x, y);
    valid = newvalid;
    xp = x; yp = y;
  }
}
```

The latter tool makes it possible to draw what is inside a buffer and to specify the parameters corresponding to the representation.

This tool will have to be placed in the file CURVES\DRAWBUFF.CPP.

```
/*===========================================================
                      DRAWBUFF.CPP :
                  DRAW A BUFFER'S CURVE
===========================================================*/

#include "armath.h"

void  ar_draw_buffer (ar_buffer &t)
{
  ar_double  xn = 0, xm = 0, yn = 0, ym = 0;
  int        axes = TRUE, grid = TRUE, ortho;

  if (t.nbelts () == 0)  {
    cerr << "The buffer is empty\n";
    ar_pause ();
    return;
  }

  ar_init_entry ("Choose the scale (or 0 for automatic
                  choice)");
  ar_fill_entry ("X min", &xn, AR_TDOU);
  ar_fill_entry ("X max", &xm, AR_TDOU);
  ar_fill_entry ("Y min", &yn, AR_TDOU);
  ar_fill_entry ("Y max", &ym, AR_TDOU);
  ar_fill_entry ("Orthonormal system", &ortho, AR_TBOO);
  if (ar_do_entry ()) return;

  ar_curve_discrete (t, xn, xm, yn, ym, axes, ortho, grid);

  ar_close_graph ();
}
```

We will not give examples of discrete curves here, since the book contains a large amount of them representing functions calculated by other programs.

---

4   Curves of Parametric Equations

4.1 Principle

The parametric curves are defined by two equations giving the coordinates x and y of a point belonging to a curve according to a parameter t which can vary:

$$\begin{cases} x = f(t) \\ y = g(t) \end{cases}$$

We notice that the curves of equation $y = f(x)$ are a particular case of curves with parameters; indeed, if we write $x = t$, then:

$$\begin{cases} x = t \\ y = g(t) = g(x) \end{cases}$$

The representation is more tricky than the one of a curve $y = f(x)$; indeed, for the latter, one had to calculate only points corresponding to equidistant values of x in order to obtain an excellent representation.

In the case of curves with parameters it is impossible to proceed in the same way with a parameter t; if we fix an increment Δt constant, it might happen, between 2 values of t separated by Δt, that the points are far from each other, or on the contrary so close as to be almost confused with each other; the only solution allowing for a precise drawing would therefore consist in choosing a very short increment Δt; the drawing would be very slow.

Thus we have decided to use an increment which varies. First, we can start a value for the increment and calculate two consecutive points and the distance between them; if that distance is greater than the fixed value, we divide the increment by 2; if on the contrary the distance is less than the fixed value we multiply it by 2.

This solution makes it possible to draw segments with an almost constant length, which finally ends up optimizing the time of calculation and the precision of the drawing.

4.2 Drawing Tool

The tool `ar_curve_parametric` has the following parameters:
- `f` and `g`, functions to be represented according to the parameter `t`;
- `tn` and `tm`, interval of variation of the parameter;
- `xn` and `xm`, scale on the axis of the abscissas;
- `yn` and `ym`, scale on the axis of the ordinates;
- `axes`, `ortho`, `grid`: booleans passed on to the drawing axes tool.

The scale is automatically calculated if `xn = xm`.

The tool will be placed in the file CURVES\PARAM.CPP.

```
/*============================================================
                     PARAM.CPP :
          DRAWING OF PARAMETRIC AND POLAR CURVES
   ==========================================================*/

#include "armath.h"

#define    DN    2
#define    DM    15
```

```
void ar_curve_parametric (
    ar_double (*f) (ar_double), ar_double (*g) (ar_double),
    ar_double tn, ar_double tm,
    ar_double xn, ar_double xm, ar_double yn, ar_double ym,
    int axes, int ortho, int grid)
{
  ar_double  step, svstep, t, r, ex, ey;
  long       d;
  int        i, k, xa, ya, xp, yp, x, y, jump;

  if (xn == xm)  {
    xm  = xn = f (tn);
    ym  = yn = g (tn);
    step = (tm - tn) / 100;
    for (i = 1; i <= 100; i++)  {
      r = f (tn + i * step);
      if (r > xm)  xm = r;
      if (r < xn)  xn = r;
      r = g (tn + i * step);
      if (r > ym)  ym = r;
      if (r < yn)  yn = r;
    }
  }

  ar_init_graph ();
  ar_draw_axes  (xn, xm, yn, ym, ex, ey, xa, ya, axes,
                 ortho, grid);

  t     = tn;
  step  = (tm - tn) / 100;
  jump  = TRUE;

  while (t + step <= tm)  {
    if (ar_stop_asked ()) return;
    if (jump)  {
      errno = 0;
      xp    = xa + ex * f (t);
      yp    = ya - ey * g (t);
    }
    k     = 0;
    jump  = FALSE;
    svstep = step;
    do  {
/*
    WARNING This graphical display slows down the drawing

      ar_grgotoxy (1, 24); ar_erase_line (24);
```

```
      sprintf (ar_temp, "Step = %10.5lf   T = %10.5lf", step,
             (t + step));
      ar_grgotoxy (1, 24); ar_outtext (ar_temp);
*/
      errno = 0;
      x  = xa + ex * f (t + step); if (errno) jump = TRUE;
      y  = ya - ey * g (t + step); if (errno) jump = TRUE;
      d  = (x - xp) * (x - xp) + (y - yp) * (y - yp);
      if (d < DN) step *= 2;
      if (d > DM) step /= 2;
      if (++k == 100) jump = TRUE;
    } while (((d < DN) || (d > DM)) && (jump == 0));

    if ((xp > 0) && (xp < ar_maxcol) && (yp > 0)
               && (yp < ar_maxlig) && (x  > 0)
               && (x  < ar_maxcol) && (y  > 0)
               && (y  < ar_maxlig) && (jump == 0))
      ar_line (xp, yp, x, y);
    if (jump) step = svstep;
    xp = x; yp = y;
    t += step;
  }
}
```

4.3 Examples

Example 1

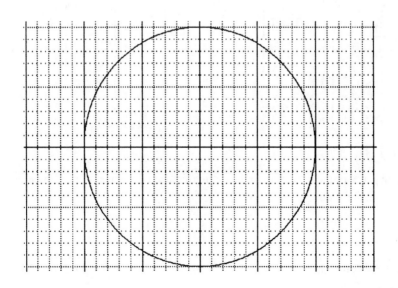

The previous curve is the circle described by equations:

$$\begin{cases} x = \cos(t) \\ y = \sin(t) \end{cases}$$

The circle is entirely obtained with $t \in [0, 2\pi]$.

Example 2

The trochoid allows for the equations with parameters:

$$\begin{cases} x = 2t - 3\sin(t) \\ y = 2 - 3\cos(t) \end{cases}$$

This time we have chosen the scale:

$$x_{min} = -17 \qquad x_{max} = 17$$
$$y_{min} = -1 \qquad y_{max} = 8$$

and $t \in [-9, 9]$.

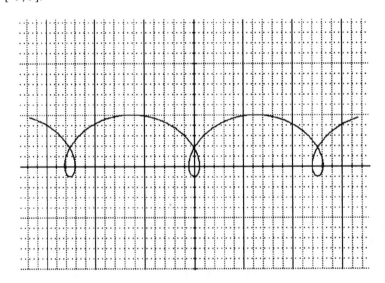

Example 3

The trajectory of a point belonging to the circumference of a wheel in movement is called a cycloid; its equations are:

$$\begin{cases} x = t - \sin(t) \\ y = 1 - \cos(t) \end{cases}$$

We have chosen $x_{min} = -7.5$, $x_{max} = 7.5$, $y_{min} = 0$, $y_{max} = 4$ and $t \in [-9, 9]$.

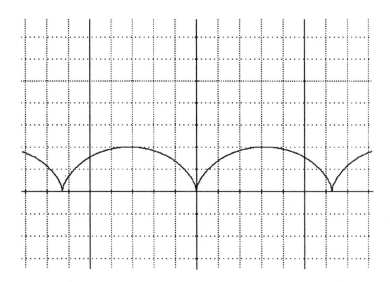

Example 4

The equations of the astroid are:

$$\begin{cases} x = \cos^3(t) \\ y = \sin^3(t) \end{cases}$$

Let us represent it for $t \in [0, 2\pi]$:

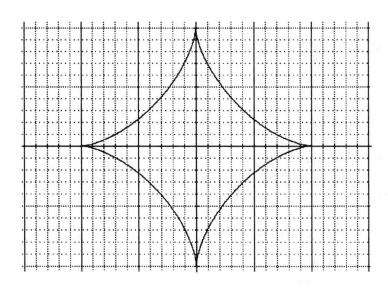

Example 5

The following curve has for equations:

$$\begin{cases} x = (1 + \cos^2(t)) \sin(t) \\ y = \sin^2(t) \cos(t) \end{cases}$$

We have represented it for $t \in [0, 2\pi]$.

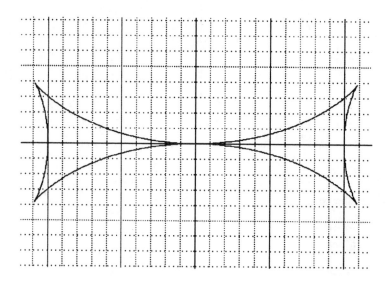

5   Cycloidal Curves

5.1 Principle

Let us consider a disk of center Ω and of radius r, turning inside and in contact with a circle of center O and of radius R. A point M belonging to the inner disk, when in movement, describes a cycloidal curve.

The cycloidal curves are a particular case of parametric curves and they have given birth to the Spirograph game.

5.2 Equations of the Curves

We will represent through M the location of the point of which we are trying to find the trajectory, through O the center of the circle, and through Ω the center of the disk in movement.

Let us consider $d = \Omega M$ to be the distance between the point M and the center of the disk and let us write:

$$d = k \frac{r}{10}$$

Thus, when k varies between 0 to 10 the point M passes from the center of the circle to a point belonging to the circumference. The nearer k is to 10, the more the curves are angular; conversely, if k approaches 0, the curves round off.

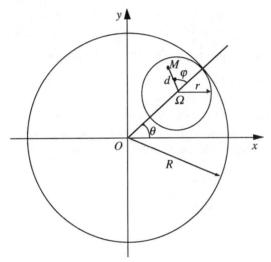

We then have:

$$\overrightarrow{OM} = \overrightarrow{O\Omega} + \overrightarrow{\Omega M}$$

That is:

$$\begin{cases} x = (R-r) \cos \theta + d \cos (\theta + \varphi) \\ y = (R-r) \sin \theta + d \sin (\theta + \varphi) \end{cases}$$

Since the disk turns inside the circle, we have the additionnal relation $r\varphi = -R\theta$. By eliminating φ, we obtain:

$$\begin{cases} x = (R-r) \cos \theta + \dfrac{k.r}{10} \cos [(1-\dfrac{R}{r}) \theta] \\ y = (R-r) \sin \theta + \dfrac{k.r}{10} \sin [(1-\dfrac{R}{r}) \theta] \end{cases}$$

By analogy with the spirograph, we will represent the radius R and r with the number of dents in the two wheels, that is, N and n respectively for the large and small wheel. We also choose the factor of scale $R = 1$. Finally the equations are:

$$\begin{cases} x = (1-\dfrac{n}{N}) \cos \theta + k \dfrac{n}{10.N} \cos [(1-\dfrac{N}{n}) \theta] \\[4mm] y = (1-\dfrac{n}{N}) \sin \theta + k \dfrac{n}{10.N} \sin [(1-\dfrac{N}{n}) \theta] \end{cases}$$

5.3 Drawing Tool

We can of course use the tool for drawing parametric curves in order to draw cycloidal curves. However, we have written a specific program which has various advantages.

First of all, the period equal to $\dfrac{2\pi n}{\text{PGCD}(n,N)}$ is automatically calculated.

Afterwards, we can superpose several curves corresponding to different values of k, which makes it possible to obtain complex figures.

Furthermore, the axes are no longer being represented, the step has stopped being variable because the evolution of the curves is regular, and the scale is fixed once and for all.

The tool will be placed in the file CURVES\CYCLOID.CPP.

```
/*==========================================================
                    CYCLOID.CPP :
               DRAWING CYCLOIDAL CURVES
==========================================================*/

#include   "armath.h"

#define   STEP   0.1

void  ar_curve_cycloid (int n1, int n2, int k)
{
   ar_double   r, x, y, rk, tm, t;
   int         a, b, d, xp, yp, xx, yy;

   r  = (ar_double) n1 / (ar_double) n2;
   rk = k * r / 10;  b  = n2; d = n1;
   do  {
     a = b; b = d; d = a % b;
   } while (d);
   tm = 2 * AR_PI * n1 / b; t  = 0;
   xp = ar_maxcol / 2 + (1-r+rk) * (ar_maxlig * ar_round / 2);
   yp = ar_maxlig / 2;
   while ((t < tm) && (! ar_stop_asked ()))  {
     t  += STEP;
     x  = (1 - r) * cos (t) + rk * cos ((1-1/r) * t);
     y  = (1 - r) * sin (t) + rk * sin ((1-1/r) * t);
     xx = ar_maxcol / 2 + x * (ar_maxlig * ar_round / 2);
```

```
    yy = ar_maxlig * (1 - y) / 2;
    ar_line (xp, yp, xx, yy); xp = xx; yp = yy;
  }
}
```

5.4 Examples

We show here a few rosettes as well as the values of the parameters which made it possible to obtain them.

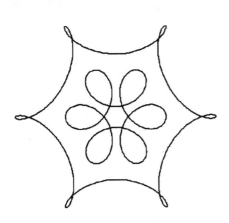

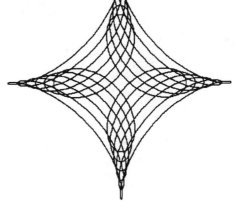

$N = 96$ $n = 80$ $N = 96$ $n = 72$
$k = 8$ $k = 3$ $k = 9$ to 4

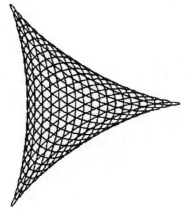

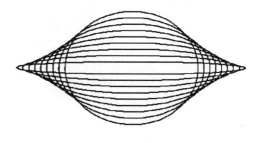

$N = 96$ $n = 64$ $N = 96$ $n = 48$
          $k = 9$ to 0 $k = 9$ to 1

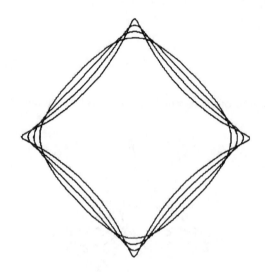

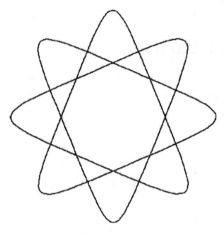

$N = 96$ $n = 24$
$k = 8, 6, 4, 2$

$N = 96$ $n = 36$
$k = 6$

$N = 96$ $n = 75$
$k = 7$

$N = 105$ $n = 24$
$k = 8$

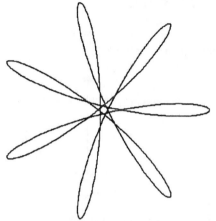

$N = 105 \qquad n = 56$
$k = 8$

$N = 105 \qquad n = 60$
$k = 8$

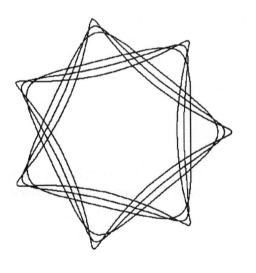

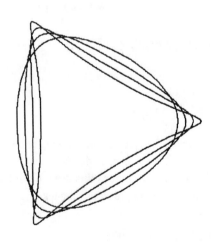

$N = 105 \qquad n = 30$
$k = 8, 6, 4$

$N = 96 \qquad n = 32$
$k = 8, 6, 4, 2$

6   Polar Curves

6.1 Principle

A polar curve is a curve whose equation is defined through the polar coordinates of the points which constitute it:

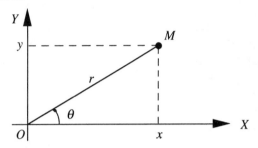

The polar coordinates are then:
– the distance r of the point M from the origin O,
– the angle θ defined by the 2 half lines Ox and $[OM)$.
The transitional formulas from the polar coordinates to the rectangular coordinates are :

$$x = r \, \cos \theta$$
$$y = r \, \sin \theta$$

A polar equation will be of the type $r = f(\theta)$.

6.2 Drawing Tool

In order to represent polar curves, the program uses the formulas:

$$x = r \, \cos \theta$$
$$y = r \, \sin \theta$$

and can be reduced to the drawing of a parametric curve.

There is no specific drawing tool for polar curves. The exploitation tool placed at the end of the chapter reduces this drawing to the representation of a parametric curve, and uses the tool seen in the previous chapter.

6.3 Examples

Example 1

Let us represent the cochleoid of equation:

$$r = \frac{\sin(\theta)}{\theta} \qquad \text{with } \theta \in [-30, 30]$$

When θ increases, the curve tends towards the point O by describing loops which are tighter and tighter.

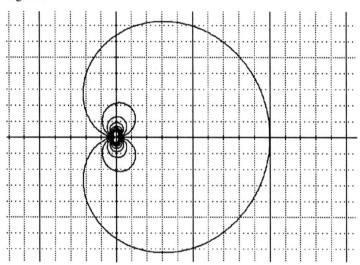

Example 2

Archimedes' spiral has a very simple equation: $r = \theta$.

The representation underneath corresponds to $\theta \in [0, 40]$.

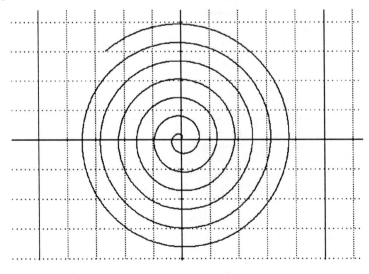

Example 3

The equation $r = \dfrac{1}{\theta}$ is that of the hyperbolic spiral. We have represented it for $\theta \in [1, 25]$. The curve winds around the point O while getting close to it; indeed $\lim\limits_{\theta \to +\infty} r(\theta) = 0$.

We then say that the point of origin is the asymptotic point of the spiral.

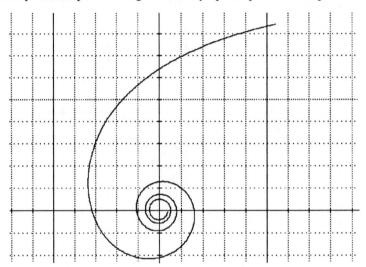

Example 4

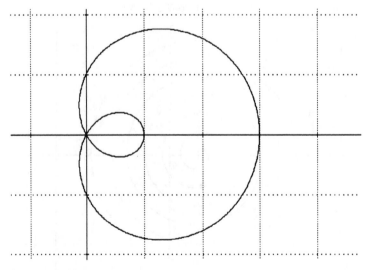

Pascal's snail has the equation $r = 1+2\cos\theta$. We have drawn it for $\theta \in [0, 2\pi]$.

Example 5

The following curve is called a scarab; its equation is:

$$r = 2\cos2\theta - \cos\theta \qquad \theta \in [0, 2\pi]$$

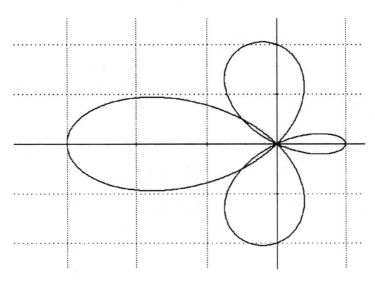

Example 6

This last curve is a rosette with four branches, of equation:

$$r = \sin 2\theta \qquad \text{with } \theta \in [0, 2\pi]$$

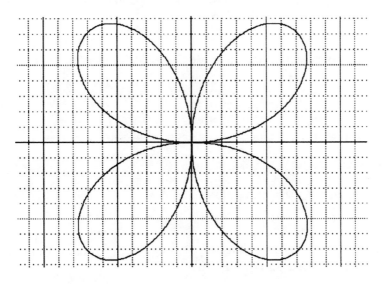

7 Exploitation Tools

The following tools make possible the direct exploitation of the tools for drawing.

The following tool must be placed in the file CURVES\UYFX.CPP:

```
/*==========================================================
                        UYFX.CPP :
              USING ANALYTICAL CURVES DRAWING
   ======================================================*/

#include "armath.h"

void ar_use_curve_yfx ()
{
  ar_double  xn, xm, yn = 0, ym = 0;
  int        axes = TRUE, grid = TRUE, ortho;

  ar_init_entry ("ANALYTIC CURVES Y=F(X)");
  ar_fill_entry ("Function to draw", &ar_glob_f, AR_TFUN);
  ar_fill_entry ("X min", &xn, AR_TDOU);
  ar_fill_entry ("X max", &xm, AR_TDOU);
  ar_fill_entry ("Y min (0 for auto calc.)", &yn, AR_TDOU);
  ar_fill_entry ("Y max (0 for auto calc.)", &ym, AR_TDOU);
  ar_fill_entry ("Orthonormal system", &ortho, AR_TBOO);

  if (ar_do_entry ()) return;

  ar_curve_yfx (ar_eval_f, xn, xm, yn, ym,axes,ortho,grid);
  ar_close_graph ();
}
```

The following tool must be placed in the file CURVES\UDISCRET.CPP:

```
/*=======================================================
                    UDISCRET.CPP :
              USING DISCRETE CURVES DRAWING
   ===================================================*/

#include "armath.h"

void ar_use_curve_discrete ()
{
  int  nt;

  if (ar_read ("Buffer number : ", &nt, AR_TINT)) return;
  if (nt > AR_MAXBUFFER) return;
```

```
  if (ar_buff [nt].nbelts () == 0)
    cin >> ar_buff [nt];

  ar_draw_buffer (ar_buff [nt]);
}
```

The following tool must be placed in the file CURVES\UPARAM.CPP:

```
/*============================================================
                        UPARAM.CPP :
              USING PARAMETRIC CURVES DRAWING
  ==========================================================*/

#include "armath.h"

void ar_use_curve_parametric ()
{
  ar_double  tn, tm, xn = 0, xm = 0, yn = 0, ym = 0;
  int        axes = TRUE, grid = TRUE, ortho;

  ar_init_entry ("PARAMETRIC CURVES");
  ar_fill_entry ("Function x (t)", &ar_glob_f, AR_TFUN);
  ar_fill_entry ("Function y (t)", &ar_glob_g, AR_TFUN);
  ar_fill_entry ("t min", &tn, AR_TDOU);
  ar_fill_entry ("t max", &tm, AR_TDOU);
  ar_fill_entry ("x min (or 0 for auto)", &xn, AR_TDOU);
  ar_fill_entry ("x max (or 0 for auto)", &xm, AR_TDOU);
  ar_fill_entry ("y min (or 0 for auto)", &yn, AR_TDOU);
  ar_fill_entry ("y max (or 0 for auto)", &ym, AR_TDOU);
  ar_fill_entry ("Orthonormal system", &ortho, AR_TBOO);

  if (ar_do_entry ()) return;

  ar_curve_parametric (ar_eval_f, ar_eval_g, tn, tm,
            xn, xm, yn, ym, axes, ortho, grid);
  ar_close_graph ();
}
```

The following tool must be placed in the file CURVES\UCYCLOID.CPP:

```
/*============================================================
                        UCYCLOID.CPP :
              USING CYCLOIDAL CURVES DRAWING
  ==========================================================*/

#include   "armath.h"
```

```
void ar_use_curve_cycloid ()
{
  int  n1, n2, nb, i, k [10];

  cout << "CYCLOIDAL CURVES\n\n";
  if (ar_read ("Number of positions for the pen : ", &nb,
      AR_TINT)) return;
  if (nb > 10) return;
  ar_init_entry ("");
  ar_fill_entry ("Large wheel", &n2, AR_TINT);
  ar_fill_entry ("Small wheel", &n1, AR_TINT);
  for (i = 0; i < nb; i++)  {
    sprintf (ar_temp, "Pen position n° %d", i + 1);
    ar_fill_entry (ar_temp, &k [i], AR_TINT);
  }
  if (ar_do_entry ()) return;
  ar_init_graph ();
  for (i = 0; i < nb; i++)
    ar_curve_cycloid (n1, n2, k [i]);
  ar_close_graph ();
}
```

The following tool must be placed in the file CURVES\UPOLAR.CPP:

```
/*============================================================
                        UPOLAR.CPP :
                   DRAWING POLAR CURVES
  ==========================================================*/

#include "armath.h"

static ar_double polar_cos (ar_double t)
{
  return (cos (t) * ar_eval_f (t));
}

static ar_double polar_sin (ar_double t)
{
  return (sin (t) * ar_eval_f (t));
}

void ar_use_curve_polar ()
{
  ar_double  tn, tm, xn = 0, xm = 0, yn = 0, ym = 0;
  int        axes = TRUE, grid = TRUE, ortho;

  ar_init_entry ("POLAR CURVES");
  ar_fill_entry ("Function r (t)", &ar_glob_f, AR_TFUN);
```

```
    ar_fill_entry ("t min", &tn, AR_TDOU);
    ar_fill_entry ("t max", &tm, AR_TDOU);
    ar_fill_entry ("x min (or 0 for auto)", &xn, AR_TDOU);
    ar_fill_entry ("x max (or 0 for auto)", &xm, AR_TDOU);
    ar_fill_entry ("y min (or 0 for auto)", &yn, AR_TDOU);
    ar_fill_entry ("y max (or 0 for auto)", &ym, AR_TDOU);
    ar_fill_entry ("Orthonormal system", &ortho, AR_TBOO);

    if (ar_do_entry ()) return;

    ar_curve_parametric (polar_cos, polar_sin, tn, tm,
                    xn, xm, yn, ym, axes, ortho, grid);
    ar_close_graph ();
}
```

12
Derivatives

This chapter is dedicated to the study of the calculation of derivatives.

The first section calculates the successive derivatives of a function f up to the order 5, at any point belonging to its field of definition. The second makes it possible to calculate the nth derivative of any function in a discrete form. The third carries out the formal differentiation of a function, that is, it obtains the derivative-function in its analytical form (according to x).

Finally, the fourth section concerns the calculation of the power series expansion of a function at a particular point x_0.

The tools used in this chapter will be placed in the subdirectory DERIV.

1   Successive Derivatives at One Point

1.1 Principle

The derivative of a function f at x_0 is given by the formula:

$$f'(x_0) = \lim_{h \to 0} \frac{f(x_0+h) - f(x_0-h)}{2h}$$

We can show that for a given h, the expression:

$$\frac{f(x_0+h) - f(x_0-h)}{2h}$$

is an approximation of order 2 at h of $f'(x_0)$.

It means that the difference between calculated value and exact value is a rough estimate of h^2, which we can write:

$$f'(x_0) = \frac{f(x_0+h) - f(x_0-h)}{2h} + O(h^2)$$

There exist other formulas of order 4, 6, 8, ... which can give better approximations of $f'(x_0)$. Thus, an approximation of order 4 of $f'(x_0)$ is:

$$f'(x_0) = \frac{1}{12h} [8(f(x_0+h) - f(x_0-h)) - (f(x_0+2h) - f(x_0-2h))] + O(h^4)$$

In the same way, for the calculation of derivatives of order greater than one, there exist formulas of approximations of order 2, 4, 6, etc. For example, an approximation of order 4 of $f''(x_0)$ is:

$$f''(x_0) = \frac{1}{8h^3} [-13 (f(x_0+h) - f(x_0-h)) + 8 (f(x_0+2h) - f(x_0-2h))$$

$$- (f(x_0+3h) - f(x_0-3h))] + O(h^4)$$

Therefore we notice in the previous examples that the formulas are of the following form:

$$f^{(n)}(x_0) = \frac{1}{A_0 h^n} \sum_{k=1}^{m} A_k [f(x_0+kh) - f(x_0-kh)] + O(h^p)$$

In this expression, m is a whole number and $A_0, A_1, ..., A_m$ are constants.

It is always possible to obtain a formula of this type for the calculation of derivatives with an odd order. The number of terms m of the sum is then linked to the order n of the derivative, as well as to the order p of the approximation by the relation:

$$m = \frac{n+p-1}{2}$$

This result is true to intuition: the approximation is all the more accurate when the number of terms in the formula is important.

For the calculation of derivatives with an even order, the formulas are of the following form:

$$f^{(n)}(x_0) = \frac{1}{A_0 h^n} \sum_{k=1}^{m} A_k [f(x_0+kh) + f(x_0-kh) - 2f(x_0)] + O(h^p)$$

This time, the number of terms of the sum is linked to the order n of the differentiation and to the order p of the approximation, by the relation:

$$m = \frac{n+p-2}{2}$$

1.2 Calculation of the Coefficients in the Formulas of Approximation

The elaboration of these formulas lies in the use of Taylor's formula:

$$f(x_0+h) = f(x_0) + h\,f'(x_0) + \frac{h^2}{2!}\,f''(x_0) +... + \frac{h^r}{r!}\,f^{(r)}(x_0) + O(h^{r+1})$$

which we can also write in a condensed form:

$$f(x_0+h) = f(x_0) + \sum_{i=1}^{r} \frac{h^i}{i!}\,f^{(i)}(x_0) + O(h^{r+1})$$

Case When the Derivatives Have an Odd Order

We then choose $r = 2m$ and we calculate the difference:

$$f(x_0+h) - f(x_0-h) = \sum_{i=1}^{m} 2\,\frac{h^{2i-1}}{(2i-1)!}f^{(2i-1)}(x_0) + O(h^{2m+1})$$

(The even powers cancel themselves in the sum.)

In the same way, we can obtain the relation (which is more general):

$$f(x_0+kh) - f(x_0-kh) = \sum_{i=1}^{m} 2k^{2i-1}\,\frac{h^{2i-1}}{(2i-1)!}f^{(2i-1)}(x_0) + O(h^{2m+1})$$

By writing this relation m times, with k varying from 1 to m, we can obtain a system of m equations with m unknowns:

$$f'(x_0), f'''(x_0),..., f^{(2m-1)}(x_0)$$

This system can be written as follows:

$$\begin{pmatrix} 1 & 1 & \cdots & 1 \\ 2 & 2^3 & \cdots & 2^{2m-1} \\ \cdots & \cdots & \cdots & \cdots \\ m & m^3 & \cdots & m^{2m-1} \end{pmatrix} \begin{pmatrix} h\,f'(x_0) \\ \frac{h^3}{3!}f'''(x_0) \\ \cdots\cdots\cdots \\ \frac{h^{2m-1}}{(2m-1)!}f^{(2m-1)}(x_0) \end{pmatrix} = \frac{1}{2} \begin{pmatrix} f(x_0+h) - f(x_0-h) \\ f(x_0+2h) - f(x_0-2h) \\ \cdots\cdots\cdots \\ f(x_0+mh) - f(x_0-mh) \end{pmatrix}$$

Therefore it is enough to invert the matrix and to solve the system in order to obtain m formulas each giving the expression of a derivative $f^{(n)}(x_0)$.

REMARK: the terms neglected in Taylor's development are of order $2m+1$; the formula obtained for $f^{(n)}(x_0)$ is therefore of order $p = (2m+1) - n$.

Therefore we find once more the result $m = \dfrac{n+p-1}{2}$.

Case When the Derivatives Have an Even Order

The calculation is similar to the previous one: now we choose $r = 2m + 1$. We obtain:

$$f(x_0+h) + f(x_0-h) - 2\,f(x_0) = \sum_{i=1}^{m} 2\,\frac{h^{2i}}{(2i)!} f^{(2i)}(x_0) \;+ O(h^{2m+2})$$

(The odd powers cancel themselves in the sum.)

$$f(x_0+kh) + f(x_0-kh) - 2\,f(x_0) = \sum_{i=1}^{m} 2k^{2i}\,\frac{h^{2i}}{(2i)!} f^{(2i)}(x_0) + O(h^{2m+2})$$

We also obtain a system of m equations with m unknowns by writing m times this relation, k varying from 1 to m:

$$\begin{pmatrix} 1 & 1 & \cdots & 1 \\ 2^2 & 2^4 & \cdots & 2^{2m} \\ \cdots & \cdots & \cdots & \cdots \\ m^2 & m^4 & \cdots & m^{2m} \end{pmatrix} \begin{pmatrix} \dfrac{h^2}{2!}f''(x_0) \\ \dfrac{h^4}{4!}f^{(4)}(x_0) \\ \cdots\cdots\cdots \\ \dfrac{h^{2m}}{(2m)!}f^{(2m)}(x_0) \end{pmatrix} = \frac{1}{2}\begin{pmatrix} f(x_0+h)+f(x_0-h)-2f(x_0) \\ f(x_0+2h)+f(x_0-2h)-2f(x_0) \\ \cdots\cdots\cdots\cdots \\ f(x_0+mh)+f(x_0-mh)-2f(x_0) \end{pmatrix}$$

The solution to this system leads to m formulas each giving an approximate expression of a derivative $f^{(n)}(x_0)$.

REMARK: the terms neglected in Taylor's development were of order $2m+2$. The formula obtained for $f^{(n)}(x_0)$ is therefore of order $p = (2m+2) - n$. For example, the formula giving $f'(x_0)$ will be of order $2m$. We find once more the result:

$$m = \frac{n+p-2}{2}$$

1.3 Calculation Tool

The coefficients of the formulas of approximation that we have just studied cannot be calculated rapidly and in a simple way by the program. We have therefore decided to limit ourselves to the derivatives of order 5, and we have included in the program the values of the coefficients of the formulas of order 6.

The tool `ar_derivative` is a function whose solution is the value of the derivative wanted. The boolean variable `errno` is positioned on TRUE if it is not possible to calculate this derivative.

The input parameters of the tool are:
– f, the function to be differentiated;
– x0, the point at which we want to evaluate the derivative;
– n, the order of the differentiation (less than or equal to 5);
– h, the step of calculation.

The tool will be placed in the file `DERIV\DERIV.CPP`.

We are going to see in the annotated examples that the calculation of derivatives is rather imprecise, and that this imprecision depends a great deal on the value of h. An acceptable compromise solution suitable for all functions is obtained with $h = 0.05$.

REMARK: the exploitation tool `ar_use_derivative` gives the first five derivatives of f at x_0, as well as the exact derivative of f at x_0 (calculated through the formal method shown in section 4).

```
/*==============================================================
                        DERIV.CPP :
          APPROXIMATION OF THE N-TH DERIVATIVE AT A POINT
   ==========================================================*/

#include "armath.h"

ar_double  ar_derivative (
          ar_double (*f) (ar_double),
            ar_double x, int n, ar_double h)
{
   static int table [5][7] =   {
        {3,  45,  -9,  1,  0,  0,  60} ,
        {3,  270,  -27,  2,  0,  0,  180} ,
        {4,  -488,  338,  -72,  7,  0,  240},
        {4,  -1952,  676,  -96,  7,  0,  240} ,
        {5,  1938,  -1872,  783,  -152,  13,  288}
        };
   int      i, *coeff;
   ar_double   fa, fb, fc, t;

   errno = 0; if (n > 5) return 0; coeff = table [n - 1];
   fa = f (x); if (errno) return (0);
   for (i = 1, t = 0; i <= coeff [0]; i++)   {
      fb = f (x - i * h); if (errno) return 0;
      fc = f (x + i * h); if (errno) return 0;
      t  = t + coeff [i] * ((n % 2) ?
             (fc - fb) : ((fc - fa) + (fb - fa)));
   }
```

```
   t /= coeff [6];
   for (i = 1; i <= n; i++)
     t /= h;

   return (t);
}
```

1.4 Annotated Examples

Example 1

CALCULATION OF THE SUCCESSIVE DERIVATIVES AT X0

```
Function to be differentiated : exp (x)
At point xo                    : 0
Value of h                     : .1

Exact derivative at xo : 1

f'       (xo)  = 1.000000007157
f''      (xo)  = 1.000000001788
f'''     (xo)  = 1.000000013594
f''''    (xo)  = 1.000000005432
f'''''   (xo)  = 1.000000023125
```

All the successive derivatives of $f(x) = e^x$ at $x_0 = 0$ are equal to 1. We notice that the error in the result is all the more important when the order of the derivative is high. This result is a general one. The derivative evaluated by the formal method is exact.

Example 2

Let us repeat the previous calculation with $h = 0.0005$:

CALCULATION OF THE SUCCESSIVE DERIVATIVES AT X0

```
Function to be differentiated : exp (x)
At point xo                    : 0
Value of h                     : .0005

Exact derivative at xo : 1
f'       (xo)  = 1
f''      (xo)  = 0.999999999562
f'''     (xo)  = 1.000001699965
f''''    (xo)  = 1.011302153131
f'''''   (xo)  = -17.948605564773
```

We notice that the first four derivatives have the correct order of magnitude, the last one, on the contrary, is totally wrong. This result is due to the too low value of h. In practice, we will never use a value of h less than 0.001.

Example 3

For certain functions, the polynomial functions in particular, the value of h must be more important. Let us calculate the successive derivatives $f(x) = x^3$ at $x_0 = 10$, with $h = 0.1$ then with $h = 1$.

```
CALCULATION OF THE SUCCESSIVE DERIVATIVES AT X0

Function to be differentiated : x^3
At point xo                    : 10
Value of h                     : .1

Exact derivative at xo : 300

f'        (xo) = 299.999999999999
f''       (xo) = 60.000000000002
f'''      (xo) = 5.999999999633
f''''     (xo) = 3.221127068779e-10
f'''''    (xo) = 2.753747847035e-07

CALCULATION OF THE SUCCESSIVE DERIVATIVES AT X0

Function to be differentiated : x^3
At point xo                    : 10
Value of h                     : 1

Exact derivative at xo : 300

f'        (xo) = 300
f''       (xo) = 60
f'''      (xo) = 6
f''''     (xo) = 0
f'''''    (xo) = 0
```

In this example, the results are exact: indeed, there is no error of method for the polynomials of order at most equal to 6 since the formulas are of order 6. In practice, the calculations will have to be done initially with a value of h close to 0.01, and eventually taken up again with other values of h, in order to confirm the result. We are going to explain, in the following section, why the value of h has such an influence on the validity of the results.

1.5 Error of Method and Numerical Errors

Error of Method

The formulas of approximation used by the program are of order 6: we could therefore think that the errors are of order 10^{-6}.

In reality, an approximation at h^6 means that the error is of the form $k.h^6$ where k is a parameter depending on the function. The values taken by k can be low and likewise they can be important.

Therefore, with $h = 0.1$, if k is of order 1000, the error on the result is 10^{-3}: this occurs for the derivatives of high order. Always with $k = 1000$, if we choose $h = 0.5$, the error is close to 15! Then the result has no significance.

In order to minimize the error, we can decide to adopt the values of h which are the lowest possible; then we encounter another cause of imprecision, the numerical errors.

Numerical Errors

When we perform the difference of two very close numbers (for example 125.00000002 and 124.99999998) the result is marred by a relative error which is very important. This phenomenon is known as an evanescent difference, and comes from the fact that the computer does not memorize a sufficient number of significant digits.

In the case of the calculation of derivatives, this phenomenon is all the more noticeable when the value of h is low. For example, if we choose $h = 0.05$ when we calculate a derivative of order 5, the significant digits of the result are in the intermediate calculations of the order 10^{-10}. Therefore, with a computer which can calculate only with 10 significant digits, the result given by the program is very approximate.

---

2 Nth Discrete Derivative of a Function

2.1 Introduction

The program in this section will give the nth derivative of a function in its discrete form, that is, in the form of a series of values taken by the derivative-function at equidistant points inside an interval $[a, b]$ which is given.

2.2 Calculation Tool

The calculation is done in two stages: the computer first tries to find the nth exact derivative of f (formal method), then this function is digitized. This method leads to a better precision compared to that obtained with the approximate method described previously.

The input parameters of the tool ar_derivative_discrete are:

– f, the function to be differentiated;

– a and b, the extremes of the interval over which f must be differentiated;

– m, the number of points to be calculated;

– n, the order of the derivative wanted;

– disp, boolean making it possible to display each point.

At the output, buffer t contains the derivative sought, in its digitized form.

The tool will be placed in the file DERIV\DERDISC.CPP.

```cpp
/*===========================================================
                       DERDISC.CPP :
          CALCULATION OF THE DERIVATIVE OF A FUNCTION
                     IN ITS DISCRETE FORM
 ==========================================================*/

#include  "armath.h"

void  ar_discrete_derivative (
            ar_function &f, ar_buffer &t,
            ar_double a, ar_double b,
            int m, int n, int disp)
{
   ar_function  h (10000);
   int          i;

   if (errno) return;  // Memory allocation for h

   h = f;

   for (i = 1; i <= n; i++)  {

      if (errno) return;
      cout << "Calculation of formal derivative " << i
           << " ...\n";
      if (! ar_glob_g [h]) {errno = TRUE; return;}
      h = ar_glob_g;
   }

   cout << "Digitization of the function ...\n";

   if (! ar_digitize_function (ar_eval_g, t, a, b, m, disp))
      errno = 1;

   return;
}
```

2.3 Annotated Examples

Example 1

Let us calculate the first derivative of the function $f(x) = \sin (3x)$ between $-\pi$ and $+\pi$, with 16 intervals:

```
CALCULATION OF DISCRETE-FORM DERIVATIVES

Function to be differentiated : SIN (3 * X)
Order of the derivative       : 1
Value of a                    : -PI
Value of b                    : PI
Number of intervals           : 16
Number of buffer              : 2
Display of the results        : y


Calculation of the formal derivative 1...
Digitization of the function...
```

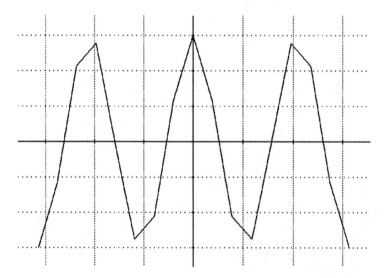

```
X0  =  -3.14159265359   Y0  =                  -3
X1  =  -2.748893571891  Y1  =  -1.148050297095  # -1737 / 1513
X2  =  -2.356194490192  Y2  =   2.12132034356   # 2378 / 1121
X3  =  -1.963495408494  Y3  =   2.771638597534  # 10183 / 3674
X4  =  -1.570796326795  Y4  =  -5.513168047089e-16
X5  =  -1.178097245096  Y5  =  -2.771638597534  # -10183 / 3674
X6  =  -0.785398163397  Y6  =  -2.12132034356   # -2378 / 1121
X7  =  -0.392699081699  Y7  =   1.148050297095  # 1737 / 1513
```

```
X8  =                     0  Y8  =                      3
X9  =   0.392699081699  Y9  =   1.148050297095  # 1737 / 1513
X10 =   0.785398163397  Y10 =  -2.12132034356   # -2378 / 1121
X11 =   1.178097245096  Y11 = -2.771638597534   # -10183 / 3674
X12 =   1.570796326795  Y12 = -5.513168047089e-16
X13 =   1.963495408494  Y13 =   2.771638597534  # 10183 / 3674
X14 =   2.356194490192  Y14 =   2.12132034356   # 2378 / 1121
X15 =   2.748893571891  Y15 = -1.148050297095   # -1737 / 1513
X16 =   3.14159265359   Y16 =                    -3
```

The tool `ar_use_derivative_discrete` (in `DERIV\UDERDISC.CPP`) makes it possible to draw the curve of this derivative (that is, 3 cos (3x)).

Therefore we obtain the curve above. We notice its angular nature. This is due to the fact that it does not have enough points.

In practice, a minimum of 100 points are necessary to obtain a curve with a proper aspect. With 600 points:

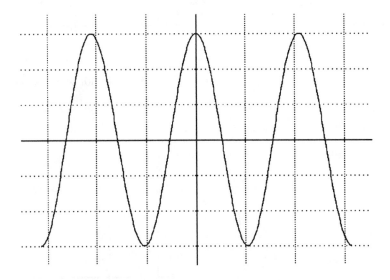

From now on, we will not give the details of the calculations, but simply the curve obtained from the results found by the program.

Example 2

The following curve represents the third derivative of $f(x) = \text{Log }(x)$, that is:

$$f'''(x) = \frac{2}{x^3}$$

calculated on the interval [1, 3] with 120 points.

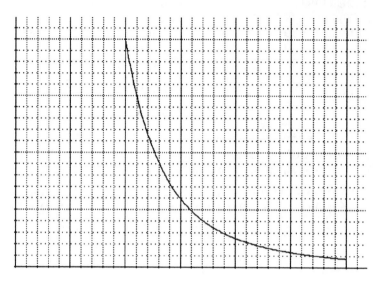

Example 3

Let us calculate the derivative of order 3 of $f(x) = \dfrac{\sin(x)}{x}$ on [–30, 30] with 180 points.

We notice that the lack of definition of the derivative-function at one point does not prevent the drawing.

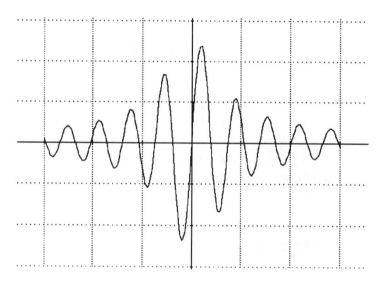

3 Formal Derivative

3.1 Introduction

We are now going to calculate a *formal* derivative of *f*, that is, its analytical expression, according to *x* (the *formal* derivative of cos 3*x* is –3 sin 3*x*).

Apart from its utilitarian and spectacular aspect, this tool makes it possible to illustrate two important notions: the recursiveness of the C language and the possibility for the computer of *creating* functions, due to the environment of manipulation of the functions which we have developed.

3.2 Method

The technique of recursiveness makes it possible in certain cases to make programs which are very powerful and very short.

Let us suppose, for example, that the function we have to differentiate is the sum of two terms *u* + *v*. We know that the result sought (*u* + *v*)' is equal to *u*' + *v*'. It is enough to apply the method of differentiation to *u* then to *v* and to do the sum of the partial results. This rule is a general one: the differentiation of an expression can be systematically applied to several differentiations of simpler expressions.

However, what is recursiveness? It is precisely the possibility, inside a function, of resorting to that same function with other parameters, without modifying the normal environment (local variables). This technique makes it possible to deal with the case of the differentiation of *u* + *v* in a very simple way: we calculate the function *u*' then *v*', due to recursiveness, and then we do the sum.

This principle can be applied whatever the operation we have to do (binary or unary), and the process stops when the expression we have to differentiate is the variable *x*, or a constant, in which case the derivative is equal to 1 or 0.

The complete tool of formal derivation obtained by using this technique is simple since it takes only about 150 lines. On the other hand, it appears necessary to simplify the derivative-function as we proceed in the calculation in order to avoid a disproportionate size of the internal representation of the function. This tool eliminates the most useless operations: for example, the derivative of sin 3*x* unsimplified gives:

```
(0 * x  + 3 * 1) * cos (3 * x)
```

After simplification, we obtain:

```
3 * cos (3 * x)
```

3.3 Calculation Tools

The operator [] is overloaded for the class ar_function. Thus, if *f* and *g* are two objects ar_function, the instruction g[f] creates in *g* the derivative of *f*.

The tool will be placed in the file DERIV\DERFORM.CPP.

```
/*==============================================================
                        DERFORM.CPP :
             FORMAL DERIVATIVE CALCULATION TOOL
--------------------------------------------------------------
   INTERNAL CODING :

   A=FMINUS, B=FPLUS, C=FSIN, D=FCOS, E=FTAN, F=FARCSIN,
   G=FARCCOS, H=FARCTAN, I=FSH,  J=FCH, K=FTH, L=FARGSH,
   M=FARGCH, N=FARGTH, O=FABS, P=FINT, Q=FFRACb, R=FFACT,
   S=FEXP, T=FLOG, U=FSQR};
==============================================================*/

#include "armath.h"

#define  REAL(u)  * (ar_double *) &u

char  descrip [] [20] = {
  "UAFu", "Fu", "B*FuUDFU", "UAB*FuUCFU", "B/FuB^UDFUC2",
  "B/FuUUB-C1B^FUC2", "UAB/FuUUB-C1B^FUC2", "B/FuB+C1B^FUC2",
  "B*FuUJFU", "B*FuUIFU", "B/FuB^UJFUC2",
  "B/FuUUB+C1B^FUC2", "B/FuUUB-B^FUC2C1", "B/FuB-C1B^FUC2",
  "C0", "C0", "C0", "C0",
  "B*FuUSFU", "B/FuFU", "B/FuB*C2UUFU"
};

static unsigned int  ptres, len_u, len_u1, len_v, len_v1;
static char          *pt_u, *pt_u1, *pt_v, *pt_v1;

static  int  fastanal       (char [], ar_function *);
static  int  ar_derive_char (char *,  ar_function *);

int fastanal (char des [], ar_function *g)
{
  char          ch, *pch = des, *pmsg;
  unsigned int  len;

  while ((ch = *(pch++)) != 0)  {
    switch (ch)  {
      case 'U' : case 'B' :
      if (ptres + 2 >= g->maxlen) return (FALSE);
        g->start [ptres ++] = ch;
```

```
        g->start [ptres ++] = (ch == 'U') ?
                 * (pch ++) - 'A' : * (pch ++);
        break;
        case 'F' :
          switch (* (pch ++))  {
          case 'U' : pmsg = pt_u;  len = len_u;  break;
          case 'u' : pmsg = pt_u1; len = len_u1; break;
          case 'V' : pmsg = pt_v;  len = len_v;  break;
          case 'v' : pmsg = pt_v1; len = len_v1; break;
          }
        if (ptres + len >= g->maxlen) return (FALSE);
          memcpy (&g->start [ptres], pmsg, len);
        ptres += len;
          break;
        case 'C' :
        if (ptres + 1 + sizeof (ar_double) >= g->maxlen)
          return (FALSE);
          g->start [ptres ++] = ch;
        REAL (g->start [ptres]) =
                            (ar_double) ((* (pch ++)) - '0');
        ptres += sizeof (ar_double);
        break;
    }
  }
  return (TRUE);
}

static  int  ar_derive_char (char *f, ar_function *g)
{
  unsigned int  loc_len;
  ar_function   u1 (-1), v1 (-1);

  if (g->maxlen < 1 + sizeof (ar_double)) return FALSE;

  switch (f [0])  {
    case 'C' : case 'V' :
      g->start [0] = 'C';
      REAL (g->start [1]) = (f [0] == 'V') ? 1 : 0;
      break;

    case 'U' :

      loc_len = ar_funclen (&f [2]);
      u1.open (40 + 5 * loc_len);
      if (errno) return FALSE;

      if (! ar_derive_char (&f [2], &u1))  return FALSE;
```

```
    pt_u  = &f [2];   len_u  = ar_funclen (pt_u);
    pt_u1 = u1.start; len_u1 = ar_funclen (pt_u1);
    ptres = 0;
    if (! fastanal (descrip [f [1]], g)) return FALSE;
    break;

case 'B' :

    loc_len = ar_funclen (&f [2]);
    u1.open (40 + 5 * loc_len);
    if (errno) return FALSE;

    len_v =  ar_funclen (&f [2 + loc_len]);
    v1.open (40 + 5 * len_v);
    if (errno) return FALSE;

    if (! ar_derive_char (&f [2], &u1)) return FALSE;
    if (! ar_derive_char (&f [2 + loc_len], &v1))
      return FALSE;
    pt_u  = &f [2];            len_u  = ar_funclen (pt_u);
    pt_u1 = u1.start;         len_u1 = ar_funclen (pt_u1);
    pt_v  = &f [2 + loc_len]; len_v  = ar_funclen (pt_v);
    pt_v1 = v1.start;         len_v1 = ar_funclen (pt_v1);
    ptres = 0;

    switch (f [1])  {
    case '+' : if (! fastanal ("B+FuFv", g))
                    return FALSE; break;
    case '-' : if (! fastanal ("B-FuFv", g))
                    return FALSE; break;
    case '*' : if (! fastanal ("B+B*FuFVB*FUFv", g))
                    return FALSE; break;
    case '/' : if (! fastanal ("B/B-B*FuFVB*FUFvB^FVC2",g))
                    return FALSE; break;
    case '^' :
      if (pt_v [0] == 'C')  {
         // Constant powers: (u^a)'=a*(u^(a-1))*u'
        if (REAL (pt_v [1]) == 0)  {
          if (! fastanal ("C0", g))
               return FALSE;
        }
        else if (REAL (pt_v [1]) == 1)  {
          if (! fastanal ("Fu", g))
               return FALSE;
        }
        else if (! fastanal ("B*B*FuFVB^FUB-FVC1", g))
            return FALSE;
      }
```

```
      else if
            (! fastanal ("B*B^FUFVB+B*FvUTFUB*FVB/FuFU", g))
            return FALSE;
         break;
      }
      break;
   }

   ar_simplify_function (g->start);

   return TRUE;
}

int ar_function::operator [] (ar_function &f)
{
   return  ar_derive_char (f.start, this);
}
```

The tool of simplification of functions `ar_simplify_function` is to be placed in the file `DERIV\DERSIMP.CPP`.

```
/*============================================================
                        DERSIMP.CPP :
              USER FUNCTION SIMPLIFICATION TOOL
                 (Eliminate some redundancies)
============================================================*/

#include  <string.h>
#include  "armath.h"

#define  REAL(u)   * (ar_double *) &u

void  ar_simplify_function (char *f)
{
   unsigned int  len_u, len_v;
   char          *u = &f [2], *v;

   switch (f [0])  {
     case 'U' :
       ar_simplify_function (u);
       len_u = ar_funclen (u);
       switch (f [1])  {
       case FMINUS :
       /*-------------------------------------- -(K) = (-K) */
         if (f [2] == 'C')  {
           f [0] = 'C';
           REAL (f [1]) = - REAL (f [3]);
         }
```

```
          /*------------------------------------------ -(-x) = x */
          else if ((f [2] == 'U') && (f [3] == (char) FMINUS))
            memcpy (f, &f [4], len_u - 2);
          break;
        }
        break;

case 'B' :
  v = &f [2 + ar_funclen (u)];
  ar_simplify_function (u); len_u = ar_funclen (u);
  ar_simplify_function (v); len_v = ar_funclen (v);
  memcpy (&f [2 + len_u], v, len_v);
  v = &f [2 + len_u];

  switch (f [1])  {
  case '+' :
    /*-------------------------------------- CNST + CNST */
    if ((u [0] == 'C') && (v [0] == 'C'))  {
      f [0] = 'C';
      REAL (f [1]) = REAL (u [1]) + REAL (v [1]);
    }
    /*---------------------------------------------- 0 + v */
    else if ((u [0] == 'C') && (REAL (u [1]) == 0))
      memcpy (f, v, len_v);
    /*---------------------------------------------- u + 0 */
    else if ((v [0] == 'C') && (REAL (v [1]) == 0))
      memcpy (f, u, len_u);
    break;

  case '-' :
    /*-------------------------------------- CNST - CNST */
    if ((u [0] == 'C') && (v [0] == 'C'))  {
      f [0] = 'C';
      REAL (f [1]) = REAL (u [1]) - REAL (v [1]);
    }
    /*---------------------------------------------- u - 0 */
    else if ((v [0] == 'C') && (REAL (v [1]) == 0))
      memcpy (f, u, len_u);
    /*---------------------------------------------- 0 - v */
    else if ((u [0] == 'C') && (REAL (u [1]) == 0))  {
      f [0] = 'U'; f [1] = FMINUS;
      memcpy (u, v, len_v);
    }
    break;

  case '*' :
    /*-------------------------------------- CNST * CNST */
    if ((u [0] == 'C') && (v [0] == 'C'))  {
```

```
      f [0] = 'C';
      REAL (f [1]) = REAL (u [1]) * REAL (v [1]);
    }
    /*--------------------------------------------- u * 1 */
    else if ((v [0] == 'C') && (REAL (v [1]) == 1))
      memcpy (f, u, len_u);
    /*--------------------------------------------- 1 * v */
    else if ((u [0] == 'C') && (REAL (u [1]) == 1))
      memcpy (f, v, len_v);
    /*--------------------------------------------- 0 * v */
    else if ((u [0] == 'C') && (REAL (u [1]) == 0))  {
      f [0] = 'C';
      REAL (f [1]) = 0;
    }
    /*--------------------------------------------- u * 0 */
    else if ((v [0] == 'C') && (REAL (v [1]) == 0))  {
      f [0] = 'C'; REAL (f [1]) = 0;
    }
    /*--------------------------------------------- -1 * v */
    else if ((u [0] == 'C') && (REAL (u [1]) == -1))  {
      f [0] = 'U'; f [1] = FMINUS;
      memcpy (u, v, len_v);
    }
    /*--------------------------------------------- u * -1 */
    else if ((v [0] == 'C') && (REAL (v [1]) == -1))  {
      f [0] = 'U'; f [1] = FMINUS;
    }
    break;

case '/' :
    /*------------------------------------- CNST / CNST */
    if ((u [0] == 'C') && (v [0] == 'C'))  {
      f [0] = 'C';
      REAL (f [1]) = REAL (u [1]) / REAL (v [1]);
    }
    /*--------------------------------------------- u / 1 */
    else if ((v [0] == 'C') && (REAL (v [1]) == 1))
      memcpy (f, u, len_u);
    /*--------------------------------------------- 0 / v */
    else if ((u [0] == 'C') && (REAL (u [1]) == 0))  {
      f [0] = 'C'; REAL (f [1]) = 0;
    }
    /*--------------------------------------------- u / -1 */
    else if ((v [0] == 'C') && (REAL (v [1]) == -1))  {
      f [0] = 'U'; f [1] = FMINUS;
    }
    break;
```

```
case '^' :
  /*--------------------------------------- CNST ^ CNST */
  if ((u [0] == 'C') && (v [0] == 'C'))   {
    f [0] = 'C';
    REAL (f[1]) = exp (log (REAL(u[1])) * REAL(v[1]));
  }
  /*------------------------------------------- u ^ 1 */
  else if ((v [0] == 'C') && (REAL (v [1]) == 1))
    memcpy (f, u, len_u);
  /*------------------------------------------- 1 ^ v */
  else if ((u [0] == 'C') && (REAL (u [1]) == 1))   {
    f [0] = 'C';
    REAL (f [1]) = 1;
  }
  /*------------------------------------------- 0 ^ v */
  else if ((u [0] == 'C') && (REAL (u [1]) == 0))   {
    f [0] = 'C';
    REAL (f [1]) = 0;
  }
  /*------------------------------------------- u ^ 0 */
  else if ((v [0] == 'C') && (REAL (v [1]) == 0))   {
    f [0] = 'C';
    REAL (f [1]) = 1;
  }
  break;
  }
 break;
 }
}
```

3.4 Annotated Examples

Here are the results given by the program for the following functions:

$$f(x) = e^{2x}$$

$$f(x) = x^4 + 3x^2 - 25x + 89$$

$$f(x) = \text{Log (Argsh } x)$$

$$f(x) = \tan (x^2)$$

```
FORMAL DIFFERENTIATION

Function to be differentiated : EXP (2*X)

The formal derivative of f is f'(x) = (2 * EXP (2 * X))
```

FORMAL DIFFERENTIATION

Function to be differentiated : X^4 + 3*X^2 - 25*X + 89

The formal derivative of f is f'(x)=(((4*(X^3)+(3*(2*X)))-25)

FORMAL DIFFERENTIATION

Function to be differentiated : LOG (ARGCH (X))

The formal derivative of f is f'(x)=(1/SQRT(X^2-1))/ARGCH(X)

FORMAL DIFFERENTIATION

Function to be differentiated : TAN (X^2)

The formal derivative of f is f'(x) = ((2*X)/(COS(X^2)^2))

---

4 Power Series Expansion of a Function at One Point

4.1 Principle

The power series expansion at the order n of the function f around the point x_0 is given by the Taylor formula:

$$f(x) = f(x_0) + (x - x_0)\frac{f'(x_0)}{1!} + (x - x_0)^2\frac{f''(x_0)}{2!} + (x - x_0)^3\frac{f'''(x_0)}{3!}$$

$$+ \ldots + (x - x_0)^n\frac{f^{(n)}(x_0)}{n!} + O((x - x_0)^{n+1})$$

that is:

$$f(x) = a_0 + a_1 (x - x_0) + a_2 (x - x_0)^2 + \ldots + a_n (x - x_0)^n + O((x - x_0)^{n+1})$$

with:

$$a_i = \frac{f^{(i)}(x_0)}{i!}$$

In the particular case where $x_0 = 0$, the formula becomes:

$$f(x) = a_0 + a_1 x + a_2 x^2 + a_3 x^3 + \ldots + a_n x^n + O(x^{n+1})$$

4.2 Calculation Tool

The tool calculates the coefficients a_i of the p.s.e. (power series expansion) of a function at any point x_0. In order to evaluate the successive derivatives, the function `ar_derivative` seen in the previous section is used, which explains the fact that we obtain p.s.e. of an order equal to 5 at the most. The exploitation tool can be found at the end of the chapter.

4.3 Annotated Examples

Example 1

The p.s.e. of order 5 at $x_0 = 0$ of the function $\dfrac{1}{1-x}$ is:

$$\frac{1}{1-x} = 1 + x + x^2 + x^3 + x^4 + x^5 + O(x^6)$$

```
POWER SERIES EXPANSION OF F AT X0

Function to be expanded : 1/(1-X)
At the point xo          : 0
Value of h               : 0.1

a1 = 1.000041625042   # 24024 / 24023
a2 = 1.000041625042   # 24024 / 24023
a3 = 1.001120792787   # 3573 / 3569
a4 = 1.001120792787   # 3573 / 3569
a5 = 1.013646846981   # 4828 / 4763
```

Here again we find that the coefficients of the terms of the highest degree are marred by the most important error. The rational approximations are in this case meaningless, since the exact values are all equal to 1.

Example 2

The p.s.e. of order 5 at $x_0 = 1$ of the function Log x is:

$$\text{Log } x = (x-1) - \frac{1}{2}(x-1)^2 + \frac{1}{3}(x-1)^3 - \frac{1}{4}(x-1)^4 + \frac{1}{5}(x-1)^5 + O((x-1)^6)$$

```
POWER SERIES EXPANSION OF F AT X0

Function to be expanded : LOG (X)
At the point xo          : 1
Value of h               : 0.1
```

```
a1 = 1.000005755205
a2 = -0.500005052039
a3 = 0.333450814231   # 946 / 2837
a4 = -0.250106233389  # -1177 / 4706
a5 = 0.201130159343   # 1139 / 5663
```

The error always stays below 1%.

4.4 Conclusion

It seems obvious that the direct method that we just studied does not make it possible to calculate the p.s.e. of just any function in a very precise manner. Furthermore, we are limited to the order 5.

The calculation of the p.s.e. of products, divisions of substitutions of functions, described in the next chapter, makes it possible to break away from those limitations and to obtain very precise results.

---

5 Exploitation Tools

The following tools make possible the direct exploitation of the tools described previously.

The following tool is to be placed in the file DERIV\UDERIV.CPP:

```
/*===========================================================
                      UDERIV.CPP :
     EXPLOITATION TOOL FOR N-TH DERIVATIVES CALCULATION
   =========================================================*/

#include  <string.h>
#include  "armath.h"

void ar_use_derivative ()
{
  ar_double  xo, h, r;
  int        n, i;

  ar_init_entry ("CALCULATION OF THE SUCCESSIVE \
                  DERIVATIVES AT XO");
  ar_fill_entry ("Function to be differentiated",
                 &ar_glob_f, AR_TFUN);
  ar_fill_entry ("At point xo", &xo, AR_TDOU);
  ar_fill_entry ("Value of h",  &h,  AR_TDOU);

  if (ar_do_entry ()) return;
```

\

```
  if (ar_glob_g [ar_glob_f])   {
    r = ar_eval_g (xo);
    if (! errno)
      cout << "Exact derivative at xo : " << r
           << ar_rational (r) << "\n";
    ar_nl;
  }

  for (n = 1; n <= 5; n++)   {
    r = ar_derivative (ar_eval_f, xo, n, h);
    if (errno)
      cout << "Non-calculable derivative\n";
    else   {
      ar_temp [0] = 'f';
      for (i = 1; i <= n;        i++)   ar_temp [i] = '\'';
      for (i = n + 1; i <= 6; i++)   ar_temp [i] = ' ';
      ar_temp [6] = 0;
      strcat (ar_temp, " (xo) = ");
      cout << ar_temp << r << "\n";
    }
  }
  ar_pause ();
}
```

The following tool will be placed in the file `DERIV\UDERDISC.CPP`:

```
/*=============================================================
                    UDERDISC.CPP :
         USING DISCRETE DERIVATIVES CALCULATIONS
=============================================================*/

#include   "armath.h"

void  ar_use_discrete_derivative ()
{
  ar_double   a, b;
  int         nt, n, m, disp;

  ar_init_entry ("CALCULATION OF DISCRETE-FORM DERIVATIVES");
  ar_fill_entry ("Function to be differentiated", &ar_glob_f,
                 AR_TFUN);
  ar_fill_entry ("Order of the derivative", &n, AR_TINT);
  ar_fill_entry ("Value of a", &a, AR_TDOU);
  ar_fill_entry ("Value of b", &b, AR_TDOU);
  ar_fill_entry ("Number of intervals", &m,  AR_TINT);
  ar_fill_entry ("Number of buffer",     &nt, AR_TINT);
  ar_fill_entry ("Display of the results", &disp, AR_TBOO);
  if ((ar_do_entry ()) || (nt > AR_MAXBUFFER)) return;
```

```
    ar_discrete_derivative(ar_glob_f,ar_buff[nt],a,b,m,n,disp);

    if (errno)  {
      cerr << "Non-calculable derivative on [a, b]\n";
      ar_pause ();
    }
    else  {
      cout << "The buffer " << nt <<
              " now contains the discrete derivative\n";
      ar_read ("Do you want the graphical representation : ",
              &disp, AR_TBOO);
      if (disp)
        ar_draw_buffer (ar_buff [nt]);
    }
}
```

The following tool will be placed in the file DERIV\UDERFORM.CPP:

```
/*==========================================================
                        UDERFORM.CPP :
                FORMAL DERIVATIVE USING TOOL
   =========================================================*/

#include  <string.h>
#include  "armath.h"

void ar_use_formal_derivative ()
{
  ar_function  g (10000);
  char         ch [200];

  if (errno) {ar_pause (); return;}
  cout << "FORMAL DERIVATION\n\n";
  if (ar_read ("Function to be differentiated :   ",
               &ar_glob_f, AR_TFUN)) return;
  ar_nl;
  if (! g [ar_glob_f])
    cerr << "Impossible derivative\n";
  else  {
    g.decompile (ch);
    if (! errno)
      cout << "The formal derivative of f is f'(x) = " << ch
           << "\n";
    else
      cout << "Result too long for display\n";
  }
  ar_pause ();
}
```

The following tool is to be placed in the file PSE\UPSEXO.CPP:

```
/*=============================================================
                      UPSEXO.CPP :
        USING TOOL FOR POWER SERIES EXPANSIONS AT XO
=============================================================*/

#include "armath.h"

void ar_use_pse_xo ()
{
  ar_double  xo, h, r, s;
  int        n;

  ar_init_entry ("POWER SERIES EXPANSION OF F AT XO");
  ar_fill_entry ("Function to be expanded", &ar_glob_f,
                  AR_TFUN);
  ar_fill_entry ("At the point xo", &xo, AR_TDOU);
  ar_fill_entry ("Value of h", &h,  AR_TDOU);
  if (ar_do_entry ()) return;

  for (n = 1, s = 1; n <= 5; n++)  {
    s *= n;
    r = ar_derivative (ar_eval_f, xo, n, h) / s;
    if (errno)
      cerr << "Non-calculable expansion\n";
    else
      cout << "a" << n << " = " << r << ar_rational (r)
           << "\n";
  }
  ar_pause ();
}
```

13

Power Series Expansions

The calculation of the power series expansion (p.s.e.) at the order 5 of a function at one point is described in the previous chapter. The power series expansions that we will calculate in this chapter will be p.s.e. at $x_0 = 0$.

The ordinary functions allow for p.s.e. which are known. Therefore we are going to use those results to find the p.s.e. of other functions.

The three following tools are going to make it possible for us to calculate precisely and at a high order the p.s.e. of the functions $f.g$, f/g and gof, knowing p.s.e. of f and g.

The tools used in this chapter will be placed in the subdirectory PSE.

The p.s.e. entry tool will be placed in the file PSE\PSEENTRY.CPP.

```
/*============================================================
                        PSEENTRY.CPP :
                ENTRY OF A POWER SERIES EXPANSION
============================================================*/

#include "armath.h"

int ar_entry_pse (ar_polynomial &p, int order, char c1,
                  char c2)
{
  ar_number   *n;
  int         i;
  if (! p.open (order)) return FALSE;
```

```
if ((n = new ar_number [order + 1]) == NULL) return FALSE;

sprintf (ar_temp,"Entry of PSE coefficients of %c : ", c1);
ar_init_entry (ar_temp);

for (i = 0; i <= order; i++)  {
   sprintf (ar_temp, "%c %2d = ", c2, i);
   ar_fill_entry (ar_temp, &n [i], AR_TNUM);
}

if (ar_do_entry ()) {delete[]n; return FALSE;}

for (i = 0; i <= order; i++)
   p.writecoeff (i, n [i]);

p.degree = order;
delete[]n;

return TRUE;
}
```

---

1   Power Series Expansion of *f.g*

1.1 Principle

Here, we are studying the case of the product of two functions *f* and *g*.

Let us suppose that we know the p.s.e. of *f* and *g* at the order *n*:

$$f(x) \quad = a_0 + a_1 x + a_2 x^2 + \dots + a_n x^n + O(x^{n+1})$$

$$= P(x) + O(x^{n+1})$$

$$g(x) \quad = b_0 + b_1 x + b_2 x^2 + \dots + b_n x^n + O(x^{n+1})$$

$$= Q(x) + O(x^{n+1})$$

Thus, the p.s.e. of order *n* of the function *f.g* is equal to:

$$(f.g)\,(x) = (a_0 + a_1 x + a_2 x^2 + \dots + a_n x^n).\,(b_0 + b_1 x + \dots + b_n x^n) + O(x^{n+1})$$

$$= c_0 + c_1 x + c_2 x^2 + \dots + c_n x^n + O(x^{n+1})$$

The coefficients c_i can be calculated by multiplying the polynomials *P* and *Q*:

$$c_i = \sum_{k=0}^{i} a_k . b_{i-k}$$

1.2 Calculation Tool

The input parameters of the tool `ar_pse_mul` are the polynomials P and Q, standing for the p.s.e. of f and g. On output, the tool gives back the coefficients of the p.s.e. of $f.g$ in the polynomial R.

The tool will be placed in the file `PSE\PSEMUL.CPP`.

```
/*==============================================================
                         PSEMUL.CPP :
            CALCULATION OF POWER SERIES EXPANSION OF f.g
       ======================================================*/

#include "armath.h"

void ar_pse_mul (ar_polynomial &p, ar_polynomial &q,
                 ar_polynomial &r)
{
  int      i;

  r = p * q;
  for (i = p.degree + 1; i <= r.degree; i++)
    r.writecoeff (i, N0);

  r.degree = p.degree;
}
```

1.3 Annotated Example

Let us calculate the p.s.e of the function $h(x) = \dfrac{e^x}{1+x}$ by considering it as the product

of $f(x) = e^x$ and $g(x) = \dfrac{1}{1+x}$, whose p.s.e. are:

$$f(x) = 1 + x + \frac{x^2}{2!} + \frac{x^3}{3!} + \dots + \frac{x^n}{n!} + O(x^{n+1})$$

$$g(x) = 1 - x + x^2 + \dots + (-1)^n x^n + O(x^{n+1})$$

Let us ask for a calculation of order 5.

```
POWER SERIES EXPANSION OF f.g

Order of series expansion desired : 5

Entry of PSE coefficients of f :
a 0 = 1
a 1 = 1
```

```
a 2 = 1/2
a 3 = 1/6
a 4 = 1/24
a 5 = 1/120

Entry of PSE coefficients of g :
b 0 = 1
b 1 = -1
b 2 = 1
b 3 = -1
b 4 = 1
b 5 = -1


- 11/30 X5 + 3/8 X4 - 1/3 X3 + 1/2 X2 + 1
```

The precision is much better than that obtained by direct calculation. We are consequently going to be able to search for developments at an order greater than 5.

This time let us ask for a calculation at order 12:

```
POWER SERIES EXPANSION OF f.g

Order of series expansion desired : 12

+ 16019531/43545600 X12 - 1468457/3991680 X11
+ 16481/44800 X10 - 16687/45360 X9 + 2119/5760 X8
- 103/280 X7 + 53/144 X6 - 11/30 X5 + 3/8 X4 - 1/3 X3
+ 1/2 X2 + 1
```

The precision is maximal for all the coefficients, which confirms the possibility of obtaining expansions at a very high order.

---

2   Power Series Expansion of *f/g*

2.1 Principle

Let us suppose we know the developments of f and g of order n:

$$f(x) = a_0 + a_1 x + a_2 x^2 + \ldots + a_n x^n + O(x^{n+1}) = P(x) + O(x^{n+1})$$

$$g(x) = b_0 + b_1 x + b_2 x^2 + \ldots + b_n x^n + O(x^{n+1}) = Q(x) + O(x^{n+1})$$

with $b_0 \neq 0$, since in the reverse case, the function f/g is not definite at $x = 0$.

The p.s.e. of the function f/g is then obtained by doing the following division according to the increasing powers at the order n of the polynomial P over the polynomial Q.

2.2 Calculation Tool

The input and output parameters are the same as for the expansion of $f.g$.

The tool `ar_pse_div` will be placed in the file `PSE\PSEDIV.CPP`.

```
/*=============================================================
                        PSEDIV.CPP :
        CALCULATION OF POWER SERIES EXPANSION OF f/g
   =========================================================*/

#include "armath.h"

void ar_pse_div (ar_polynomial &p, ar_polynomial &q,
                 ar_polynomial &r)
{
  ar_polynomial  remainder;

  if (p.degree == q.degree)
    r = ar_dcr_pol (p, q, p.degree + 1, remainder);
}
```

2.3 Annotated Examples

Example 1

Let us take up again the function $h(x) = \dfrac{e^x}{1+x}$ but this time we will look upon it as the ratio of the functions $f(x) = e^x$ and $g(x) = 1+x$.

```
POWER SERIES EXPANSION OF f/g

Order of desired series expansion : 6

Entry of PSE coefficients of f :
a 0 = 1
a 1 = 1
a 2 = 1/2
a 3 = 1/6
a 4 = 1/24
a 5 = 1/120
a 6 = 1/720

Entry of PSE coefficients of g :
b 0 = 1
b 1 = 1
b 2 = 0
```

```
b 3 = 0
b 4 = 0
b 5 = 0
b 6 = 0
```

```
+ 53/144 X6 - 11/30 X5 + 3/8 X4 - 1/3 X3 + 1/2 X2 + 1
```

The results are identical to those given by the previous program; here again the precision is maximal, and the rational approximations are the exact values.

Example 2

Let us calculate the p.s.e. of order 6 of the function:

$$h(x) = \frac{1}{1+\text{sh}x}$$

```
POWER SERIES EXPANSION OF f/g

Order of desired series expansion : 6

Entry of PSE coefficients of f :
a 0 = 1
a 1 = 0
a 2 = 0
a 3 = 0
a 4 = 0
a 5 = 0
a 6 = 0

Entry of PSE coefficients of g :
b 0 = 1
b 1 = 1
b 2 = 0
b 3 = 1/6
b 4 = 0
b 5 = 1/120
b 6 = 0
```

```
+ 77/45 X6 - 181/120 X5 + 4/3 X4 - 7/6 X3 + X2 - X + 1
```

Here again the approximations are exact.

Example 3

Let us calculate the development of tan x, by writing $f(x) = \sin x$ and $g(x) = \cos x$.

```
POWER SERIES EXPANSION OF f/g

Order of desired series expansion : 10

Entry of PSE coefficients of f :
a   0 = 0
a   1 = 1
a   2 = 0
a   3 = -1/6
a   4 = 0
a   5 = 1/120
a   6 = 0
a   7 = -1/5040
a   8 = 0
a   9 = 1/362880
a  10 = 0

Entry of PSE coefficients of g :
b   0 = 1
b   1 = 0
b   2 = -1/2
b   3 = 0
b   4 = 1/24
b   5 = 0
b   6 = -1/720
b   7 = 0
b   8 = 1/40320
b   9 = 0
b  10 = -1/3628800

+ 62/2835 X9 + 17/315 X7 + 2/15 X5 + 1/3 X3 + X
```

The expansion obtained, at the order 10, is exact.

3 Power Series Expansion of $g \circ f$

3.1 Principle

Let us suppose that we know the expansions of f and g of order n:

$$g(x) = a_0 + a_1 x + a_2 x^2 + \ldots + a_n x^n + O(x^{n+1})$$

$$= P(x) + O(x^{n+1})$$

$$f(x) = 0 + b_1 x + b_2 x^2 + \ldots + b_n x^n + O(x^{n+1})$$

$$= Q(x) + O(x^{n+1})$$

The term b_0 must be necessarily equal to 0, in order for $f(x)$ to tend to 0 when x tends to 0; otherwise, we could not speak of the expansion of *gof* at 0.

The expansion of *gof* is then:

$$(gof)\,(x) = P[Q(x)] + O(x^{n+1})$$

or again, in a more explicit form:

$$(gof)\,(x) = a_0 \;\; + a_1[b_1x + b_2x^2 + ... + b_nx^n]$$

$$+ \, a_2[b_1x + b_2x^2 + ... + b_nx^n]^2$$

$$+ \;\; ....$$

$$+ \, a_n[b_1x + b_2x^2 + ... + b_nx^n]^n + O(x^{n+1})$$

This expansion contains terms of degree 0 at n^2. In order to obtain the p.s.e. of order n, it is advisable not to keep in this expansion terms of degree less than or equal to n.

3.2 Calculation Tool

The input and output parameters are the same as for those of the expansion of *f.g.*

The tool `ar_pse_comp` will be placed in the file `PSE\PSESUBST.CPP`.

```
/*============================================================
                      PSESUBST.CPP :
        CALCULATION OF POWER SERIES EXPANSION OF gof
  ==========================================================*/

#include "armath.h"

void ar_pse_comp (ar_polynomial &p, ar_polynomial &q,
                  ar_polynomial &r)
{
  int  i;

  r = ar_subst_pol (q, p);
  for (i = q.degree + 1; i <= r.degree; i++)
    r.writecoeff (i, N0);
  r.degree = q.degree;
}
```

3.3 Annotated Examples

Example 1

Let us calculate the p.s.e. of order 10 of the function $h(x) = e^{\sin x}$.

```
POWER SERIES EXPANSION OF gof

Order of desired series expansion : 10

- 2951/3628800 X10 + 1/5670 X9 + 31/5760 X8 + 1/90 X7
- 1/240 X6 - 1/15 X5 - 1/8 X4 + 1/2 X2 + X + 1
```

We can verify through calculation the exactitude of each of the coefficients.

Example 2

Here, we have tried to find, once more, the results of the previous program relating to the function $h(x) = \dfrac{1}{1+\mathrm{sh}x}$ by considering it this time of the composition of the function:

$$f(x) = \mathrm{sh}\ x$$

and the function:

$$g(x) = \frac{1}{1+x}$$

```
CALCULATION OF THE POWER SERIES EXPANSION OF gof

Order of the expansion wanted : 6

+ 77/45 X6 - 181/120 X5 + 4/3 X4 - 7/6 X3 + X2 - X + 1
```

Once more we find the same results.

---

4 Conclusion

We have seen that the direct calculation of derivatives could meet with several drawbacks:
 – a lack of precision in the calculations,
 – a great influence of the parameter h on the precision,
 – a limitation of the order of the differentiation.
  Furthermore, the three tools presented in this chapter, using the class `ar_polynomial` and its member functions, make it possible, as we have seen, to calculate the p.s.e. of an important order with an excellent precision.
  We will therefore systematically use one of these three tools when it is possible and we will resort to direct calculation only if the function studied cannot be expressed with the help of more simple functions.

5 Exploitation Tools

The following tools make posssible the direct exploitation of the calculation tools.
The following tool must be placed in the file PSE\UPSEMUL.CPP:

```
/*==========================================================
                        UPSEMUL.CPP :
        POWER SERIES EXPANSION OF f.g EXPLOITATION TOOL
==========================================================*/

#include "armath.h"

void ar_use_pse_mul ()
{
  ar_polynomial   p, q, r;
  int             order;

  cout << "POWER SERIES EXPANSION OF f.g\n\n";

  if (ar_read ("Order of series expansion desired : ",
               &order, AR_TINT)) return;
  if (! ar_entry_pse (p, order, 'f', 'a')) return;
  if (! ar_entry_pse (q, order, 'g', 'b')) return;
  ar_pse_mul (p, q, r);
  if (errno)
    cout << "\nNon-calculable series expansion\n";
  else
    cout << r;
  ar_pause ();
}
```

The following tool must be placed in the file PSE\UPSEDIV.CPP:

```
/*==========================================================
                        UPSEDIV.CPP :
        POWER SERIES EXPANSION OF f/g EXPLOITATION TOOL
==========================================================*/

#include "armath.h"

void ar_use_pse_div ()
{
  ar_polynomial   p, q, r;
  int             order;

  cout << "POWER SERIES EXPANSION OF f/g\n\n";
```

```
  if (ar_read ("Order of desired series expansion : ",
               &order, AR_TINT)) return;
  if (! ar_entry_pse (p, order, 'f', 'a')) return;
  if (! ar_entry_pse (q, order, 'g', 'b')) return;

  ar_pse_div (p, q, r);

  if (errno)
    cout << "\nNon-calculable series expansion\n";
  else
    cout << r;

  ar_pause ();
}
```

The following tool must be placed in the file PSE\UPSESUBS.CPP:

```
/*===========================================================
                    UPSESUBS.CPP :
     POWER SERIES EXPANSION OF gof EXPLOITATION TOOL
=============================================================*/

#include "armath.h"

void ar_use_pse_comp ()
{
  ar_polynomial   p, q, r;
  int             order;

  cout << "POWER SERIES EXPANSION OF gof\n\n";

  if (ar_read ("Order of desired series expansion : ",
               &order, AR_TINT)) return;

  if (! ar_entry_pse (q, order, 'g', 'b')) return;
  if (! ar_entry_pse (p, order, 'f', 'a')) return;

  ar_pse_comp (p, q, r);

  if (errno)
    cout << "\nNon-calculable series expansion\n";
  else
    cout << r;

  ar_pause ();
}
```

14

Integrals and Primitives

We will now concern ourselves with the approximate calculation of integrals and primitives.

The first two tools will enable us to work out the approximate calculation of integrals with functions defined analytically according to Cotes' formulas. Those consist in dividing the interval of integration into subintervals and in substituting a polynomial for the function to be integrated on each of those subintervals. We will study two different methods: the method of Simpson and that of Villarceau.

Later we will study Romberg's method which affords the advantage of allowing the user to fix the precision of the result. Next we will examine the way Simpson's method can be applied to discrete functions. And finally, we will determine the discrete expression of the primitives of functions defined analytically, this by applying Simpson's method.

The tools are grouped together in the subdirectory named `INTEGRAL`.

---

1 Simpson's Method

1.1 Principle

Simpson's method belongs to the wider family of Cotes' methods. The principle of these methods consists in dividing the interval of integration $[a, b]$ into n subintervals of which the length is $h = \dfrac{b-a}{n}$, and replacing the curve with a polynomial interpolation on each subinterval.

The trapezoidal rule which is one of the simplest of Cotes' methods uses a polynomial of degree 1 for the interpolation, that is, the segment of a straight line.

As for Simpson's method, it uses a polynomial of degree 2, which amounts to replacing the function with an arc of a parabola on each of the subintervals. Thus one can prove that the approximation found in that way is of order h^4, which means that the difference between the exact value of the integral and its calculated value is proportional to h^4.

Let us write:

$$h = \frac{b-a}{2n} \qquad \text{and} \qquad x_i = a + ih.$$

Therefore, there are $(2n+1)$ points x_i, with $x_0 = a$ and $x_{2n} = b$. Thus we can show that on an interval $[x_{2i}, x_{2i+1}]$, the integral:

$$\int_{x_{2i}}^{x_{2i+2}} f(x) \, dx$$

can be approximated to:

$$T_{2i} = \frac{h}{3} \left[f(x_{2i}) + 4 f(x_{2i+1}) + f(x_{2i+2}) \right]$$

The integral I then equals:

$$I = T_0 + T_2 + T_4 + \dots + T_{2(n-1)} = \sum_{i=0}^{n-1} T_{2i}$$

1.2 Calculation Tool

The tool `ar_integral_simpson` is a function whose solution is the value of the integral sought. The boolean variable `errno` is positioned on `TRUE` if it has not been possible to evaluate the function at one point or other.

The parameters of the tool are:
- `f`, the function;
- `a` and `b`, the extremes of the interval of integration;
- `n`, the number of steps of integration.

The tool will be placed in the file `INTEGRAL\SIMPSON.CPP`.

```
/*==============================================================
                        SIMPSON.CPP :
            SIMPSON'S METHOD INTEGRATION CALCULATION TOOL
    ===========================================================*/

#include "armath.h"
```

```
ar_double ar_integral_simpson (ar_double  (*f) (ar_double),
                         ar_double a ,ar_double b, long n)
{
  long        i;
  ar_double   pas, r, res;

  errno = 0;
  pas = (b - a) / 2 / n;
  res  = f (a);                      if (errno) return (0);
  res += f (b);                      if (errno) return (0);
  res /= 2;
  for (i = 1; i < 2 * n; i++)  {
    r = f (a + i * pas);            if (errno) return (0);
    if (i % 2)  res += r + r;
    else res += r;
  }

  return (res * pas * 2 / 3);
}
```

1.3 Annotated Examples

Example 1

Let us calculate:

$$I = \int_5^{11} \frac{1}{\sqrt{x^2-6x+8}}\, dx$$

The exact value is:

$$I = \text{Log}\, \frac{8+\sqrt{63}}{2+\sqrt{3}} = 1.4517014864$$

```
INTEGRATION WITH SIMPSON'S METHOD

Function to be integrated : 1/sqrt(x^2 - 6*x + 8)
Enter a                   : 5
Enter b                   : 11
Enter n                   : 100

Value of the integral     : 1.451701492722  # 2645 / 1822
```

The value obtained with 100 steps of integration reveals a very slight error.

Example 2

Let us calculate:

$$I = \int_1^{12} x \sin^2 x \, dx$$

The exact value is:

$$I = \frac{1}{8} [288 - 24 \sin(24) - \cos(24) - 2 + 2 \sin(2) + \cos(2)]$$

or again:

$$I = 38.589018712241$$

```
INTEGRATION WITH SIMPSON'S METHOD

Function to be integrated : x*SIN(x)^2
Enter a                   : 1
Enter b                   : 12
Enter n                   : 1000

Value of the integral     : 38.589018712506  # 23192 / 601
```

The value obtained with 1000 steps of integration is already very precise.

---

2 Villarceau's Method

2.1 Principle

This second method belonging to Cotes that we are now studying is still based on the division into n subintervals of $[a, b]$, but this time the function is replaced by a polynomial of degree 4. Thus we write:

$$h = \frac{b-a}{4n} \quad \text{and} \quad x_i = a + ih.$$

Then we can show that on each interval $[x_{4i}, x_{4i+4}]$, the integral:

$$\int_{x_{4i}}^{x_{4i+4}} f(x) \, dx$$

can be approximated to:

$$T_{4i} = \frac{2h}{45} [7 f(x_{4i}) + 32 f(x_{4i+1}) + 12 f(x_{4i+2}) + 32 f(x_{4i+3}) + 7 f(x_{4i+4})]$$

The integral I is:

$$I = \sum_{i=0}^{n-1} T_{4i}$$

This approximation of $\int_{a}^{b} f(x)\, dx$ is of order h^6.

2.2 Calculation Tool

The parameters of the tool `ar_integral_villarceau` are the same as those for the tool `ar_integral_simpson`, that is:
- f, the function;
- a and b, the extremes of the interval of integration;
- n, the number of steps of integration.

The tool will be placed in the file `INTEGRAL\VILLARC.CPP`.

```
/*================================================================
                         VILLARC.CPP :
        VILLARCEAU'S METHOD INTEGRATION CALCULATION TOOL
  ==============================================================*/

#include "armath.h"

ar_double ar_integral_villarceau (ar_double  (*f)
(ar_double),
                  ar_double a , ar_double b, long n)
{
  int          i;
  ar_double    step, step4, x, res;

  errno = 0;
  step4 = (b - a) / (double) n;
  step  = step4  / (double) 4;
  res   = 7 * f (a); if (errno) return (0);
  res  -= 7 * f (b); if (errno) return (0);

  for (i = 0; i < n; i++)   {
    x = a + i * step4;
    x += step; res += 32 * f (x); if (errno) return (0);
    x += step; res += 12 * f (x); if (errno) return (0);
    x += step; res += 32 * f (x); if (errno) return (0);
    x += step; res += 14 * f (x); if (errno) return (0);
  }
  return (res * step * 2 / (double) 45);
}
```

2.3 Annotated Examples

Example 1

Let us consider once more the calculation of:

$$I = \int_1^{12} x \sin^2 x \, dx$$

by taking 50 intervals:

```
INTEGRATION WITH VILLARCEAU'S METHOD

Function to be integrated : x*SIN(x)^2
Enter a                    : 1
Enter b                    : 12
Enter n                    : 50

Value of the integral      : 38.589018699145  # 23192 / 601
```

The result found is accurate up to 10^{-7} with only 50 intervals:

$$I = 38.589018712241$$

Example 2

Let us work out the calculation of:

$$I = \int_1^2 (x^{14} - 8x^{11} + 3x^3) \, dx = -\frac{32057}{60}$$

by taking successively 15 then 100 intervals. The integral found is accurate up to 10^{-6} with only 15 steps of integration.

```
INTEGRATION WITH VILLARCEAU'S METHOD

Function to be integrated : x^14 - 8*x^11 + 3*x^3
Enter a                    : 1
Enter b                    : 2
Enter n                    : 15

Value of the integral      : -534.283329045278  # -32057 / 60

INTEGRATION WITH VILLARCEAU'S METHOD

Function to be integrated : x^14 - 8*x^11 + 3*x^3
Enter a                    : 1
```

```
Enter b                   : 2
Enter n                   : 100

Value of the integral     : -534.283333333285   # -32057 / 60
```

2.4 Conclusion on Cotes' Methods

There exist many other formulas by Cotes (in reality, an infinite number of them) giving approximations of order h^n with $n > 6$.

However, the numerical errors due to these methods can outweigh the additional precision that they bring. In general, one will use 20 or so intervals with Villarceau's method, and 100 or so intervals with Simpson's method; those values represent a good compromise between errors of method, numerical errors and speed.

Generally, the formulas of order higher than 6 are little used, and Romberg's method is preferred.

---

3   Romberg's Method

3.1 Introduction

The major drawback concerning Cotes' method lies in the fact that we do not know the precision of the result.

Romberg's method gives the opportunity to choose this precision *a priori*. Thus the iterations can be made until the precision needed is obtained.

3.2 Principle

This method is based on the trapezoidal rule, but it is carried out in an unusual way.

Considering a step h, an estimation $T_0(h)$ of the integral I being sought can be obtained by this method. If we divide the step h by 2, the estimation $T_0\left(\dfrac{h}{2}\right)$ will be more accurate and we can in the same way calculate $T_0\left(\dfrac{h}{4}\right)$, $T_0\left(\dfrac{h}{8}\right)$ ... and $T_0\left(\dfrac{h}{2^n}\right)$.

This series converges towards I. We can demonstrate that a second series $T_1\left(\dfrac{h}{2^{n-1}}\right)$ can be obtained for which the term $T_1\left(\dfrac{h}{2^k}\right)$ is a better approximation of the integral $T_0\left(\dfrac{h}{2^k}\right)$.

We can obtain $T_1\left(\dfrac{h}{2^k}\right)$ by:

$$T_1\left(\frac{h}{2^k}\right) = \frac{4\,T_0\left(\frac{h}{2^{k+1}}\right) - T_0\left(\frac{h}{2^k}\right)}{4-1} \qquad k \in [0,\, n-1]$$

We can obtain the third series in this way:

$$T_2\left(\frac{h}{2^k}\right) = \frac{4^2\,T_1\left(\frac{h}{2^{k+1}}\right) - T_1\left(\frac{h}{2^k}\right)}{4^2-1} \qquad k \in [0,\, n-2]$$

and as a general rule:

$$T_p\left(\frac{h}{2^k}\right) = \frac{4^p\,T_{p-1}\left(\frac{h}{2^{k+1}}\right) - T_{p-1}\left(\frac{h}{2^k}\right)}{4^p-1} \qquad k \in [0,\, n-p]$$

Therefore we can compose a table as follows:

$T_0(h)$	$T_0\left(\frac{h}{2}\right)$	....	$T_0\left(\frac{h}{2^{n-2}}\right)$	$T_0\left(\frac{h}{2^{n-1}}\right)$	$T_0\left(\frac{h}{2^n}\right)$
$T_1(h)$	$T_1\left(\frac{h}{2}\right)$	....	$T_1\left(\frac{h}{2^{n-2}}\right)$	$T_1\left(\frac{h}{2^{n-1}}\right)$	
$T_2(h)$	$T_2\left(\frac{h}{2}\right)$	....	$T_2\left(\frac{h}{2^{n-2}}\right)$		
$T_{n-1}(h)$	$T_{n-1}\left(\frac{h}{2}\right)$				
$T_n(h)$					

We can demonstrate that $T_k(h)$ converges much more rapidly towards I than $T_0\left(\frac{h}{2^k}\right)$.

Use of the Method

Therefore we start by calculating $T_0(h)$ with the help of the trapezoidal rule.

We then proceed to calculate $T_0\left(\frac{h}{2}\right)$ and we deduce from it $T_1(h)$, then $T_0\left(\frac{h}{4}\right)$, $T_1\left(\frac{h}{2}\right)$ and $T_2(h)$... More generally, we obtain a table of order $(n+1)$ from the table of order n by calculating $T_0\left(\frac{h}{2^{n+1}}\right)$ and by deducing from it $T_k\left(\frac{h}{2^{n+1-k}}\right)$ where $k \in [1,\, n+1]$. The calculation is finished when the difference between $T_{n+1}(h)$ and $T_n(h)$ is lower than the fixed limit.

3.3 Calculation Tool

The tool `ar_integral_romberg` is a function whose solution is the value of the integral sought. The boolean variable `errno` is positioned on `TRUE` if it has not been possible to evaluate the function at one point.

The input parameters of the tool are:

– `f`, the function to be integrated;

– `a` and `b`, the extremes of the interval of integration;

– `prec`, the precision wanted (difference between two successive estimations which causes the interruption of the iterations);

– `iter_min`, the minimal number of iterations (makes it possible to avoid a premature output in certain circumstances: see the calculation of the coefficients of a Fourier series);

– `iter_max`, the maximal number of iterations beyond which the computer gives up. The maximal calculation time varies in an exponential way according to this parameter (2^{iter_max}), and a value of 12 leads to a reasonable time of calculation whatever the circumstances (8000 evaluations of the function at most);

– `disp`, boolean indicator making it possible to display the number of the iteration, which is pleasing during lengthy calculations.

On output, the variable `prec_reached` contains the precision reached, in fact the difference between the last two estimations of the integral.

The tool will be placed in the file `INTEGRAL\ROMBERG.CPP`.

```
/*=========================================================
                        ROMBERG.CPP :
          ROMBERG'S METHOD INTEGRATION CALCULATION TOOL
   =======================================================*/

#include "armath.h"

#define  MAXITER  13

ar_double  ar_integral_romberg (ar_double  (*f) (ar_double),
        ar_double a, ar_double b, ar_double prec,
        ar_double &prec_reached, int iter_min, int iter_max,
        int disp)
{
   static ar_double  t [MAXITER+1] [MAXITER+1];
   ar_double         pas, r, s, ta;
   int               n, i, j;

   errno    = 0;
   iter_max = min (iter_max, MAXITER);
   r        = f (a);              if (errno) return (0);
```

```
ta        = (r + f (b)) / 2; if (errno) return (0);
pas       = (b - a);
t [0][0]  = ta * pas;
for (n = 1; n < iter_max; n++)  {
  if (disp)
    cout << "n=" << n << " : " << t [n-1] [0] << "\n";
  pas /= 2;
  s     = ta;
  for (i = 1; i < (1 << n); i++) {
    s += f (a + pas * i); if (errno) return (0);
  }
  t [0] [n] = s * pas;
  for (i = 1, r = 1; i <= n; i++)  {
    r *= 4;
    j = n - i;
    t [i][j] = (r * t [i-1][j+1] - t [i-1][j]) / (r - 1);
  }
  prec_reached = fabs (t [n][0] - t [n-1][0]);
  if ((prec_reached < prec) && (n >= iter_min)) break;
}
if (prec_reached > prec) errno = 1;
return (t [n][0]);
}
```

3.4 Annotated Example

Let us consider once more the calculation of:

$$I = \int_1^{12} x \sin^2 x \, dx$$

by specifying a precision of 10^{-6}:

```
INTEGRATION WITH ROMBERG'S METHOD

Function to be integrated : x*SIN(x)^2
Enter a                   : 1
Enter b                   : 12
Precision desired         : 1e-6

n=1 : 22.896496558384
n=2 : 9.838017228232
n=3 : 9.888116064244
n=4 : 47.825876540865
n=5 : 38.077778023714
n=6 : 38.595594934826
n=7 : 38.588997958751
n=8 : 38.589018728513
```

```
Value of the integral : 38.589018712238  # 23192 / 601
Precision reached     : 1.627578427588e-08
```

We notice that in the series of estimations the terms 2 and 3, totally false, differ by less than 10^{-1}. Thus, if the calculation is started again by requiring a precision of 1, the program stops at the second iteration, by displaying as a result:

```
INTEGRATION WITH ROMBERG'S METHOD

Function to be integrated : x*SIN(x)^2
Enter a                   : 1
Enter b                   : 12
Precision desired         : 0.1

n=1 : 22.896496558384
n=2 : 9.838017228232

Value of the integral : 9.888116064244  # 15643 / 1582
Precision reached     : 0.050098836012
```

That is why one will always have to work out the calculation with a sufficient precision.

---

4 Integration of Discrete Functions

4.1 Introduction

The previous programs allow us to integrate functions whose expression $f(x)$ is known, valid for every point x belonging to their field of definition.

But there are functions whose value is known only for a finite number of points: those are the *discrete functions*.

We will now examine the adaptation of Simpson's method to this type of function.

4.2 Principle

We know the values $f(x_i)$ taken by the function at n points x_i not necessarily equidistant. The number of these values must be odd: $n = 2m + 1$. Then we demonstrate that:

$$T_{2i} = \int_{x_{2i-1}}^{x_{2i+1}} f(x)\, dx$$

$$T_{2i} = \frac{h_1+h_2}{6h_1} \left[(2h_1-h_2)\, f(x_{2i-1}) + \frac{(h_1+h_2)^2}{h_2}\, f(x_{2i}) + \frac{h_1}{h_2} (2h_2-h_1)\, f(x_{2i+1}) \right]$$

with:

$$h_1 = x_{2i} - x_{2i-1} \qquad \text{and} \qquad h_2 = x_{2i+1} - x_{2i}$$

and consequently:

$$I = \int_{x_1}^{x_{2m+1}} f(x)\, dx = \sum_{i=1}^{m} T_{2i}$$

This formula is *correct* for the polynomials of degree 2.

4.3 Calculation Tool

This tool does its calculation on a set of n points $(x_i, f(x_i))$.

If the number n of points is even, Simpson's method is applied on the $(n-1)$ first points; the trapezoidal method is then used on the last interval, which generally reduces the precision.

It will therefore be preferable to use, as much as possible, the program with an odd number of points.

Furthermore, the highest the number of points, the least noticeable will be the perturbation caused by the trapezoidal method.

The tool `ar_integral_discrete` is a function whose solution is the value of the integral sought. The boolean variable `errno` is positioned on TRUE if it is not possible to calculate this integral.

The only parameter of input of the function is a data-buffer, which contains the number of points defining the function, and their coordinates.

The tool will be placed in the file `INTEGRAL\DISCINT.CPP`.

```
/*===========================================================
                       DISCINT.CPP :
           SIMPSON'S METHOD DISCRETE INTEGRATION
 ========================================================*/

#include "armath.h"

ar_double ar_integral_discrete (ar_buffer &t)
{
   int         i = t.start, i1, i2, n = t.nbelts ();
   ar_double   h, k, j, r = 0;

   errno = 1;

   do {
      i1 = i + 1; i2 = i + 2;
      h  = t.readx (i1) - t.readx (i);
```

```
    k   = t.readx (i2) - t.readx (i1);
    j   = h + k;
    if (h == 0) return (0);
    r += ((h + h - k) * t.ready (i) + (j * j * t.ready (i1) +
        h * (k + k - h) * t.ready (i2)) / k) * j / 6 / h;
    i   = i2;
} while (i < n - 1);

if (! (n % 2))
    r += (t.readx (n) - t.readx (n - 1)) *
         (t.ready (n) + t.ready (n - 1)) / 2;
errno = 0;
return (r);
}
```

4.4 Annotated Examples

Example 1

Let us first try to find an estimation of:

$$I = \int_{1}^{10} x^2 \, dx$$

which is equal to 333, by taking the values of a function at the points 1, 2, 5, 7 and 10.

```
SIMPSON'S DISCRETE INTEGRATION

Number of buffer : 1

INPUT BUFFER :

Title                 : x2
Index of first point  : 1
Index of last point   : 5

x1 = 1
y1 = 1

x2 = 2
y2 = 4

x3 = 5
y3 = 25

x4 = 7
y4 = 49
```

```
x5 = 10
y5 = 100

Value of the integral : 333
```

The result obtained is correct: this is always the case with Simpson's method concerning polynomials of second degree. Then, with six points, we have calculated:

$$I = \int_1^{20} x^2 \, dx$$

which equals 2666.33…

```
SIMPSON'S DISCRETE INTEGRATION

Number of buffer : 2

INPUT BUFFER :

Title               : x2
Index of first point : 1
Index of last point  : 6

x1 = 1
y1 = 1

x2 = 2
y2 = 4

x3 = 5
y3 = 25

x4 = 7
y4 = 49

x5 = 10
y5 = 100

x6 = 20
y6 = 400

Value of the integral : 2833
```

This time the result obtained is not accurate: the number of points is even, and Simpson's method is applied only to the first five.

Example 2

We will show in this example an application of the method to a practical example: the charging of an accumulator.

The experiment is as follows: an accumulator is charged over a period of 15 hours and the intensity going through it being measured at certain instants t_k.

We then endeavor to determine the charge q accumulated by the accumulator (disregarding the losses).

The total charge of the accumulator is given by:

$$q = \int_{t_0}^{t_f} i(t)\, dt$$

We only have to enter into the program the instants t_k in hours and the corresponding intensities i_k in amperes, and it will provide the estimation of a charge in Ah.

This is the experimental reading:

t (in h)	0	0.25	0.5	1	4	10	13	14	14.5	15
I (in A)	4	3	2.7	2.5	2.4	2.3	2.1	1.8	1.5	1

```
SIMPSON'S DISCRETE INTEGRATION

Number of buffer   : 3

INPUT BUFFER :

Title                   : acc
Index of first point : 1
Index of last point   : 10

x1 = 0
y1 = 4

x2 = .25
y2 = 3

x3 = .5
y3 = 2.7

x4 = 1
y4 = 2.5

x5 = 4
y5 = 2.4
```

```
x6 = 10
y6 = 2.3

x7 = 13
y7 = 2.1

x8 = 14
y8 = 1.8

x9 = 14.5
y9 = 1.5

x10 = 15
y10 = 1

Value of the integral : 34.097222222222  # 2455 / 72
```

The program provides the result $q = 34.1$ Ah. The data have been entered with the buffer entry tool, which made it possible to draw the curve before calculating its integral :

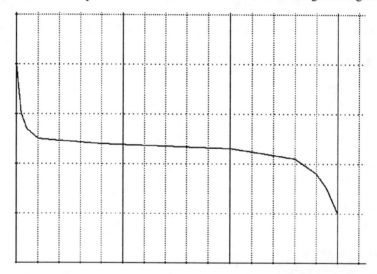

5 The Calculation of a Discrete Primitive

5.1 Introduction

A program for the search for a formal primitive would be much larger and more complicated than a program of numerical differentiation. Indeed the calculation of a derivative is submitted to a set of precise rules systematically applicable.

On the other hand, the method allowing for the exact calculation of a primitive is not dictated at all by the expression of a function, and therefore the search is a matter for artificial intelligence. In addition to that, there are functions whose primitive we don't know how to calculate.

We will therefore try to find primitives in their discrete expression, that is, in the form of a succession of values taken by the function sought on a given interval. Let us remind you however that a calculation worked out with a sufficient number of points (a few hundred) provides a graphical representation as accurate as that of a function calculated in an analytical way.

5.2 Principle

The search for a primitive is a particular case of finding the solution of an explicit differential equation of the first order.

Indeed, the general expression of an explicit differential equation of the first order is as follows:

$$y' = f(y, x)$$

The search for a primitive therefore corresponds to a particular case where f does not depend on y.

Here we will use Runge-Kutta's method of order 4 (explained in chapter 17 concerning differential equations) which can be greatly simplified. Starting from a known point (x_n, y_n) belonging to the solution curve the following point is determined by:

$$x_{n+1} = x_n + h$$

$$y_{n+1} = y_n + \frac{h}{6} \left[f(x_n) + 4 f(x_n + \frac{h}{2}) + f(x_n + h) \right]$$

REMARK: the method obtained through the simplification of the Runge-Kutta method of order 4 is none other than Simpson's method.

5.3 Calculation Tool

The input parameters of the tool `ar_primitive` are:
 – `f`, the function to be integrated;
 – `a` and `b`, the extremes of the interval on which the primitive must be calculated;
 – `fa`, the initial value of the primitive at point a;
   (Let us indeed remind ourselves of the fact that a given function does not have only one primitive but an infinite number of them, all equal to each other but for a constant; this makes it compulsory to fix the value of the primitive at one point)
 – `n`, the number of points to be calculated;

– fi, the finesse of the calculation;

(The notion of finesse is explained in detail in the chapter concerning differential equations. We will sum up by saying that the finesse characterizes the precision of the calculation. The higher the finesse, the more precise is the result. On the other hand, the time of execution is proportional to the finesse. The calculation of the primitives is precise, and a finesse of a few units is generally quite satisfactory; the following examples have been obtained with a finesse of 1 or 2.)

– disp, boolean making it possible to display the primitive in real time, that is, of each point, as the calculation proceeds.

On output, the tool gives back the buffer, which contains the digitized primitive-function (the number of points and their coordinates). The boolean indicator errno indicates if it is possible to calculate the integral or not.

REMARK: the formula uses three evaluations of the function for each calculated point. The last of these evaluations for a given point is identical to the first for the following point. The program optimizes its time of calculation by saving this value, and does only two evaluations for each point calculated.

The tool will be placed in the file INTEGRAL\PRIMITIV.CPP.

```
/*=============================================================
                        PRIMITIV.CPP :
              CALCULATION OF DISCRETE PRIMIVES
     =========================================================*/

#include "armath.h"

void  ar_primitive  (ar_double        (*f) (ar_double),
      ar_buffer  &t, ar_double a, ar_double b,
      ar_double fa, int n, int fi, int aff)
{
   ar_double  h, h2, h6, ly, lr, x, y, u;
   int        i, j, ni;

   errno = TRUE;
   if (! t.open ("Discrete primitive", 0, n)) return;
   if (fi < 1)              return;

   h    = (b - a) / fi / n;
   h2   = h / 2; h6 = h / 6;

   t.addcouple (a, fa);
   lr   = fa;
   ly   = f (a);              if (errno)  return;

   for (i = 1; i <= n; i++)  {
      ni = (i - 1) * fi - 1;
```

```
for (j = 1; j <= fi; j++)  {
   x  = a + h * (ni + j);
   u  = 4 * f (x + h2);
   if (errno)  return;

   x  += h;
   y  = f (x);
   if (errno)  return;
   lr += h6 * (ly + u + y);
   ly = y;
}

t.addcouple (x, lr);
if (aff)
   cout << "x = " << setw (25) << x << " y = " <<
        setw (25) << lr << ar_rational (lr) << "\n";
}

errno = FALSE;
}
```

5.4 Annotated Examples

Example 1

We will try to find the primitive of the function $y = x$ on the interval $[-5, 5]$. We know that the primitive is a parabola whose equation is:

$$F(x) = \frac{x^2}{2} + k$$

Let us fix the initial value $F(-5) = \dfrac{25}{2}$, in order to obtain the parabola $y = \dfrac{x^2}{2}$.

The exploitation tool enables us to obtain simply the graphical representation of the primitive once it has been calculated.

```
CALCULATION OF PRIMITIVES IN THEIR DISCRETE EXPRESSION

Input function        : X
Value of a            : -5
Value of b            : 5
Initial value in  a   : 25/2
Number of points      : 20
Finesse               : 2
N° of buffer          : 1
Display of the points : y
```

```
X =       -4.5    Y =        10.125   # 81 / 8
X =         -4    Y =             8
X =       -3.5    Y =         6.125   # 49 / 8
X =         -3    Y =           4.5   # 9 / 2
X =       -2.5    Y =         3.125   # 25 / 8
X =         -2    Y =             2
X =       -1.5    Y =         1.125   # 9 / 8
X =         -1    Y =           0.5   # 1 / 2
X =       -0.5    Y =         0.125   # 1 / 8
X =          0    Y = 8.673617379884e-18
X =        0.5    Y =         0.125   # 1 / 8
X =          1    Y =           0.5   # 1 / 2
X =        1.5    Y =         1.125   # 9 / 8
X =          2    Y =             2
X =        2.5    Y =         3.125   # 25 / 8
X =          3    Y =           4.5   # 9 / 2
X =        3.5    Y =         6.125   # 49 / 8
X =          4    Y =             8
X =        4.5    Y =        10.125   # 81 / 8
X =          5    Y =          12.5   # 25 / 2
```

The buffer number 1 now contains the discrete primitive.
Graphical representation ? y

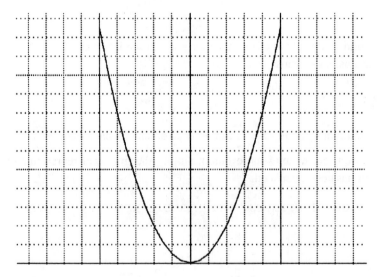

Example 2

The following curves represent:
   – The function $y = x \sin^3 x$ drawn by the tool for drawing analytical curves, on the interval $[-10, 10]$;

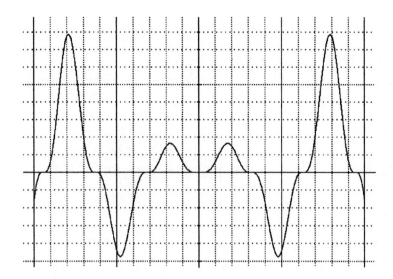

– its primitive, calculated by the program on the interval $[-3\pi, 3\pi]$, with 100 points and $F(-3\pi) = -2\pi$.

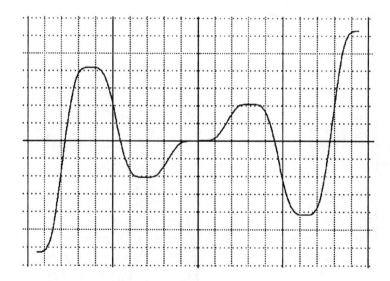

The exact expression of the primitive is as follows:

$$F(x) = \frac{1}{4}\left[3\,(\sin x - x\,\cos x) + \frac{1}{9}\,(3x\,\cos 3x - \sin 3x) \right] + C$$

Example 3

The three following curves represent successively:

– the function $y = \left(\dfrac{x}{x^2+1}\right)^3$ represented by the tool for drawing analytical curves:

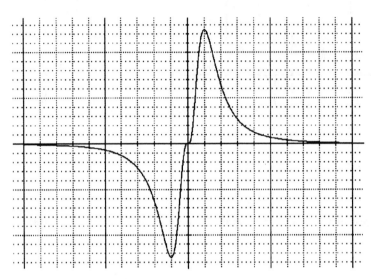

– its exact primitive, obtained by the tool for drawing analytical curves:

$$y = \dfrac{x^4}{4(x^2+1)^2}$$

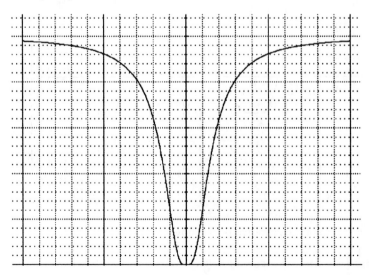

– its primitive calculated (with 80 points) and represented by the buffer drawing tool.

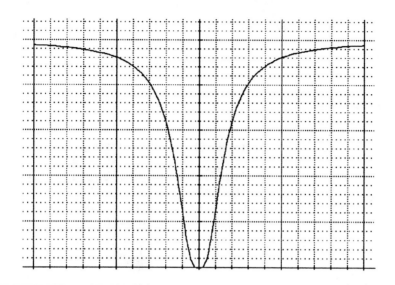

---

6 Exploitation Tools

The following tools make possible the direct exploitation of the calculation tools.

The following tool must be placed in the file `INTEGRAL\USIMPSON.CPP`:

```
/*===========================================================
                      USIMPSON.CPP :
           SIMPSON'S METHOD EXPLOITATION TOOL
=============================================================*/

#include "armath.h"

void ar_use_simpson ()
{
  ar_double   a, b, r;
  long        n;

  ar_init_entry ("INTEGRATION WITH SIMPSON'S METHOD");
  ar_fill_entry ("Function to be integrated", &ar_glob_f,
                 AR_TFUN);
  ar_fill_entry ("Enter a", &a, AR_TDOU);
  ar_fill_entry ("Enter b", &b, AR_TDOU);
  ar_fill_entry ("Enter n", &n, AR_TLON);
  if (ar_do_entry ()) return;
```

```
    r = ar_integral_simpson (ar_eval_f, a, b, n);

    if (errno)
      cerr << "Non-calculable integral\n";
    else
      cout << "Value of the integral : " << r <<
                      ar_rational (r) << "\n";

    ar_pause ();
}
```

The following tool must be placed in the file INTEGRAL\UVILLARC.CPP:

```
/*==========================================================
                        UVILLARC.CPP :
            VILLARCEAU'S METHOD EXPLOITATION TOOL
==========================================================*/

#include "armath.h"

void ar_use_villarceau ()
{
  ar_double    a, b, r;
  long         n;

  ar_init_entry ("INTEGRATION WITH VILLARCEAU'S METHOD");
  ar_fill_entry ("Function to be integrated", &ar_glob_f,
                 AR_TFUN);
  ar_fill_entry ("Enter a", &a, AR_TDOU);
  ar_fill_entry ("Enter b", &b, AR_TDOU);
  ar_fill_entry ("Enter n", &n, AR_TLON);
  if (ar_do_entry ()) return;

  r = ar_integral_villarceau (ar_eval_f, a, b, n);
  if (errno)
    cerr << "Non-calculable integral\n";
  else
    cout << "Value of the integral : " << r <<
                    ar_rational (r) << "\n";
  ar_pause ();
}
```

The following tool must be placed in the file INTEGRAL\UROMBERG.CPP:

```
/*==========================================================
                        UROMBERG.CPP :
            ROMBERG'S METHOD EXPLOITATION TOOL
==========================================================*/
```

```
#include "armath.h"

void ar_use_romberg ()
{
  ar_double  a, b, p, q, r;

  ar_init_entry ("INTEGRATION WITH ROMBERG'S METHOD");
  ar_fill_entry ("Function to be integrated", &ar_glob_f,
                 AR_TFUN);
  ar_fill_entry ("Enter a", &a, AR_TDOU);
  ar_fill_entry ("Enter b", &b, AR_TDOU);
  ar_fill_entry ("Precision desired", &p, AR_TDOU);
  if (ar_do_entry ()) return;

  r = ar_integral_romberg (ar_eval_f,a,b,p,q,2,12,TRUE);

  if (errno)
    cerr << "Non-calculable integral\n";
  else
    cout << "Value of the integral : " << r <<
                 ar_rational (r) << "\n" <<
            "Precision reached     : " << q << "\n";

  ar_pause ();
}
```

The following tool must be placed in the file INTEGRAL\UDISCINT.CPP:

```
/*============================================================
                       UDISCINT.CPP :
           DISCRETE INTEGRATION EXPLOITATION TOOL
============================================================*/

#include "armath.h"

void ar_use_integral_discrete ()
{
  int        nt;
  ar_double  r;

  cout << "SIMPSON'S DISCRETE INTEGRATION\n\n";
  if (ar_read ("Number of buffer : ", &nt, AR_TINT)) return;
  if ((nt < 0) || (nt > AR_MAXBUFFER)) return;

  if (ar_buff [nt].nbelts () == 0)
    cin >> ar_buff [nt];

  r = ar_integral_discrete (ar_buff [nt]);
```

```
  if (errno)
    cerr << "Non-calculable integral\n";
  else
    cout << "Value of the integral : " << r
         << ar_rational (r) << "\n";

  ar_pause ();
}
```

The following tool must be placed in the file INTEGRAL\UPRIMITI.CPP:

```
/*=========================================================
                        UPRIMITI.CPP :
     DISCRETE PRIMITIVE CALCULATION EXPLOITATION TOOL
=========================================================*/

#include "armath.h"

void ar_use_primitive ()
{
  ar_double  a, b, fa;
  int        n, nt, fi, disp;

  ar_init_entry ("CALCULATION OF PRIMITIVES IN THEIR \
                  DISCRETE EXPRESSION");
  ar_fill_entry ("Enter function       ",&ar_glob_f,AR_TFUN);
  ar_fill_entry ("Value of a           ", &a, AR_TDOU);
  ar_fill_entry ("Value of b           ", &b, AR_TDOU);
  ar_fill_entry ("Initial value in a   ", &fa, AR_TDOU);
  ar_fill_entry ("Number of points     ", &n, AR_TINT);
  ar_fill_entry ("Finesse              ", &fi, AR_TINT);
  ar_fill_entry ("N° of buffer         ", &nt, AR_TINT);
  ar_fill_entry ("Display of the points", &disp, AR_TBOO);

  if (ar_do_entry ()) return;
  ar_primitive (ar_eval_f,ar_buff[nt],a,b,fa,n,fi,disp);
  if (errno)   {
    cerr << "Non-calculable primitive\n";
    ar_pause  ();
  }
  else  {
    cout << "The buffer number " << nt << " now contains"
         << " the discrete primitive\n\n";
    ar_read ("Graphical representation ? ", &disp, AR_TBOO);
    if (disp)
      ar_draw_buffer (ar_buff [nt]);
  }
}
```

15

The Drawing of Surfaces

The graphic representation of functions with one variable necessitates a space of two dimensions; one for the function, another for the variable. The graphic displays of computers are thus particularly adapted to their representation.

On the other hand, the representation of functions with two variables necessitates three dimensions; still one for the function, but two with the variables. The result obtained is a surface. It is therefore necessary to use a trick in order to represent in two dimensions a geometric object with three dimensions.

Therefore we use projections to display the image of the surface on the screen. There are several types of them, which of course give different results. We will study in detail three of these projections: the isometric projection, the Cavalieri projection and the projection in perspective.

However, another problem emerges when we want to draw surfaces: the representation of the hidden lines. Indeed according to the type of equation and the nature of the projection, a part of the surface can be hidden from the eyes of the observer. Therefore we have to create an algorithm which will render possible the omission of the drawing of the hidden lines.

This chapter will therefore be made up as follows: first we will explain the different projections which we have previously cited. Then, we will go into the details of the functioning of an algorithm designed for the representation of the hidden lines, this by using the method of "the peak lines". Finally, we will provide the program and show how to use it with the help of some examples.

1   The Different Projections

A projection is an affine transformation whose image of a group of points belonging to a space of dimension N is a group of points belonging to a sub-space of dimension M, with $M<N$. We distinguish two main families of projections: those whose lines of projection are parallel (parallel projections) and those whose lines of projection are secant at a point called center of projection (projections in perspective).

1.1   The Projection in Perspective

To carry out the projection in perspective, we define three orthornormal coordinates system: (O, x, y, z) is the coordinates system of the object, (O_O, x_O, y_O, z_O) is the coordinates system of the observer, and (O_E, x_E, y_E) is the coordinates system of the display.

We locate the observer through his spherical coordinates (R, θ, ϕ). The display is placed at the distance D from the observer, perpendicular to the axis OO_O.

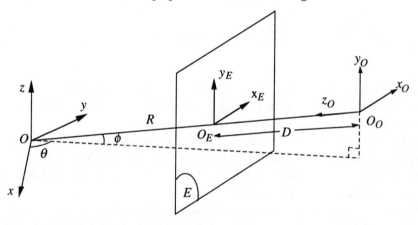

In this system of axes, we obtain rapidly the coordinates in the coordinate system of the display, according to the coordinates in the coordinate system of the observer (property of the similar triangles):

$$x_E = \frac{D.x_O}{z_O} \qquad y_E = \frac{D.y_O}{z_O}$$

Furthermore, the coordinates in the coordinate system of the observer are obtained from the coordinates in the coordinate system of the object through the relations:

$$x_O = -x.\sin \theta \quad + y.\cos \theta$$

$$y_O = -x.\cos \theta.\sin \phi \quad - y.\sin \theta.\sin \phi \quad + z.\cos \phi$$

$$z_O = -x.\cos \theta.\cos \phi \quad - y.\sin \theta.\cos \phi \quad - z.\sin \phi \quad + R$$

1.2 The Isometric Projection

The coordinates in the coordinate system of the display are obtained immediately according to those given in the coordinate system of the observer, because the projection is parallel:

$$x_E = x_O \qquad\qquad y_E = y_O$$

The coordinates in the coordinate system of the observer are obtained from the formulas of the previous case, by taking:

$$\theta = 45° \qquad\qquad \phi = 35.26°$$

1.3 The Cavalieri Projection

This projection is the most simple of the three, since two axes are common both to the coordinates system of the object and to the coordinates system of the display (Oy and Oz).

The third axis goes through a reduction ($k = 0.5$ generally) and is represented by an angle θ in relation to the horizontal ($\theta = 45°$ or $\theta = 30°$ generally).

$$x_E = -x_O.k.\cos\theta + y_O$$

$$y_E = -x_O.k.\sin\theta + z_O$$

---

2   The Problem of Hidden Lines

The surface is represented by a succession of curves obtained through the intersection of parallel planes, either at the plane (xOz), or at the plane (yOz), according to the position of the observer. The curves are drawn successively from the nearest to the observer to the farthest.

Each curve is itself made up of a succession of straight line segments linking certain calculated points belonging to the surface. For the majority of surfaces, a satisfactory accuracy is obtained by drawing about 50 curves, with a sufficient number of calculated points (about a hundred).

To render the representation of a surface more pleasant and realistic, it is preferable not to draw the lines which are hidden by another part of the surface.

In order to do so, we use the following principle. As we progress in the drawing, we will determine two peak lines, which represent respectively the maxima and minima reached by the different curves representing the surface. When a new curve is drawn, the position of the points belonging to the segment in the process of being drawn is compared to the hidden area bounded by the two peak lines.

Several cases present themselves: either the two points are in the hidden area, and no drawing can be done, or the two points belong to the same side of the visible area, and the segment can drawn in full, or one of the points is in the hidden area, and we can draw a part of the segment, or the points are on either side of the hidden area, and we have to draw two segments.

This necessitates the presence of a function to work out the calculation of the intersection of the segment in the process of being drawn with the peak line.

3 Drawing Tool

The tool `ar_perspective` does the drawing of the surface corresponding to the following parameters:
- `f`, the function with two variables to be represented;
- `xn`, `xm`: interval of representation on the axis of the *x*;
- `yn`, `ym`: interval of representation on the axis of the *y*;
- `nb_curves`: the number of curves to be drawn;
- `nb_points`: the number of points to use for each curve;
- `d`: the distance between the observer and the plane of projection;
- `r`: the distance between the object and the observer;
- `theta`, `phi`: angular and spherical coordinates of the observer;
- `proj`: nature of the projection (1: perspective, 2: cavalieri, 3: isometric).

This tool will be placed in the file SURFACES\PERSPECT.CPP.

In order to improve the readability of the program, we have used subfunctions.

The function `calculate_point` does the calculation of the changing of the coordinate system according to the projection wanted.

The function `init` mostly takes charge of the initialization of the values of the coefficients of projection, which for reasons of efficiency are calculated only once at the beginning of the drawing.

The function `intersection` calculates the coordinates of the point of intersection between the segment in the process of being drawn and one of the peak lines (according to the parameters *n* and *m* which it is being given).

Finally, the function `draw` does the calculation. The main difficulty comes from the necessity to repeatedly bring the peak lines up to date each time a segment has been drawn.

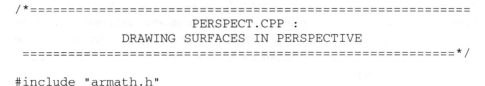

```
/*==============================================================
                     PERSPECT.CPP :
            DRAWING SURFACES IN PERSPECTIVE
==============================================================*/

#include "armath.h"
```

```
static void sline (int, int, int, int);
static void intersection (int, int);
static void update_max_min (int, int);
static void sdraw (int, int);
static int  init (void);
static void calculate_point (void);

static int      *mini, *maxi;
static int      xs, ys, xp, yp, rx, ry, u;
static ar_double  x, y, dx, dy,
               xorg, yorg, cav1, cav2,
               p1, q1,/*r1, s1,*/
               p2, q2, r2,/*s2,*/
               p3, q3, r3, s3;

/*===============================================
   Parameters through global static variables
   =============================================*/
static  ar_double  (*f) (ar_double, ar_double);
static  int      nb_curves, nb_points, proj;
static       ar_double  xi, xm, yi, ym, d, r, theta, phi;

/*-----------------------
Input  : x, y
Output : xs, ys
Uses   : p1, q1, ...
         and cav1, cav2, xorg, yorg, dist, proj
-----------------------*/

static void calculate_point ()
{
  ar_double  xo, yo, zo, u1, u2;
  ar_double  z = (*f) (x, y);

  switch (proj)  {

    case 1 :
      xo = p1 * x + q1 * y/*+ r1 * z + s1*/;
      yo = p2 * x + q2 * y + r2 * z/*+ s2*/;
      zo = p3 * x + q3 * y + r3 * z + s3 ;
      u1 = xo / zo;
      u2 = yo / zo / ar_round;
      break;

    case 2 :
      u1 = cav1 * x + y;
      u2 = cav2 * x + z;
      break;
```

```
   case 3 :
      xo = p1 * x + q1 * y/*+ r1 * z + s1*/;
      yo = p2 * x + q2 * y + r2 * z/*+ s2*/;
      u1 = xo;
      u2 = yo / ar_round;
      break;
  }
  xs = xorg + d * u1;
  ys = yorg - d * u2;
}


static int init ()
{
  int  k;

  ar_init_graph ();

  if ((mini = (int *) calloc (ar_maxcol+1,sizeof(int))) == 0)
    return (FALSE);
  if ((maxi = (int *) calloc (ar_maxcol+1,sizeof(int))) == 0)
{
    free (mini); return (FALSE);
  }

  dx = xm - xi; dy = ym - yi;
  xorg = ar_maxcol / 2;
  yorg = ar_maxlig / 2;

  for (k = 0; k <= ar_maxcol; k++)   {
    maxi [k] = 0;
    mini [k] = ar_maxlig;
  }
  if (proj == 3)   {
    theta  = 45 * AR_PI / 180;
    phi = 35.26 * AR_PI / 180;
  }

  if (proj == 2)   {
    cav1 = - cos (theta) * phi;
    cav2 = - sin (theta) * phi;
  }

  p1 = - sin (theta);
  q1 =   cos (theta);
/*r1 =   0;
  s1 =   0; */
```

```
  p2 = - cos (theta) * sin (phi);
  q2 = - sin (theta) * sin (phi);
  r2 =   cos (phi);
/*s2 =   0; */

  p3 = - cos (theta) * cos (phi);
  q3 = - sin (theta) * cos (phi);
  r3 = - sin (phi);
  s3 =   r;

  return (TRUE);
}

static void sline (int x1, int y1, int x2, int y2)
{
  if ((x1 >= 0) && (x1 <= ar_maxcol) && (x2 >= 0)
              && (x2 <= ar_maxcol) && (y1 >= 0)
              && (y1 <= ar_maxlig) && (y2 >= 0)
              && (y2 <= ar_maxlig) && (errno == 0))
    ar_line (x1, y1, x2, y2);
}

static void intersection (int n, int m)
{
  ar_double  a = (ar_double) (ys-yp) / (ar_double) (xs - xp);
  ar_double  b = (ar_double) ys - a * xs;
  ar_double  c = (ar_double) (m - n) / (ar_double) (xs - xp);
  ar_double  d = m - c * xs;
  rx = (int) ((d - b) / (a - c));
  ry = (int) ((b * c - d * a) / (c - a));
}

static void update_max_min (int x, int y)
{
  if ((x >= 0) && (x <= ar_maxcol))  {
    if (y > maxi [x])  maxi [x] = y;
    if (y < mini [x])  mini [x] = y;
  }
}

static void sdraw (int sens, int mode)
{
  int   beg_loop, end_loop, index1, index2, k;
  int ymp, yms, yip, yis, pl, mm;

  if ((mode == 1) && (sens == -1))  {
    beg_loop = nb_points; end_loop = 0;
  }
```

```
else  {
  beg_loop = 0;
  end_loop = nb_points;
}

for (index1 = 0; index1 <= nb_curves; index1++)  {
  if (mode == 1)  {
    x = xm - index1 * dx / nb_curves;
    y = (sens == 1) ? yi : ym;
  }
  else  {
    y = (sens == 1) ?
        yi + index1 * dy / nb_curves :
          ym - index1 * dy / nb_curves;
    x = xi;
  }
  calculate_point ();
  if (index1 == 0)  mm = xs;
  xp = xs; yp = ys;
  ymp = maxi [xp]; yip = mini [xp];
  update_max_min (xp, yp);
  index2 = beg_loop;
  do  {
    if (mode == 1)  {
      index2 += sens;
    y = yi + index2 * dy / nb_points;
    }
    else  {
      index2 ++;
    x = xi + index2 * dx / nb_points;
    }
    calculate_point ();
    if (xs != xp)  {
    yms = maxi [xs]; yis = mini [xs];
      if (((xs > mm) && (sens == 1)) ||
          ((xs < mm) && (sens == -1)) ||
          ((ys > maxi [xs]) || (ys < mini [xs])))  {
        k = xp;
        do  {
          k += sens;
          u = (int) (yp + (k - xp) * (ys-yp) / (xs - xp));
          update_max_min (k, u);
        } while (k != xs);
      }
      if (((xs > mm) && (sens == 1)) ||
          ((xs < mm) && (sens == -1)))  {
      mm = xs; yis = ys; yms = ys;
      }
```

```
      pl = 0;
      if (ys > yms) pl = 10;
      if (ys < yis) pl = 20;
      if (yp > ymp) pl ++;
      if (yp < yip) pl += 2;
      if (index1 == 0)  pl = 11;
      switch (pl)  {
        case  1 : intersection (ymp, yms);
                sline (xp, yp, rx, ry);
                break;
        case  2 : intersection (yip, yis);
                sline (xp, yp, rx, ry);
                break;
        case 10 : intersection (ymp, yms);
                sline (rx, ry, xs, ys);
                break;
        case 20 : intersection (yip, yis);
                sline (rx, ry, xs, ys);
                    break;
        case 12 : intersection (yip, yis);
                sline (xp, yp, rx, ry);
                    intersection (ymp, yms);
                sline (rx, ry, xs, ys);
                break;
        case 21 : intersection (ymp, yms);
                sline (xp, yp, rx, ry);
                intersection (yip, yis);
                sline (rx, ry, xs, ys);
                break;
        case 11 :
      case 22 : sline (xp, yp, xs, ys);
                break;
      }
    xp = xs; yp = ys; ymp = yms; yip = yis;
    }
    if (ar_stop_asked ()) return;
  } while (index2 < end_loop);
 }   /* du for index1 */
}   /* de sdraw */

void  ar_perspective (
    ar_double (*par_f) (ar_double, ar_double),
    int par_nb_curves, int par_nb_points,
    ar_double par_xi, ar_double par_xm,
    ar_double par_yi, ar_double par_ym,
    ar_double par_d, ar_double par_r,
    ar_double par_theta, ar_double par_phi,
    int par_proj)
```

```
{
    f            = par_f;
    nb_curves    = par_nb_curves;
    nb_points    = par_nb_points;
    xi           = par_xi;
    xm           = par_xm;
    yi           = par_yi;
    ym           = par_ym;
    d            = par_d;
    r            = par_r;
    theta        = par_theta;
    phi          = par_phi;
    proj         = par_proj;

    if (init ())  {
       if ((theta >= 0) && (theta < AR_PI/3)) sdraw (1,1);
       if ((theta >= -AR_PI/3) && (theta < 0)) sdraw(-1,1);
       if ((theta >= -AR_PI/2) && (theta < -AR_PI/3))
          sdraw(1,-1);
       if ((theta >= AR_PI/3) && (theta <= AR_PI/2))
          sdraw(-1,-1);

       free ((char *) mini);
       free ((char *) maxi);
    }
}
```

4   Examples

The following examples have been obtained on a VGA graphics card. Slightly different parameters are necessary for other video cards: the scale is indeed different, and the drawing can turn out to be impossible in certain cases with the parameters indicated in the text.

Example 1

Let us consider the equation $z = 5 \cdot \dfrac{\sin x}{x} \cdot \dfrac{\sin y}{y}$ and let us represent it with the following parameters:

$$x_{min} = -9.42 \qquad x_{max} = 9.42 \qquad y_{min} = -9.42 \qquad y_{max} = 9.42$$

Number of curves: 41   Number of points: 81

$$D = 28 \qquad\qquad \theta = 22 \qquad\qquad \phi = 22$$

The fact of choosing an odd number of curves and points makes it possible to avoid the singularity of the origin.

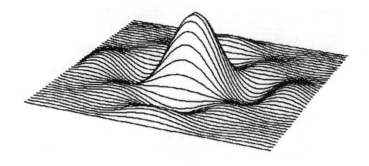

Example 2

Let us consider the equation $z = 1 - \dfrac{1}{\sqrt{x^2+y^2}}$ and let us represent it with the parameters:

$x_{min} = -2$ $x_{max} = 2$ $y_{min} = -2$ $y_{max} = 2$

Number of curves: 41   Number of points: 81

$D = 28$ $\theta = 22°$

We are going to make a drawing by taking an angle ϕ negative, which makes it possible to see the surface from underneath. Let us begin with the view from above with $\phi = 22°$:

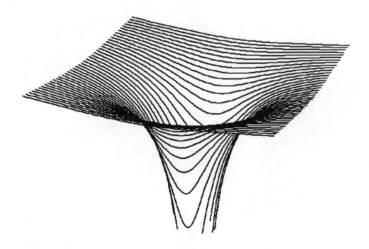

Then let us draw the view from underneath with $\phi = -22°$:

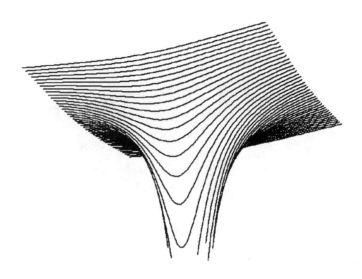

Example 3

Let us consider the equation $z = 7.x^2.e^{-(x^2+y^2)}$ and let us represent it with the parameters:

$x_{min} = -2.5$ $\quad$ $x_{max} = 2.5$ $\quad$ $y_{min} = -2.5$ $\quad$ $y_{max} = 2.5$

Number of curves: 50 $\qquad$ Number of points: 80

$D = 28$ $\qquad$ $\theta = 60$ $\qquad$ $\phi = 40$

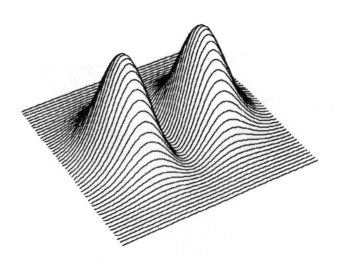

Example 4

Let us consider the equation:
$$z = 5 . \frac{\sin(\sqrt{x^2+y^2})}{\sqrt{x^2+y^2}}$$

We make a projection in perspective with the following parameters:

$x_{min} = -10$ $x_{max} = 10$ $y_{min} = -10$ $y_{max} = 10$

Number of curves: 51   Number of points: 81

$D = 28$ $\theta = 22$ $\phi = 22$

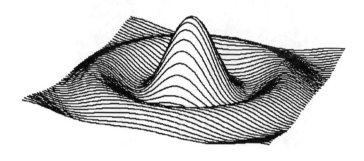

Example 5

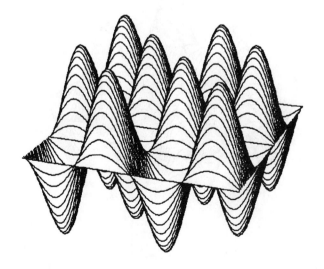

The previous surface has for equation: $z = 5.\sin x.\sin y$

We have represented it by using the three projections available, with the parameters:

$x_{min} = -6.28$ $x_{max} = 6.28$ $y_{min} = -6.28$ $y_{max} = 6.28$

Number of curves: 80   Number of points: 150

$D = 25$

For the projection in perspective, we have chosen $\theta = 22°$ and $\phi = 22°$.

For the Cavalieri projection, we choose $\theta = 45°$ and $k = 0.5$.

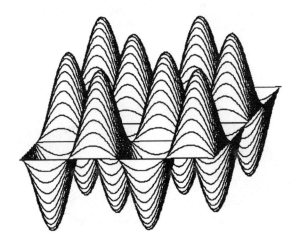

For the isometric projection, we obtain:

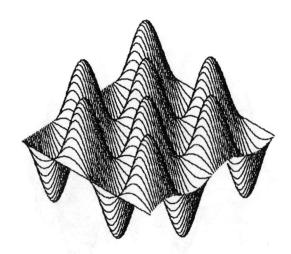

Example 6

Let us consider the equation: $z = 0.5.y^2.\dfrac{\sin(\sqrt{x^2+y^2})}{\sqrt{x^2+y^2}}$

We make a projection in perspective with the following parameters:

Number of curves: 45   Number of points: 80

$x_{min} = -4$ $x_{max} = 4$ $y_{min} = -4$ $y_{max} = 4$

$D = 32$ $\theta = 22$ $\phi = 22$

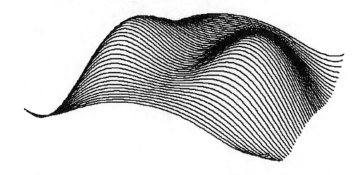

5   Exploitation Tool

The following tool makes possible the direct exploitation of the tool for drawing.
It must be placed in the file SURFACES\UPERSPEC.CPP:

```
/*==============================================================
                        UPERSPEC.CPP :
      DRAWING SURFACES IN PERSPECTIVE EXPLOITATION TOOL
   ==========================================================*/

#include <conio.h>
#include "armath.h"

void ar_use_perspective ()
{
   ar_double   xn, xm, yn, ym, r, d, theta, phi;
   int         proj, nb_curves, nb_points;
   do {
      clrscr (); cout << "DRAWING SURFACES IN PERSPECTIVE\n\n";
```

```
    cout << "Choose the projection type\n\n\n";
    cout << "1 : Projection in perspective\n\n";
    cout << "2 : Cavalieri projection\n\n";
    cout << "3 : Isometric projection\n\n";
    if (ar_read ("Your choice : ", &proj, AR_TINT)) return;
  } while ((proj > 3) || (proj <= 0));
  ar_nl; ar_init_entry ("Entry of limits is MANDATORY");
  ar_fill_entry ("Function z (x, y)", &ar_glob_f, AR_TFYI);
  ar_fill_entry ("x min", &xn, AR_TDOU);
  ar_fill_entry ("x max", &xm, AR_TDOU);
  ar_fill_entry ("y min", &yn, AR_TDOU);
  ar_fill_entry ("y max", &ym, AR_TDOU);
  ar_fill_entry ("Number of curves  (ou 0)", &nb_curves,
                 AR_TINT);
  ar_fill_entry ("Number of points  (ou 0)", &nb_points,
                 AR_TINT);
  ar_fill_entry ("Distance to plane (0<d<100)", &d, AR_TDOU);
  switch (proj)  {
    case 1 :
      ar_fill_entry ("Theta (from  -90 to  90°)", &theta,
                     AR_TDOU);
      ar_fill_entry ("Phi   (from -180 to 180°)", &phi,
                     AR_TDOU); break;
    case 2 :
      ar_fill_entry ("Theta (from   0 to  90°)", &theta,
                     AR_TDOU);
      ar_fill_entry ("Reduction (from  0 to   1)", &phi,
                     AR_TDOU); break;
  }
  ar_do_entry (); if (nb_curves <= 0)  nb_curves = 50;
  if (nb_points <= 0)  nb_points = 200;
  if ((d > 100) || (xm < xn) || (ym < yn)) return;
  switch (proj)  {
    case 1 :
      if ((theta < -90) || (theta > 90)) return;
      if ((phi  < -180) || (phi  > 180)) return;
      theta *= AR_PI / 180; phi   *= AR_PI / 180;
      r = 2.5 * (fabs(xn) + fabs(xm) + fabs(yn) + fabs(ym));
      d *= 70; break;
    case 2 :
      if ((theta <= 0) || (theta >= 90)) return;
      if ((phi  <= 0) || (phi  >= 1))  return;
      theta *= AR_PI / 180; break;
  }
  ar_perspective (ar_eval_fxy, nb_curves, nb_points,
                  xn, xm, yn, ym, d, r, theta, phi, proj);
  ar_close_graph ();
}
```

16

Fourier Series

The fact that a periodic function can be expressed as a sum of sinusoidal functions is a result which can only draw our attention to it: in this way, how can it be possible to obtain a square, triangular, or switchback signal?

But nevertheless, most of the periodic functions (of period T) can be broken up into their fundamental harmonics, that is, can be developed into series such as:

$$f(x) = a_0 + \sum_{n=1}^{+\infty} \left(a_n \cos n\frac{2\pi}{T}x + b_n \sin n\frac{2\pi}{T}x \right)$$

Such series are called Fourier series.

We will start by studying the calculation of the coefficients a_n and b_n of the Fourier series for a function f.

Then we will represent the spectrum of the function which enables us, among other things, to estimate the speed of converging of that Fourier series.

The last tool will represent the signal given by the coefficient of that Fourier series; it will then be possible to compare directly the reconstituted signal with the initial signal.

We will conclude this study by examining several examples.

The tools of this chapter will be placed in the subdirectory FOURIER.

---

1   Calculation of the Coefficients

1.1 Introduction

We will start by studying the fundamental problem concerning Fourier series, that is, the determination of the coefficients of the Fourier series corresponding to a given periodic function.

The function can be defined in two different ways:
- in an analytical way; it will therefore have to be represented by an equation on each segment;
- in a discrete way; the program will therefore consider only a restricted number of points having to define completely the function, as well as its discontinuities.

Although the results wanted are identical in both cases, the methods of resolution used in each case are totally different, and consequently the time needed to calculate in both cases also differs very much.

1.2 Principle

When a periodic function f of period T allows for a developement into a Fourier series the latter is unique.

Then the coefficients are given by:

$$f(x) = a_0 + \sum_{n=1}^{+\infty} \left(a_n \cos n\frac{2\pi}{T} x + b_n \sin n\frac{2\pi}{T} x \right)$$

with:

$$a_0 = \frac{1}{T} \int_{-T/2}^{T/2} f(x)\, dx$$

$$\begin{cases} a_n = \frac{2}{T} \int_{-T/2}^{T/2} f(x) \cos\left(n\frac{2\pi}{T}x \right) dx \\[2mm] b_n = \frac{2}{T} \int_{-T/2}^{T/2} f(x) \sin\left(n\frac{2\pi}{T}x \right) dx \end{cases}$$

In the case where the function $f(x)$ is known on an interval $[a, b]$ of length T, but which does not coincide with $[-T/2, T/2]$, those formulas become:

$$a_0 = \frac{1}{T} \int_{a}^{a+T} f(x)\, dx$$

$$\begin{cases} a_n = \frac{2}{T} \int_{a}^{a+T} f(x) \cos\left(n\frac{2\pi}{T}(x-C) \right) dx \\[2mm] b_n = \frac{2}{T} \int_{a}^{a+T} f(x) \sin\left(n\frac{2\pi}{T}(x-C) \right) dx \end{cases}$$

by writing:

$$C = \frac{a+b}{2} = a + \frac{T}{2}$$

corresponding to the point located in the middle of the interval of definition.

The calculation of integrals is worked out with Romberg's method in the case of analytical functions. In the case of discrete functions, those integrals are calculated rigorously, and the tool applies only the formulas.

1.3 Rank of the Calculated Harmonics

The approximate calculation of integrals with Romberg's method concerning the analytical functions is rather slow, and the time needed for the calculation is generally quite considerable. For example, the calculation of the coefficients of the 500 harmonics for an analytical function which is of average complexity takes a few hours, with a maximal precision. The first few are calculated quickly enough, but the time of calculation increases with the rank of the calculated harmonic.

The determination of the coefficients of a discrete function is much faster, but the calculation of the first 50 harmonics of the defined function with 500 points still necessitates a few minutes. The exploitation tool, before working out the calculations, asks for the range of harmonics wanted. At that point one has to give it only the lower and upper bounds of the harmonics to be calculated. This option makes it possible not to calculate the first two hundred harmonics if the only one needed is the two-hundred-and twenty-third!

1.4 Discrete Functions

1.4.1 Principle

A discrete function is in reality affine by fragments, which amounts to saying that its graphic representation is made up of a succession of straight line segments.

Integrals can be broken up into a sum of integrals on a segment, of the type:

$$\begin{cases} A_j = \displaystyle\int_{x_j}^{x_{j+1}} (\lambda x + \mu) \cos[\omega n(x-C)] \, dx \\ \\ B_j = \displaystyle\int_{x_j}^{x_{j+1}} (\lambda x + \mu) \sin[\omega n(x-C)] \, dx \end{cases} \qquad \omega = \frac{2\pi}{T}$$

Two partial integrations lead us to the following formulas:

$$\begin{cases} A_j = \dfrac{1}{\omega n} \left[\dfrac{\lambda}{\omega n} \cos[\omega n(x-C)] + (\lambda x + \mu) \sin[\omega n(x-C)] \right]_{x_j}^{x_{j+1}} \\ \\ B_j = \dfrac{1}{\omega n} \left[\dfrac{\lambda}{\omega n} \sin[\omega n(x-C)] - (\lambda x + \mu) \cos[\omega n(x-C)] \right]_{x_j}^{x_{j+1}} \end{cases}$$

The coefficients λ and μ corresponding to the straight line segment linking the points (x_j, y_j) to (x_{j+1}, y_{j+1}) satisfy:

$$\lambda = \frac{y_{j+1}-y_j}{x_{j+1}-x_j} \quad \text{and} \quad \begin{cases} \lambda x_j + \mu = y_j \\ \lambda x_{j+1} + \mu = y_{j+1} \end{cases}$$

and we obtain finally:

$$A_j = \frac{1}{\omega n}\left[\frac{\lambda}{\omega n}(\cos[\omega n(x_{j+1}-C)]-\cos[\omega n(x_j-C)])+y_{j+1}\sin[\omega n(x_{j+1}-C)]-y_j\sin[\omega n(x_j-C)]\right]$$

$$B_j = \frac{1}{\omega n}\left[\frac{\lambda}{\omega n}(\sin[\omega n(x_{j+1}-C)]-\sin[\omega n(x_j-C)])-y_{j+1}\cos[\omega n(x_{j+1}-C)]+y_j\cos[\omega n(x_j-C)]\right]$$

1.4.2 Program

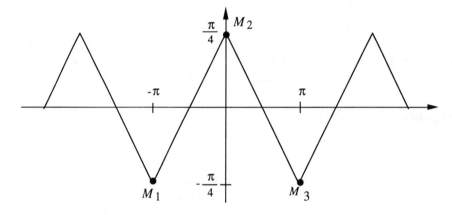

Description of the function

The function must be defined over a period, with the necessary and sufficient number of points.

For example, the previous "switchback graph" is defined by the three points M_1, M_2, M_3 of coordinates:

$$M_1 \left(-\pi, -\frac{\pi}{4}\right) \qquad M_2 \left(0, \frac{\pi}{4}\right) \qquad M_3 \left(\pi, -\frac{\pi}{4}\right)$$

Therefore its period is implicitly $x(M_3) - x(M_1)$, that is, 2π.

One will have to give only the following parameters to the tool: the number of definition points of the function and the coordinates of each point.

REMARK: it is not necessary for the interval of definition of the function to be symmetric with respect to the origin.

Description of the discontinuities

The input of a discontinuity is very simple: one has to input only the two points corresponding to the abscissa where the discontinuity occurs.

For example, the following signal will be entirely defined by the four points:

$$M_1 \left(-\pi, \frac{\pi}{4}\right) \qquad M_2 \left(-\frac{\pi}{2}, \frac{\pi}{4}\right) \qquad M_3 \left(-\frac{\pi}{2}, -\frac{\pi}{4}\right) \qquad M_4 \left(\pi, -\frac{\pi}{4}\right)$$

REMARK: the order of the points is natural and imperative. The discontinuities at the end of an interval (that is, $-\pi$ or π for the previous example) are automatically dealt with by the program.

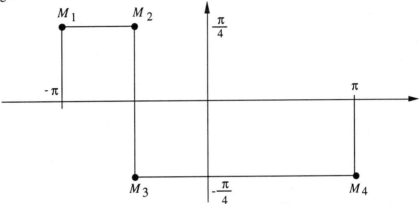

Input of points

The points defining the function are contained in a buffer, which makes it possible, among other things, to calculate the Fourier series corresponding to a function whose analytical expression is unknown, and which has been calculated by the program concerning differential equations for example.

Speed

The time of calculation is proportionate to the number of harmonics n calculated, as well as to the number of points np defining the function.

The tool `ar_fourier_discrete` admits as parameters:

– `tp`, buffer containing the description of the function over a period;

– `n`, number of the harmonic wanted;

At the output, a and b contain respectively the cosine term and the sin term of the harmonic. The tool will be placed in the file `FOURIER\CALCDISC.CPP`.

```
/*===============================================================
                      CALCDISC.CPP :
          CALCULATE ONE FOURIER'S SERIES HARMONIC
                   FOR A DISCRETE FUNCTION
   =============================================================*/
```

```
#include "armath.h"

void ar_fourier_discrete (ar_buffer &tp, int n,
                          ar_double &a, ar_double &b)
{
  ar_double  xi,  T, om, wa, wb, wc, wd,
             wg, wh, wi, wl, wm, wn, wp;
  int        i;

  T  = (tp.readx (tp.end) - tp.readx (tp.start));
  xi = (tp.readx (tp.start) + tp.readx (tp.end)) / 2;
  om = 2 * AR_PI * n / T;
  a = 0; b = 0;

  for (i = tp.start; i < tp.end; i++)  {
    wa = tp.readx (i); wb = tp.readx (i + 1);
    wc = tp.ready (i); wd = tp.ready (i + 1);
    if (wa != wb)  {
      wg = (wd - wc) / (wb - wa);
      wh = om * (wa - xi);
      wi = om * (wb - xi);
      if (n == 0)
        a += (wb - wa) * (wc + wg / 2 * (wb - wa));
       else  {
          wl = cos (wh); wm = sin (wh);
          wn = cos (wi); wp = sin (wi);
          a += wg / om * (wn - wl) + wd * wp - wc * wm;
          b += wg / om * (wp - wm) - wd * wn + wc * wl;
       }
    }
  }
  a /= T; b /= T;
  if (n)  {
    a *= 2 / om;
    b *= 2 / om;
  }
}
```

1.5 Analytical Functions

1.5.1 Calculation Tools

The tool of calculation of the Fourier coefficients concerning analytical functions uses the representation of functions already seen in this book. However, it is often interesting to work with analytical functions defined by intervals.

We have therefore provided for this option, by using an array of functions.

The following function is an arc of parabola, defined on the interval [–2, 2].

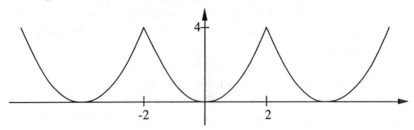

Over a period, the functions studied can be broken up into several segments. For example, the following function is made up of three segments:

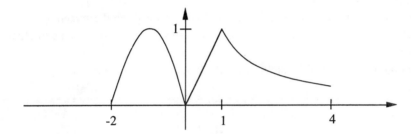

– on the interval [–2, 0], $f(x) = 1 - (x+1)^2$
– on the interval [0, 1], $f(x) = x$
– on the interval [1, 4], $f(x) = \dfrac{1}{x}$

We have to provide the tool with the abscissas of the limits of the segments, as well as the expression of the function on each segment. The period must not be entered. It is calculated by the program and is equal to XS(NS)–S(0). It is not compulsory to describe the function on the interval [–T/2, T/2].

Discontinuities
The fact of being able to study the functions defined on several segments solves the problem of discontinuities: each point of discontinuity will have to be the border between two segments.

For example, the function $f(x) = \dfrac{E(x)}{x}$ between 1 and 6 wil have to be broken up into 5 segments. Its expression will be:

$\dfrac{1}{x}$ on the interval [1, 2[;

$\dfrac{2}{x}$ on the interval [2, 3[;   etc...

Indeed Romberg's method used for the approximate calculation of integrals converges much slower when the interval of calculation contains a discontinuity, and it becomes unusable in practice. *That is why we will have to make sure that the function studied is continuous on each segment.*

The parameters of the tool `ar_fourier_analytic` are:

– `ns`, number of segments of the function over a period;

– `xs`, array of the points containing the limits of the segments;

– `f`, array of the functions containing the expression of the function on each of the segments;

– `n`, rank of the harmonic to be calculated;

– `iter`, maximal number of iterations in the integration;

– `p`, precision wanted;

– `disp`, boolean making possible the following through on the screen.

On output, the tool puts back in a and b the terms in cosine and in sine of the harmonic calculated.

The tool will be placed in the file `FOURIER\CALCANAL.CPP`.

```
/*============================================================
                       CALCANAL.CPP :
            CALCULATE ONE FOURIER'S SERIES HARMONIC
                    FOR AN ANALYTIC FUNCTION
   ==========================================================*/

#include "armath.h"

static   int             ss;
static   ar_double       om, xi;
static   ar_function     *tf;

static ar_double g (ar_double x)
{
   ar_glob_x = x;
   return (tf [ss] (ar_val_var) * cos (om * (x - xi)));
}

static ar_double h (ar_double x)
{
   ar_glob_x = x;
   return (tf [ss] (ar_val_var) * sin (om * (x - xi)));
}

void ar_fourier_analytic (ar_function *f,
      ar_double *xs, int ns, int n, int iter, ar_double &p,
      ar_double &a, ar_double &b, int disp)
```

```
{
  ar_double   T, r;

  tf = f;

  T  = (xs [ns] - xs [0]);
  xi = (xs [0]  + xs [ns]) / 2;
  om = 2 * AR_PI * n / T;

  a = 0; b = 0;
  for (ss = 1; ss <= ns; ss++)   {
    if (disp)
      cout << "Segment "<< ss
              << " - calculation of cosine term\n";

    a += ar_integral_romberg (g, xs [ss-1], xs [ss], p, r,
            3 + (int) log ((double) n + 1), iter, FALSE);
    if (disp)
      cout << "Segment "<< ss
              << " - calculation of sine term\n";

    b += ar_integral_romberg (h, xs [ss-1], xs [ss], p, r,
            3 + (int) log ((double) n + 1), iter, FALSE);
  }

  if (disp) ar_nl;

  a *= (double) 2 / T;
  b *= (double) 2 / T;
  if (n == 0) a /= 2;
}
```

1.5.2 The Regulation of the Precision

Let us first remind ourselves of the principle of Romberg's method.

The calculation is worked out through several iterations. At each iteration, the integral is estimated by the trapezoidal rule over a number of intervals corresponding to the power of 2.

This estimation is used, together with the previous ones, for the deduction of a new and more accurate approximated value of the result. This result is then compared with the previous estimation.

If the difference between the two values is higher in absolute value than a fixed limit defined beforehand which characterises the precision of the search, a new iteration starts, with a number of intervals, and consequently a time of calculation twice the previous one.

In the opposite case, the calculation is finished, and the value of the integral corresponds to the last estimation.

1.5.3 The Regulation of the Time of Calculation

The advantage of Romberg's method with respect to a more traditional method of integration, like Simpson's method, is that we can look for a result with a given precision and not with a given time of calculation (the number of intervals for example).

The drawback is obvious when we want to calculate 500 complex integrals: we do not know in advance the necessary time of calculation.

We have provided for an option making it possible to have better control of the time of calculation: if after a certain number of iterations, the precision wanted is still not reached, the program "gives up", gives the result as it is, providing, however, the precision obtained.

The integrals used are relatively complex, because of the presence of trigonometric functions, and in practice 8 or 9 iterations are the minimum necessary in order to reach a satisfactory precision for the calculation of harmonics of high order. That is why the maximal number of iterations can change from 10 to 15.

For information only, the calculation of an harmonic for a function of average complexity will be worked out therefore in a *maximum* time of:

Maximal number of iterations	*max* time of calculation of an harmonic
10	1 mn × number of segments
11	2 mn × number of segments
12	4 mn × number of segments
13	8 mn × number of segments
14	1/4 h × number of segments
15	1/2 h × number of segments

Those times, which depend a lot on the type of computer used, have been measured with an entry-level machine (286 at 16 MHz).

1.5.4 Programming Particularities

Minimum number of iterations
We have seen that it was possible to fix a maximum time of calculation, beyond which the program gives up its iterations.

Conversely, there exists in the program a lower limit to the number of iterations. This limit depends on the rank n of the harmonic calculated by the relation:

$$l = 3 + \log_2(n)$$

Explanation
At the ith iteration, the integral is estimated through the trapezoidal rule with 2^i intervals.

On $\left[-\frac{T}{2}, \frac{T}{2}\right]$, the trigonometric functions $\sin(nx\frac{2\pi}{T})$ and $\cos(nx\frac{2\pi}{T})$ used in the integral have a $2n$ arch. It is not conceivable for the trapezoidal rule to give a significant result with less than four points by arch.

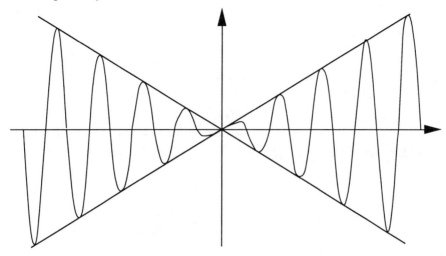

Therefore a minimum of 8 n points will be necessary to obtain a significant result, thus $\log_2(8n)$ iterations, that is, $3 + \log_2(n)$.

REMARK: if $n > 128$, the calculation is worked out with a *minimum* of 10 iterations...

Calculation and preliminary storage of the sine
By developing and simplifying the formulas used through the trapezoidal rule to work out those calculations, we end up with the following formulas:

$$
\begin{cases}
a_n = \dfrac{(-1)^n}{T} \left[\displaystyle\sum_{i=1}^{2^q-1} f\left(a+\dfrac{it}{2^q}\right) \cos\left(i\,\dfrac{2\pi n}{2^q}\right) + \dfrac{f(a)+f(b)}{2} \right] \\[4ex]
b_n = \dfrac{(-1)^n}{T} \displaystyle\sum_{i=1}^{2^q-1} f\left(a+\dfrac{it}{2^q}\right) \sin\left(i\,\dfrac{2\pi n}{2^q}\right)
\end{cases}
$$

where n represents the rank of the harmonic and q the number of the iteration.

It so happens that the calculation of trigonometric functions is very penalizing if we consider the time of execution, since generally a micro-computer can only calculate a 100 sines (or cosines) per second. It appears quite clearly in the formulas that the values used are equidistant, and are a multiple of $\dfrac{2\pi}{2^q}$.

This observation leads us to think that we could store the values of the sine in the memory for the execution. The accurate calculation of the coefficients of high order necessitates, for some functions, a minimum of 14 iterations. The number of values to be stored is therefore 2^{14}, that is, 16184, which necessitates 128 KB of memory...

However, by storing exclusively the values of the sine corresponding to angles contained between 0 and $\frac{\pi}{2}$, we divide by four the memory necessary, which is quite possible.

Unfortunately, the time then necessary to obtain the value of a given sine, by successive comparisons and symmetries, is approximately the same as the time needed for the direct calculation of the sine: that is why we have not chosen this solution.

2 Representation of the Spectrum

2.1 Principle

We have seen that the Fourier series of a function f could be written as follows:

$$f(x) = a_0 + \sum_{n=1}^{+\infty} \left(a_n \cos n\frac{2\pi}{T}x + b_n \sin n\frac{2\pi}{T}x \right)$$

It can also be expressed in this way:

$$f(x) = \sum_{n=-\infty}^{+\infty} c_k\, e^{ik\frac{2\pi}{T}x}$$

Where the coefficients c_k are complex and are given by:

$$c_0 = a_0 \qquad\qquad a_0 = c_0$$

$$c_k = \frac{a_k - ib_k}{2} \qquad \Leftrightarrow \qquad a_k = c_k + c_{-k} \qquad \text{with } k > 0$$

$$c_{-k} = \frac{a_k + ib_k}{2} \qquad\qquad b_k = i\,(c_k - c_{-k})$$

The modulus of the coefficient c_k represents, so to speak, the "weight" of the harmonic k in the development of f into a Fourier series.

Let us write on a graph the modulus of the coefficients c_k according to the frequency: we obtain the spectrum of the function f. A spectrum appears therefore as a series of parallel segments (which we call rays); each segment corresponds to an harmonic and its length is proportionate to the modulus of the coefficient c_k.

It is possible to estimate the convergence of the series by considering the decrease of the rays; the faster this decrease, the faster is also the convergence of the series towards the function.

2.2 Tools for Drawing

The tool `ar_fourier_spectrum` draws the spectrum on the screen from the coefficients of the series present in the buffer `tp`. The number of rays represented is the other parameter in this program. This option makes it possible to draw a partial spectrum in order to emphasize a more interesting aspect.

In order to maintain a constant factor of scale and to make possible direct comparisons between different spectrums, we have systematically attributed the maximum length on the segments (that is, 10 graduations) to the harmonic with the highest coefficient; it is generally the fundamental term (order one). The corresponding value is displayed under the spectrum.

The tool will be placed in the file FOURIER\SPECTRUM.CPP.

```
/*==========================================================
                       SPECTRUM.CPP :
            DRAW THE SPECTRUM OF A FOURIER SERIES
  =========================================================*/

#include   "armath.h"

void ar_fourier_spectrum (ar_buffer &tp, int n)
{
  ar_double   *y, mx, r;
  int         i, 12, 11, xa, ya, za, zb, e;

  y = new ar_double [n + 1];
  if (y == NULL) {
    errno = 1;
    cerr << "Not enough memory\n";
    ar_pause ();
    return;
  }
  if (n > tp.nbelts ())   n = tp.nbelts ();
  for (i = 1, mx = 0; i <= n; i++)   {
    y [i] = sqrt (tp.readx (i) * tp.readx (i) +
                  tp.ready (i) * tp.ready (i));
    if (y [i] > mx)   mx = y [i];
  }
  if (mx == 0) {delete[]y; return;}
  r = (ar_maxlig - 20) / mx;
  for (i = 1; i <= n; i++)
    y [i] *= r;
  e = (ar_maxcol - 20) / (n + 1);

  ar_init_graph ();
```

```
   xa = 10;
   ya = ar_maxlig - 10;
   l2 = ar_maxlig - 20;
   ar_line (xa, 0, xa, ar_maxlig);
   za = xa + (n + 1) * e;
   ar_line (za, 0, za, ar_maxlig);
   ar_line (0, ya, xa+za, ya);
   for (i=1; i<=n; i++)   {
      ll = (i % 5) ? 3 : 6;
      ar_line (xa + i * e, ya, xa + i * e, ya + ll);
   }
   zb = ya;
   for (i = 1; i <= 10; i++)   {
      ll = (i % 5) ? 4 : 8;
      zb -= (l2 / 10);
      ar_line (xa, zb, xa - ll, zb);
      ar_line (za, zb, za + ll, zb);
   }
   for (i = 1; i <= n; i++)
      ar_line (xa + i * e, ya, xa + i * e, ya - y[i]);

   ar_close_graph ();
   delete[]y;
}
```

3   The Synthesis of the Signal

3.1 Principle

We have studied up to now the transformation of the function f into its Fourier series; we are now going to adopt the reverse process: from the Fourier coefficients, we are going to calculate and then represent the function f.

This will enable us, among other things, to verify the results of the calculations and to estimate the speed of convergence of the Fourier series towards the function.

3.2 Tools for Drawing the Signal

The harmonics are added together and visualized one after the other, which makes it possible to represent all the intermediate stages of reconstitution. During a drawing, the previous curve is progressively cleared from the screen.

The coefficients of a series are not enough for the reconstitution of the function: the period must be provided to the program, before the drawing starts.

The fact of doing a reconstitution with a period different from that of the initial period simply causes a dilatation (or a contraction) on the axis of the abscissas.

We have seen, during the calculation of coefficients, that the lateral position of the interval of definition of the function had no influence on the coefficients. The reconstitution is done on the interval $[-\frac{T}{2}, \frac{T}{2}]$, and the function is completed by the sucessive translations.

The bottom line of the screen permanently displays the number of the harmonic used, as well as the corresponding coefficients a and b.

The parameters of the tool `ar_fourier_synthesis` are:
– `tp`, buffer containing the coefficients of the series;
– `n`, maximal number of harmonics to be added up;
– `t`, period of reconstitution of the signal;
– `xn` and `xm`, scale of the abscissas;
– `yn` and `ym`, scale of the ordinates;
– `axes`, `ortho`, `grid`: booleans passed on to the tool for the drawing of the axis.

REMARK: it is necessary to provide the tool with the extremes of the interval of representation, as much on the axis of the abscissas (which makes it possible in particular to obtain a reconstitution over several periods) as on that of the ordinates (because the extremal values of the function are known only after having done all the calculations).

The tool must be placed in the file FOURIER\SYNTHES.CPP.

```
/*============================================================
                    SYNTHES.CPP :
    SYNTHESIS OF A FOURIER SERIES FROM ITS COEFFICIENTS
 ============================================================*/

#include <conio.h>
#include "armath.h"

void ar_fourier_synthesis (ar_buffer &tp, int n, ar_double t,
        ar_double xn, ar_double xm, ar_double yn,
        ar_double ym, int axes, int ortho, int grid)
{
  ar_double  k, kx, ex, ey, *p;
  int        i, j, xi, xf, xp, yp, ua, ub, db, xa, ya, *r;

  ar_init_graph ();   // Imperatively BEFORE memory allocation
  p = new ar_double [ar_maxcol + 1];
  r = new int        [ar_maxcol + 1];

  if ((p == NULL) || (r == NULL))  {
    ar_outtext ("Not enough memory... Press a key\n");
    getch ();
    return;
  }
```

```
ar_draw_axes (xn,xm,yn,ym,ex,ey,xa,ya,axes,ortho,grid);
xi = xa + xn * ex;
xf = xa + xm * ex;
ua = ya - tp.readx (0) * ey;

for (i = xi; i <= xf; i++)   {
  p [i] = tp.readx (0);
  r [i] = ua;
}
db = 1;
if ((tp.readx (0) != 0) && (ua > 0) && (ua < ar_maxlig))   {
  db = 0;
  ar_line (xi, ua, xf, ua);
}
for (i = 1; i <= n; i++)   {
  ar_draw_axes (xn,xm,yn,ym,ex,ey,xa,ya,axes,ortho,grid);
  ar_erase_line (24);
  ar_grgotoxy (1, 24);
  sprintf (ar_temp, "Current harmonic : %3d", i);
  ar_outtext (ar_temp);
  sprintf (ar_temp, "   a = %20.10lf", tp.readx (i));
  ar_outtext (ar_temp);
  sprintf (ar_temp, "   b = %20.10lf", tp.ready (i));
  ar_outtext (ar_temp);
  if ((tp.readx (i) != 0) || (tp.ready (i) != 0))   {
    k = i * 2 * AR_PI / t;
    if ((i > db) && (r[xi] >= 0) && (r[xi + 1] >= 0)
      && (r[xi] <= ar_maxlig) && (r[xi + 1] <= ar_maxlig))
{
        ar_setcolor (0);
        ar_line (xi, r [xi], xi + 1, r [xi + 1]);
        ar_setcolor (ar_getmaxcolor ());
    }
    j  = xi;
    kx = k / ex * (j - xa);
    p [j] += tp.readx(i) * cos(kx) + tp.ready(i) * sin(kx);
    r [j] = ya - p [j] * ey;
    xp = xi; yp = r [j];
    for (j = xi + 1; j <= xf; j++)   {
      ua = r [j];
      ub = r [j + 1];
      if ((i > db) && (j < xf) && (ua >= 0) && (ub >= 0)
        && (ua <= ar_maxlig) && (ub <= ar_maxlig))   {
        ar_setcolor (0);
        ar_line (j, ua, j+1, ub);
        ar_setcolor (ar_getmaxcolor ());
      }
      kx = k / ex * (j - xa);
```

```
      p [j] += tp.readx(i)*cos(kx) + tp.ready(i)*sin(kx);
      r [j] = ya - p [j] * ey; ua = r [j];
      if ((yp >= 0) && (yp <= ar_maxlig) &&
         (ua >= 0) && (ua <= ar_maxlig))
           ar_line (xp, yp, j, ua);
      xp = j; yp = ua;
   }
   if (ar_stop_asked ())
   ar_close_graph ();
  }
 }
 delete[]p; delete r;
}
```

4 Examples

4.1 Introduction

We are now going to apply the previous programs to the study of different segments.

We will give the spectrum obtained, and a few stages of the reconstitution will enable us to estimate the convergence of the series towards the functions (*n* will represent the number of harmonics used for each curve). In some examples, we will compare the Fourier coefficients calculated by the program with the exact values.

4.2 Discrete Functions

4.2.1 Rectangular Signal of Cyclic Ratio 1/4

First of all here is the graphic representation of such a signal, like the one we could see on an oscilloscope connected to a generator of signals:

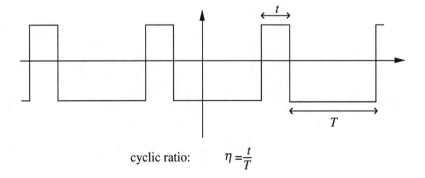

$$\text{cyclic ratio:} \qquad \eta = \frac{t}{T}$$

We will restrict our study to one period of this signal:

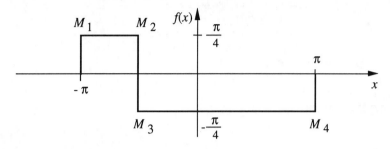

The theoretical coefficients of this signal are as follows:

$$a_n = -\frac{1}{2n} \quad \text{if } n = 4p + 1; \qquad\qquad 0 \quad \text{if } n \text{ is even;}$$

$$a_0 = -\frac{\pi}{8} \qquad\qquad \frac{1}{2n} \quad \text{if } n = 4p + 3;$$

$$b_n = \quad 0 \quad \text{if } n = 4p; \qquad\qquad -\frac{1}{2n} \quad \text{if } n = 4p + 1;$$

$$\frac{1}{n} \quad \text{if } n = 4p + 2; \qquad\qquad -\frac{1}{2n} \quad \text{if } n = 4p + 3.$$

We will give only the first 10 harmonics calculated because of the shortage of space.

```
FOURIER : CALCULATION OF COEFFS OF A DISCRETE SERIES

Number of buffer where the function is stored ? 1

INPUT BUFFER :

Title                : Rectangle
Index of first point : 0
Index of last point  : 3

x0 = -PI
y0 = PI / 4

x1 = -PI / 2
y1 = PI / 4

x2 = -PI / 2
y2 = -PI / 4

x3 = PI
y3 = -PI / 4
```

```
Low harmonic            : 0
High harmonic           : 10
N° of saving buffer     : 2
Display of the harmonics : y

a0  =   -0.392699081699  # - 355 / 904
b0  =                0
a1  =             -0.5  # -1 / 2
b1  =             -0.5  # -1 / 2
a2  =   -3.062871137272e-17
b2  =              0.5  # 1 / 2
a3  =    0.166666666667  # 1 / 6
b3  =   -0.166666666667  # -1 / 6
a4  =    3.062871137272e-17
b4  =                0
a5  =             -0.1  # -1 / 10
b5  =             -0.1  # -1 / 10
a6  =   -3.062871137272e-17
b6  =    0.166666666667  # 1 / 6
a7  =    0.071428571429  # 1 / 14
b7  =   -0.071428571429  # 1 / 14
a8  =    3.062871137272e-17
b8  =                0
a9  =   -0.555555555556  # -1 / 18
b9  =   -0.555555555556  # -1 / 18
a10 =   -3.062871137272e-17
b10 =              0.1  # 1 / 10
```

Representation of the spectrum with the first hundred rays:

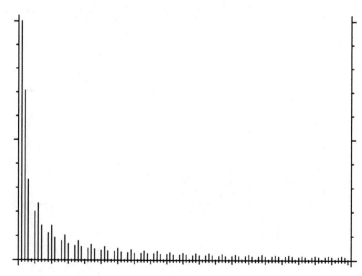

Reconstitution of the signal:

$n = 1$:

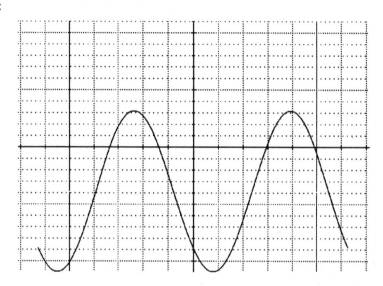

$n = 5$:

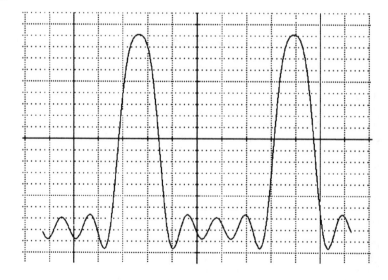

$n = 25$:

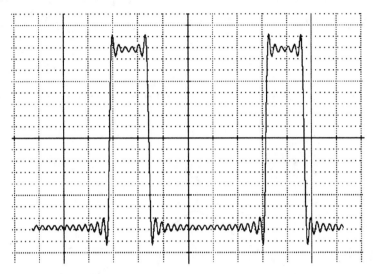

$n = 125$:

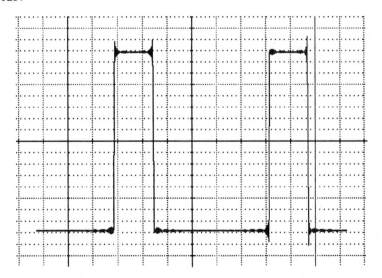

4.2.2 Triangular Signal

We would get the following on the oscilloscope:

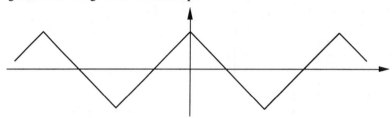

For a period, we will therefore consider:

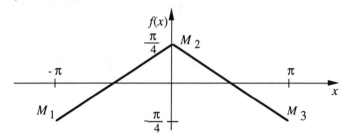

The theoretical values of the coefficients are:

$$a_n = \frac{2}{\pi n^2} \quad \text{if } n \text{ is odd} \qquad\qquad b_n = 0$$

$$0 \quad \text{if } n \text{ is even}$$

Let us work out the calculation of the first 20 harmonics:

```
FOURIER : CALCULATION OF THE COEFFS OF A DISCRETE SERIES

Number of buffer where the function is stored : 3

INPUT BUFFER :

Title                 : Triangle
Index of first point  : 1
Index of last point   : 3

x1 = -PI
y1 = -PI / 4

x2 = 0
y2 = PI / 4

x3 = PI
y3 = -PI / 4
```

```
Low harmonic            : 0
High harmonic           : 10
N° of saving buffer     : 4
Display of the harmonics : y

a0  =                    0
b0  =                    0
a1  =    0.636619772368  # 226 / 355
b1  =                    0
a2  =   6.125742274543e-17
b2  =   9.749421631005e-18
a3  =    0.070735530263  # 226 / 3195
b3  =                    0
a4  =   6.125742274543e-17
b4  =   4.874710815503e-18
a5  =    0.025464790895  # 226 / 8875
b5  =                    0
a6  =   6.125742274543e-17
b6  =   3.249807210335e-18
a7  =    0.012992240252  # 226 / 17395
b7  =                    0
a8  =   6.125742274543e-17
b8  =   2.437355407751e-18
a9  =    0.007859503363  # 226 / 28755
b9  =                    0
a10 =   6.125742274543e-17
b10 =   1.949884326201e-18
```

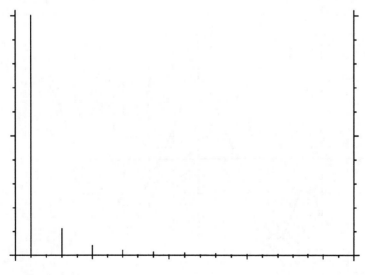

Let us compare the spectrum below with that of the square signal: the decrease of the rays is more marked in the first case and the series converges much more rapidly towards the function.

Indeed, the coefficients of the triangle are at $\frac{1}{n^2}$ whereas those of the square are only at $\frac{1}{n}$.

Reconstitution of the signal

We notice the rapid convergence of the series:

$n = 1$:

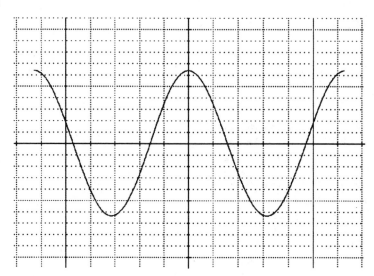

$n = 3$:

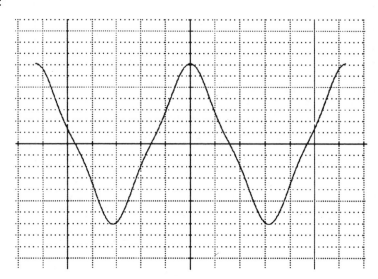

$n = 7$:

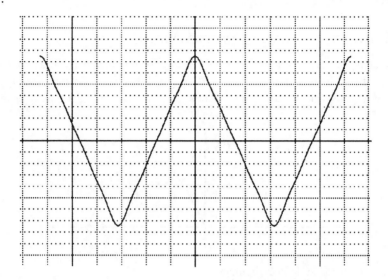

$n = 20$:

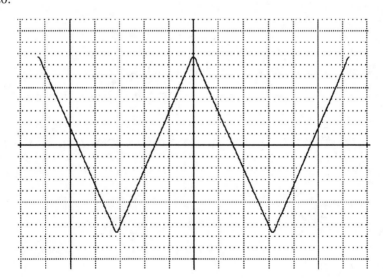

4.3 Analytical Functions

4.3.1 Upwards Sinusoid of Simple Alternation

The first analytical function that we will study is the upwards sinusoid of simple alternation. This signal could be observed by visualising the tension which is at the terminals of a perfect diode used at a sinusoidal rate. We will consider only a period of that signal:

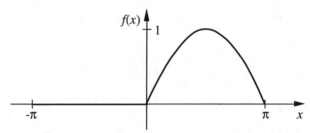

This function is made up of 2 segments:
– on the segment $[-\pi, 0]$, its expression is $y = 0$
– on the segment $[0, \pi]$, its expression is $y = \sin x$
The theoretical calculations provide the following values:

$$a_0 = \frac{1}{\pi} \qquad a_n = 0 \quad \text{if } n \text{ is odd;} \qquad -\frac{2}{\pi(n^2-1)} \quad \text{if } n \text{ is even;}$$

$$b_1 = \frac{1}{2} \qquad b_n = 0 \quad \text{for } n \geq 2$$

The coefficients being at $\frac{1}{n^2}$, the reconstitution will be quick; we will therefore calculate only 10 harmonics. With a specified precision of 10^{-4}, the program gives the exact values up to 10^{-7}:

```
FOURIER: CALCULATION OF THE COEFFS OF AN ANALYTICAL SERIES

Number of segments ? 2

Abscissa beginning segment 1 : -PI
Abscisse end segment 1        : 0
Function on segment 1         : 0

Abscissa end segment 2        : PI
Function on segment 2         : sin (x)

Low harmonic                  : 0
High harmonic                 : 20
Saving buffer                 : 5
```

```
Precision                    : 1e-4
Max number iterations        : 10

Display harmonics            : y
Display countdown            : y

a0  =      0.318309885322   # 113 / 355
b0  =                    0
a1  =     -1.93338679257e-17
b1  =      0.500000000676
a2  =     -0.212206647948   # -2559 / 12059
b2  =      8.663503708659e-18
a3  =     -2.780244395421e-17
b3  =      9.014463612568e-10
a4  =     -0.042441325047   # -557 / 13124
b4  =      1.306874278883e-17
a5  =     -1.06846348027e-16
b5  =     -9.014462387685e-10
a6  =     -0.018189136201   # -226 / 12425
b6  =     -2.526920972124e-16
a7  =      6.682673208259e-17
b7  =      9.613226516921e-10
a8  =     -0.010105078085   # -276 / 27313
b8  =     -7.524384258844e-18
a9  =      9.119073445256e-17
b9  =     -9.613226317325e-10
a10 =     -0.006430507937
b10 =      1.672297728688e-16
```

Representation of the spectrum:

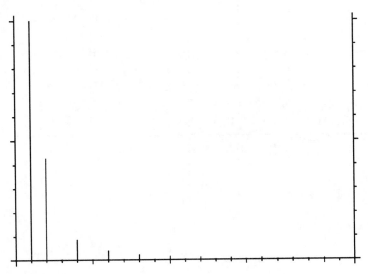

Reconstitution of the signal:

$n = 1$:

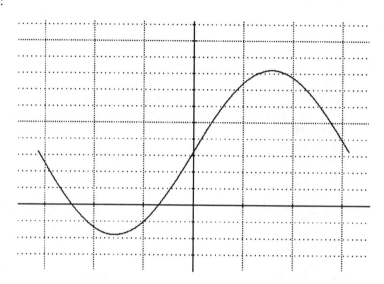

$n = 2$:

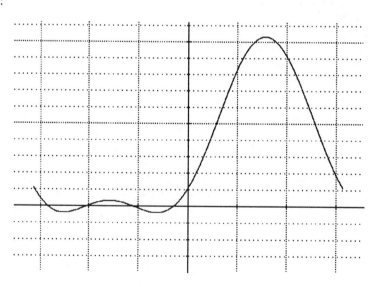

$n = 6$:

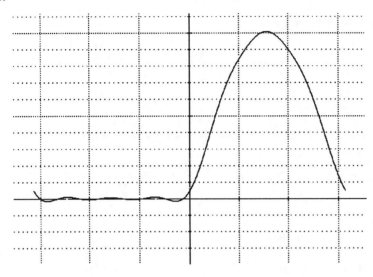

$n = 20$:

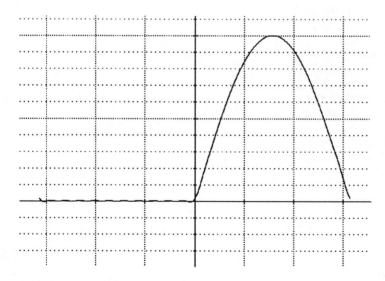

4.3.2 Parabola-Exponential Curve

Let us consider the following curve:

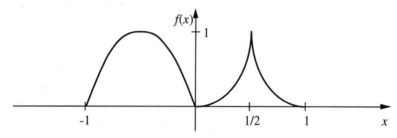

It can be broken up into 3 segments:

– on the interval $[-1, 0]$, $f(x) = -4x\,(x+1)$

– on the interval $[0, \frac{1}{2}]$, $f(x) = e^{10x-5}$

– on the interval $[\frac{1}{2}, 1]$, $f(x) = e^{-10x+5}$

We have calculated 50 harmonics, and here are the first 10:

```
FOURIER : CALCULATION OF THE COEFFS OF AN ANALYTICAL SERIES

Number of segments ? 3

Abscissa beginning segment 1: -1
Abscissa end segment 1         : 0
Function on segment 1          : -4 * x * (x + 1)

Abscissa end segment 2         : 0.5
Function on segment 2          : exp (10 * x - 5)

Abscissa end segment 3         : 1
Fonction on segment 3          : exp (5 - 10 * x)

Low harmonic                   : 0
High harmonic                  : 10

Saving buffer                  : 6

Precision                      : 1e-6
Max number iterations          : 10

Display harmonics              : y
Display countdown              : y
```

```
a0  =    0.432659538639   # 1905 / 4403
b0  =                0
a1  =    5.20417042793e-17
b1  =   -0.333605256039
a2  =   -0.346999890781   # -3013 / 8683
b2  =    3.469446951954e-17
a3  =    6.938893903907e-18
b3  =   -0.124356777857
a4  =    0.026362238462   # 463 / 17563
b4  =                0
a5  =    1.040834085586e-16
b5  =    0.054162374139
a6  =   -0.066738318588   # -621 / 9305
b6  =   -6.938893903907e-18
a7  =   -6.245004513517e-17
b7  =   -0.035266082448
a8  =    0.014485968299
b8  =   -2.081668171172e-17
a9  =    1.318389841742e-16
b9  =    0.021951879242
a10 =   -0.026629606136   # -297 / 11153
b10 =    1.283695372223e-16
```

Let us represent the spectrum with 20 rays; we notice that the series converges quickly.

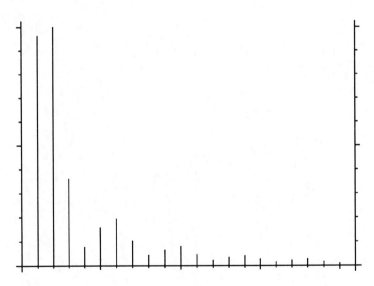

Reconstitution of the signal:

$n = 2$:

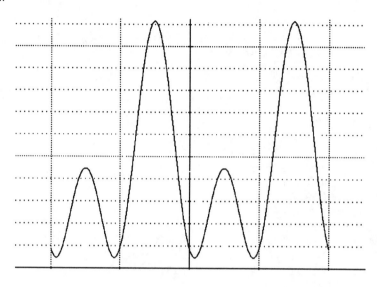

$n = 8$:

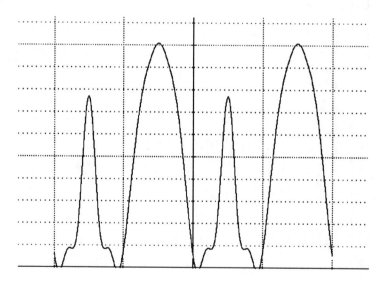

$n = 15$:

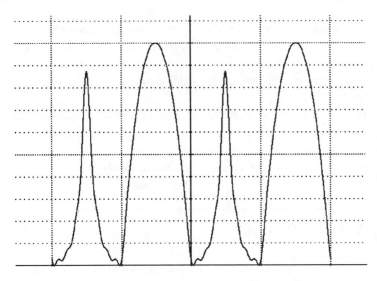

$n = 50$:

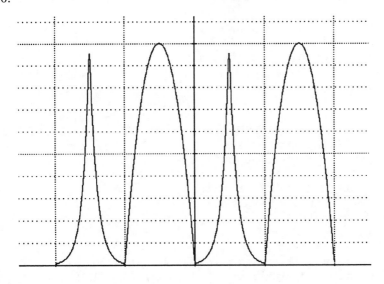

4.4 Conclusion

The speed and the precision of the calculation of the coefficients for a discrete function are two undeniable assets in comparison with the approximated calculation of the coefficients for an analytical function.

In the previous examples, we applied this method only to very simple functions, affine by fragments.

However, one has to be aware of the fact that all the functions sampled, calculated by other programs (especially that concerning the solution of differential equations), are likened to functions affine by fragments.

The spectral decomposition of these functions will therefore be fast and accurate.

---

5 Exploitation Tools

The following tools make possible the direct exploitation of the previous tools.

This tool must be placed in the file FOURIER\UCALCDIS.CPP:

```
/*============================================================
                        UCALCDIS.CPP :
      DISCRETE FUNCTIONS FOURIER'S SERIES EXPLOITATION TOOL
  ============================================================*/

#include "armath.h"

void ar_use_fourier_discrete ()
{
  ar_double  a, b;
  int        i, bn, bm, nt, ns, disp;

  cout << "FOURIER : CALCULATION OF COEFFS OF A DISCRETE
           SERIES\n\n";
  if (ar_read ("Number of buffer where the function is \
              stored ? ", &nt, AR_TINT)) return;
  if (nt > AR_MAXBUFFER) return;
  if (ar_buff [nt].nbelts () == 0)
    cin >> ar_buff [nt];

  ar_init_entry ("");
  ar_fill_entry ("Low harmonic", &bn, AR_TINT);
  ar_fill_entry ("High harmonic", &bm, AR_TINT);
  ar_fill_entry ("N° of saving buffer", &ns, AR_TINT);
  ar_fill_entry ("Display harmonics", &disp, AR_TBOO);
  if (ar_do_entry ()) return;
```

```
    if (ns > AR_MAXBUFFER) return;
    if (! ar_buff [ns].open ("Discrete harmonics", bn, bm))
      return;

    for (i = bn; i <= bm; i++)  {
      ar_fourier_discrete (ar_buff [nt], i, a, b);
      ar_buff [ns].writecouple (i, a, b);
      if (disp)  {
        cout << "a " <<  i << " = " << setw (15) << a
             << ar_rational (a) << "\n";
        cout << "b " <<  i << " = " << setw (15) << b
             << ar_rational (b) << "\n\n";
      }
    }
    ar_pause ();
}
```

This tool must be placed in the file FOURIER\UCALCANA.CPP:

```
/*=========================================================
                      UCALCANA.CPP :
  ANALYTIC FUNCTIONS FOURIER'S SERIES EXPLOITATION TOOL
  =======================================================*/

#include "armath.h"

void ar_use_fourier_analytic ()
{
  ar_function  f [10];
  ar_double    xs [10], a, b, p;
  int          i, bn, bm, nt, ns, iter, aff, affh;

  cout << "FOURIER: CALCULATION OF THE COEFFS OF AN \
            ANALYTICAL SERIES\n\n";

  if (ar_read ("Number of segments  ? ", &ns, AR_TINT))
    return;
  if (ns > 9) return;
  ar_init_entry ("");
  ar_fill_entry ("Abscissa beginning segment 1", &xs [0],
                  AR_TDOU);

  for (i = 1; i <= ns; i++)  {
   sprintf (ar_temp, "Abscissa end segment %d", i);
   ar_fill_entry (ar_temp, &xs [i], AR_TDOU);
   sprintf (ar_temp, "Function on segment %d", i);
   ar_fill_entry (ar_temp, &f [i], AR_TFUN);
  }
```

```
ar_fill_entry ("Low  harmonic",          &bn,   AR_TINT);
ar_fill_entry ("High harmonic",          &bm,   AR_TINT);
ar_fill_entry ("Saving buffer",          &nt,   AR_TINT);
ar_fill_entry ("Precision",              &p,    AR_TDOU);
ar_fill_entry ("Max number iterations", &iter, AR_TINT);
ar_fill_entry ("Display harmonics",      &affh, AR_TBOO);
ar_fill_entry ("Display countdown",      &aff,  AR_TBOO);

if (! ar_do_entry ())  {
  if (! ar_buff [nt].open ("Analytic harmonics", bn, bm))
    return;
  for (i = bn; i <= bm; i++)  {
    ar_fourier_analytic (f, xs, ns, i, iter, p, a, b, aff);
    if (errno)
      cerr << "Error during calculation\n";
    else  {
      if (affh)  {
        cout << "a " << i << " = " << setw (15) << a
             << ar_rational (a) << "\n";
        cout << "b " << i << " = " << setw (15) << b
             << ar_rational (b) << "\n";
      }
      ar_buff [nt].writecouple (i, a, b); ar_nl;
    }
  }
  ar_pause ();
}
}
```

This tool must be placed in the file FOURIER\USPECTRU.CPP:

```
/*============================================================
                       USPECTRU.CPP :
    FOURIER'S SERIES SPECTRUM DRAWING EXPLOITATION TOOL
============================================================*/

#include "armath.h"

void ar_use_fourier_spectrum ()
{
  int  nt, nr;

  cout << "FOURIER : DRAWING THE SPECTRUM\n\n";
  if (ar_read ("Number of buffer where the function is \
               stored : ", &nt, AR_TINT)) return;
  if (nt > AR_MAXBUFFER) return;
  if (ar_buff [nt].nbelts () == 0)
    cin >> ar_buff [nt];
```

```
  if (ar_read ("Number of rays (0 for all the rays)   : ",
        &nr, AR_TINT)) return;
  if (nr == 0)
    nr = ar_buff [nt].nbelts ();

  ar_fourier_spectrum (ar_buff [nt], nr);
}
```

This tool must be placed in the file FOURIER\USYNTHES.CPP:

```
/*==========================================================
                        USYNTHES.CPP :
          FOURIER SERIES SYNTHESIS EXPLOITATION TOOL
==========================================================*/

#include "armath.h"

void  ar_use_fourier_synthesis ()
{
  ar_double  t, xn, xm, yn, ym;
  int        nt, n, axes = TRUE, ortho, grid = TRUE;

  cout << "FOURIER : THE SYNTHESIS OF THE SIGNAL\n\n";
  if (ar_read ("Number of the buffer where the coefficients \
                are stored : ", &nt, AR_TINT)) return;
  if (nt > AR_MAXBUFFER) return;
  if (ar_buff [nt].nbelts () == 0)
    cin >> ar_buff [nt];

  ar_init_entry ("");
  ar_fill_entry ("Period of the signal", &t, AR_TDOU);
  ar_fill_entry ("Number of harmonics", &n, AR_TINT);
  ar_fill_entry ("X min", &xn, AR_TDOU);
  ar_fill_entry ("X max", &xm, AR_TDOU);
  ar_fill_entry ("Y min", &yn, AR_TDOU);
  ar_fill_entry ("Y max", &ym, AR_TDOU);
  ar_fill_entry ("Orthonormal system", &ortho, AR_TBOO);
  if (ar_do_entry ()) return;
  n = min (n, ar_buff [nt].nbelts ());
  n = max (n, 0);

  ar_fourier_synthesis (ar_buff [nt], n, t,
    xn, xm, yn, ym, axes, ortho, grid);

  ar_close_graph ();
}
```

17

Differential Equations

A differential equation is an equation in which occur, besides the variable x and the function y, the successive derivatives of the function y, up to an order n, called order of the differential equation.

Thus, a differential equation generally presents itself as follows:

$$G\ (x, y, y', y'', ..., y^{(n)}) = 0$$

To solve the differential equation, we must find the set of functions y satisfying the equation above.

At present we know how to solve only differential equations, that is, in a perfect way, in certain particular cases; and most of the time we have to resort to the numerical methods in order to obtain the solutions of any equations.

In this chapter we will give the methods and the tools making it possible to solve the most frequently found equations.

First we will study the way to solve differential equations of first degree, through the method of Runge-Kutta, then through the predictor-corrector method. We will then study differential equations of degree n. Finally, we will solve systems of differential equations of p equations of first degree. We will also explain how this latter program can be generalized to systems of p equations of degree n.

The tools of the chapter will be placed in the subdirectory EQUADIFF.

1 Reminders of Theoretical Principles

1.1 The Initial Conditions

A differential equation does not generally allow for only one solution, but for an infinite number of solutions. The determination of one function as a solution therefore necessitates the incorporation of additional data concerning that function which are usually the initial conditions.

Let us consider x_0 a point at random. Those initial conditions are then:

– for an equation of order one, the value of y at x_0, that is, $y(x_0)$.

– for an equation of order n, $y(x_0)$ and the values of the $(n-1)$ first derivatives of y at the point x_0, that is, $y'(x_0)$, $y''(x_0)$, ..., $y^{(n-1)}(x_0)$.

The initial conditions being fixed, there generally remains only one solution. In reality, the problems in physics involving differential equations make those initial conditions appear naturally.

For example, an object moving quickly through the air obeys the law:

$$m\, z'' + k\, z' - g = 0$$

The initial conditions are then the position $z_0 = z(t_0)$ and the speed $z'_0 = z'(t_0)$ of the moving object at the instant of origin t_0, essential values for the complete determination of the law on movements.

1.2 Explicit Equations

All the equations we are going to study are called *explicit* equations. It means that the derivative of order n can be expressed through the use of the $(n-1)$ other derivatives, of the function and of the variable. An explicit equation therefore appears as follows:

$$y^{(n)} = F\left(y^{(n-1)}, y^{(n-2)}, ..., y', y, x\right)$$

An equation such as:

$$y'' + e^{y''} = y'' - y$$

is not an explicit equation and will not be therefore dealt through the methods shown here.

1.3 Analytical Form and Discrete Form

To solve a differential equation in a theoretical way gives a solution in its *analytical* form.

The solution given by the program will be in the *discrete* form, that is, in the form of a series of values taken by the function for equidistant values of the variable x.

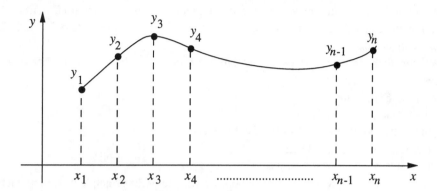

The solution will be the series of the values $y_1, y_2, ..., y_n$.

---

2   Runge-Kutta Method

2.1 Introduction

The equation to be solve appears as follows:

$$y' = f(y, x)$$

with the initial condition at a point x_0, that is:

$$y(x_0) = y_0$$

Furthermore we will fix the final value x_f of the variable. Therefore it amounts to the determination of the solution for values of the variable contained between x_0 and x_f.

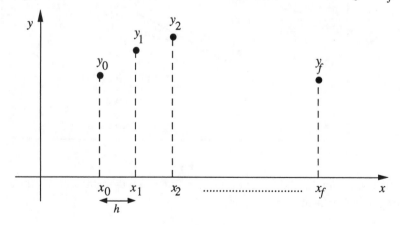

We know that the answer given by the computer is a discrete function, defined for a certain number of values of the variable. We have to fix the number n of points calculated between x_0 and x_f.

We can then define a "step of calculation" h equal to the difference between two successive values of x.

In short, the data are:

.– the equation $y' = f(y, x)$

– the initial point (x_0, y_0) and the final abscissa x_f

– the number of points to calculate

and the result is the set of the values y_i.

Before studying the Runge-Kutta method, we will study the principle of Euler's method, which is easier to interpret, without, however, giving a program because the results given by this method are poor.

2.2 Euler's Method

Let us assume a point (x_0, y_0) which is known. Euler's method consists in writing:

$$y_1 = y_0 + h\ f(y_0, x_0)$$

$$y_2 = y_1 + h\ f(y_1, x_1)$$

$$\dots\dots\dots\dots\dots\dots\dots\dots$$

$$y_n = y_{n-1} + h\ f(y_{n-1}, x_{n-1})$$

Therefore the principle consists in comparing the curve to its tangent at each point x_i, since $f(x_i, y_i)$ is the coefficient of the directrix of this tangent.

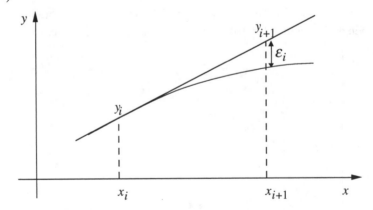

This method is simple, and in contrast to the Runge-Kutta method, it has the advantage of allowing for a graphical interpretation.

2.3 Runge-Kutta Method

The method shown here is a method of order: indeed the development of y around x_n coincides with its Taylor expansion at the order 4:

$$y_{n+1} = y_n + h\, y_n' + \frac{h^2}{2}\, y_n'' + \frac{h^3}{6}\, y_n''' + \frac{h^4}{24}\, y_n''''$$

Of course, there exist other methods according to the order of coincidence with Taylor's formula; in particular, we can note that Euler's method is none other than a Runge-Kutta method of order 1.

We generally use the formula of order 4 because it represents a good compromise between complexity, speed of calculation and precision.

From a known point (x_n, y_n), the next point is determined by the formulas:

$$K_0 = h\, f(x_n, y_n)$$

$$K_1 = h\, f(x_n + \frac{h}{2}, y_n + \frac{K_0}{2})$$

$$K_2 = h\, f(x_n + \frac{h}{2}, y_n + \frac{K_1}{2})$$

$$K_3 = h\, f(x_n + h, y_n + K_2)$$

which by substitution lead to:

$$y_{n+1} = y_n + \frac{1}{6}\, (K_0 + 2\, K_1 + K_3)$$

The significance of the formulas is no longer intuitive as it was in Euler's method. However, the precision is much better. We can show that the error on one step, for Euler's method, is of order h^2; for the fourth order Runge-Kutta method, this error is of order h^5.

The main drawback of the latter method is the length of time it takes to calculate. Four evaluations of the function are indeed necessary for each step, and they take all the more time if the functions are complicated.

2.4 Calculation Tool

The parameters of the tool `ar_equadiff_11` are the following:
- f, equation to be solved, as a function in C of the form:
  ```
  ar_double f(ar_double x, ar_double y)
  {
  ...
  }
  ```
- xi and xf, interval studied;

– yi, initial value at xi;

– m, number of points to be calculated;

– fi, finesse;

– disp, boolean making possible the display of the results in real time.

On output, buffer t contains the digitized result-function. The boolean variable errno indicates if it has not been possible to evaluate the function at one point or other.

The finesse is a way to increase the precision of the calculation. The precision is of course directly linked to the number of terms calculated. In order to get a better precision without, however, saturating the buffer with useless results, only a part of the points calculated will be memorized.

The finesse then represents the number of points calculated between two memorized points. For a finesse of 5, for example, the program will calculate five times more points than it will keep. If on the contrary we want all the points calculated to be memorized, one has to ask for a finesse of only 1.

Particularities

One can stop the calculation at any time by pressing a key at random.

The exploitation tool makes it possible to represent the solution with in fact a discrete curve. In order to use a function captured as a succession of characters by the tool of capture in the variable ar_glob_f, the function ar_eval_fxy must be passed as a parameter to the calculation tool.

These particularities are equally valid concerning the other programs in this chapter.

The tool will have to be placed in the file EQUADIFF\EQUA11.CPP.

```
/*===========================================================
                      EQUA11.CPP:
            SOLVING DIFFERENTIAL EQUATIONS
          ONE VARIABLE - ORDER 1 (RUNGE-KUTTA)
  ===========================================================*/

#include "armath.h"

void  ar_equadiff_11 (
      ar_double (*f) (ar_double, ar_double), ar_buffer &t,
      ar_double xi, ar_double xf, ar_double yi,
      int m, int fi, int disp)
{
  ar_double  h, a, b, c, d, x, y;
  int        i, j;
  long       ni;

  if (fi < 1) return;
  h    = (xf - xi) / fi / m;
  if (! t.open ("Diff.Equa.1,1", 0, m)) return;
```

```
y = yi; t.addcouple (xi, yi);
for (i = 1; i <= m; i++)  {
  if (ar_stop_asked ())  {
    errno = TRUE;
    return;
  }
  ni = (long) (i - 1) * fi - 1;
  for (j = 1; j <= fi; j++)  {
    x = xi + h * (ni + j);
    a  = h * f (x, y);                      if (errno)  return;
    b  = h * f (x + h / 2, y + a / 2);  if (errno)  return;
    c  = h * f (x + h / 2, y + b / 2);  if (errno)  return;
    x  = x + h;
    d  = h * f (x, y + c);                  if (errno)  return;
    y  = y + (a + b + b + c + c + d) / 6;
  }
  t.addcouple (x, y);
  if (disp)
    cout << "x = " << setw (20) << x << "    y = "
         << setw (20) << y << ar_rational (y) << "\n";
}
errno = FALSE;
}
```

2.5 Annotated Examples

Example 1

We are going to try to find the solution of a Bernoulli equation:

$$y' = \frac{4xy + 4x\sqrt{y}}{1+x^2}$$

with the initial condition $y(0) = 1$.

The exact solution of this equation is:

$$y = (2x^2 + 1)^2$$

Thus:

$$y(10) = 40401$$

Let us start on a first search between 0 and 10, with a finesse of 1:

```
SOLVING DIFFERENTIAL EQUATIONS WITH 1 VARIABLE OF ORDER 1

Enter equation : y' =    : 4 * x * (y + sqrt (y)) / (1 + x*x)
Value of xo              : 0
```

```
Value of xf              : 10
Initial value at xo      : 1
Number of points         : 10
Finesse                  : 1
Number of buffer         : 1
Display of the numbers   : y

x =         1     y =           7.820638858478   # 3183 / 407
x =         2     y =          67.530066695508   # 30321 / 449
x =         3     y =         298.711911397742
x =         4     y =         900.02936914674    # 30601 / 34
x =         5     y =        2149.79618032392
x =         6     y =        4405.834959753912
x =         7     y =        8105.457295827604
x =         8     y =       13765.466309859752
x =         9     y =       21982.160896779613
x =        10     y =       33431.338761420018
The buffer number 1 now contains the solution function.
```

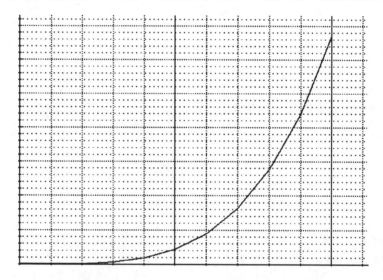

We notice that the rough estimate is correct but the precision is poor.

Let us start on a second search with a finesse of 500:

```
SOLVING DIFFERENTIAL EQUATIONS WITH 1 VARIABLE OF ORDER 1

Enter equation : y' =    : 4 * x * (y + sqrt (y)) / (1 + x*x)
Value of xo              : 0
Value of xf              : 10
Initial value at xo      : 1
Number of points         : 10
Finesse                  : 500
```

```
Number of buffer        : 1
Display of numbers      : y

x =        1    y =           8.999999999937
x =        2    y =          80.999999999099
x =        3    y =         360.999999995857
x =        4    y =        1088.999999987533
x =        5    y =        2600.999999970363
x =        6    y =        5328.999999939501
x =        7    y =        9800.999999889007
x =        8    y =       16640.999999811866
x =        9    y =       26568.999999699994
x =       10    y =       40400.999999544299
The buffer number 1 now contains the solution function.
```

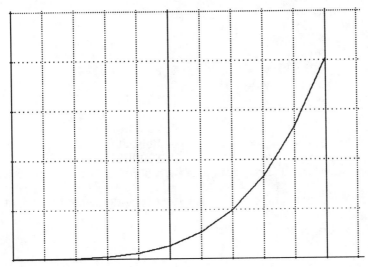

This time the precision is excellent.

Of course the time needed to calculate depends on the function itself, but generally a rough estimate is of about the tenth of a second by calculated point.

Therefore a finesse of 10 represents a good compromise between precision and calculation time since the computer displays a point about every second.

A finesse of 100 or more will of course give a very precise result but will necessitate 10 or so seconds of calculations per point displayed.

Example 2

The equation studied is:

$$y' = -y^2 \qquad \text{with } y(1) = 1$$

The exact solution is:

$$y = \frac{1}{x}$$

```
SOLVING DIFFERENTIAL EQUATIONS WITH 1 VARIABLE OF ORDER 1

Enter equation : y' =      : - y * y
Value of xo                : 1
Value of xf                : 10
Initial value at xo        : 1
Number of points           : 9
Finesse                    : 10
Number of buffer           : 1
Display of numbers         : y

x =            2      y =            0.50000029758
x =            3      y =            0.333333479093
x =            4      y =            0.250000083844
x =            5      y =            0.200000054083
x =            6      y =            0.166666704354
x =            7      y =            0.142857170595
x =            8      y =            0.125000021257
x =            9      y =            0.111111127917
x =           10      y =            0.100000013618
The buffer number 1 now contains the solution function.

SOLVING DIFFERENTIAL EQUATIONS WITH 1 VARIABLE OF ORDER  1

Enter equation : y' =      : - y * y
Value of xo                : 1
Value of xf                : 10
Initial value at xo        : 1
Number of points           : 9
Finesse                    : 200
Number of buffer           : 1
Display of numbers         : y

x =            2      y =            0.500000000002  # 1 / 2
x =            3      y =            0.333333333334  # 1 / 3
x =            4      y =            0.250000000001  # 1 / 4
x =            5      y =                       0.2  # 1 / 5
x =            6      y =            0.166666666667  # 1 / 6
x =            7      y =            0.142857142857  # 1 / 7
x =            8      y =                     0.125  # 1 / 8
x =            9      y =            0.111111111111  # 1 / 9
x =           10      y =                       0.1  # 1 / 10
The buffer number 1 now contains the solution function.
```

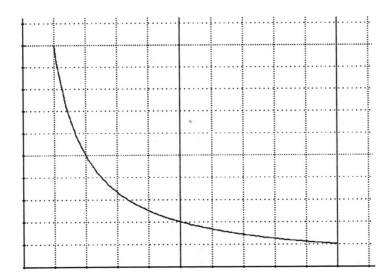

The results here again are satisfactory with a finesse of 10, and are better with a finesse of 200. The previous curve has been obtained from 180 points, with a finesse of one.

REMARK: if the curve is the primary requirement, it is better to start on the search with a large number of points (at least a hundred). The finesse can in that case take low values (one or several units).

3 Predictor-Corrector Method

3.1 Principle

In the Runge-Kutta method, the term y_{n+1} is calculated from only one point (x_n, y_n). That is, of all the points previously calculated only the last is used. This type of method is called one with "single steps" or "separated steps".

The methods we are going to study now are "multiple steps" methods, that is, that the calculation of y_{n+1} uses more than one point y_n, it also uses $y_{n-1}, y_{n-2}, ...,$ the number of points needed depending on the formula studied.

We distinguish between two types of formulas:

– the explicit formulas, of the kind:

$$y_{n+1} = y_n + h \left[a_0 y'_n + a_1 y'_{n-1} + ... + a_k y'_{n-k} \right]$$

– the implicit formulas, of the kind:

$$y_{n+1} = y_n + h \left[b_{-1} y'_{n+1} + b_0 y'_n + ... + b_k y'_{n-k} \right]$$

In the implicit formulas the value of $y'_{n+1} = f(y_{n+1}, x_{n+1})$ which intervenes is unknown, since y_{n+1} has not yet been calculated. It is therefore necessary to inject a first estimated value $^0y'_{n+1}$ into the formula, which makes it posssible to calculate $^1y_{n+1}$; we reinject this value into the equation in order to calculate $^1y'_{n+1}$, and so on until we obtain two values $^{i-1}y_{n+1}$ and $^iy_{n+1}$ sufficiently close.

The interest of the implicit methods is not obvious at first sight, since they necessitate several iterations, whereas only one iteration is necessary for the explicit methods, which means a longer time of calculation for the former methods.

In reality, those methods are much more accurate than the explicit methods of the same order; furthermore they are generally stable while the explicit methods are often unstable.

The formulas we will study are of order 4 (as in the Runge-Kutta method):

– explicit formula:

$$y_{n+1} = y_n + \frac{h}{24} [55y'_n - 59y'_{n-1} + 37y'_{n-2} - 9y'_{n-3}]$$

– implicit formula:

$$y_{n+1} = y_n + \frac{h}{24} [9y'_{n+1} + 19y'_n - 5y'_{n-1} + y'_{n-2}]$$

In reality, we will use neither explicit formulas nor implicit formulas, but a combination of both, in order to benefit from the advantages of both: this is called the predictor-corrector method.

Indeed, we have seen that the drawback of implicit formulas was the necessity to make several iterations. But if the value injected $^0y'_{n+1}$ is close to the real value, the number of iterations is low (around 2 or 3).

Therefore we will proceed in two stages:

– the initial estimation $^0y'_{n+1}$ will be calculated through the explicit method;

– this value will be inserted into the implicit formula which will then necessitate only a few iterations.

The formulas with linked steps have the drawback of not "starting" by themselves. Indeed, only the value y_0 is initially known, while the calculation of y_1 would necessitate the knowledge of $y_0, y_{-1}, y_{-2}, y_{-3}$. The first values y_1, y_2, y_3 will therefore be calculated through a Runge-Kutta method, which will make it possible to start the process.

In short, the algorithm used is as follows:

– calculation of y_1, y_2 and y_3 through a Runge-Kutta method to start the process,

– from the point (x_n, y_n) onwards, calculation of the next point with the formulas:

$$^0y_{n+1} = y_n + \frac{h}{24} (55y'_n - 59y'_{n-1} + 37y'_{n-2} - 9y'_{n-3})$$

$$^1y_{n+1} = y_n + \frac{h}{24} (9\,^0y'_{n+1} + 19y'_n - 5y'_{n-1} + y'_{n-2})$$

then until convergence:

$$^{r+1}y_{n+1} = y_n + \frac{h}{24} (9\ ^r y'_{n+1} + 19y'_n - 5y'_{n-1} + y'_{n-2})$$

3.2 Calculation Tool

The parameters of the tool `ar_equadiff_pc` are the following:
- f, equation to be solved, as a function in C of the form:

```
ar_double f(ar_double x, ar_double y)
{
...
}
```

- xi and xf, interval studied;
- yi, initial value at xi;
- m, number of points to be calculated;
- fi, finesse;
- disp, boolean making it possible to display the result in real time.

On output the buffer t contains the digitized result-function. The boolean variable errno indicates if has not been possible to evaluate the function at one point or other.

In order to use a function captured as a succession of characters by the capture tool in the variable `ar_glob_f`, the function `ar_eval_fxy` must be passed as a parameter to the calculation tool.

The tool will have to be placed in the file EQUADIFF\EQUAPC.CPP.

```
/*=========================================================
                      EQUAPC.CPP:
              SOLVING DIFFERENTIAL EQUATIONS
         ONE VARIABLE - ORDER 1 - PREDICTOR-CORRECTOR
=========================================================*/

#include "armath.h"

static double  h, x;

static  void runge_kutta (
      ar_double (*f) (ar_double, ar_double), ar_double &y)
{
   ar_double  a, b, c, d;

   a = h * f (x, y);                     if (errno)  return;
   b = h * f (x + h / 2, y + a / 2);     if (errno)  return;
   c = h * f (x + h / 2, y + b / 2);     if (errno)  return;

   x += h;
```

```
    d = h * f (x, y + c);                if (errno)  return;
    y += (a + b + b + c + c + d) / 6;
}

void  ar_equadiff_pc (
       ar_double (*f) (ar_double, ar_double),
       ar_buffer &t,
       ar_double xi, ar_double xf, ar_double yi,
       int m, int fi, int disp)
{
  int        i, j, k;
  long       ni;
  ar_double  z = yi, y, w, p [4];

  if (fi < 1) return;
  h    = (xf - xi) / fi / m;
  p [3] = f (xi, yi); if (errno) return;

  if (! t.open ("Diff.Equa.PC", 0, m)) return;
  t.addcouple (xi, yi);

  for (k = 0, i = 1; i <= m; i++)  {
    if (ar_stop_asked ())  {
      errno = TRUE;
      return;
    }
    ni = (long) (i - 1) * fi - 1;
    for (j = 1; j <= fi; j++)  {
      x = xi + h * (ni + j);
      if (++k < 4)  {
      runge_kutta (f, z);     if (errno) return;
      p [3 - k] = f (x, z);   if (errno) return;
      }
      else  {
      x += h;
      w = z + h / 24 * (55 * p [0] - 59 * p [1]
                  + 37 * p [2] -  9 * p [3]);
      do  {
        y = w;
        w = z + h / 24 * (9 * f (x, y)
            + 19 * p [0] - 5 * p [1] + p [2]);
        if (errno) return;
      } while (fabs (y - w) > 1E-10);
      z = w; p [3] = p [2]; p [2] = p [1];
      p [1] = p [0]; p [0] = f (x, z); if (errno) return;
      }
    }
    t.addcouple (x, z);
```

```
    if (disp)
       cout << "x = " << setw (20) << x << "     y = "
            << setw (20) << z << ar_rational (z) << "\n";
    }
  errno = FALSE;
}
```

3.3 Annotated Examples

Example 1

Let us use once more the Bernouilli equation which we have solved through the Runge-Kutta method:

$$y' = \frac{4xy + 4x\sqrt{y}}{1 + x^2}$$

```
SOLVING DIFFERENTIAL EQUATIONS - PREDICTOR/CORRECTOR

Enter equation : y' =      : 4 * x * (y + SQRT(y)) / (1 + x*x)
Value of xo                : 0
Value of xf                : 10
Initial value at xo        : 1
Number of points           : 10
Finesse                    : 10
Number of buffer           : 1
Display of numbers         : y
```

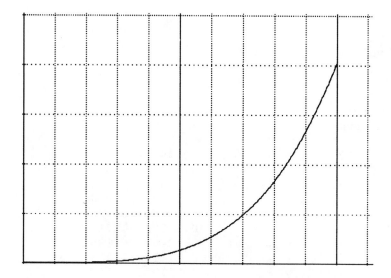

```
x =            1       y =              8.999984090629
x =            2       y =             80.999880679707
x =            3       y =            360.999496203196
x =            4       y =           1088.998512473634
x =            5       y =           2600.996484028578
x =            6       y =           5328.992838130595
x =            7       y =           9800.986874767275
x =            8       y =          16640.977766651216
x =            9       y =          26568.964559220036
x =           10       y =          40400.946170636365
Now the buffer 1 contains the solution-function.
```

With the same number of calculated points, the precision is 50 times better for the last value.

Example 2

In certain cases, in particular for the previous example, the preditor-corrector method gives better results than the Runge-Kutta method. However, in other cases, the reverse phenomenon occurs. Let us resume with the equation:

$$y' = -y^2 \qquad \text{with } y\,(1) = 1$$

whose exact solution is $y = \dfrac{1}{x}$.

```
SOLVING DIFFERENTIAL EQUATIONS - PREDICTOR/CORRECTOR

Enter equation : y' =    : - y * y
Value of xo              : 1
Value of xf              : 10
Initial value at xo      : 1

Number of points         : 9
Finesse                  : 10
Number of buffer         : 1
Display of numbers       : y

x =            2       y =              0.49998800127
x =            3       y =             0.333326725875
x =            4       y =             0.249996120144
x =            5       y =             0.199997480954
x =            6       y =             0.166664906526
x =            7       y =             0.142855845716
x =            8       y =             0.124999005185
x =            9       y =             0.111110324283
x =           10       y =             0.099999362257
The buffer 1 now contains the solution function.
```

```
SOLVING DIFFERENTIAL EQUATIONS  -  PREDICTOR/CORRECTOR

Enter equation : y' =    : - y * y
Value of xo              : 1
Value of xf              : 10
Initial value at xo      : 1

Number of points points : 9
Finesse                  : 50
Number of buffer         : 1
Display of numbers       : y

x =         2        y =          0.499999967608  # 1 / 2
x =         3        y =          0.333333317218  # 1 / 3
x =         4        y =          0.249999990697  # 1 / 4
x =         5        y =          0.199999993991  # 1 / 5
x =         6        y =          0.166666662477  # 1 / 6
x =         7        y =          0.142857139773  # 1 / 7
x =         8        y =          0.124999997636  # 1 / 8
x =         9        y =          0.111111109242  # 1 / 9
x =        10        y =          0.099999998485  # 1 / 10
The buffer 1 now contains the solution function.
```

This time the precision is better with the Runge-Kutta method.

In the following programs we will generalise the Runge-Kutta method rather than the predictor-corrector method, although the latter sometimes gives better results.

4 Equations of Order *n*

4.1 Principle

We will now study equations of the form:

$$y^{(n)} = f(y^{(n-1)}, y^{(n-2)},..., y', y, x)$$

Let us make the following change of variables; let us write:

$$y_1 = y$$

$$y_2 = y'$$

....

$$y_n = y^{(n-1)}$$

The starting equation is then equivalent to the system:

$$y'_1 = y_2 \qquad\qquad y_1(0) = y(0)$$

$$y'_2 = y_3 \qquad\qquad y_2(0) = y'(0)$$

$$\dots\dots \qquad \text{with} \qquad \dots\dots$$

$$y'_{n-1} = y_n \qquad\qquad y_{n-1}(0) = y^{(n-2)}(0)$$

$$y'_n = f(y_n, y_{n-1},\dots, y_2, y_1, x) \qquad\qquad y_n(0) = y^{(n-1)}(0)$$

which is a system with n coupled equations of order 1. This system can be solved through the method described in the following section.

4.2 Calculation Tools

The parameters of the tools `ar_equadiff_1n` are the following:
- f, equation to be solved as a function in C of the form:

```
ar_double f(ar_double x, ar_double y)
{
...
}
```

   In this function C, y is represented by y[0], y' by y[1], etc.
- xi and xf, interval studied;
- m, number of points to be calculated;
- n, order of the equation;
- fi, finesse;
- disp, boolean making it possible to display the results in real time.
- yi, array of real numbers having to contain the initial conditions, that is:

$$y(x_0), y'(x_0),\dots, y^{(n-1)}(x_0)$$

On output, buffer t contains the digitized result-function. The boolean variable `errno` indicates if it has not been possible to evaluate the function at one point or other.

   In order to use a function captured as a succession of characters by the capture tool in the variable `ar_glob_f`, the function `ar_eval_fyi` must be passed as a parameter to the calculation tool.

   The tool of interpretation of functions shown in chapter 4 takes care of the interpretation of the notation y', y", etc. for the successive derivatives. For example the equation:

$$y'''' = 3y''' + y' + 3y - x$$

will be entered as follows:

```
3 * Y''' + Y' + 3 * Y - X
```

The maximal order of the system is limited to 9.

The tool will have to be placed in the file EQUADIFF\EQUA1N.CPP.

```
/*===========================================================
                        EQUA1N.CPP:
                SOLVING DIFFERENTIAL EQUATIONS
            ONE VARIABLE - ORDER N (RUNGE-KUTTA)
   ========================================================*/

#include "armath.h"

#define   compute(tx, b)   \
          tx [n1] = h * f (x, y);  if (errno)  return; \
          for (k = 0; k < n1; k++)  {   \
            tx [k] = h * y [k + 1];     \
            y  [k] = z [k] + ((b) ? tx [k] : (tx [k] / 2));\
          }                                             \
          y  [n1] = z [n1] + ((b) ? tx [n1] : (tx [n1] / 2))

void  ar_equadiff_1n (
      ar_double (*f) (ar_double, ar_double []),
      ar_buffer &t,
      ar_double xi, ar_double xf, ar_double yi [],
      int m, int order, int fi, int disp)
{
  ar_double  ta[10], tb[10], tc[10], td[10], y[10], z[10];
  ar_double  h, x;
  long       ni;
  int        i, j, k, n1;

  if ((fi < 1) || (order > 9)) return;
  h        = (xf - xi) / fi / m;
  if (! t.open ("Diff.Equa.1,N", 0, m)) return;
  n1 = order - 1; t.addcouple (xi, yi [0]);
  for (k = 0; k <= n1; k++) z [k] = yi [k];
  for (i = 1; i <= m; i++)  {
    if (ar_stop_asked ())  {
      errno = TRUE; return;
    }
    ni = (long) (i - 1) * fi - 1;
    for (j = 1; j <= fi; j++)  {
      x = xi + h * (ni + j);
      for (k = 0; k <= n1; k++) y [k] = z [k];
      compute (ta,FALSE); x = x + h / 2; compute (tb,FALSE);
      compute (tc, TRUE); x = x + h / 2;
      compute (td, TRUE);
      for (k = 0; k <= n1; k++)
        z[k] = z[k] + (ta[k] + 2*tb[k] + 2*tc[k] + td[k])/6;
    }
```

```
      t.addcouple (x, z [0]);
      if (disp)
        cout << "x = " << setw (20) << x << "    y = "
                << setw (20) << z [0] <<
                    ar_rational (z [0]) << "\n";
    }
  errno = FALSE;
}
```

4.3 Annotated Examples

Example 1

Let us consider the following equation of second order:

$$y'' = \frac{2y'^2 + y^2}{y} \qquad \text{with } y(4) = 2 \text{ and } y'(4) = -2 \text{ tg}(1)$$

The exact solution is:

$$y = \frac{2\cos(1)}{\cos(x-5)}$$

```
SOLVING DIFFERENTIAL EQUATIONS WITH 1 VARIABLE OF ORDER N

Order of the equation     : 2

Input equation : y(n) =   : (2 * y'^2 + y^2) / y

Value of xo               : 4
Value of xf               : 6
Value at xo of y          : 2
Value at xo of y'         : -2*tan(1)

Number of points          : 10
Finesse                   : 20

Number of buffer          : 1
Display of numbers        : y

x =         4.2      y =         1.551017960256   # 12875 / 8301
x =         4.4      y =         1.309291154276   # 7370 / 5629
x =         4.6      y =         1.173217220757   # 4985 / 4249
x =         4.8      y =         1.102582868759   # 4525 / 4104
x =         5        y =         1.080604618374   # 429 / 397
x =         5.2      y =         1.102582867491   # 4525 / 4104
x =         5.4      y =         1.173217217943   # 4985 / 4249
```

```
x =            5.6      y =      1.309291149204   # 7370 / 5629
x =            5.8      y =      1.551017951301   # 12875 / 8301
x =              6      y =      1.999999983452
```

```
The buffer 1 now contains the solution function
```

We can verify that the results are exact up to 10^{-8}.

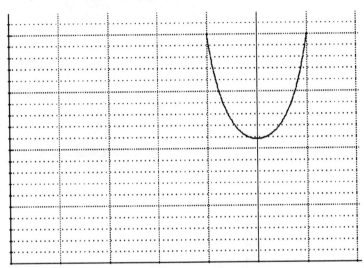

Example 2

Let us consider the equation of third order:

$$y''' = y \qquad \text{with} \qquad y(0) = 2, \, y'(0) = -1, \, y''(0) = -1$$

The exact solution is:

$$y = 2 \, e^{\frac{-x}{2}} \cos\frac{\sqrt{3}}{2} x$$

```
SOLVING DIFFERENTIAL EQUATIONS WITH 1 VARIABLE OF ORDER N

Order of the equation       : 3

Input equation : y(n) =     : y

Value of xo                 : 0
Value of xf                 : -5
Value at xo of y            : 2
Value at xo of y'           : -1
Value at xo of y''          : -1
```

```
Number of points          : 10
Finesse                   : 50

Number of buffer          : 2
Display of numbers        : y
x =          -0.5    y =        2.331034428222    # 338 / 145
x =            -1    y =        2.136278964291    # 3433 / 1607
x =          -1.5    y =        1.136513769663    # 3097 / 2725
x =            -2    y =       -0.872875843199    # -2671 / 3060
x =          -2.5    y =        -3.90849806847    # -18581 / 4754
x =            -3    y =        -7.67171459094    # -14185 / 1849
x =          -3.5    y =      -11.439006933262    # -15660 / 1369
x =            -4    y =      -14.016199957799    # -9517 / 679
x =          -4.5    y =      -13.812510608692
x =            -5    y =       -9.088630765181    # -10152 / 1117
```

One notices in this example the possibility of introducing a final abscissa x_f less than the initial abscissa x_0.

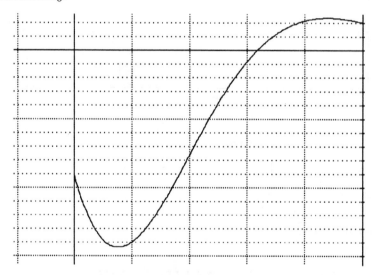

5   Differential Systems of Order 1

5.1 Principle

Now we are interested in determining not *one*, but p functions, solutions of a differential system of first order of the form:

$$y'_1 = f_1(x, y_1, y_2,..., y_p)$$

$$y'_2 = f_2(x, y_1, y_2,..., y_p)$$

....

$$y'_p = f_p(x, y_1, y_2,..., y_p)$$

The equations are here again in a solved form.

The system can be written more simply by using the vectorial form:

Let us write;   then:

$$\vec{y} = \begin{pmatrix} y_1 \\ y_2 \\ \vdots \\ y_p \end{pmatrix} \qquad \vec{y'} = \begin{pmatrix} y'_1 \\ y'_2 \\ \vdots \\ y'_p \end{pmatrix}$$

The system can therefore be written as follows:

$$\vec{y'} = \vec{f}(x, \vec{y})$$

The solution is found in the same way as for a differential equation of order 1, the only difference being the vectorial nature of the unknowns y and of the functions f.

5.2 Calculation Tools

The parameters of the tool `ar_equadiff_p1` are the following:
- f, array of the functions;
- xi and xf, interval studied;
- m, number of points to be calculated;
- p, number of variables;
- fi, finesse;
- disp, boolean making it possible to display the results in real time.
- yi, array which must contain the initial conditions, that is:

$$y_1(x_0), y_2(x_0),..., y_p(x_0)$$

On output, buffers t1 and t2 contain the first two digitized result-functions.

The boolean variable errno indicates if it is possible to evaluate the function at one point or other. The tool of interpretation of the functions shown in chapter 4 will take care of the interpretation of the rotations y_1, y_2, etc. for the successive variables.

The maximum number of equations is 9.

The tool will have to be placed in the file EQUADIFF\EQUAP1.CPP.

```
/*============================================================
                        EQUAP1.CPP:
                 SOLVING DIFFERENTIAL SYSTEMS
  ==========================================================*/

#include  "armath.h"

#define  compute(tx, b)  \
        for (k = 0; k < p; k++)  {   \
          tx [k] = h * (f [k]) (x, y);  if (errno)  return; \
          }  \
        for (k = 0; k < p; k++)    \
          y [k] = z [k] + ((b) ? tx [k] : (tx [k] / 2));

void  ar_equadiff_p1 (
      ar_double (*f []) (ar_double, ar_double []),
      ar_buffer &t1, ar_buffer &t2,
      ar_double xi, ar_double xf, ar_double yi [],
      int m, int p, int fi, int disp)
{
  int      i, j, k;
  long     ni;
  ar_double  h, x;
  ar_double  ta[10], tb[10], tc[10], td[10], y[10], z[10];

  if ((fi < 1) || (p > 9)) return;
  h        = (xf - xi) / fi / m;
  if (! t1.open ("Diff.Syst.Sol.1", 0, m)) return;
  if (! t2.open ("Diff.Syst.Sol.2", 0, m)) return;
  t1.addcouple (xi, yi [0]);
  t2.addcouple (xi, yi [1]);
  for (k = 0; k < p; k++) z [k] = yi [k];
  for (i = 1; i <= m; i++)  {
    if (ar_stop_asked ())  {
      errno = TRUE; return;
    }
    ni = (long) (i - 1) * fi - 1;
    for (j = 1; j <= fi; j++)  {
      x = xi + h * (ni + j);
      for (k = 0; k < p; k++) y [k] = z [k];
      compute (ta,FALSE); x = x + h / 2; compute (tb,FALSE);
      compute (tc,TRUE); x = x + h / 2; compute (td,TRUE);
      for (k = 0; k < p; k++)
        z[k] = z[k] + (ta[k] + 2*tb[k] + 2*tc[k] + td[k])/6;
    }
```

```
      t1.addcouple (x, z [0]); t2.addcouple (x, z [1]);
      if (disp)  {
        cout << "\nx = " << setw (20) << x << "\n";
        for (k = 0; k < p; k++)
          cout << "      y " << (k + 1) << " = " << setw (20) <<
              z [k] << ar_rational (z [k]) << "\n";
      }
   }
   errno = FALSE;
}
```

5.3 Annotated Examples

Example 1

Let us consider the system:

$$y'_1 = y_2 + y_3 - 3y_1 \qquad\qquad y_1(0) = 1$$

$$y'_2 = y_1 + y_3 - 3y_2 \qquad \text{with} \qquad y_2(0) = 2$$

$$y'_3 = y_1 + y_2 - 3y_3 \qquad\qquad y_3(0) = -1$$

The exact solution is:

$$y_1 = \frac{1}{3} (e^{-4x} + 2e^{-x})$$

$$y_2 = \frac{1}{3} (4e^{-4x} + 2e^{-x})$$

$$y_3 = \frac{1}{3} (-5e^{-4x} + 2e^{-x})$$

```
SOLVING DIFFERENTIAL SYSTEMS

Number of variables        :

Function y1'               : y2 + y3 - 3*y1
Function y2'               : y1 + y3 - 3*y2
Function y3'               : y1 + y2 - 3*y3
Value of xo                : 0
Value of xf                : 3
Value at xo of y1          : 1
Value at xo of y2          : 2
Value at xo of y3          : -1
Number of points           : 6
Finesse                    : 100
Display results            : y
```

```
x =                   0.5
   y1 =       0.449465534344   # 925 / 2058
   y2 =       0.584800817948   # 6841 / 11698
   y3 =       0.178794967137   # 2371 / 13261

x =                    1
   y1 =       0.251358173778   # 2591 / 10308
   y2 =       0.269673812766   # 2224 / 8247
   y3 =       0.214726895802   # 1773 / 8257

x =                   1.5
   y1 =       0.149579690832   # 1726 / 11539
   y2 =       0.152058443029   # 229 / 1506
   y3 =       0.144622186439   # 1112 / 7689

x =                    2
   y1 =       0.090335343036   # 959 / 10616
   y2 =       0.090670805667   # 761 / 8393
   y3 =       0.089664417773   # 1873 / 20889

x =                   2.5
   y1 =       0.054738465727   # 923 / 16862
   y2 =       0.054783865657   # 493 / 8999
   y3 =       0.054647665866   # 418 / 7649

x =                    3
   y1 =       0.033193426983
   y2 =       0.033199571196
   y3 =       0.033181138558   # 734 / 22121
```

Example 2

Let us now visualise the phenomenon of divergence. Let us consider the following system:

$$y'_1 = y_1 + y_2 + \sin x$$

$$y'_2 = -y_1 + 3y_2$$

The solutions are of the following type:

$$y_1 = (\lambda + \mu - \delta x)\, e^{2x} - \frac{1}{25}\,(13 \sin x + 9 \cos x)$$

$$y_2 = (\mu - \lambda x)\, e^{2x} - \frac{1}{25}\,(3 \sin x + 4 \cos x)$$

where λ and μ are arbitrary constants determining the initial conditions.

Thus, if we impose as initial conditions:

$$y_1(0) = -\frac{9}{25} \qquad \text{and} \qquad y_2(0) = -\frac{4}{25}$$

we must obtain the solution:

$$y_1 = -\frac{1}{25}\,(13 \sin x + 9 \cos x)$$

$$y_2 = -\frac{1}{25}\,(3 \sin x + 4 \cos x)$$

which is a periodic solution.

In contrast, the solution given by the program is not periodic and diverges. This is because the numerical results are not exact and the terms $x\, e^{2x}$ which should not exist gradually become preponderant until they completely conceal the required solution. This phenomenon occurs relatively often with systems of differential equations. Therefore one has to repeat the calculation with a better finesse in order to obtain a satisfactory result.

```
SOLVING DIFFERENTIAL SYSTEMS

Number of variables    : 2

Function y1'           : y1 + y2 + sin (x)
Function y2'           : - y1 + 3 * y2
Value of xo            : 0
Value of xf            : 5 * PI
Value at xo of y1      : -9 / 25
Value at xo of y2      : -4 / 25

Number of points       : 10
Finesse                : 20
```

```
Display of numbers    : y

x =     1.570796326795
   y1 =              -0.519991941219   # -2575 / 4952
   y2 =              -0.11998353279    # -583 / 4859

x =     3.14159265359
   y1 =               0.360506964547   # 2304 / 6391
   y2 =               0.160711718545   # 1111 / 6913

x =     4.712388980385
   y1 =               0.539165690002   # 4123 / 7647
   y2 =               0.143895364626

x =     6.28318530718
   y1 =               0.255400587818   # 934 / 3657
   y2 =               0.564836823929   # 4517 / 7997

x =     7.853981633974
   y1 =              17.698395073445   # 15433 / 872
   y2 =              20.630798365209   # 11120 / 539

x =     9.424777960769
   y1 =             513.988240941306
   y2 =             572.38899769782

x =    10.995574287564
   y1 =           14016.088400430566
   y2 =           15371.731525853791

x =    12.566370614359
   y1 =          373614.544933754543
   y2 =          404994.083198167267

x =    14.137166941154
   y1 =         9786163.006386153401
   y2 =        10512292.872169887648

x =    15.707963267949
   y1 = 252848802.561488240968
   y2 = 269651706.12672019004
```

The buffers 0 and 1 now contain the 2 first solution functions

   The following representations clearly show the phenomenon of divergence and the effect of the finesse on the abscissa. The first corresponds to a finesse of 20, the second to a finesse of 200.

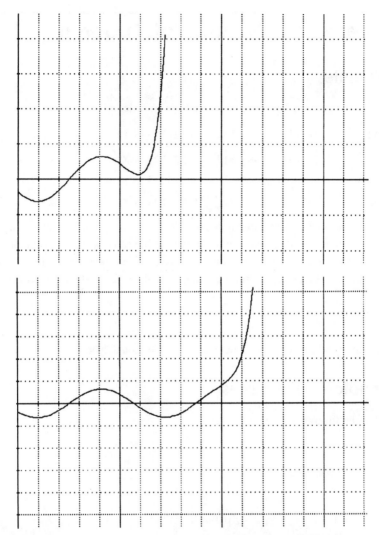

REMARK: it is impossible to increase the finesse too much. Indeed regardless of the considerable calculation time needed, the advantage brought by the error of method no longer suffices to compensate for the accumulation of numerical errors. For example, we have verified that the previous calculation, made with a finesse of 30 000, does not converge more rapidly than that made with a finesse of 5 000.

5.4 Conclusion

The phenomenon of divergence is the only problem one meets when numerically solving systems of differential equations. It is therefore better to be very critical of the results obtained, and when in doubt not to hesitate to repeat the calculation with a higher finesse.

6 Differential Systems of Order *n*

6.1 Principle

The general form of solved systems of p equations of order n is as follows:

$$y_1^{(n-1)} = f_1(x, y_1, y_1', ..., y_1^{(n-1)}, y_2, y_2', ..., y_2^{(n-1)}, ..., y_p, y_p', ..., y_p^{(n-1)})$$

$$y_2^{(n-1)} = f_2(x, y_1, y_1', ..., y_1^{(n-1)}, y_2, y_2', ..., y_2^{(n-1)}, ..., y_p, y_p', ..., y_p^{(n-1)})$$

$$\cdots\cdots\cdots\cdots\cdots\cdots\cdots\cdots\cdots\cdots\cdots\cdots\cdots\cdots\cdots\cdots\cdots\cdots\cdots\cdots$$

$$y_p^{(n-1)} = f_p(x, y_1, y_1', ..., y_1^{(n-1)}, y_2, y_2', ..., y_2^{(n-1)}, ..., y_p, y_p', ..., y_p^{(n-1)})$$

We have seen that solving equations of order n could be done by changing the initial equation into a coupled system with n equations. In the same way, the previous system can be changed into a coupled system with n equations. The unknowns of this system are no longer scalars, but vectors. By using vectorial formalism the system can still be written as follows:

$$\vec{y}' = \vec{f}(x, \vec{y})$$

The vectors y and f belong this time to a two-dimentional space.

6.2 Annotated Examples

Let us solve the following system:

$$z''_1 = -4z_1 - 3z_2$$

$$z''_2 = -8z_1 - 2z_2$$

with:

$$z_1(0) = 3 \qquad\qquad z'_1(0) = 0$$

$$z_2(0) = 4 \qquad\qquad z'_2(0) = 0$$

Let us return to a system of equations of order 1 by writing:

$$y_1 = z_1 \qquad\qquad y_3 = z_2$$

$$y_2 = z'_1 \qquad\qquad y_4 = z'_2$$

The initial system is therefore equivalent to the following:

$$y'_1 = y_2 \qquad\qquad y_1(0) = 3$$

$$y'_2 = -4y_1 - 3y_3 \qquad\qquad y_2(0) = 0$$

$$y'_3 = y_4 \qquad\qquad y_3(0) = 4$$

$$y'_4 = -8y_1 - 2y_3 \qquad y_4(0) = 0$$

This system, of first order, can then be solved by the program. The exact solution is:

$$y_1 = 3\cos(2\sqrt{2}\,x)$$

$$y_3 = 4\cos(2\sqrt{2}\,x)$$

The variable defining the interval $[0, \dfrac{4\pi}{2\sqrt{2}}]$, the results for y_1 and y_3 must be:

$$(0, 0), (-3, -4), (0, 0), (3, 4), (0, 0), \dots$$

```
SOLVING DIFFERENTIAL SYSTEMS

Number of variables    : 4

Function y1'           : y2
Function y2'           : - 4 * y1 - 3 * y3
Function y3'           : y4
Function y4'           : -8 * y1 - 2 * y3

Value of xo            : 0
Value of xf            : PI * sqrt (2)

Value at xo of y1      : 3
Value at xo of y2      : 0
Value at xo of y3      : 4
Value at xo of y4      : 0

Number of points       : 8
Finesse                : 100

Display of numbers     : y

x =        0.55536036727
  y1 =          2.39056883548e-09
  y2 =         -8.48528137415   # -9512 / 1121
  y3 =          3.187423568141e-09
  y4 =        -11.313708498867   # -12875 / 1138

x =        1.11072073454
  y1 =         -2.999999999937
  y2 =         -1.35231018189e-08
  y3 =         -3.999999999917
  y4 =         -1.803078064171e-08
```

```
x  =        1.666081101809
  y1 =       -7.171711211007e-09
  y2 =        8.485281373973    # 9512 / 1121
  y3 =       -9.562256000906e-09
  y4 =       11.313708498631    # 12875 / 1138

x  =        2.221441469079
  y1 =        2.999999999875
  y2 =        2.704615620353e-08
  y3 =        3.999999999833
  y4 =        3.606163491432e-08

x  =        2.776801836349
  y1 =        1.195279679169e-08
  y2 =       -8.485281373796    # -9512 / 1121
  y3 =        1.593719884535e-08
  y4 =      -11.313708498395    # -12875 / 1138
x  =        3.332162203619
  y1 =       -2.999999999812
  y2 =       -4.056940429431e-08
  y3 =       -3.999999999749
  y4 =       -5.409211668861e-08

x  =        3.887522570889
  y1 =       -1.673417055273e-08
  y2 =        8.485281373619    # 9512 / 1121
  y3 =       -2.231157006372e-08
  y4 =       11.313708498159    # 12875 / 1138

x  =        4.442882938158
  y1 =        2.999999999749
  y2 =        5.409176186133e-08
  y3 =        3.999999999667
  y4 =        7.212438325281e-08
```

7   Exploitation Tools

The following tools make possible the direct exploitation of the tools of calculation.

The following tool is to be placed in the file EQUADIFF\UEQUA11.CPP:

```
/*============================================================
                      UEQUA11.CPP:
        1-1 DIFFERENTIAL EQUATIONS EXPLOITATION TOOL
                     (RUNGE-KUTTA)
 ============================================================*/
```

```cpp
#include "armath.h"

void ar_use_equadiff_11 ()
{
  ar_double  xi, xf, yi;
  int        fi, nt, m, disp;

  ar_init_entry ("SOLVING DIFFERENTIAL EQUATIONS WITH \
                  1 VARIABLE OF ORDER 1");
  ar_fill_entry ("Enter equation :  y' = ", &ar_glob_f,
                  AR_TFYI);
  ar_fill_entry ("Value of xo",            &xi,   AR_TDOU);
  ar_fill_entry ("Value of xf",            &xf,   AR_TDOU);
  ar_fill_entry ("Initial value at xo",    &yi,   AR_TDOU);
  ar_fill_entry ("Number of points",       &m,    AR_TINT);
  ar_fill_entry ("Finesse",                &fi,   AR_TINT);
  ar_fill_entry ("Number of buffer",       &nt,   AR_TINT);
  ar_fill_entry ("Display results",        &disp, AR_TBOO);

  if (ar_do_entry ())     return;
  if (nt > AR_MAXBUFFER)  return;

  ar_equadiff_11(ar_eval_fxy,ar_buff[nt],xi,xf,yi,m,fi,disp);

  if (errno)  {
    cout << "Equation not defined at some points\n";

    ar_pause ();
  }
  else  {
    cout << "The buffer number " << nt << " now contains "
         << "the solution function\n\n";

    if (ar_read ("Graphical representation ? ", &disp,
                 AR_TBOO)) return;

    if (disp)
      ar_draw_buffer (ar_buff [nt]);
  }
}
```

The following tool is to be placed in the file EQUADIFF\UEQUAPC.CPP:

```cpp
/*==============================================================
                      UEQUAPC.CPP:
          1-1 DIFFERENTIAL EQUATION EXPLOITATION TOOL
                  (PREDICTOR - CORRECTOR)
  ==============================================================*/
```

```
#include "armath.h"

void ar_use_equadiff_pc ()
{
  ar_double  xi, xf, yi;
  int        fi, nt, m, disp;

  ar_init_entry ("SOLVING DIFFERENTIAL EQUATIONS -
                  PREDICTOR/CORRECTOR");
  ar_fill_entry ("Enter equation :  y' = ", &ar_glob_f,
                  AR_TFYI);
  ar_fill_entry ("Value of xo",          &xi,   AR_TDOU);
  ar_fill_entry ("Value of xf",          &xf,   AR_TDOU);
  ar_fill_entry ("Initial value at xo", &yi,   AR_TDOU);
  ar_fill_entry ("Number of points",    &m,    AR_TINT);
  ar_fill_entry ("Finesse",             &fi,   AR_TINT);
  ar_fill_entry ("Number of buffer",    &nt,   AR_TINT);
  ar_fill_entry ("Display results",     &disp, AR_TBOO);

  if (ar_do_entry ())     return;
  if (nt > AR_MAXBUFFER)  return;

  ar_equadiff_pc(ar_eval_fxy,ar_buff[nt],xi,xf,yi,m,fi,disp);

  if (errno)  {
    cerr << "Equation not defined at certain points\n";
    ar_pause ();
  }
  else  {
    cout << "The buffer " << nt << " now contains the"
         << " solution function\n\n";

    if (ar_read ("Graphical representation ? ", &disp,
                AR_TBOO)) return;
    if (disp)
      ar_draw_buffer (ar_buff [nt]);
  }
}
```

The following tool is to be placed in the file EQUADIFF\UEQUA1N.CPP:

```
/*=============================================================
                      UEQUA1N.CPP:
       ORDER N DIFFERENTIAL EQUATIONS EXPLOITATION TOOL
 =============================================================*/

#include <string.h>
#include "armath.h"
```

```
void ar_use_equadiff_1n ()
{
  ar_double  xi, xf, yi [10];
  int        fi, nt, m, disp, i;

  cout << "SOLVING DIFFERENTIAL EQUATIONS WITH \
          1 VARIABLE OF ORDER N\n\n";
  if (ar_read ("Order of the equation  : ", &ar_glob_dim,
              AR_TINT)) return;
  if (ar_glob_dim > 9) return;

  ar_init_entry ("");
  ar_fill_entry ("Enter equation :  y (n) = ", &ar_glob_f,
              AR_TFYI);
  ar_fill_entry ("Value of xo",             &xi,  AR_TDOU);
  ar_fill_entry ("Value of xf",             &xf,  AR_TDOU);
  strcpy (ar_temp, "Value at xo of y");

  for (i = 0; i < ar_glob_dim; i++)  {
    ar_fill_entry (ar_temp, &yi [i], , AR_TDOU);
    strcat (ar_temp, "'");
  }

  ar_fill_entry ("Number of points", &m,   AR_TINT);
  ar_fill_entry ("Finesse",          &fi,  AR_TINT);
  ar_fill_entry ("Number of buffer", &nt,  AR_TINT);
  ar_fill_entry ("Display results",  &disp, AR_TBOO);

  if (ar_do_entry ())     return;
  if (nt > AR_MAXBUFFER)  return;

  ar_equadiff_1n (ar_eval_fyi, ar_buff [nt], xi, xf,
            yi, m, ar_glob_dim, fi, disp);

  if (errno)  {
    cerr << "Equation not defined at certain points\n";
    ar_pause ();
  }
  else  {
    cout << "The buffer " << nt << " now contains the"
          << " solution function\n\n";

    if (ar_read ("Graphical representation ? ", &disp,
                AR_TBOO)) return;
    if (disp)
      ar_draw_buffer (ar_buff [nt]);
  }
}
```

The following tool is to be placed in the file EQUADIFF\UEQUAP1.CPP:

```
/*===========================================================
                        UEQUAP1.CPP:
            DIFFERENTIAL SYSTEMS EXPLOITATION TOOL
  =========================================================*/

#include "armath.h"

static ar_function  loc_f [10];


static ar_double loc_eval_f0 (ar_double x, ar_double y [])
{
  int  i;

  ar_glob_x   = x;
  for (i = 0; i < ar_glob_dim; i++) ar_glob_arr_y [i] = y[i];
  return (loc_f [0] (ar_val_arr));
}

static ar_double loc_eval_f1 (ar_double x, ar_double y [])
{
  int  i;

  ar_glob_x   = x;
  for (i = 0; i < ar_glob_dim; i++) ar_glob_arr_y [i] = y[i];
  return (loc_f [1] (ar_val_arr));
}

static ar_double loc_eval_f2 (ar_double x, ar_double y [])
{
  int  i;

  ar_glob_x   = x;
  for (i = 0; i < ar_glob_dim; i++) ar_glob_arr_y [i] = y[i];
  return (loc_f [2] (ar_val_arr));
}

static ar_double loc_eval_f3 (ar_double x, ar_double y [])
{
  int  i;

  ar_glob_x   = x;
  for (i = 0; i < ar_glob_dim; i++) ar_glob_arr_y [i] = y[i];
  return (loc_f [3] (ar_val_arr));
}
```

```
static ar_double loc_eval_f4 (ar_double x, ar_double y [])
{
  int  i;

  ar_glob_x  = x;
  for (i = 0; i < ar_glob_dim; i++) ar_glob_arr_y [i] = y[i];
  return (loc_f [4] (ar_val_arr));
}

static ar_double loc_eval_f5 (ar_double x, ar_double y [])
{
  int  i;

  ar_glob_x  = x;
  for (i = 0; i < ar_glob_dim; i++) ar_glob_arr_y [i] = y[i];
  return (loc_f [5] (ar_val_arr));
}

static ar_double loc_eval_f6 (ar_double x, ar_double y [])
{
  int  i;

  ar_glob_x  = x;
  for (i = 0; i < ar_glob_dim; i++) ar_glob_arr_y [i] = y[i];
  return (loc_f [6] (ar_val_arr));
}

static ar_double loc_eval_f7 (ar_double x, ar_double y [])
{
  int  i;

  ar_glob_x  = x;
  for (i = 0; i < ar_glob_dim; i++) ar_glob_arr_y [i] = y[i];
  return (loc_f [7] (ar_val_arr));
}

static ar_double loc_eval_f8 (ar_double x, ar_double y [])
{
  int  i;

  ar_glob_x  = x;
  for (i = 0; i < ar_glob_dim; i++) ar_glob_arr_y [i] = y[i];
  return (loc_f [8] (ar_val_arr));
}

static ar_double loc_eval_f9 (ar_double x, ar_double y [])
{
  int  i;
```

```
  ar_glob_x    = x;
  for (i = 0; i < ar_glob_dim; i++) ar_glob_arr_y [i] = y[i];
  return (loc_f [9] (ar_val_arr));
}

void ar_use_equadiff_p1 ()
{
  ar_double  (*f [10]) (ar_double, ar_double []);
  ar_double  xi, xf, yi [10];
  int        i, fi, m, disp;

  cout << "SOLVING DIFFERENTIAL SYSTEMS\n\n";
  if (ar_read ("Number of variables : ", &ar_glob_dim,
               AR_TINT)) return;
  if (ar_glob_dim > 9) return;

  ar_init_entry ("");
  for (i = 0; i < ar_glob_dim; i++)  {
    sprintf (ar_temp, "Function y%d'", i + 1);
    ar_fill_entry (ar_temp, &loc_f [i], AR_TFYI);
  }
  ar_fill_entry ("Value of xo",  &xi,   AR_TDOU);
  ar_fill_entry ("Value of xf",  &xf,   AR_TDOU);

  for (i = 0; i < ar_glob_dim; i++)  {
    sprintf (ar_temp, "Value at xo of y%d", i + 1);
    ar_fill_entry (ar_temp, &yi [i], AR_TDOU);
  }

  ar_fill_entry ("Number of points", &m,     AR_TINT);
  ar_fill_entry ("Finesse",          &fi,    AR_TINT);
  ar_fill_entry ("Display results",  &disp, AR_TBOO);

  if (ar_do_entry ()) return;

  f [0] = loc_eval_f0; f [1] = loc_eval_f1;
  f [2] = loc_eval_f2; f [3] = loc_eval_f3;
  f [4] = loc_eval_f4; f [5] = loc_eval_f5;
  f [6] = loc_eval_f6; f [7] = loc_eval_f7;
  f [8] = loc_eval_f8; f [9] = loc_eval_f9;

  ar_equadiff_p1 (f, ar_buff [0], ar_buff [1],
             xi, xf, yi, m, ar_glob_dim, fi, disp);

  if (errno)  {
    cerr << "Equation not defined at certain points\n";
    ar_pause ();
  }
```

```
  else  {
    cout << "The buffers 0 and 1 now contain the "
         << "2 first solution functions\n\n";
    if (ar_read ("Graphical representation of y1  ? ", &disp,
                AR_TBOO)) return;
    if (disp)
      ar_draw_buffer (ar_buff [0]);
    if (ar_read ("Graphical representation of y2  ? ", &disp,
                AR_TBOO)) return;
    if (disp)
      ar_draw_buffer (ar_buff [1]);
  }
}
```

The Companion Diskette

The optional diskette accompanying this book contains:
- all the source modules (approximately 10 000 lines of programming divided into 200 files),
- a library (ARMATH.LIB) and a library regeneration file (ARMATH.RSP), which allow direct utilisation of all the tools, in the same way as standard C libraries,
- two directly executable programs, ANALYSI.EXE and ALGEBRA.EXE, .
- a trial program and a project file specific to each chapter,
- a text file README.DOC which provides all the instructions necessary for the configuration and the utilisation of the diskettes.

You may contact us at the following address if you wish to comment on this book or its companion diskette:

Alain Reverchon - (C++)
25, rue de Bezons
92400 COURBEVOIE
FRANCE